CREATING AND CAPTURING VALUE THROUGH CROWDSOURCING

Creating and Capturing Value through Crowdsourcing

Edited by
CHRISTOPHER L. TUCCI, ALLAN AFUAH,
AND GIANLUIGI VISCUSI

OXFORD
UNIVERSITY PRESS

OXFORD
UNIVERSITY PRESS

Great Clarendon Street, Oxford, OX2 6DP,
United Kingdom

Oxford University Press is a department of the University of Oxford.
It furthers the University's objective of excellence in research, scholarship,
and education by publishing worldwide. Oxford is a registered trade mark of
Oxford University Press in the UK and in certain other countries

Published in the United States of America by Oxford University Press
198 Madison Avenue, New York, NY 10016, United States of America

British Library Cataloguing in Publication Data
Data available

Library of Congress Control Number: 2017952316

ISBN 978-0-19-881622-5

Printed and bound by
CPI Group (UK) Ltd, Croydon, CR0 4YY

Foreword to Creating and capturing value through crowdsourcing

Henry Chesbrough[1]

Innovation has come a long way in a short period of time. Just thirty years ago, thinkers like Michael Porter of Harvard were telling innovators to invest heavily in internal R&D to use as a barrier against their competitors. The idea was that this investment would differentiate the company in the market, and that only those companies who made similar levels of investment could keep up. This R&D activity was organized inside the company, and its results shared with no one until the products that resulted from innovation went to market.

The leading companies of the day were distinguished in part by the level of their internal R&D spending. Computer makers like IBM poured their dollars into new computer hardware and software. AT&T built out its Bell Laboratories research system, perhaps the most accomplished industrial lab of its day. Auto makers such as Ford, GM, and Chrysler spent billions each year in rolling out new cars and trucks. Pharmaceutical giants such as Merck created powerful research arms that reached back into the basic sciences of biology and chemistry, and filled their product pipelines with compounds they discovered and developed inside their own four walls.

Today things are very different in most industries, not only in the US but around the world. The model of industrial innovation has moved on from this inwardly focused, vertically integrated approach that I call a Closed Innovation system. Open Innovation today prevails, as organizations make extensive use (and re-use) of external ideas and technologies in their own innovation activities, while unused or under-used ideas and technologies internally are allowed to go to the outside for others to utilize. The result is a much deeper division of innovation labor, where specialist firms contribute discoveries and innovations that connect together to form a web of innovation. Startups and small to medium-sized enterprises and even individuals

---

[1] Chesbrough is "the father of Open Innovation", according to Wikipedia. He is the author of the award-winning book, *Open Innovation* (Harvard Business School Press, 2003), *Open Business Models* (Harvard Business School Press, 2006), *Open Services Innovation* (Jossey-Bass, 2011), and the newest book, *New Frontiers in Open Innovation* (Oxford University Press, 2014, with Wim Vanhaverbeke and Joel West). He is the founder and executive director of the Center for Open Innovation at the Haas School of Business at UC Berkeley in California.

play a far more significant role, while the large firms seek to attract and collaborate with these small, agile, skilled participants.

Data from the National Science Foundation on R&D spending in the US over the past thirty years bears out the extent of this shift (see Figure 1).

This chart shows that large firms with more than 25,000 employees were responsible for 70% of the industrial R&D spending done in the US in 1981. But their share of R&D spending shrank by half to 35% in 2007. In contrast, small firms with less than 1,000 employees increased their share of R&D spending from 4% to 24% during that period. Note that large firms are still important in industrial R&D because their share is still very big (35%). The amount of R&D spending in large firms increased from $21.2 billion in 1981 to $94.8 billion in 2011, a factor of 4.

However, the increase in R&D expenditures of small firms is even more impressive. Firms with less than 1,000 employees spent $64.7 billion on R&D in 2011 compared to $1.3 billion in 1981—50 times as much spending! Another way to look at this is smaller firm R&D spending overall has grown 10 times as fast as large company spending over these 26 years. Clearly, the world of innovation has changed.

You can see this new, deeper division of innovation labor in practice, as well as in the statistics. IBM now makes more money from its services business (where it supports the hardware and software of many other companies,

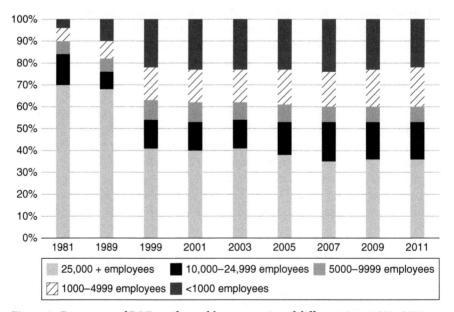

Figure 1. Percentage of R&D performed by companies of different sizes, 1981–2011

Sources: National Science Foundation, Science Resource Studies, Survey of Industrial Research Development 1999, 2001, 2003, 2006, 2008, 2011.

including its competitors) than it does from its traditional product businesses. Cell phone manufacturers strive to attract applications developers to their platforms to boost the range and quality of services that customers can install on their phones. The pharmaceutical industry now licenses in most of its compounds in its product pipeline from external sources such as universities and young biotech firms, rather than carrying projects from the laboratory bench all the way through to market. Auto makers now rely primarily upon their suppliers and their suppliers' suppliers for new innovations.

Within this overall shift toward more open innovation, crowdsourcing is also growing in importance. The fundamental insight underlying crowdsourcing—which is shared by open innovation—is that useful knowledge is widely distributed around the world. No one has a monopoly on that knowledge. Once you accept that, you must face the question of how best to access the wealth of knowledge around the globe.

Crowdsourcing is a powerful answer to that question. Done right, it taps into the knowledge, creativity, insight, and skill of the world around you. It can find solutions to previously intractable problems. It can help you predict next month's sales, or next season's fashions. It can improve the management of your supply chain. It can enhance your customers' experience of your products and services. It even frequently outperforms polling in predicting the winners of elections. And often these improved outcomes can be created with surprisingly modest investments.

You will read about many crowdsourcing examples in this book, so I will confine myself here to one, the company Innocentive. Innocentive has built an online network of more than 200,000 people around the world who go to its website to consider challenges that companies have posted prizes to have solved. These problems are usually technical in nature, and quite difficult to solve, which is why leading companies that have not found answers internally have reached out to the Innocentive community for solutions.

One intractable problem arose from the aftermath of the Exxon Valdez oil spill in Alaska. The crude oil spilled had settled on the ocean floor, hundreds of feet below the surface in very cold water. The combination of pressure and cold temperatures made it impossible to suck up the oil from the ocean floor. This was the challenge presented to the Innocentive community.

Happily, a solution was found from Innocentive's crowd of hundreds of thousands of experts. But that solution came from an unlikely place, one that suggests the value of the crowdsourcing approach. An engineer with extensive experience in the cement industry realized that cement companies employed vibration to keep cement from setting before it had been delivered and deployed in its final location. That same vibration could make the oil on the ocean floor more viscous, allowing it to be sucked off of the ocean floor. A test of the idea demonstrated that it actually worked. The prize was paid, and the technique recovered a great deal of oil that might otherwise have lingered for decades, continuing to damage the surrounding environment.

As you will also read in this book, crowdsourcing is not a panacea for all ills, and can lead to terrible results if it is not managed properly. If, for example, the "crowd" of contributors are not independent of one another, the crowd can become a herd, charging off in a single direction, instead of balancing the different perspectives of people to provide a reliable prediction of a future event or activity.

Crowdsourcing is thus a powerful resource for innovators. Like most powerful resources, this power can be mismanaged as well. That is why you would be well advised to read this book, drink in its insights, and then apply it to your own challenges. A world of people and organizations are available to assist you, if you have the commitment and care to engage them properly.

Acknowledgments

The authors would like to thank their Editor, Clare Kennedy, the production staff including Gayathri Manoharan, and the anonymous referees for their support and contributions to this volume. They are also grateful for the support of EPFL and the University of Michigan.

Contents

PART I. CROWDSOURCING: FUNDAMENTALS AND THE ROLE OF CROWDS AND COMMUNITIES

PART III. COLLABORATION-BASED CROWDSOURCING

PART IV. HYBRIDS: TOURNAMENT-BASED AND COLLABORATION-BASED CROWDSOURCING

List of Figures and Tables

Figures

Tables

List of Contributors

Allan Afuah is Professor of Corporate Strategy and International Business at the Ross School of Business at the University of Michigan. He received his Ph.D. from MIT. His honors include the 1999 MBA Teacher of the Year, at Michigan. His 2012 article "Crowdsourcing as solution to distant search"— co-authored with Christopher Tucci—won the 2012 AMR Best Paper Award, when the journal was ranked the number one scholarly journal in the categories of Management and Business. His first book, *Innovation Management: Strategies, Implementation and Profits*, published by Oxford University Press, has been translated into several languages. His second book, *Internet Business Models*—co-authored with Christopher Tucci and published by McGrawHill—has also been translated into many languages and has over 2,500 Google citations. His latest book is *Business Model Innovation*, published by Routledge. His research has been published in the *Academy of Management Annals, Academy of Management Journal* (AMJ), *Academy of Management Review* (AMR), *Strategic Management Journal, Journal of Management, Research Policy, Industrial and Corporate Change, IEEE Transactions on Engineering Management*, and *Sloan Management Review*.

Marcel Bogers is Professor of Innovation and Entrepreneurship at the Department of Food and Resource Economics (Unit for Innovation, Entrepreneurship and Management at the Section for Production, Markets and Policy), University of Copenhagen. He obtained a combined B.Sc. and M.Sc. in Technology and Society (Innovation Sciences) from Eindhoven University of Technology and a Ph.D. in Management of Technology from Ecole Polytechnique Fédérale de Lausanne (Swiss Federal Institute of Technology). He previously held (visiting) positions at the University of Southern Denmark (where most of his research for this book was conducted), Chalmers University of Technology, and the University of Trento. His main interests center on the design, organization, and management of technology, innovation, and entrepreneurship in general, and on openness and participation in innovation and entrepreneurial processes in particular. More specifically, he has studied areas such as business models, open innovation, users as innovators, collaborative prototyping, family firms, improvization, and university-industry relations.

Alexander Brem holds the Chair of Technology Management at the Friedrich-Alexander-Universität Erlangen-Nürnberg. Moreover, he is Honorary Professor at the University of Southern Denmark (Sønderborg, Denmark). His research interest is in technology and innovation management, with a special focus on boundaries to psychology, marketing, and entrepreneurship.

Vincenzo Butticè is a Ph.D. student at the School of Management of Politecnico di Milano. He graduated in management and production engineering from Politecnico di Milano. His interests are in the area of entrepreneurship, particularly in the cultural and creative industries. He is also studying ways in which crowdfunding supports innovative entrepreneurial ventures.

Antonio Cordella is an associate professor at the London School of Economics and Political Science (LSE), and a visiting professor at the Maastricht Graduate School of Governance, UNMERIT, The Netherlands. His research interests cover the areas of e-government, economic theories of information systems, and the social studies of information systems. His publications address problems related to the adoption of ICTs in the public sector and discuss the institutional and organizational implication of such adoptions. An Italian national, he holds a Ph.D. in Information Systems from Gothenburg University, Sweden.

Daniel Curto-Millet recently completed his Ph.D. at the London School of Economics and Political Science. His research interests include open source phenomena, development processes, and the collaborative economy. He is currently Marie Curie Research Fellow at the Spanish National Research Council and retains an affiliation to the UAM-Accenture Chair at the Universidad Autónoma de Madrid. Before that, he was Research Fellow at ESCP Europe working on Stars4All, a Horizon 2020-funded project under the CAPS2020 call for advancing collective social innovation platforms that he helped draft. He has published in the *Journal of Information Technology* and has presented at major IS and management conferences.

Anne-Laure Fayard is Associate Professor of Management in the Department of Technology Management and Innovation at NYU Tandon School of Engineering, and is affiliated with the Department of Management and Organizations at NYU Stern Business School. Her research interests involve communication, collaboration, design, culture, and space, with a focus on interactions, particularly those between people and technology. Her work has been published in several leading journals, such as *Organization Science, Information Systems Research, Organization Studies and Harvard Business Review*. She is also the author with Anca Metiu of *The Power of Writing in Organizations* (Routledge, 2012). Prior to joining NYU Tandon, Fayard was a faculty member at INSEAD in Singapore and France. She holds a Ph.D. in Cognitive Science from the Ecole des Hautes-Etudes en Sciences Sociales (Paris), an M.Phil. in Cognitive Science from Ecole Polytechnique (Paris), and an M.A. and M.Phil. in Philosophy from La Sorbonne (Paris).

Chiara Franzoni is Associate Professor at the School of Management of Politecnico di Milano. Her research expertise is in the area of economics of science and innovation. She has conducted research on the financing of science and innovation, including crowdfunding. She also studies crowd science and online participation of citizens in public watch and policy-making. Her research has been published in *Science, Nature Biotechnology, Entrepreneurship Theory and Practice, PNAS, Economics Letters, Research Policy, Industrial and Corporate Change*, and elsewhere.

Christian Horn is working at the Department of Strategy at the business software company DATEV eG in Nuremberg, Germany. He received his Diploma in Business Administration at the Otto-Friedrich-University of Bamberg, where he also gained his Ph.D. in Marketing and Innovation Management. During his time at university, he worked as a lecturer and research assistant at several national and international higher education institutions, e.g. in South Korea, Belgium, and Germany. Also, he was active in consulting and cooperation projects with large companies such as Adidas AG, Siemens AG, and several small- and medium-sized enterprises. Christian is author, reviewer, and presenter for international journals, books, and conferences in his fields of research, including innovation management, open innovation, crowdsourcing, prediction markets, strategic management, and marketing and technology management.

Karl-Heinz Leitner is Senior Scientist at the Austrian Institute of Technology and Professor for Innovation Management at the University of Graz. His main research interests cover changing R&D and innovation processes, science–industry relations, research policy, and the valuation of intellectual capital. Karl-Heinz Leitner has conducted research and consultancy projects funded by agencies, ministries, and the European Commission. Between 2009 and 2012 he coordinated a FP7 funded foresight project about the future of innovation (INFU). His research has been published in, amongst others, *R&D Management, Management Accounting Research, International Journal of Innovation Management*, and *Small Business Economics*.

Natalia Levina is Toyota Motors Corporation Term Chair and Professor of Information Systems at New York University Stern School of Business. Her research has appeared in *Information Systems Research, MIS Quarterly, Organization Science*, and *Academy of Management Journal*, among others. Her main research interest is in understanding how people span organizational, professional, cultural, and other boundaries in order to generate innovative ideas and products, and how boundary-spanning practices impact firm sourcing strategy. She primarily uses qualitative methods and practice theory in her research and is a co-founder of the Grounded Theory Methods group within the Association of Information Systems. She has served as a senior editor for *Information Systems Research*, and on the editorial boards of the *Organization Science* and *Information and Organization* journals. She received her Ph.D. in Information Systems from Massachusetts Institute of Technology, and B.A. and M.A. degrees in Mathematics and Computer Science from Boston University.

Arsalan Nisar is an assistant professor at the Enterprise Institute where he holds the Chair of Energy and Innovation Management. Prior to this, he completed his postdoctoral fellowship at the Centre for Social and Sustainable Innovation, Gustavson School of Business at University of Victoria, conducting research on the role of open innovation in business sustainability. Furthermore, he was a postdoctoral fellow at the School of Economics and Business, Norwegian University of Life Sciences, exploring the role of storytelling in crowd-based platforms for scaling new ventures. He has a Ph.D. in Industrial Management from the School of Industrial Engineering, Technical University of Madrid and an MBA from University of Aberdeen. During his doctoral studies, he was a visiting scholar to ESCP Europe Business School and the Chair of Strategy and Innovation at the Swiss Federal Institute of Technology, Zurich. Currently, Arsalan is exploring the role of innovation and business model design within the energy industry. Further, he remains interested in broadening the research on hybrid organizations, the paradox of multiple organizational forms, and crowd-based platforms.

Andrea Paletti is a Ph.D. candidate in Information Systems and Innovation at the Department of Management at the London School of Economics and Political Science (LSE). He holds a Masters' degree in Management of Information Systems and Digital Innovation (MISDI) from LSE and a Master of Public Administration (MPA) from Tsinghua University in Beijing, China. He received his B.A. in Political Science from LUISS University in Rome, Italy. Andrea's research focuses on digital strategy in the private and public sectors, and design of information systems (IS). Andrea examines different forms of co-creation that can increase the value of products and services. He is also researching how to design IS to create new forms of private and public organizations that directly involve citizens and clients in the production of services and products. Prior to joining the LSE, Andrea served for three years in the Italian Navy. And finally, during his studies he also worked in several start-up projects in Italy and China.

Gireeja V. Ranade is a postdoctoral researcher at Microsoft Research, Redmond. Before this she was a lecturer in EECS at UC Berkeley, working on designing and teaching the pilot version for 16AB, the new first-year EECS classes. She received an M.S. and Ph.D. in EECS from UC Berkeley and an S.B. in EECS from MIT. She has worked on topics in brain–machine interfaces, information theory, control theory, wireless communications, and crowdsourcing.

Cristina Rossi-Lamastra is Associate Professor at Politecnico di Milano School of Management. Her research interests deal with entrepreneurship and organizational economics. Cristina has published on these topics in *Management Science, Entrepreneurship Theory and Practice, California Management Review,* and *Research Policy,* among others. She is Associate Editor of the *Journal of Small Business Management* and the *Journal of Industrial and Business Economics.*

Paola Rovelli is a Ph.D. student at Politecnico di Milano School of Management. In 2013, she was awarded a Masters' degree in Management Engineering at Politecnico di Milano summa cum laude. She carries out research on organizational design and on TMTs' functioning, with a specific focus on delegation.

Maha Shaikh is Associate Professor at Warwick Business School (WBS), University of Warwick. Maha has a Ph.D. in Information Systems from the London School of Economics and Political Science (LSE). Maha is also a research associate at the LSE. Her past affiliations include the University of Limerick, where she worked on a number of projects including the OPAALS project with Professor Brian Fitzgerald. She has also worked with Professor Leslie Willcocks at the LSE studying the relationship of open source to outsourcing, open innovation, and open business models. Dr Shaikh has been focused on open source, open innovation, and new forms of sourcing for a number of years and has published in the *Journal of the Association of Information Systems, Information Systems Research,* and *Government Information Quarterly.* Dr Shaikh is a co-author of *Adopting Open Source Software: A Practical Guide,* published by the MIT Press.

Jan Henrik Sieg holds a Ph.D. in Innovation Management from ETH Zurich, Department of Management, Technology, and Economics, where his research focused on open innovation and the knowledge-based view of the firm. He currently works as a management consultant, serving banks, asset managers, and institutional investors in Europe and the Middle East.

Jonathan Sims is Assistant Professor of Strategy at Babson College. He holds a Ph.D. in Management from the McCombs School of Business at the University of Texas at Austin, an M.B.A. from the Smith School of Business at the University of Maryland, and a B.A. in Political Science from Emory University. Jonathan's research and teaching interests lie at the intersection of strategy, entrepreneurship, and technology innovation. Specifically, he studies how entrepreneurial companies develop and implement technology strategies in cooperation with external communities. He has organized and moderated several conference workshops on researching open innovation. Prior to returning to academia, Jonathan was an entrepreneur and consultant to both non-profit and for-profit ventures.

Milica Šundić is devoted to building bridges between academic research and industrial practices in the field of crowdsourcing. She has been engaged in several projects dealing with transformation and innovation management in large enterprises, with the goal of attaining and retaining cutting-edge operations. Milica holds Masters' degrees in Informatics and Business Informatics and a postgraduate diploma from Vienna University of Technology and the Innovation Incubation Center. Her extensive experience in applied research was gained through her work as junior researcher and lecturer at Vienna University of Technology and her research work related to open and user innovation, crowdsourcing, and idea contests. She has published in scientific journals and conference proceedings in Austria, Germany, France, and the USA. Milica was awarded the Young Innovators Professional Award by the Austrian Federal Ministry of Science, Research and Economy in 2012. She has several years of industry experience in the fields of information technology, financial services, and telecommunication, with an emphasis on digital services, early-stage innovation projects, and above all, web and mobile app development.

Christopher L. Tucci is Dean of the College of Management of Technology at the Ecole Polytechnique Fédérale de Lausanne (EPFL), where he holds the Corporate Strategy & Innovation. He received the degrees of Ph.D. in Management from the Sloan School of Management, MIT; SM (Technology & Policy) from MIT; and B.S. (Mathematical Sciences), A.B. (Music), and M.S. (Computer Science) from Stanford University. Before returning for his Ph.D., he was an industrial computer scientist involved in developing Internet protocols and applying artificial intelligence tools to solving industrial problems. Professor Tucci joined EPFL in 2003, where he teaches courses in technology and innovation management (TIM), information technology strategy, and research methods. His primary areas of interest are business models, open innovation, crowdsourcing, and dynamic capabilities. He is also studying how the popularization of the Internet affects firms in different industries. He has published articles in, among others, *Academy of Management Review* (AMR), *Strategic Management Journal*, *Management Science*, *Research Policy*, *Communications of the ACM*, *Strategic Entrepreneurship Journal*, and *Journal of Product Innovation Management*. His 2012 article "Crowdsourcing as solution to distant search" won the Best Paper of 2012 for AMR, which was ranked the number one scholarly journal in the categories of Management and Business. He was the TIM Department Editor for the *IEEE Transactions on Engineering Management* and is Associate Editor of *Academy of Management Discoveries*. In 2004, he was elected to the five-year division leadership track of the Academy of Management's (AOM) TIM Division. In 2010, he was elected to the leadership track of the SMS' Strategy & Entrepreneurship Division. In 2013, he was elected to the AOM's board of governors.

Lav R. Varshney is an assistant professor of electrical and computer engineering at the University of Illinois at Urbana-Champaign. His research centers on the science and engineering of sociotechnical systems and is driven by a desire to improve individual and collective intelligence in modern environments. He draws on techniques from information theory, statistical signal processing, and data analytics. He was previously a research staff member at the IBM Thomas J. Watson Research Center (Yorktown Heights, NY), where he developed analytical techniques to improve IBM's internal crowdsourcing platform and global service delivery system. He also previously conceptualized IBM's computational creativity system for producing novel and flavorful culinary recipes, and led its design and development. He received his B.S. degree from Cornell University and his S.M., E.E., and Ph.D. degrees from the Massachusetts Institute of Technology.

Gianluigi Viscusi (Ph.D.) is a research fellow at the Chair of Corporate Strategy and Innovation (CSI) of the EPFL. His areas of expertise include information systems strategy and planning, business modeling, public policy and ICT-enabled innovation, e-government, information quality and value, service management and engineering, and social study of information systems. Currently, he is specifically interested in four research streams: *crowd-driven innovation*, investigating how crowdsourcing affects organizations in different industries; *cognitive economy and digital innovation* impacts on business and society; *translational research and science communication*; *policy and technology innovation* (focus on social value and open government). He has been a consultant on e-government planning, policy design, and implementation roadmaps for international organizations such as, e.g. the OECD. His research has been published in a range of books, conference proceedings, and journals such as, e.g. *Government Information Quarterly*. In 2010 he co-authored with Carlo Batini and Massimo Mecella the book *Information Systems for eGovernment: A Quality of Service Perspective* (Springer, Heidelberg).

Georg von Krogh is full Professor of Strategic Management and Innovation at ETH Zurich. He is also a member of the National Research Council at the Swiss National Science Foundation. His research interests include competitive strategy, technological innovation, and organizational knowledge creation.

Martin W. Wallin is Professor of Innovation Management at Chalmers University of Technology, Department of Technology Management and Economics in Sweden, and faculty member at ETH Zurich, Department of Management, Technology, and Economics, Switzerland. His research examines organizational and motivational implications of distributed innovation.

Joel West is Professor of Innovation & Entrepreneurship at the Keck Graduate Institute School of Applied Life Sciences, after holding a similar position at

San Jose State University. His research on open innovation includes co-editing *Open Innovation: Researching a New Paradigm* (Oxford, 2006), *New Frontiers in Open Innovation* (Oxford, 2014), and a 2014 special issue of *Research Policy*. His research focuses on how firms manage communities, ecosystems, and platforms, including research on 3-D printing, open source software, and mobile telecommunications. He has published articles in *Industry & Innovation, Information Systems Research, Journal of Management Studies, Journal of Product Innovation Management, Journal of Technology Transfer, R&D Management, Research Policy, Strategic Entrepreneurship Journal, Strategic Management Journal, Technological Forecasting & Social Change,* and *Telecommunications Policy,* among other journals. He has a Ph.D. from UC Irvine, an S.B. from MIT and more than 20 years' experience in the software industry.

1

Introduction to *Creating and Capturing Value Through Crowdsourcing*

Christopher L. Tucci, Allan Afuah, and Gianluigi Viscusi

Abstract
Partly fueled by the pervasiveness of information technologies that facilitate the broadcasting of problems to crowds, and by anecdotal examples of phenomenally high-value solutions from outsourcing some problems to crowds, growth in the research and practice of crowdsourcing for problem solving has been remarkable. Research streams have been emerging in different disciplines. In this introduction to the volume, we introduce twelve chapters by scholars—from different disciplines—who explore interesting topics from some of these emerging research streams. The chapters fall into different groups distinguished by whether value is created and captured via tournament-based, collaboration-based, or hybrid crowdsourcing activities. We also offer future research directions and conclusions.

INTRODUCTION

For decades, transaction cost economics, the problem-solving view, and other theoretical perspectives have been used to understand, explain, and make predictions about why and when a firm would want to solve a problem through hierarchies, hybrids, or markets (e.g., Williamson, 1985, 2002; Nickerson & Zenger, 2004). In that research, getting a problem solved through "markets" has meant that a focal firm finds someone whom it believes can solve the problem, and designates that someone—through an *ex ante* contract or other agreement/commitment specific to the problem—as the contractor to solve the problem (Afuah, 2018a). The challenge is that, for many problems, finding that someone to solve a problem can be as difficult as finding a needle in a haystack (Afuah & Tucci, 2012; Afuah, 2016). Even more challenging is the fact that some problems require a collection of solvers that the focal firm cannot identify, *ex ante*, to collaborate with and solve the problem.

This is where *crowdsourcing*—a portmanteau of the words "crowd" and "outsourcing," as in outsourcing to a crowd rather than a designated contractor (Howe, 2006)—comes in. Because it can be difficult for focal firms, individuals, or even nations to identify, *ex ante*, who can solve a problem, they broadcast the problem to a crowd so that potential solvers can self-select to solve it with no *ex ante* agreements/commitments to solving the problem (Afuah & Tucci, 2012).

Partly fueled by the pervasiveness of information technologies that facilitate the broadcasting of problems to crowds, and by anecdotal examples of phenomenally high-value solutions from outsourcing some problems to crowds, growth in the research and practice of crowdsourcing has been remarkable. Importantly, different crowdsourcing research streams have emerged. Some scholars see crowdsourcing as an online phenomenon (e.g., Brabham, 2008), while others see it as a governance mechanism that goes back to at least the Longitude Prize of 1714, with information technology only serving as an enabler (Afuah & Tucci, 2012). Yet others see crowdsourcing as a mechanism for selling and buying on-demand labor that has the potential to disrupt the way firms create and capture value. Symbolic of these differences are the different research silos that explore crowdsourcing and the different terms that have been used to describe the phenomenon. Authors have used terms such as *broadcast search, distributed innovation, crowdfunding, collective intelligence, innovation tournaments, innovation contests,* and so on to describe crowdsourcing.

Fortunately, much research has been conducted on outsourcing and crowds—research that can help us to better theorize about crowdsourcing. In particular, much has been written about using tournaments to get crowds to solve problems, how crowds collaborate in solving problems, and what motivates crowds to solve problems—that is, much has been written about using crowds to create and capture value. The chapters in this volume fall into different groups, distinguished by whether value is created and captured via tournament-based, collaboration-based, or hybrid crowdsourcing activities.

The papers in Part I introduce the reader to crowdsourcing and the crowds and communities that are foundational to the phenomenon. More specifically, Afuah (2018a) presents a crowdsourcing primer and framework with the goal of introducing scholars to some of the constructs and concepts that academics may find useful in exploring theoretically interesting research questions. Viscusi & Tucci (2018) examine some important *characteristics of crowds* such as the goal orientation and the "seriality" of interactions and activities, thus clarifying how crowds may differ from communities and other kinds of collective entities. This difference is particularly relevant for identifying which kind of collective entity would be most effective when designing crowdsourcing initiatives, especially considering the different kinds of investments that might be required by the different kinds of crowds and communities.

West & Sims (2018) focus on the role that crowds and communities play during open innovation, especially focusing on *problem formulation* in innovation contests and the role of managerial actions in facilitating it. To this end, the authors analyze multiple case studies to inductively build a theoretical framework defining mechanisms for seeker firms' formulations of sharable problems in innovation contests. The last chapter in Part I, by Butticè et al. (2018), provides an extensive overview of crowdfunding, which is one of the most popular forms of crowdsourcing (if one conceptualizes a lack of funding as a problem to be solved). In particular, the chapter specifies the main characteristics of crowdfunding and how they relate to crowdfunding success.

The papers in Part II of the volume are about tournament-based crowdsourcing and extend the arguments discussed in Part I. In the first paper in the group, Wallin et al. (2018) remind us that *problem formulation* is so fundamental to problem solving that—for some problems—formulation can be more important than the solution. Using seven case studies, they detail rare accounts of the intra-organizational activities and implications of problem formulation for contests. Ranade & Varshney (2018) consider the other side of the spectrum of crowdsourcing contests, focusing on the *utility* generated for different types of tasks, including but not limited to idea generation. In particular, the authors identify a set of relevant factors for crowdsourcing contest design such as knowledge about the relative strengths of the participating solvers/workers and their awareness of the strength of internal competitors.

The papers in Part III are about collaboration-based crowdsourcing. Cordella et al. (2018) focus on the public sector to understand how and why co-production can be a valuable solution to delivering public services, improving both their public value *and* the administrative activities behind them. The authors propose that collaboration-based crowdsourcing in the public sector implies a change of perspective from focusing merely on the production processes of public services to first targeting public value creation. Levina & Fayard (2018) consider digital platforms enabling crowdsourcing contests and compare how consulting companies approach the translation and integration of diverse ideas and expertise to how they are addressed in innovation-focused crowdsourcing platforms. In particular, the authors analyze the role of boundary-spanning practices for knowledge collaboration, necessary due to the complexity of the task in crowdsourcing exercises where many new boundaries must be managed, in comparison with, e.g., online communities (cf. Faraj et al., 2011).

To conclude Part III, Šundić & Leitner (2018) analyze cases from A1 Telekom Austria to understand co-creation in both public and internal crowdsourcing initiatives, thus also contributing to the literature on internal crowdsourcing (cf. Zuchowski et al. 2016). The three approaches proposed comprise: (1) the open, external co-creation approach with customers and users of the A1 Support Community; (2) the semi-open, internal tool-based co-creation approach with selected employees; and (3) the internal offline co-creation approach with employees.

The papers in Part IV are about hybrid crowdsourcing—that is, they explore questions that involve both tournament- and collaboration-based crowdsourcing. Afuah (2018b) argues that simultaneous competition to solve modules of a decomposable problem and collaboration to aggregate the module solutions produce a higher-value solution to the problem than collaboration alone. Just as important, simultaneous cooperation to reduce crowdsourcing frictions, and competition to solve a non-decomposable problem yield a higher-value solution than competition alone. Horn et al. (2018) take us into the world of prediction markets, and demonstrate how these markets can be used as a crowdsourcing mechanism to get crowds that will more effectively solve problems. More specifically, they demonstrate that when prediction markets are used in getting internal crowds to solve a problem, the crowd can outperform external crowds in solving some problems.

To round out the book, Curto-Millet & Nisar (2018) review the extent to which stakeholder theory might be applicable to understanding the ethical dimension of crowdsourcing. They discuss many of the ethical consequences of crowdsourcing and propose recommendations on how stakeholder theory can provide a response to such ethical dilemmas, and they provide one of the first attempts to debate the role of stakeholder theory for future research directions in the context of crowdsourcing.

As shown in Table 1.1, we have identified seven key cross-cutting topics from the chapters in this book that represent potential research themes and challenges for disciplines such as Innovation Management and Strategy, but also Organization Science, Political Science, and Information Systems. The first theme draws out some of the distinctions and similarities between crowds and communities, what they have in common, and how to take advantage of some of the differences for firms' innovation processes. The second theme is about the relation between open innovation and crowdsourcing, how companies might think about crowdsourcing as part of their open innovation portfolio, and when crowdsourcing might be different from open innovation. The third theme has to do with the differences and commonalities between internal and external crowds and many of the nuances of using external and internal agents in different contexts.

The fourth cross-cutting theme is concerned with an exploration of the co-production and co-creation processes enabled by crowdsourcing and how they might differ from more traditional problem-solving approaches. The fifth theme is about capturing value from crowdsourcing: who are the stakeholders, how is the contest governed, how is the contest designed to increase overall value, and how is the value shared? If crowdsourcing is about problem solving, the sixth theme revolves around "non-traditional" problems

Table 1.1. Cross-cutting themes developed in this book.

Cross-cutting topic	Chapters	Disciplinary areas
1. The relation and difference between crowds and communities	• Chapter 3 (Viscusi & Tucci) • Chapter 4 (West & Sims)	• Innovation Management • Organization Science • Information Systems
2. The relation and difference between open innovation and crowdsourcing	• Chapter 2 (Afuah) • Chapter 4 (West & Sims) • Chapter 9 (Levina & Fayard) • Chapter 13 (Curto-Millet & Nisar)	• Innovation Management • Organization Science • Strategy
3. The advantages and disadvantages of internal versus external crowds; inter- and intra-organizational processes to facilitate crowdsourcing	• Chapter 2 (Afuah) • Chapter 9 (Levina & Fayard) • Chapter 6 (Wallin et al.) • Chapter 10 (Šundić & Leitner) • Chapter 12 (Horn et al.)	• Innovation Management • Organization Science • Information Systems • Strategy
4. The different ways to organize crowds from the common sense understanding of crowdsourcing as an input into the problem-solving process to co-production and co-creation	• Chapter 3 (Viscusi & Tucci) • Chapter 8 (Cordella et al.) • Chapter 10 (Šundić & Leitner)	• Innovation Management • Organization Science • Political Science
5. Governance of and value capture from crowdsourcing	• Chapter 11 (Afuah) • Chapter 13 (Curto-Millet & Nisar)	• Strategy • Organization Science • Ethics
6. "Non-traditional problems" solved by crowdsourcing, from monetary value in crowdfunding to public value in the public sector	• Chapter 5 (Butticè et al.) • Chapter 8 (Cordella et al.)	• Innovation Management • Strategy • Political Science • Entrepreneurship
7. The role of information and information systems capacity in designing and managing crowdsourcing	• Chapter 3 (Viscusi & Tucci) • Chapter 7 (Ranade & Varshney) • Chapter 11 (Afuah)	• Innovation Management • Information Systems

to be solved and expands our repertoire of what constitutes effective contexts of crowdsourcing. Finally, the seventh cross-cutting theme is about the role of information and how information systems can be used in designing crowdsourcing exercises. Table 1.1 links each of these themes to multiple chapters as a convenient cross-reference and suggests different disciplines to which the themes might be relevant.

CONCLUSIONS AND FUTURE RESEARCH DIRECTIONS

Together, these chapters provide critical elements for pursuing research in crowdsourcing, and constitute an excellent starting point for crowdsourcing scholarship. Because the research opportunities in crowdsourcing are inherently large, and there are only twelve further chapters in this volume, there are still many research gaps and therefore many opportunities for future research. These gaps fall within four generic domains. First, although the volume is entitled *Creating and Capturing Value through Crowdsourcing*, there is still a bigger emphasis in the volume on value creation relative to value capture. This asymmetrical attention to value creation at the expense of value capture in crowdsourcing literature has been recognized for a while, but to date little has been accomplished towards addressing it (Afuah & Tucci, 2013; Bloodgood, 2013). Future research could more explicitly focus on value capture questions, especially the roles of complementary assets and business models (Teece, 1986; Massa et al., 2017).

Second, little attention has been given to date to how seekers could organize to better formulate, delineate, and broadcast problems, so as to evaluate and assimilate the solutions from crowds. We know very little about the types of organizational structures, systems, culture, and strategies that seeker organizations may want to pursue to increase their chances of creating and capturing superior value via crowdsourcing. Third, although internal crowdsourcing research has recently attracted some interest (including at least two of the chapters in this volume), much of the attention has been focused on external crowdsourcing. Future research could tease apart many of the nuances that distinguish internal from external crowds. Fourth, these chapters, like most crowdsourcing research so far, have focused largely on the advantages of the phenomenon, with less of an emphasis on its pitfalls. Future research could look into the disadvantages of crowdsourcing and how they might be mitigated, or the contingencies that might distinguish success from failure.

Fifth and most important, good research explains and predicts. However, as mentioned previously, most of the chapters in this book are conceptual, qualitative, or descriptive, focusing on the "pre-theorizing" that is natural at this stage of evolution of the field. The emphasis in this book was not on clearly defining constructs, developing and testing hypothesized relationships, or on linking constructs with causal logic. The full potential—both scientific and practical—of crowdsourcing is likely to be attained when researchers take the field to the next level and explore explanation and prediction. Luckily, as the identified research gaps suggest, there are plenty of opportunities to write papers that make meaningful contributions to advancing knowledge in crowdsourcing.

We hope this volume stimulates even more interest in the topic so that our research community can grow into a large, open crowd, teeming with excitement about crowdsourcing's potential!

REFERENCES

Afuah A. (2018a). Crowdsourcing: A primer and research framework. In C. Tucci, A. Afuah, & G. Viscusi (eds.), *Creating and Capturing Value Through Crowdsourcing.* Oxford: Oxford University Press, pp. 11–38.

Afuah A. (2018b). Co-opetition in crowdsourcing: When simultaneous cooperation and competition deliver superior solutions. In C. Tucci, A. Afuah, & G. Viscusi (eds.), *Creating and Capturing Value Through Crowdsourcing. Oxford*: Oxford University Press, pp. 271–91.

Afuah, A. N. (2016). The extreme-value and aggregated-contribution potential of a crowd. Working paper, Ross School of Business, University of Michigan, Ann Arbor, MI.

Afuah, A. & Tucci, C. L. (2012). Crowdsourcing as a solution to distant search. *Academy of Management Review, 37*(3), 355–75.

Afuah, A. & Tucci, C. L. (2013). Value capture and crowdsourcing. *Academy of Management Review, 38*(3), 457–60.

Bloodgood, J. (2013). Crowdsourcing: Useful for problem solving, but what about value capture? *Academy of Management Review, 38*(3), 455–7.

Brabham, D. C. (2008). Crowdsourcing as a model for problem solving an introduction and cases. *Convergence: International Journal of Research into Mew Media Technologies, 14*(1), 75–90.

Butticè, V., Franzoni, C., Rossi-Lamastra, C., & Rovelli, P. (2018). The road to crowdfunding success: A review of extant literature. In C. Tucci, A. Afuah, & G. Viscusi (eds.), *Creating and Capturing Value Through Crowdsourcing.* Oxford: Oxford University Press, pp. 97–126.

Cordella, A., Palletti, A., & Shaikh, M. (2018). Renegotiating public value with co-production. In C. Tucci, A. Afuah, & G. Viscusi (eds.), *Creating and Capturing Value Through Crowdsourcing.* Oxford: Oxford University Press, pp. 181–203.

Curto-Millet, D. & Nisar, A. (2018). Ethics in crowdsourcing: Revisiting and revising the role of stakeholder theory. In C. Tucci, A. Afuah, & G. Viscusi (eds.), *Creating and Capturing Value Through Crowdsourcing.* Oxford: Oxford University Press, pp. 310–34.

Faraj, S. Jarvenpaa, S. L, & Majchrzack, A. (2011). Knowledge collaboration in online communities. *Organization Science 22*(5): 1224–39.

Horn, C., Bogers, M., & Brem, A. (2018). Prediction markets for crowdsourcing. In C. Tucci, A. Afuah, & G. Viscusi (eds.), *Creating and Capturing Value Through Crowdsourcing.* Oxford: Oxford University Press, pp. 292–309.

Howe, J. (2006). Crowdsourcing: A definition. *Crowdsourcing: Tracking the rise of the amateur* (weblog, June 2), http://crowdsourcing.typepad.com/cs/2006/06/crowdsourcing_a.html (accessed January 20, 2017).

Levina, N. & Fayard, A-L. (2018). Tapping into diversity through open innovation platforms: The emergence of boundary spanning practices. In C. Tucci, A. Afuah, & G. Viscusi (eds.), *Creating and Capturing Value Through Crowdsourcing.* Oxford: Oxford University Press, pp. 204–35.

Massa, L., Tucci, C. L., & Afuah, A. (2017). A critical assessment of business model research. *Academy of Management Annals, 11*(1), 73–104.

Nickerson, J. A. & Zenger, T. R. (2004). A knowledge-based theory of the firm—The problem-solving perspective. *Organization Science, 15*(6), 617–32.

Ranade, G. & Varshney, L. (2018). The role of information patterns in designing crowdsourcing contests. In C. Tucci, A. Afuah, & G. Viscusi (eds.), *Creating and Capturing Value Through Crowdsourcing.* Oxford: Oxford University Press, pp. 154–80.

Šundić, M. & Leitner, K-H. (2018). Co-creation from a telecommunication provider's perspective: A comparative study on innovation with customers and employees. In C. Tucci, A. Afuah, & G. Viscusi (eds.), *Creating and Capturing Value Through Crowdsourcing.* Oxford: Oxford University Press, pp. 236–70.

Teece, D. J. (1986). Profiting from technological innovation: Implications for integration, collaboration, licensing and public policy. *Research Policy, 15*(6), 285–305.

Viscusi, G. & Tucci, C. (2018). Three's a crowd? In C. Tucci, A. Afuah, & G. Viscusi (eds.), *Creating and Capturing Value Through Crowdsourcing.* Oxford: Oxford University Press, pp. 39–57.

Wallin, M., von Krogh, G., & Sieg, J. (2017). A problem in the making: How firms formulate sharable problems for open innovation contests. In C. Tucci, A. Afuah, & G. Viscusi (eds.), *Creating and Capturing Value Through Crowdsourcing.* Oxford: Oxford University Press, pp. 39–57.

West, J. & Sims, J. (2018). How firms leverage crowds and communities for open innovation. In C. Tucci, A. Afuah, & G. Viscusi (eds.), *Creating and Capturing Value Through Crowdsourcing.* Oxford: Oxford University Press, pp. 58–96.

Williamson, O. E. (1985). *The Economic Institutions of Capitalism.* New York: Free Press.

Williamson, O. E. (2002). The theory of the firm as governance structure: From choice to contract. *Journal of Economic Perspectives, 16*(3), 171–95.

Zuchowski, O., Posegga, O., Schlagwein, D., & Fischbach, K. (2016). Internal crowdsourcing: conceptual framework, structured review, and research agenda. *Journal of Information Technology, 31*(2, SI), 166–84.

Part I

Crowdsourcing: Fundamentals and the Role of Crowds and Communities

2

Crowdsourcing: A Primer and Research Framework

Allan Afuah

Abstract

Managers are regularly confronted with unsolved problems. If managers know who can solve a problem, they can assign the problem to the correct person to have it solved under an *ex ante* contract or other form of agreement/commitment, inside or outside the organization. If they do not know who can solve it, they can crowdsource it, broadcasting the problem to an undefined set of people (the crowd) to self-select and solve it with no *ex ante* contract or other commitment. Although the practice of crowdsourcing goes back to at least the Longitude Prize of 1714, research on the phenomenon has only recently flourished, thanks, in part, to advances in information technology, globalization, and other macro-environmental factors. Herein I present a crowdsourcing primer and framework with the goal of providing management scholars with some of the fundamentals needed to pursue their research interests in this compelling phenomenon.

INTRODUCTION

At a very general and intuitive level, crowdsourcing is the act of having an *undefined* set of people self-select and perform a task with no *ex ante* contracts or other commitments to get the task performed (Howe, 2006; Malone et al., 2010; Afuah & Tucci, 2012; Afuah, 2016). Solving the problem is not restricted to one person in particular—it is *open* to anyone. Beyond this intuitive level, definitions of the phenomenon can vary considerably (for a summary of definitions, see: Estellés-Arolas & González-Ladrón-De-Guevara, 2012; Majchrzak &

Malhotra, 2013). Importantly, many of these definitions are derived from the first definition of crowdsourcing offered by Howe, who coined the term and defined it as:

> The act of a company or institution taking a function once performed by employees and outsourcing it to an undefined (and generally large) network of people in the form of an open call.   (2006: 1)

Three popular examples illustrate the meaning of the phenomenon. First, in 1714, rather than select some of its employees to solve the longitude problem or contract the task to those it believed were talented enough to perform the task, the UK government crowdsourced the problem—it outsourced the task in the form of an open call to anyone anywhere in the kingdom who could solve it (Sobel, 2007). George Harrison, a clock maker, solved the problem, delivering a solution that, for decades, gave the British a competitive advantage at sea.

Second, about three centuries after the Longitude Prize, in 2009, Facebook decided to translate its website from English to other languages to open up its social network to non-English-speakers. Rather than assigning the task to specific employees, or contracting the job to designated translation houses, Facebook crowdsourced the problem in the form of an open call to anyone anywhere in the world interested in performing the task. The site was translated from English to French in twenty-four hours and to Spanish in two weeks. By the end of 2011, the site had been translated into more than seventy languages, launching Facebook on its way to having more than one billion visitors to its site. Third, in 2005, rather than asking its forecasting group to predict sales of its gift cards, Best Buy sent emails—together with readily available straightforward data—to hundreds of its employees asking those who were interested to voluntarily perform the task (Dye, 2008). A straight average of the forecasts from those who self-selected to perform the task was 99.5 percent accurate, compared to a forecast of 94.5 percent from the company's internal expert forecasters (Dye, 2008).

In each of the three examples, a problem was broadcast to an *undefined* set of people. With no *ex ante* commitments about solving the specific problem, solvers self-selected and solved it, delivering high-value solutions. The issuer of the task did not specifically identify a person and assign the task to him or her to perform under a contract or other agreement/commitment specific to the task. The call to solve the problem was open.

One way to conceptualize crowdsourcing is to consider an organization that has a problem that it would like to solve. Such a problem could be to develop an app for a smartphone platform, design a new product, create a new algorithm for recommending videos or apps, provide hotel accommodation for someone in a strange city, catch a criminal, diagnose a rare disease, forecast sales of a new product, fund a new venture, identify people in a museum's photo archives, and so on (Afuah, 2016). That is, these "problems" can be just about any task that contributes to value creation and capture (Allen, 1966; Nickerson et al., 2012).

If a manager knows who can solve such a problem, s/he can assign the problem to the designated solver—inside or outside the organization—to solve it under some form of authority or *ex ante* contract/commitment (Malone, et al., 2010). If a manager does not know who can solve the problem, s/he can *crowdsource* it—outsource it in the form of an *open call* to an *undefined* group of solvers to self-select and solve the problem, *without* the manager specifically assigning the task to someone that they believe can solve the particular problem (Howe, 2006; Afuah & Tucci, 2012).

Types of Crowdsourcing

Crowdsourcing can be tournament based, collaboration based, or a hybrid of both. In tournament-based crowdsourcing, each actor that self-selects to solve a problem generates a solution to the problem (Che & Gale, 2003; Scotchmer, 2004; Afuah & Tucci, 2012). Thus, if there are a hundred solvers that self-select to solve the problem, about one hundred solutions are likely to be generated. These solutions are evaluated for winners. The Longitude Prize example falls in this category. Much of the crowdsourcing research conducted to date has been tournament based (e.g., Terwiesch & Xu, 2008; Boudreau et al., 2011; Lampel et al., 2012). Some of that research has yielded some rather interesting results (Poetz & Schreier, 2012; Lang et al., 2016). For example, Poetz & Schreier (2012) found that product innovation ideas from a crowd of external non-experts outperformed those from internal experts in some key performance measures. Tournament-based crowdsourcing research has drawn on neoclassical economic theory, tournament theory, and all-pay auction theory to explore theoretically interesting questions (e.g., Connelly et al., 2014; Liu et al., 2014; Ranade & Varshney, 2018).

In collaboration-based crowdsourcing, each solver provides only a component of the solution, and the different components are aggregated to obtain the solution to the problem (e.g., Afuah & Tucci, 2012; Levine & Prietula, 2013; Franzoni & Sauermann, 2014; Bauer & Gegenhuber, 2015). For example, in the crowdsourcing of the translation of a document from one language to another, different translators translate different passages and their contributions are aggregated to produce the translated document. Crowdfunding and open source projects are largely collaboration-based crowdsourcing (Mollick, 2014; Butticè et al., 2018).

Crowdsourcing can also be a hybrid of tournament-based and collaboration-based activities. Witness Wikipedia, where people can compete to write each entry and the "winning" entries are aggregated to produce the encyclopedia. The use of prediction markets to solve problems often involves both types of crowdsourcing (Christiansen, 2007; Borison & Hamm, 2010; Horn et al., 2018).

The Crowdsourcing Process

As a process, crowdsourcing has four major steps (Afuah & Tucci, 2012). First, the managers of a seeker organization get the problem formulated, delineated, and broadcast to an undefined set of people in the form of an open call (e.g., Chiu, Liang, & Turban, 2014; Frederiksen & Rullani, 2015; Wallin et al., 2017). Second, those people who want to solve the problem self-select to do so without being specifically assigned to the task by the seeker. These solvers are on their own and incur their own cost of solving the problem, with no guarantees about what happens if they are not successful in providing the solution that the seeker wants.

Third, in the case of tournament-based crowdsourcing, the solutions generated are evaluated to determine a winner. Note that a crowd can also be used to formulate the problems or evaluate the solutions generated. For example, a firm can have its T-shirt designed by conducting design contests in which anyone can submit a design, and the designs are evaluated by its community of registered users, many of whom are customers (Brabham, 2008). In collaboration-based or hybrid crowdsourcing, component solutions are aggregated—often through implicit coordination (Rico et al., 2008)—to obtain the solution. Wikipedia entries are aggregated to produce an encyclopedia, with the help of its editors' implicit coordination activities. The final step in the crowdsourcing process is solution assimilation and implementation, in which the winning solutions are transferred to the seeker to incorporate into its value creation and capture activities (Lüttgens et al., 2014; Levina & Fayard, 2018).

Theoretical Rationale Behind Crowdsourcing

As the Longitude Prize, Google translations, Best Buy, and other anecdotal examples illustrate (e.g., Masters & Delbecq, 2008; Jeppesen & Lakhani, 2010), crowdsourcing can deliver extraordinarily high-value solutions to some problems. The rationale behind why crowdsourcing can deliver such superior-value solutions to some problems is rooted in well-established insights and theoretical perspectives about the resources—including knowledge—needed to solve problems, as well as the incentives for solving problems. How? First, according to von Hayek (1937), knowledge is heterogeneously distributed among members of society, and according to the resource-based view (RBV), heterogeneously distributed resources can be scarce, valuable (uniquely superior at performing some tasks), immobile, and difficult to imitate or substitute (cf., Barney, 1991; Mahoney & Pandian, 1992; Grant, 1996; Peteraf & Barney, 2003).

Therefore, sooner or later, some units or organizations will face problems whose solutions require knowledge and resources that they do not have—solutions that require scarce, valuable, and difficult to imitate or substitute resources that someone else has. If the scarce knowledge/resources are also immobile, a unit or organization that does not already have them is not likely to obtain them (Barney, 1991). In the ideal world of unlimited cognition, a manager would know which individual, units, or organizations have these resources and could assign the tasks to them to be performed under some form of authority, *ex ante* contract, or other commitment/agreement. In a boundedly rational world, managers often cannot tell, *ex ante*, who is capable of solving which problems, and finding out who can solve such problems can be as difficult as finding a needle in a haystack, with all the challenges associated with distant search (Katila & Ahuja, 2002; Afuah & Tucci, 2012; Piezunka & Dahlander, 2015). In crowdsourcing, managers broadcast the problem in the form of an open call, and the people with the superior knowledge/resources for solving the problem self-select to solve it. The "needles" in the haystacks identify themselves.

The second reason why crowdsourcing can deliver high-value solutions to some problems is rooted in the heterogeneity of incentives. Contrary to neoclassical economic theory, not everyone is motivated by money. Although many solvers are motivated by immediate monetary payments, many others solve problems to build new skills, improve their expertise, signal their skills to potential employers, build reputations, have fun, and to make a difference in the world (Lerner & Tirole, 2002; Lakhani & Wolf, 2005; Shah, 2006). Effectively, each solver may be motived by some combination of monetary, non-monetary, extrinsic, intrinsic, identity-based, or need-based incentives that can be very different from what motivates other solvers (e.g., Shah, 2006; Ren et al., 2007; von Krogh et al., 2012; Belenzon & Schankerman, 2015). Just as it is difficult for cognitively limited managers to tell in advance who has the resources to solve which problems, it can be difficult for these mangers to tell in advance who has the incentives to solve what problems. In crowdsourcing, managers do not need to know who has the right incentives for solving a problem. The problem is broadcast to an undefined set of people so that potential solvers with the right incentives self-select to solve it. A solver with the right knowledge, resources, and incentives can deliver a superior value solution that is also very low cost.

Internal Versus External Crowdsourcing

In a world in which people are hyper-rational, with no cognitive limitations, any manager with a problem knows, *ex ante*, who can solve it. If the solver is an employee, s/he can be assigned to the task under an employee contract or other agreement, and if from outside, s/he can be assigned to perform the task as a designated contractor. However, in a boundedly rational world, managers are cognitively limited and therefore may not be able to tell in advance who (inside or outside) can solve a problem. In internal crowdsourcing, the problem would be broadcast internally in the form of an open call to an undefined set of employees who can self-select to solve the problem without managers specifically assigning the task to them; and the employees not making any *ex ante* commitments to management about performing that specific task. For example, rather than ask the unit that has traditionally designed new cars, an automaker may decide to crowdsource the task internally. It may broadcast the problem within the firm for anyone, anywhere in the firm, to self-select to produce a new design without being specifically assigned to the task by the firm's managers, and without making any commitments to management about designing the car—that is, with no advance agreement with authorities on what to do, or when and how to do it. The Best Buy example from the introduction falls into the category of internal crowdsourcing. Zuchowski et al. (2016) provide an excellent review of the internal crowdsourcing literature.

In external crowdsourcing, a seeker broadcasts a problem to an outside crowd, and members of the crowd self-select and solve the problem with no *ex ante* contracts with the seeker. Much of the earlier research in crowdsourcing was about external crowdsourcing. A critical question that has not been explored is: when is a seeker better off crowdsourcing a problem internally rather than externally? According to Surowiecki (2004), an important criterion for a crowd to be "wise" is independence—that is, for a crowd to be wise, each of its members should be able to act independently of other members when self-selecting and solving a problem. Because an organization's goals, strategy, culture, and other attributes can influence the independence of its members in self-selecting and solving some problems, a seeker organization may be better off using external crowdsourcing to solve such problems. External crowds may be less likely to have one central authority dictating what they can do.

The Relationship Between Open Innovation and Crowdsourcing

If something here reminds you of open innovation, that feeling may be because crowdsourcing and open innovation are very related. Open innovation has been defined as "the use of purposive inflows and outflows of knowledge to accelerate internal innovation, and expand the markets for external use of innovation, respectively" (Chesbrough, 2006: 1). That is, open innovation is about two things: (1) purposive knowledge flowing into an organization to be used to complement and/or replace internal knowledge stocks to improve innovation performance (Chesbrough, 2003; West & Bogers, 2014); and (2) purposive knowledge outflows to leverage external complementary assets and business models so as to better profit from internally generated innovations (Chesbrough, 2003; Chesbrough et al., 2006; Alexy et al., 2013; Henkel et al., 2014; Bogers et al., 2016; Massa, Tucci, & Afuah, 2017).

So what has open innovation to do with crowdsourcing? A lot! Recall that crowdsourcing is the act of having an undefined set of people self-select and perform a task with no *ex ante* contracts or other commitments to get the particular task performed. That is, crowdsourcing is the act of *opening* up the solving of a problem to anyone who wants to self-select and solve it. In external crowdsourcing, a problem is broadcast to a crowd outside the focal organization and therefore, problems can be viewed as purposive knowledge outflows from the organization, and solutions as purposive knowledge inflows (Alexy et al., 2013). Therefore, open innovation and external crowdsourcing are both about purposive knowledge inflows/outflows, with crowdsourcing being more limiting since outflows are largely problems and inflows are largely solutions to the problems. That is, crowdsourcing involves both knowledge inflows and outflows into and out of a focal organization—it involves so-called "coupled" open innovation (cf., Gassmann & Enkel, 2004).

There are two important differences between open innovation and crowdsourcing. First, the knowledge inflows/outflows of open innovation often take place between parties *with ex ante* contracts or other commitments. For example, technology alliances, strategic alliances, licensing agreements, venture capital investments, joint ventures, and other forms of "teaming up" formally are popular mechanisms for pursuing knowledge inflows/outflows and are rooted in *ex ante* contracts/commitments (e.g., Faems et al., 2010; Felin & Zenger, 2014). These governance forms are critical to open innovation. A defining property of crowdsourcing is the absence of these contracts/commitments. Second, crowdsourcing can be internal to an organization but open innovation has not been viewed as such. By definition, open innovation is about knowledge inflows into and outflows from a focal organization, and therefore open innovation scholars do not see open innovation as an internal phenomenon (e.g., Bogers et al., 2016; West & Sims, 2018). Internal crowdsourcing can be a critical organizational strategy for solving problems, and is increasingly attracting much scholarly attention (Zuchowski et al., 2016).

Advantages of Crowdsourcing

From the crowdsourcing research that has been conducted so far, the phenomenon has many advantages for solvers and seekers (Afuah, 2014). Here, I focus on five of these advantages: higher-value solutions at lower costs, potential recruiting tool, opportunity to deploy slack resources, opportunity to solve problems from the long tails of problem distributions, and an opportunity to signal strategic moves.[1] More advantages should emerge as more crowdsourcing research is conducted.

Higher-value solutions at lower cost. Because crowdsourcing enables solvers with the incentives and the valuable, immobile, difficult to imitate or substitute resources to self-select to solve problems, there is a high likelihood of obtaining superior-value solutions to problems that seekers do not know how to solve and who can solve them. Additionally, since solvers may have non-monetary incentives for solving some problems, and solvers whose solutions do not win have to incur their own costs, the cost of solutions to seekers can be very low. Therefore, crowdsourcing has the potential to deliver very *high-value* solutions to some problems at very *low cost*. Many examples confirm this dual advantage of crowdsourcing (Masters & Delbecq, 2008; Brabham, 2010, 2013). Witness the GoldCorp challenge (Tischler, 2002; Tapscott & Williams, 2006; Marjanovic et al., 2012), Wikipedia experiment, protein folding (Cooper et al., 2010), and so on. Imagine how much less comprehensive and less dependable Wikipedia entries would be, and how much more it would cost to produce the entries if the organization had to hire experts to produce them internally or contract the writing out to them.

Potential recruiting tool. Recall that one of the incentives for some solvers who participate in crowdsourcing is to signal their skills to potential employers (Lerner & Tirole, 2002; Lakhani & Wolf, 2005). Thus, some seekers can use crowdsourcing as a recruiting venue and tool. For example, after the tournament in which solutions from solvers enabled it to find enough gold on its property to catapult its value from $300 million to $9 billion, GoldCorp hired ten of the semifinalists in the contests (Marjanovic et al., 2012). Its competitors hired some of the other winning contestants.

Opportunity for solvers to deploy slack or underemployed resources. Slack resources are assets that have not been committed to a specific use. A microchip design engineer's forecasting skills and spare time are slack or underemployed resources. They can use them to solve crowdsourced problems that they enjoy solving, thereby utilizing resources that might have been wasted (Afuah, 2016).

Opportunity to solve problems from long tails. In each organization's portfolio of problems to solve, there are likely to be some that languish in its long tail of problems because it cannot solve them and does not know who can solve them. Crowdsourcing can be a good mechanism for experimenting with such problems (Jeppesen & Lakhani, 2010).

---

[1] This section draws on chapter 4 of Afuah (2014).

Opportunity for a seeker to signal its strategy to its competitors. A seeker can use crowdsourcing to signal strategic moves (Connelly et al., 2011). For example, if a seeker's competitors introduce a new product and it wants to assure its loyal customers that it has something better in the works, it can crowdsource selective aspects of its version of the new product.

Disadvantages of Crowdsourcing

Both solvers and seekers face disadvantages during crowdsourcing.[2] First, by broadcasting a problem to an undefined group of solvers, there is always the chance that very few or no solvers will self-select to solve the problem and the seeker will end up with no solution at all. This threat of no solution is one reason why problem formulation/design can be such a critical step in crowd-sourcing. For example, a problem that is in a language—communications codes (Monteverde, 1995)—that solvers cannot understand or that has the wrong incentives for solvers, has a higher risk of not being solved. A crowd can also deliver a solution but the solution can be wrong. For example, if solvers in a crowd cannot act independently, a powerful solver's ideas can dominate, leading to so-called herding in which solvers' thinking converges to the leader of the herd's solution path, producing a solution that reflects the individual's thinking rather than that of the crowd (Surowiecki, 2004).

Second, since there are no *ex ante* agreements/contracts between solvers and seekers; the seeker is taking extra risks. An opportunistic solver may decide to keep his or her solution to a problem or, where possible, sell it to the highest bidder. Opportunistic competitors can target a seeker's problems with malicious solutions. Also, because many solutions are knowledge, a seeker that obtains solutions to evaluate already has the solutions. Therefore an opportunistic seeker may not have the incentive to pay for a solution that it already has—that is, the Arrow (1962) paradox and its associated challenges come into play. Then there is the risk that broadcasting one's problem to an undefined set of solvers—some of whom may be opportunistic—can threaten one's intellectual property protec-tions. Effectively, opportunistic behavior can be problematic in crowdsourcing (e.g., Curto-Millet & Nisar, 2018). Third, it can be very difficult integrating a solution from outside a unit or organization into the unit or organization. One hurdle is the "not invented here" syndrome (NIHS). Another is that the receiving unit may not have the absorptive capacity to value and assimilate the new solution. Later, I will have more to say about these two hurdles.

Note that some of these crowdsourcing disadvantages can be mitigated (Afuah, 2014; Wallin et al., 2018). For example, using an intermediary, such

---

[2] This section also draws heavily on Afuah (2014).

as InnoCentive, may prove helpful to a seeker because the intermediary can hide the identity of seekers, thereby reducing the chances that competitors will target them for malicious activities. An intermediary can also guarantee to pay a tournament reward, thereby reassuring solvers that if a seeker ran away with a solution, the solver would still be paid, thereby mitigating the Arrow (1962) enigma.

Why the Interest in Crowdsourcing?

There are several reasons why scholars from biochemistry to computer science to marketing are interested in crowdsourcing (e.g., Simula & Ahola, 2014). First, early research published in journals that require manuscripts to make a contribution to theory has been just as fascinating as the anecdotal accounts of high-value solutions from crowdsourcing. For example, Jeppesen & Lakhani (2010)—in their study of scientific problem solving at InnoCentive—concluded that "the provision of a winning solution was positively related to increasing distance between the solver's field of technical expertise and the focal field of the problem." Female solvers—known to be in the "outer circle" of the scientific establishment—"performed significantly better than men in developing successful solutions" (p. 1016).

Second, crowdsourcing's potential dual advantage of delivering very *high-value* solutions at very *low cost* is particularly interesting to those strategy scholars whose research is rooted in understanding performance differences. Third, the low cost of ubiquitous information technologies (IT) such as the Internet and smartphones facilitates the process of crowdsourcing by aiding the formulation, delineation, and broadcasting of problems, enabling solvers to enhance their problem-solving capabilities and be more effective at solving problems. In fact, the prominent role played by IT has prompted some scholars to define crowdsourcing as an IT phenomenon (Brabham, 2008; Estellés-Arolas & González-Ladrón-De-Guevara, 2012). Fourth, to some scholars, crowdsourcing may be an answer to some age-old problems. For example, an important question for technology and innovation management scholars has revolved around what incumbents may want to do in the face of competence-destroying, radical, or disruptive technological innovations to better achieve their goals (Tushman & Anderson, 1986; Henderson & Clark, 1990; Christensen, 1997). Preliminary research suggests that crowdsourcing could be a viable mechanism for incumbents to overcome their handicaps in the face of such innovations (Poetz & Schreier, 2012; Bayus, 2013; Franke et al., 2013).

The question is: how can these scholars who have been attracted to crowdsourcing identify and explore theoretically interesting questions about the phenomenon—the type of questions that have the potential to advance the field, and that managers and scholars find valuable? One step towards answering this question is the framework that I will now present. Note that this is not intended to be a full-fledged theoretical framework with theory-grounded causal logic and propositions for a theory journal. Rather, it is intended to be an intuitive framework to introduce some of the core constructs in crowdsourcing and a step towards potentially identifying meaningful relationships among the constructs and the causal logic that underpins the relationships.

A CONCEPTUAL FRAMEWORK FOR IDENTIFYING AND EXPLORING THEORETICALLY INTERESTING CROWDSOURCING QUESTIONS

When a manager formulates, delineates, and broadcasts a problem to a crowd, they are contributing to value creation, and hope to capture value for their organization/unit through the solutions that solvers generate. When solvers self-select and solve a problem, they too are contributing to value creation and hope to capture value through the rewards associated with solving the problem (Afuah & Tucci, 2013; Bloodgood, 2013). Thus, when seekers and solvers come together, they create and capture value. Therefore, because the activities that seekers and solvers perform are a function of their characteristics and those of the problem, crowdsourcing can be conceptualized as shown in Figure 2.1—as value created and/or captured driven by the characteristics of seekers, crowds, solvers, and problems. That is, at a general and intuitive level, the value created and/or captured during crowdsourcing is a function of the characteristics of the seeker, the crowd and the problem—a relationship that is moderated by the seeker's crowdsourcing strategy and its overarching meso- and macro-environments (Figure 2.1).

I now quickly describe each component and some of the relationships among them. Again, note that a full-blown framework—with detailed relationships among constructs and propositions backed by the relevant causal logic—is beyond the scope of this crowdsourcing primer. Rather, my intention here is to introduce the reader to the core constructs and the potential relationships among them, with little or none of the causal logic linking them that would be required by a journal that requires manuscripts to make a contribution to theory. I start by defining value created and value captured during crowdsourcing.

Value Created and/or Captured during Crowdsourcing

An actor creates value when the benefits that it offers its customers exceed its cost of providing the benefits; it captures value when the price that it

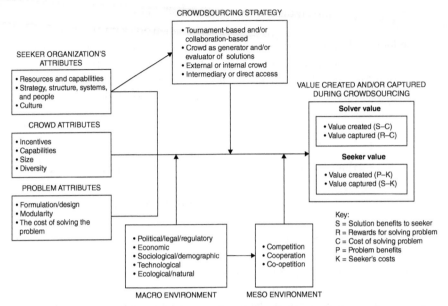

Figure 2.1. Framework for identifying and exploring theoretically interesting crowdsourcing questions.

obtains for the benefits exceeds its cost of providing the benefits (Bowman & Ambrosini, 2000; Lepak, Smith, & Taylor et al., 2007). During crowdsourcing, a solver creates value when the benefits (S) to the seeker from the solution that the solver produces exceed its cost (C) of solving the problem (Figure 2.1). A solver captures value if the rewards (R) that it obtains from solving a problem exceed its cost (C) of solving the problem. Rewards here include both monetary and non-monetary, as well as extrinsic and intrinsic rewards (von Krogh et al., 2012; Belenzon, & Schankerman, 2015). A seeker creates value when the benefits (P) perceived by solvers in a problem that the seeker formulates, delineates, and broadcasts exceed its cost (K) of performing these activities. A seeker captures value when the benefits (S) that it obtains from the solution exceed the cost (K) of getting solvers to solve the problem. Note that the seeker's cost (K) includes the monetary part of the reward such as the prize money that the seeker has to pay out. With these definitions in place, the question is: what drives this value creation and capture for seekers and solvers?

Seeker Organization's Attributes

One driver of value creation and capture is the attributes of the unit or organization that has a problem to solve (Figure 2.1). To keep the chapter tractable, I focus on only a few of these constructs: (1) resources and capabilities, (2) strategy, structure, systems, and people, and (3) culture. These attributes are critical to an organization's ability to formulate, delineate, and broadcast a problem to a crowd, have solvers self-select to solve its problems rather than competitors' problems, and evaluate and assimilate the final solution. That is, a unit's or an organization's attributes drive its ability to create and/or capture value during crowdsourcing (e.g., Palacios et al., 2016; Kornberger, 2017). How?

Resources and capabilities. Clearly, without the appropriate knowledge, skills, and other resources, a seeker would have a difficult time formulating, delineating, and broadcasting a problem to crowds, and getting members of the crowd to self-select and solve the problem. For example, a seeker organization's brand name reputation assures potential solvers that if they were to win a problem-solving tournament, the seeker would pay the reward promised, and not run away with the solution and reward. To evaluate and assimilate a solution, a seeker needs the absorptive capacity—an ability to recognize the value of the solution to the organization, assimilate it, and convert it into new end-products/services for its customers (Cohen & Levinthal, 1990). Importantly, a firm's complementary assets (Teece, 1986) and business model (Massa et al., 2017) play a critical role in its ability to capture value created during crowdsourcing.

Strategy, structure, systems, and people. An organization's strategy is its plan to achieve its goals. Depending on its goals, an organization may or may not want to use crowdsourcing. For example, Wikipedia's goal is to offer a free encyclopedia that is available to everyone everywhere in the world. Therefore, a plan that involves hiring people and paying them to write the entries is likely to be out of the question for Wikipedia, because such a plan is likely to cost too much for the product to be free. On the contrary, one of IBM's earlier goals was to protect its intellectual property. Thus, IBM was less likely to crowdsource core activities that might risk its intellectual property protections. Later, when IBM started participating in some open source activities, it was because it had the tightly held complementary assets to profit from open source technologies despite the imitability of these technologies (Teece, 1986; West & Gallagher, 2006).

An organization's structure is about who has authority over whom and who is accountable for what activities. Its systems are about how performance is measured and rewarded and, just as importantly, what information flows to whom, when, and how (Afuah, 2014). Structure and systems complement and often reinforce each other. Thus, the structure and systems at the old IBM and those at today's Wikipedia are very different, and we can expect the impact of these structures on value creation and capture through crowdsourcing to be different.

In this framework (Figure 2.1), the construct "people" refers to the roles that individuals—tempered by their cognitive frames—play in formulating and implementing an organization's strategy. The leadership roles played by developers, advisors, coordinators, champions, sponsors, boundary spanners, project managers, and gatekeepers can have a significant influence on a seeker organization's ability to formulate, delineate, and broadcast problems, have solvers self-select and solve problems, evaluate solutions, and assimilate winners (Allen, 1977; Afuah, 2003; Fleming & Waguespack, 2007). For example, an important hurdle at some seeker organizations is the *not invented here syndrome* (NIHS) in which some functional units may not want to adopt a solution from outside the unit that has traditionally solved similar problems (Katz & Allen, 1982; Antons & Piller, 2015; Chua et al., 2015). In fact, some units may fight formulation, delineation, and broadcast of a problem to a crowd. This can impact not only on the likelihood of pursuing crowdsourcing but also that of obtaining a high-value solution. Champions that can articulate a vision of why a problem is being solved through crowdsourcing can mitigate the NIHS effect (Afuah, 2003). Boundary spanners play an important role (Howell & Higgins, 1990; Levina & Fayard, 2018). Developers, advisors, and coordinators who help to formulate a problem can also play major roles in assimilating a solution (Wallin et al., 2018).

Culture. One definition of organizational culture is "a set of shared mental assumptions that guide interpretation and action in organizations by defining appropriate behavior for various situations" (Ravasi & Schultz, 2006: 437). This set of guiding assumptions can have a significant effect on an organization's ability to formulate problems for crowdsourcing, and to evaluate and assimilate solutions. For example, consider the evaluation and assimilation of solutions. Organizational attitudes and beliefs about where solutions come from, how to evaluate them, and how to assimilate them can have a significant impact on the value created during crowdsourcing (Chua et al., 2015; Fayard et al., 2016).

Crowd Attributes

One of the first scholars to explore those characteristics of a crowd that makes it wise—more effective in solving crowdsourced problems—was Surowiecki (2004). According to him, a "wise" crowd has to meet four criteria: diversity of opinion, independence, decentralization, and an aggregation mechanism for getting information out of the crowd. Subsequent research suggests that a crowd's attributes are strong determinants of the value that can be created and/or captured when its members solve problems for seekers (e.g., Bonabeau, 2009; Liu et al., 2014; Riedl & Woolley, 2017; Viscusi & Tucci, 2018). Four of these attributes stand out: incentives, resources/capabilities, size, and diversity (Figure 2.1).

Incentives. Solvers that self-select and solve problems have an incentive to do so. Incentives can be extrinsic or intrinsic (for an excellent review, see von Krogh et al., 2012). If a solver is motivated by the outcome of solving a problem, he or she is said to be extrinsically motivated. That is, extrinsic motivations are associated with outcomes and include the prize for winning a crowdsourcing contest, the joy and thrill of winning, the reputation gained by winning, and so on (Lerner & Tirole, 2002; Lakhani & Wolf, 2005; Shah, 2006). Intrinsic incentives are those associated with the process of self-selecting and solving problems. These include the fun that a solver has when solving a problem, what solvers learn as they solve problems, the reputation built during problem solving, and so on. Incentives can also be monetary or non-monetary. Monetary incentives are money or anything that can be converted into money. These include the incentives to solve a problem so as to acquire a reputation that can lead to employment. The joy of solving a problem or of having a winning solution is non-monetary. Effectively, solvers' incentives for self-selecting to solve problems can be monetary, non-monetary, intrinsic, extrinsic or some combination of thesde. Thus, a solver's likelihood of producing a high-value solution to a problem depends on how the incentives embodied in solving the problem are consistent with what motivates the solver. Note that a solver's incentives for solving a problem can also be identity-based or need-based (Shah, 2006; Ren et al., 2007; Nagaraj & Piezunka, 2017).

Resources and capabilities. To solve a problem, a solver needs the relevant resources—expertise, tools, time, and other assets—as well as an ability (capability) to integrate these resources to deliver a solution on time. For example, a solver's absorptive capacity to understand what a broadcast problem means can be critical since, by definition, solvers are not likely to have access to the seeker to answer questions. Note that resources and capabilities in this context go beyond those defined by the resource-based view of the firm, and include resources such as trust (Ye & Kankanhalli, 2017) and social capital—"the sum of the actual and potential resources embedded within, available through, and derived from the network of relationships possessed by an individual or social unit" (Nahapiet & Ghoshal, 1998: 243).

Size. The size of a crowd is critical. In tournament-based crowdsourcing, the larger the crowd, the higher the likelihood that someone in the crowd will have what it takes to self-select and deliver a winning solution (Terwiesch & Xu, 2008; Afuah, 2016). In collaboration-based crowdsourcing, having a large crowd increases the likelihood that there will be enough solvers to tackle the critical number of components of the problem to produce an aggregated solution that meets the expectations of the seeker.

Diversity. Early research suggests that a heterogeneous crowd is more likely to deliver high-value solutions to problems than a homogeneous one (Surowiecki,

2004; Jeppesen & Lakhani, 2010; Levina & Fyard, 2018). Imagine how incomplete Wikipedia's encyclopedia entries would be if the crowd of writers was made up of only particle physicists.

Note that beyond these attributes of a crowd, there are questions about what constitutes a crowd (e.g., Viscusi & Tucci, 2018). More work is also needed on the other attributes of crowds and communities (West & Sims, 2018).

Problem Attributes

The attributes of the problem being crowdsourced also have an impact on the value created and/or captured. I focus on three of these characteristics: formulation, modularity, and the expected cost of producing a solution (Figure 2.1).

Formulation. Obtaining a superior solution to a problem starts with the right formulation/design of the problem (Che & Gale, 2003; Lakhani et al., 2007; Olsen & Carmel, 2013; Ranade & Varshney, 2018; Wallin et al., 2018). Several factors about the formulation of a problem increase the likelihood of solvers self-selecting to solve the problem. First, incorporation of language—e.g., communications codes—that solvers can understand is important (Monteverde, 1995). Second, incorporating the types of incentives that are likely to motivate the crowd is also important (Liu et al., 2014). These incorporations can be difficult to achieve because, in crowdsourcing, a problem is broadcast to a set of undefined people and therefore knowing their incentives can be challenging. Just as important, there is little chance that the unspecified solvers can interact with the seeker to answer questions about the problem. The roles played by developers, advisors, sponsors, and other key players in the seeker organization can be critical in formulating the right problem (Wallin et al., 2018).

Modularity. The modularity of a problem is the degree to which the problem can be parceled into component problems, the components solved, and component solutions (re)combined to obtain the solution to the problem. For example, the problem of producing an encyclopedia is modularizable since it can be separated into component problems of producing entries for different subjects, and the produced entries aggregated to produce the encyclopedia. The more modularizable a problem, the higher the likelihood of creating value through crowdsourcing (Afuah & Tucci, 2012).

Expected cost of producing a solution. Each solver that self-selects to solve a problem incurs costs. These costs have to be weighed against expected rewards. For example, consider solvers that are motivated by money and self-select to solve a problem for a contest in which the winner is awarded prize money. Those who do not win are not reimbursed for their efforts. Therefore, rational potential solvers have to carefully weigh their expected costs of solving the problem against their chances of winning and the salvage value of their solution. Effectively, solvers' expected costs of solving a problem impact their likelihood of self-selecting to solve the problem, and therefore the likelihood of obtaining a solution to the problem. All else being equal, the lower the cost of solving a problem, the higher the likelihood of solvers self-selecting to solve the problem.

Moderating Effect of Crowdsourcing Strategy

An organization that decides to crowdsource a problem usually also has to make choices about four approaches to crowdsourcing (Figure 2.1): whether to (1) pursue tournament-based and/or collaboration-based crowdsourcing; (2) use crowds for generating solutions to the problem, for evaluating the solutions, or both; (3) utilize external and/or internal crowds; and (4) use an intermediary to access the crowd or pursue direct access. The choice of crowdsourcing strategy moderates the degree to which the attributes of seekers, crowds, and problems impact the value created and/or captured during crowdsourcing (Figure 2.1).

Tournament-based and/or collaboration-based. The decision to crowdsource a problem is often accompanied by whether to use tournament-based, collaboration-based, or hybrid crowdsourcing. As we saw earlier, if a problem is modularizable, it can be parceled into its components, each of which can be solved separately and the component solutions aggregated to produce the solution to the problem; making collaboration-based crowdsourcing more conducive to solving the problem than tournament-based crowdsourcing. Thus, if the seeker organization were to choose to use tournament-based crowdsourcing to solve a modularizable problem, value creation and capture is likely to be less efficient/effective relative to using collaboration-based crowdsourcing. That is, the type of crowdsourcing that a seeker chooses to pursue moderates the impact of problem attributes on value creation and capture (Figure 2.1).

Crowd as generator and/or evaluator of solutions. A seeker organization that chooses to crowdsource a problem also has to decide whether to use crowds only for generating the solution or also for evaluating the solution. This choice also moderates the impact of the attributes of the problem, crowd, and seeker on value creation and capture. For example, if a crowd is diverse and therefore produces diverse solutions to a problem, it may make sense to have a diverse crowd—rather than a few individual experts—evaluate the solutions.

External and/or internal crowds. Recall that the crowd which an organization uses to solve a problem can be internal, external, or some combination of both (Zuchowski et al., 2016; Šundić & Leitner, 2018). The choice of an internal or external crowd moderates the impact of the characteristics of a problem, crowd, and seeker on value creation and capture. How? On the one hand, for some problems, solvers are more likely to deliver winning solutions to some problems—for example, problems that seekers cannot solve—when their field of technical expertise is far from the focal field of the problem than when it is close (Jeppesen & Lakhani, 2010). Since the field of technical expertise of solvers from a particular organization is more likely to be close to the focal field of a problem from the same organization, the organization may be better off using an external crowd to solve such problems. On the other hand, there may be problems that involve information that the seeker may like to keep proprietary. In that case, an internal crowd may be better than an external one. Using an internal crowd might also mitigate some of the other disadvantages of external crowdsourcing. That is, the more that the choice of internal or external crowd is consistent with the characteristics of the problem, the crowd, and the seeker, the more that these characteristics are likely to have a positive impact on value creation and capture. The internal crowd versus external crowd debate is in its infancy and promises to be very enlightening (Zuchowski et al., 2016; Horn et al., 2018; Šundić & Leitner, 2018).

Intermediary or direct access. An organization that decides to crowdsource a problem can go directly to the crowd (e.g., Huston & Sakkab, 2006), or pass through an intermediary (Jeppesen & Lakhani, 2010; Sieg, Wallin, & von Krogh, 2010; Lauritzen, 2017). Although passing through an intermediary has extra costs associated with paying the intermediary for its services, there are advantages to using an intermediary. First, as we saw earlier, by going through an intermediary, a seeker can protect its identity by remaining anonymous. Second, an intermediary can help the seeker better formulate/design a problem, delineate it, and broadcast it to solvers in terminology that they can understand. Third, by providing a marketplace where solvers and seekers can go to find each other, an intermediary reduces search costs for both seekers and solvers (Afuah, 2018). Solvers do not have to search through the websites of thousands of seekers to see if they have problems to solve. Thus, going through an intermediary can influence the degree to which the attributes of a problem, crowd and seeker impact value creation and capture.

Moderating Effect of Meso Environment

An organization's meso environment—also called industry or competitive environment in strategy—is made up of rivals, suppliers, customers, complementors, and potential new entrants into the organization's market space. Organizations have some control over their meso environments through the activities that they choose to perform when they engage in competition, cooperation, or co-opetition (Brandenburger & Stuart, 1996). Solvers also engage in competition, cooperation, and co-opetition (Afuah, 2018). These activities can influence the effect of problem, crowd, and seeker attributes on value creation and capture (Figure 2.1). How? It depends on the activities—on whether they are competitive, cooperative, or co-opetitive.

Competition. Competition among seekers for solutions is good for solvers because it is likely to increase the rewards for solvers, thereby increasing the value that they capture. Competition among seekers also means that they may end up with solutions that are easy to imitate. Such imitability can reduce the value captured by a seeker, unless it has tightly held and difficult to imitate complementary assets or business models to help it profit from the solution (Teece, 1986; Massa et al., 2017).

Cooperation. Seekers can cooperate with solvers, but only indirectly because of the nature of crowdsourcing. How? Take multi-sided platforms, for example. Rather than develop its own apps or contract the task to designated developers, smartphone platform owners crowdsource app development to anyone any-where in the world that wants to develop apps for the platform. These platform owners (seekers) cooperate with app developers (solvers) by providing them with software tools and details of the interfaces to which the apps have to mesh to function efficiently. Such cooperation can increase the quality and number of apps developed for the platform—that is, increase the value created.

Co-opetition. In co-opetition, actors cooperate to create value and compete to capture it (Branderburger & Stuart, 1996; Afuah, 2000, 2018). The idea here is that, wherever there is cooperation to make a pie, there is likely to be compe-tition for a piece of the pie to take home. In the smartphone example, platform owners cooperate with app developers to populate the platform with superior apps, but also compete for how much of the share of revenue the owner gets to keep compared to the developer. Co-opetition can also have an impact on the degree to which the attributes of crowds, problems, and seekers impact value creation and capture.

Moderating Effect of Macro-Environmental Factors

A seeker organization's macro environment consists of the political/legal/regulatory, economic, sociological/demographic, technological, and natural/ecological (PESTN) forces, over which most organizations have very little or no control. Each of these environmental forces moderates the degree to which the attributes of seekers, solvers, and problems impact value creation and capture during crowdsourcing. Because very little has been written about the role of the macro environment on value creation and capture during crowd-sourcing, I will focus on defining the components of this overarching environment, and leave the actual moderating effect to future research.

Political/legal/regulatory. An organization's political/legal/regulatory environment is about the forces from political activism, nationalism, laws, lobbying, ideological beliefs, legislation, and so on that impact the organization's ability to pursue its goals. Employment laws, intellectual property protection, and mergers and acquisitions regulations can impact a seeker's ability to successfully crowdsource problems. For example, strong intellectual property laws can mean that seekers do not have to forego crowdsourcing for fear of imitation. Governments can also promote grand challenges that produce the types of discoveries that can move a nation forward. In fact, the first crowdsourcing challenges, such as the Longitude Prize of 1714, were launched by governments (Masters & Delbecq, 2008).

Economic. The economic environment of a seeker refers to the forces associated with employment, inflation, factors of production, interest rates, monetary policies, exchange rates, and inflation that impinge on seeker organizations and their co-opetitors, thereby influencing the degree to which the attributes of solvers, seekers, and problems impact value creation and capture during crowdsourcing. For example, higher interest rates and cost of borrowing may make some entrepreneurs more likely to turn to crowdsourcing, either to seek funding through crowdfunding or to compete to win prize money to finance their ventures. High unemployment may make some people more likely to use their time to perform crowdsourced tasks, such as driving for Uber, and so on. The impact of economic effects on crowdsourcing is an area that is wide open for future research.

Sociological/demographic. The sociological/demographic environment consists of the level and quality of education, wealth distribution, population growth and diversity, age distribution, and so on. It also moderates the impact that the attributes of problems, seekers, and solvers can have on value created and captured during crowdsourcing.

Technological. The technological forces that impinge on organizations include advances in information technology, materials, knowledge generation, product development, and the processes for making, distributing, and marketing products and services. These forces can have a huge impact on not only the likelihood of crowdsourcing problems, but also the value created and/or captured. Witness the role that the Internet and smartphones have played in enabling organizations to use crowdsourcing to create and capture value.

Natural/ecological. Natural/ecological environmental factors include the pollution of air, sea, water, and land through poor/wrong use of/overuse of resources. These factors can also moderate the impact of the character-istics of solvers, seekers, and problems on value created and/or captured during crowdsourcing (Figure 2.1).

As the impact of the technological environment on value creation and capture illustrates, the macro environment can have a significant effect on both seeker and solver value creation and capture. Unfortunately, very little attention has been given to macro-environmental factors beyond technological factors such as information technology (IT), offering yet more opportunities for future research anchored on the role of these other factors.

CONCLUSIONS AND FUTURE RESEARCH

The act of broadcasting a problem to an undefined set of people to self-select and solve the problem with no *ex ante* contracts/commitments, goes back to at least 1714, well before the institution of in-house R&D labs by organizations to solve problems. Advances in information and communications technologies have facilitated the degree to which problems can be formulated, delineated, and broadcast to crowds, and the degree to which these crowds can solve problems and evaluate solutions. This has led to not only an increase in the practice of crowdsourcing, but also an increase in researching the phenom-enon. My goal in this essay has been to provide scholars with the type of crowdsourcing primer and framework that can help them better generate and explore theoretically interesting questions about the phenomenon—the type of questions that can also help advance the practice of crowdsourcing.

Some of these research questions are obvious. For example, what problems are more usefully solved using both tournament-based and collaboration-based crowdsourcing, rather than one on its own? In addition to the characteristics of problems, crowds, and seekers already identified, what other characteristics would impact value creation and capture during crowdsourcing, when and how? What is the causal logic linking each pair of constructs in Figure 2.1? Other questions are not as obvious. For example, to formulate/design a problem effectively, a seeker needs information about the crowd to which the problem will be broadcast. However, according to Jeppesen & Lakhani (2010), the likelihood of solving some problems increases with the distance between the solver's field of technical expertise and the focal field of the problem? This raises an interesting question: How can a seeker obtain information about a crowd whose field of technical expertise is far from that of its problems—the type of information that it needs to better formulate/design problems? In addition to prediction markets, what other crowdsourcing mechanisms are there?

Like most of the works in crowdsourcing so far, this primer focuses largely on "content" issues—on the activities and decisions involving the attributes of seekers, crowds, problems, crowdsourcing strategy, meso environment, and macro environment, and their impact on value creation and capture. The primer has paid little attention to "process" issues—to the sequence of events that unravel as seekers formulate, delineate, and broadcast problems; as solvers self-select and solve problems; and as solutions are evaluated and assimilated. Future research could look into crowdsourcing process research questions.

Indeed, the list of research questions is long, and research about the phenomenon promises to be fascinating. Hopefully, this primer and framework have provided scholars with some of the crowdsourcing fundamentals that they need to consider writing papers that make a contribution to theory—enough for the papers to be published in journals that require manuscripts to make a contribution to theory. As Van de Ven put it, "Good theory is practical precisely because it advances knowledge in a scientific discipline, guides research toward crucial questions, and enlightens the profession of management" (1989: 486). Hopefully, this chapter is helpful to those whose goal is to produce works that contain *good theory*.

REFERENCES

Afuah, A. (2003). *Innovation Management: Strategies, Implementation, and Profits.* New York: Oxford University Press.

Afuah, A. (2014). *Business Model Innovation: Concepts, Analysis and Cases.* New York, NY: Routledge.

Afuah, A. (2016). The extreme-value and aggregated-contribution potentials of crowds. Working Paper, Stephen M. Ross School of Business, University of Michigan.

Afuah, A. (2018). Co-opetition in crowdsourcing: When simultaneous cooperation and competition deliver superior solutions. In C. Tucci, A. Afuah, & G. Viscusi (eds.), *Creating and Capturing Value Through Crowdsourcing.* Oxford: Oxford University Press, pp. 271–91.

Afuah, A. (2000). How much do your co-opetitors' capabilities matter in the face of technological change? *Strategic Management Journal, 21*(3), 387–404.

Afuah, A. & Tucci, C. L. (2012). Crowdsourcing as a solution to distant search. *Academy of Management Review, 37*(3), 355–75.

Afuah, A. & Tucci, C. L. (2013). Value capture and crowdsourcing. *Academy of Management Review, 38*(3), 457–60.

Alexy, O., George, G., & Salter, A. J. (2013). Cui bono? The selective revealing of knowledge and its implications for innovative activity. *Academy of Management Review, 38*(2), 270–91.

Allen, T. J. (1966). Studies of the problem-solving process in engineering design. *IEEE Transactions on Engineering Management, EM13*(2), 72–83.

Allen, T. J. (1977). *Managing the Flow of Technology: Technology Transfer and the Dissemination of Technological Information within the R and D Organization.* Cambridge, MA: MIT Press.

Antons, D. & Piller, F. (2015). Opening the black box of Not-Invented-Here: Attitudes, decision biases, and behavioral consequences. *Academy of Management Perspectives*, *29*(2), 193–217.

Arrow, K. (1962). Economic welfare and the allocation of resources for invention. In *The rate and direction of inventive activity: Economic and Social Factors*. Princeton, NJ: Princeton University Press, pp. 609–26.

Barney, J. B. (1991). Firm resources and sustained competitive advantage. *Journal of Management, 17*(1), 99–120.

Bauer, R. M. & Gegenhuber, T. (2015). Crowdsourcing: Global search and the twisted roles of consumers and producers. *Organization, 22*(5), 661–81.

Bayus, B. L. (2013). Crowdsourcing new product ideas over time: An analysis of the Dell IdeaStorm community. *Management Science, 59*(1), 226–44.

Belenzon, S. & Schankerman, M. (2015). Motivation and sorting of human capital in open innovation. *Strategic Management Journal, 36*(6), 795–820.

Bogers, M., Zobel, A. K., Afuah, A. et al. (2016). The open innovation research landscape: Established perspectives and emerging themes across different levels of analysis. *Industry and Innovation, 24*(1), 8–40.

Bloodgood, J. (2013). Crowdsourcing: Useful for problem solving, but what about value capture? *Academy of Management Review, 38*(3), 455–7.

Bonabeau, E. (2009). Decisions 2.0: The power of collective intelligence. *MIT Sloan Management Review, 50*(2) 45–52.

Borison, A. & Hamm, G. (2010). Prediction markets: A new tool for strategic decision making. *California Management Review, 52*(4), 125–41.

Boudreau, K. J., Lacetera, N., & Lakhani, K. R. (2011). Incentives and problem uncertainty in innovation contests: An empirical analysis. *Management Science, 57*(5), 843–63.

Bowman, C. & Ambrosini, V. (2000). Value creation versus value capture: Towards a coherent definition of value in strategy. *British Journal of Management, 11*(1), 1–15.

Brabham, D. C. (2008). Crowdsourcing as a model for problem solving an introduction and cases. *Convergence: International Journal of Research into New Media Technologies, 14*(1), 75–90.

Brabham, D. C. (2010). Moving the crowd at Threadless: Motivations for participation in a crowdsourcing application. *Information, Communication & Society, 13*(8), 1122–45.

Brabham, D. C. (2013). *Crowdsourcing*. Cambridge MA: MIT Press.

Brandenburger, A. M. & Stuart, H. W. (1996). Value-based business strategy. *Journal of Economics & Management Strategy, 5*(1), 5–24.

Butticè, V., Franzoni, C., Rossi-Lamastra, C., & Rovelli, P. (2018). The road to crowdfunding success: A review of extant literature. In C. Tucci, A. Afuah, & G. Viscusi (eds.), *Creating and Capturing Value Through Crowdsourcing*. Oxford: Oxford University Press, pp. 97–126.

Che, Y. K. & Gale, I. (2003). Optimal design of research contests. *American Economic Review, 93*(3), 646–71.

Chesbrough, H. (2003). Open innovation: A new paradigm for understanding industrial innovation, in H. Chesbrough, W. Vanhaverbeke, & J. West (eds.). *Open Innovation: Researching a New Paradigm*. Oxford: Oxford University Press, pp. 1–12.

Chesbrough, H., Vanhaverbeke, W., & West, J. (2006). *Open Innovation: Researching a New Paradigm.* Oxford, UK: Oxford University Press on Demand.

Chesbrough, H. W. (2003). *Open Innovation: The New Imperative for Creating and Profiting from Technology.* Boston, MA: Harvard Business School Press.

Chiu, C. M., Liang, T. P., & Turban, E. (2014). What can crowdsourcing do for decision support? *Decision Support Systems, 65,* 40–9.

Christensen, C. M. (1997). *The Innovator's Dilemma.* Boston, MA: Harvard Business School Press.

Christiansen, J. D. (2007). Prediction markets: Practical experiments in small markets and behaviours observed, *Journal of Prediction Markets, 1*(1), 17–41.

Chua, R.Y.J., Roth, Y., & Lemoine, J.-F. (2015). The impact of culture on creativity: How cultural tightness and cultural distance affect global innovation crowdsourcing work. *Administrative Science Quarterly, 60*(2), 189–227.

Cohen, W. M. & Levinthal, D. A. (1990). Absorptive capacity: A new perspective on learning and innovation. *Administrative Science Quarterly, 35,* 128–52.

Connelly, B. L., Certo, S. T., Ireland, R. D., & Reutzel, C. R. (2011). Signaling theory: A review and assessment. *Journal of Management, 37*(1), 39–67.

Connelly, B. L., Tihanyi, L., Crook, T. R., & Gangloff, K. A. (2014). Tournament theory: Thirty years of contests and competitions. *Journal of Management, 40*(1), 16–47.

Cooper, S., Khatib, F., Treuille, A. et al. (2010). Predicting protein structures with a multiplayer online game. *Nature, 466*(7307), 756–60.

Curto-Millet, D. & Nisar, A. (2018). Ethics in crowdsourcing: Revisiting and revising the role of stakeholder theory. In C. Tucci, A. Afuah, & G. Viscusi (eds.), *Creating and Capturing Value Through Crowdsourcing.* Oxford: Oxford University Press, pp. 310–34.

Dye, R. (2008). The promise of prediction markets: A roundtable. *McKinsey Quarterly, 2,* 83–93.

Estellés-Arolas, E. & González-Ladrón-De-Guevara, F. (2012). Towards an integrated crowdsourcing definition. *Journal of Information Science, 38*(2), 189–200.

Faems, D., de Visser, M., Andries, P., & van Looy, B. (2010). Technology alliance portfolios and financial performance: Value-enhancing and cost-increasing effects of open innovation. *Journal of Product Innovation Management, 27*(6), 785–96.

Fayard, A. L., Gkeredakis, E., & Levina, N. (2016). Framing innovation opportunities while staying committed to an organizational epistemic stance. *Information Systems Research, 27*(2), 302–23.

Felin, T. & Zenger, T. R. (2014). Closed or open innovation? Problem solving and the governance choice. *Research Policy, 43*(5), 914–25.

Fleming, L. & Waguespack, D. M. (2007). Brokerage, boundary spanning, and leadership in open innovation communities. *Organization Science, 18*(2), 165–80.

Franke, N., Poetz, M. K., & Schreier, M. (2013). Integrating problem solvers from analogous markets in new product ideation. *Management Science, 60*(4), 1063–81.

Franzoni, C. & Sauermann, H. (2014). Crowd science: The organization of scientific research in open collaborative projects. *Research Policy, 43*(1), 1–20.

Frederiksen, L. & Rullani, F. (2015). Problem-formulation and problem-solving in self-organized communities: How modes of communication shape project behaviors in the free open-source software community. *Strategic Management Journal, 37*(13), 2589–610.

Gassmann, O. & Enkel, E. (2004). Towards a theory of open innovation: Three core process archetypes. In Paper presented at R&D Management Conference, Lisbon.

Grant, R. M. (1996). Toward a knowledge-based theory of the firm. *Strategic Management Journal, 17*(Winter special issue), 109–22.

Henderson, R. M. & Clark, K. B. (1990). Architectural innovation: The reconfiguration of existing product technologies and the failure of established firms. *Administrative Science Quarterly, 35*(1), 9–30.

Henkel, J., Schöberl, S., & Alexy, O. (2014). The emergence of openness: How and why firms adopt selective revealing in open innovation. *Research Policy, 43*(5), 879–90.

Horn, C., Bogers, M., & Brem, A. (2018). Prediction markets for crowdsourcing. In C. Tucci, A. Afuah, & G. Viscusi (eds.), *Creating and Capturing Value Through Crowdsourcing*. Oxford: Oxford University Press, pp. 292–309.

Howe, J. (2006). Crowdsourcing: A Definition, *Crowdsourcing: Tracking the rise of the amateur* (weblog, 2 June), http://crowdsourcing.typepad.com/cs/2006/06/crowd sourcing_a.html (accessed January 20, 2017).

Howell, J. M. & Higgins, C. A. (1990). Champions of technological innovation. *Administrative Science Quarterly, 35*(2), 317–41.

Huston, L. & Sakkab, N. (2006). Connect and develop. *Harvard Business Review, 84*(3), 58–66.

Jeppesen, L. B. & Lakhani, K. R. (2010). Marginality and problem-solving effectiveness in broadcast search. *Organization Science, 21*(5), 1016–33.

Katila, R. & Ahuja, G. (2002). Something old, something new: A longitudinal study of search behavior and new product introduction. *Academy of Management Journal, 45*(6), 1183–94.

Katz, R. & Allen, T.J. (1982). Investigating the not invented here (NIH) syndrome: A look at the performance, tenure, and communication patterns of 50 R&D project groups. *R&D Management, 12*(1), 7–19.

Kornberger, M. (2017). The visible hand and the crowd: Analyzing organization design in distributed innovation systems. *Strategic Organization, 15*(2), 174–93.

Lakhani, K. R. & Wolf, R. G. (2005). Why hackers do what they do: Understanding motivation and effort in free/open source software projects, In *Perspectives on Free and Open Source Software*, J. Feller, B. Fitzgerald, S. Hissam, and K. R. Lakhani (eds.), pp. 3–22. Cambridge MA: MIT Press.

Lakhani, K. R., Jeppesen, L. B., Lohse, P. A., & Panetta, J. A. (2007). *The Value of Openness in Scientific Problem Solving*. Cambridge, MA: Harvard Business School.

Lampel, J., Jha, P. P., & Bhalla, A. (2012). Test-driving the future: How design competitions are changing innovation. *Academy of Management Perspectives, 26*(2), 71–85.

Lang, M., Bharadwaj, N., & Di Benedetto, C. A. (2016). How crowdsourcing improves prediction of market-oriented outcomes. *Journal of Business Research, 69*(10), 4168–76.

Lauritzen, G. D. (2017). The role of innovation intermediaries in firm–innovation community collaboration: Navigating the membership paradox. *Journal of Product Innovation Management*, DOI: 10.1111/jpim.12363.

Lepak, D. P., Smith, K. G., & Taylor, M. S. (2007). Value creation and value capture: a multilevel perspective. *Academy of Management Review, 32*(1), 180–94.

Lerner, J. & Tirole, J. (2002). Some simple economics of open source. *The Journal of Industrial Economics, 50*(2), 197–234.

Levina, N. & Fayard, A-L. (2018). Tapping into diversity through open innovation platforms: The emergence of boundary spanning practices. In C. Tucci, A. Afuah, & G. Viscusi (eds.), *Creating and Capturing Value Through Crowdsourcing*. Oxford: Oxford University Press, pp. 204–35.

Levine, S. S. & Prietula, M. J. (2013). Open collaboration for innovation: Principles and performance. *Organization Science, 25*(5), 1414–33.

Liu, T. X., Yang, J., Adamic, L. A., & Chen, Y. (2014). Crowdsourcing with all-pay auctions: a field experiment on taskcn. *Management Science, 60*(8), 2020–37.

Lüttgens, D., Pollok, P., Antons, D., & Piller, F. (2014). Wisdom of the crowd and capabilities of a few: Internal success factors of crowdsourcing for innovation. *Journal of Business Economics, 84*(3), 339–74.

Mahoney, J. T. & Pandian, J. R. (1992). The resource-based view within the conversation of strategic management. *Strategic Management Journal, 13*(5), 363–80.

Majchrzak, A. & Malhotra, A. (2013). Towards an information systems perspective and research agenda on crowdsourcing for innovation. *Journal of Strategic Information Systems, 22*(4), 257–68.

Malone, T. W., Laubacher, R., & Dellarocas, C. (2010). The collective intelligence genome. *MIT Sloan Management Review, 51*(3), 21.

Marjanovic, S., Fry, C., & Chataway, J. (2012). Crowdsourcing based business models: In search of evidence for innovation 2.0. *Science and Public Policy, 39*(3), 318–32.

Massa, L., Tucci, C., & Afuah, A. (2017). A critical assessment of business model research. *Academy of Management Annals, 11*(1), 73–104.

Masters, W. A. & Delbecq, B. (2008). *Accelerating Innovation with Prize Rewards: History and Typology of Technology Prizes and a New Contest Design for Innovation in African Agriculture* (Vol. 835). Intl Food Policy Res Inst.

Mollick, E. (2014). The dynamics of crowdfunding: An exploratory study. *Journal of Business Venturing, 29*(1), 1–16.

Monteverde, K. (1995). Technical dialog as an incentive for vertical integration in the semiconductor industry. *Management Science, 41*(10), 1624–38.

Nagaraj, A. & Piezunka, H. (2017). The impact of competition on contributions in online communities: Evidence from digital mapping platforms. Working Paper, INSEAD.

Nahapiet, J. & Ghoshal, S. (1998). Social capital, intellectual capital, and the organizational advantage. *Academy of Management Review, 23*(2), 242–66.

Nickerson, J. A., Yen, C. J., & Mahoney, J. T. (2012). Exploring the problem-finding and problem-solving approach for designing organizations. *Academy of Management Perspectives, 26*(1), 52–72.

Olsen, T. & Carmel, E. (2013). The process of atomization of business tasks for crowdsourcing, *Strategic Outsourcing, 6*(3), 208–12.

Palacios, M., Martinez-Corral, A., Nisar, A., & Grijalvo, M. (2016). Crowdsourcing and organizational forms: Emerging trends and research implications. *Journal of Business Research, 69*(5), 1834–9.

Peteraf, M. A. & Barney, J. B. (2003). Unraveling the resource-based tangle. *Managerial and Decision Economics, 24*(4), 309–23.

Piezunka, H. & Dahlander, L. (2015). Distant search, narrow attention: How crowding alters organizations' filtering of suggestions in crowdsourcing. *Academy of Management Journal, 58*(3), 856–80.

Poetz, M. K. & Schreier, M. (2012). The value of crowdsourcing: Can users really compete with professionals in generating new product ideas? *Journal of Product Innovation Management, 29*(2), 245–56.

Ranade, G. & Varshney, L. (2018). The role of information patterns in designing crowdsourcing contests. In C. Tucci, A. Afuah, & G. Viscusi (eds.), *Creating and Capturing Value Through Crowdsourcing*. Oxford: Oxford University Press, pp. 154–80.

Ravasi, D. & Schultz, M. (2006). Responding to organizational identity threats: Exploring the role of organizational culture. *Academy of Management Journal, 49*(3), 433–58.

Ren, Y., Kraut, R., & Kiesler, S. (2007). Applying common identity and bond theory to design of online communities. *Organization Studies, 28*(3), 377–408.

Rico, R., Sánchez-Manzanares, M., Gil, F., & Gibson, C. (2008). Team implicit coordination processes: A team knowledge-based approach. *Academy of Management Review, 33*(1), 163–84.

Riedl, C. & Woolley, A. (2017). Teams vs. crowds: A field test of the relative contribution of incentives, member ability, and collaboration to crowd-based problem solving performance. Academy of Management Discoveries, https://papers.ssrn.com/sol3/papers.cfm?abstract_id=2384068

Scotchmer, S. (2004). *Innovation and Incentives*. Cambridge, MA: MIT Press.

Shah, S. K. (2006). Motivation, governance, and the viability of hybrid forms in open source software development. *Management Science, 52*(7), 1000–14.

Sieg, J. H., Wallin, M. W., & von Krogh, G. (2010). Managerial challenges in open innovation: A study of innovation intermediation in the chemical industry. *R & D Management, 40*(3), 281–91.

Simula, H. & Ahola, T. (2014). A network perspective on idea and innovation crowdsourcing in industrial firms. *Industrial Marketing Management, 43*(3), 400–8.

Sobel, D. (2007). *Longitude: True Story of a Lone Genius Who Solved the Greatest Scientific Problem of His Time*. London, UK: HarperCollins.

Šundić, M. & Leitner, K-H. (2018). Co-creation from a telecommunication provider's perspective: A comparative study on innovation with customers and employees. In C. Tucci, A. Afuah, & G. Viscusi (eds.), *Creating and Capturing Value Through Crowdsourcing*. Oxford: Oxford University Press, pp. 236–70.

Surowiecki, J. (2004). *The Wisdom of Crowds*. New York: Doubleday.

Tapscott, D. & Williams, A. D. (2006). *Wikinomics: How Mass Collaboration Changes Everything*. New York: Portfolio.

Teece, D. J. (1986). Profiting from technological innovation: Implications for integration, collaboration, licensing and public policy. *Research Policy, 15*(6), 285–305.

Terwiesch, C. & Xu, Y. (2008). Innovation contests, open innovation, and multiagent problem solving. *Management Science, 54*(9), 1529–43.

Tischler, L. 2002. He struck gold on the net (really). Fast Company, http://www. fastcompany.com/magazine/59/mcewen.html (accessed February 20, 2017).

Tushman, M. L. & Anderson, P. (1986). Technological discontinuities and organizational environments. *Administrative Science Quarterly*, *31*(3), 439–65.

Van de Ven, A. H. (1989). Nothing is quite so practical as a good theory. *Academy of Management Review*, *14*(4), 486–9.

Viscusi, G. & Tucci, C. (2018). Three's a crowd? In C. Tucci, A. Afuah, & G. Viscusi (eds.), *Creating and Capturing Value Through Crowdsourcing*. Oxford: Oxford University Press, pp. 39–57.

Von Hayek, F. A. (1937). Economics and knowledge. *Economica*, *4*(13), 33–54.

Von Krogh, G., Haefliger, S., Spaeth, S., & Wallin, M. W. (2012). Carrots and rainbows: Motivation and social practice in open source software development. *MIS Quarterly*, *36*(2), 649–76.

Wallin, M., von Krogh, G., & Sieg, J. (2017). A problem in the making: How firms formulate sharable problems for open innovation contests. In C. Tucci, A. Afuah, & G. Viscusi (eds.), *Creating and Capturing Value Through Crowdsourcing*. Oxford: Oxford University Press, pp. 39–57.

West, J. & Bogers, M. (2014). Leveraging external sources of innovation: A review of research on open innovation. *Journal of Product Innovation Management*, *31*(4), 814–31.

West, J. & Gallagher, S. (2006). Challenges of open innovation: The paradox of firm investment in open-source software. *R&D Management*, *36*(3), 319–31.

West, J. & Sims, J. (2018). How firms leverage crowds and communities for open innovation. In C. Tucci, A. Afuah, & G. Viscusi (eds.), *Creating and Capturing Value Through Crowdsourcing*. Oxford: Oxford University Press, pp. 58–96.

Ye, H. J. & Kankanhalli, A. (2017). Solvers' participation in crowdsourcing platforms: Examining the impacts of trust, and benefit and cost factors. *Journal of Strategic Information Systems*, *26*(2), 101–17.

Zuchowski, O., Posegga, O., Schlagwein, D., & Fischbach, K. (2016). Internal crowdsourcing: Conceptual framework, structured review, and research agenda. *Journal of Information Technology*, *31*(2), 166–84.

3

Three's a Crowd?

Gianluigi Viscusi and Christopher L. Tucci

Abstract
According to conventional wisdom on crowdsourcing, the number of people defines the crowd and maximization of this number is often assumed to be the goal of any crowdsourcing exercise. However, some structural characteristics of the crowd might be more important than the sheer number of participants. These characteristics include (1) the growth rate and its attractiveness to members, (2) equality among members, (3) density within provisional boundaries, (4) goal orientation of the crowd, and (5) "seriality" of the interactions between members. Therefore, a typology is proposed that may allow managers to position their companies' initiatives among four strategic types for driving innovation: crowd crystals, online communities, closed crowds, and open crowds. Incumbent companies may prefer closed and controlled access to the crowd, limiting the potential for gaining results and insights from fully open crowd-driven innovation initiatives. Thus, the effects on industries and organizations by open crowds are still to be explored.

INTRODUCTION

"There is nothing that man fears more than the touch of the unknown. He wants to *see* what is reaching towards him, and to be able to recognize or at least classify it . . . All the distances which men create round themselves are dictated by this fear . . . It is only in a crowd that man can become free of this fear of being touched. That is the only situation in which the fear changes into its opposite.

(Canetti, 1962: 15)

These sentences, from the beginning of *Crowds and Power* by the philosopher Elias Canetti look either prophetic or explanatory today, with regard to the impact of crowdsourcing in current digital business scenarios. Indeed, in spite of the hype, diffusion, and adoption of the diverse forms of crowdsourcing, it represents an activity that blurs the boundaries of organizations in an as yet poorly understood fashion. In many cases perceived as being related to sourcing activities such as a low-cost labor/ideation force, crowdsourcing has not yet been investigated for its potential for shaping yet unknown organizational forms that are not only virtual but also go beyond being purely distributed to agents holding multiple roles across multiple crowds. To anticipate changes in organization and business innovation, we propose an analysis of the terms related to crowds to provide a classification scheme suitable to reduce the distance between formal organizations as we know them and "crowded" organizations. It is worth noting, however, that in spite of such questions being widely discussed by scholars and practitioners interested in, for example, models for the simulation of pedestrian dynamics and crowd management (Batty et al., 2003; Challenger et al., 2009; Bandini et al., 2011), management perspectives seem to rely mainly on the "sourcing" part of the crowdsourcing. This can be seen in the most cited definition by Howe: "*crowdsourcing is the act of taking a job traditionally performed by a designated agent (usually an employee) and outsourcing it to an undefined, generally large group of people in the form of an open call*" (Howe, 2006b, 2008), further stating "*the labor isn't always free, but it costs a lot less than paying traditional employees. It's not outsourcing; it's crowdsourcing*" (Howe, 2006a). This framing of the concept is often done without questioning the other terms or defining them in a rather general manner, and not analytically considering crowd organizational behavior, structure, and social impact (Wexler, 2011), nor providing precise figures on how many members are necessary to form a crowd, from thousands of people, to perhaps a hundred in the case of businesses dealing with confidential information (Estélles-Arolas & González-Ladrón-de-Guevara, 2012). We believe that a further clarification of the "crowd" component of crowdsourcing is relevant to fostering its innovation potential, moving beyond the premise of decision-making that makes crowdsourcing out to be only another low cost form of sourcing enabled by digital infrastructures.

Thus the questions we consider are: *What are the characteristics that allow a proper identification of a crowd with regard to other forms of collective or group organizations? How can organizations adapt to crowd-driven market and technological change? Is crowdsourcing yet another sourcing innovation or rather an integrated whole with tech startups and digital business organizations?*

ONLINE DISTRIBUTED INNOVATION:
A CROWD IS NOT A GROUP

How many people constitute a *crowd* compared to a *group*? In what follows, we introduce a summary of the key issues suitable for supporting these distinctions and a set of parameters to identify a crowd, based on prior work on real-life crowds. Then we extend the insights from real crowds to digital crowds. The first issue is to identify the attributes of a given entity as part of a social collective, if such attributes exist. The second issue, reconceptualizing social collectivity or the meaning of social groups as a phenomenon of *serial collectivity* (each member of the collective operates autonomously but inter-dependently to achieve a goal as developed below), has been investigated, e.g., by political scientists such as Iris Marion Young (1994). This stance relies on Sartre's distinction between *series*, a specific kind of social collectivity, and *groups* (Sartre, 1960/2004).

According to that perspective, a *group* is a collection of people who recognize themselves as being unified in relation to one another, i.e., the mutual acknowledgment that they are undertaking a common project or action (e.g., storming the Bastille, building an amphitheater), thus all sharing the same goals (Young, 1994). Also, this acknowledgment usually tends to be made explicit as a collective project through some form of agreement, such as, for example, a statement of purpose, a contract, a pledge, etc. Consequently, a group can be defined as a "self-consciously, mutually acknowledging collective with a self-conscious purpose" (Young, 1994). However, as Sartre noticed, some groups are often emergent from a kind of collective unity characterized by being less organized and certainly unselfconscious: a *series* (Young, 1994; Sartre, 1960/2004).

Members of a series are unified passively by a response to the environment, the target of their actions, or by the effects of the structures resulting from past actions produced by others, either persons or organizations (routines, habits, protocols, etc.). As an example of a series, Sartre considered people waiting for a bus. Their being part of a collective is governed and bounded by the rules (routines related to social practices of public transportation) of "waiting for a bus" (the target material object of their action). However different they are in their experience, class, identity, work, and education, they are unified by the goal of taking a specific bus following a given route. In a series, the individual experiences him- or herself and the others as *anonymous* and *interchangeable* (it is irrelevant whether I can go on the bus first, or within a second line of passengers, or sitting in the back or the front, depending on the time). As pointed out by Young (1994), in a series, individuals are isolated but not alone, or in a more modern context of diffusion of mobile and social network technologies, *alone together* (Turkle, 2011).

Coming now to the potential emergence of a group from a series; the bus series may become an organized group if the bus fails to arrive (thinking about a collective complaint against the transportation company, sharing a taxi, etc.). The breakdown contributes to the creation of a mutual identification and agreed-upon goals typical of a group. Another example of seriality developed by Sartre (1960/2004) concerns listening to the radio. Here the series is characterized by the orientation toward a radio and its function of sound transmission, and is made up of isolated listeners, who may be aware of the presence of other listeners linked through broadcasting. Also, note the role of the host or DJ who explicitly refers to the series of listeners for competitions, announcements, etc. The set of objects and practices that generate and are reproduced by the series are called by Sartre the *milieu of action*, which delimits and constrains individual action without defining the person's identity in terms of goals, projects, and sense of self in relation to others (Young, 1994).

Thus, seriality seems to be a feature that may distinguish a group (self-aware as a group) from a crowd (anonymous and interchangeable). A series is characterized by the *lack of salience* of individual differences; general *equality* characterizes its crowd members. The process of self-selection in crowdsourcing discharges the elements that are not at an appropriate level for the anonymous goals orienting the crowd, thus creating the right series. To investigate the implications of seriality, we rely on the conceptualization of Canetti (1962), arguing for two diverse types of crowd. The natural and true crowd is the *open crowd*, having no limits to its growth, open everywhere and in any direction. The open crowd exists as long as it can grow, collapsing as soon as it cannot grow anymore. Digital channels increase the chances of serial collectivity with regard to growth rate and its attractiveness to the members.

In contrast, the *closed crowd* is characterized by permanence, a renunciation of growth, and self-established boundaries, protected from outside influence, preventing disorganized growth (size) as well as dispersion and consequent dissolution. The boundaries of the closed crowd are their entry points, which can be accessed by a limited number of people until capacity is reached. Closed crowd interactions are based on repetition, which makes the dispersion of some of its members acceptable, the important thing being its internal density. The *eruption* is the sudden transition from a closed into an open crowd, due to a blurring of the boundaries by the tendency of the individuals in the crowd to transcend the physical limitations of the crowd's space. This introduces the *destructiveness* of the crowd as its most prominent quality, when members push and extend its boundaries. Destructiveness as an intrinsic quality of a crowd is worth considering for understanding the potential of the open crowd as creative destroyer, compared with the controlled nature of the closed crowd.

Groups on the other hand can be seen as what Canetti defines as *crowd crystals* (the *milieu of action* of a series in Sartre's view), that are "the small, rigid groups of men, strictly delimited and of great constancy, which serve to precipitate the crowd...Their unity is more important than their size. Their role must be familiar" (Canetti, 1962: 73). A crowd, therefore, can originate from groups; however, a group would differ from a closed crowd because it is smaller, less spontaneous, with specific functions allocated to its members, and their identity survives the disintegration of the crowd.

Thus, the structural characteristics of a crowd might be:

1. *Growth* rate and its attractiveness to the members;
2. *Equality* among members;
3. *Density* within provisional boundaries;
4. *Goal* orientation (a crowd exists as long as it has an unattained goal, no matter the type of goal (Canetti, 1962: 22)); and
5. *Seriality* of the interactions.

Density is particularly relevant because it emphasizes the role of space (whether virtual as in a digital platform or else physical) in determining the characterization of a number of people as an open/closed crowd rather than a group. As pointed out, e.g., by the Cabinet Office (2009) of the UK, density and size are interrelated in the definition of what forms a crowd (e.g., a flow rate of people per meter per minute), as well as connected to the perception of crowding by an external observer. Consider for example fifty people located over a very large area such as a park (very low density) and the same number in a small area such as the counter of a kiosk in the same park (high density); in the second case we have a crowd, given the same number of people. One could probably arrive at a threshold effect of the density of the number of people per square meter that would give the impression of having a crowd (which might differ from country to country, depending on perceptions of "personal distance").

Consider now fifty participants in an idea competition discussing online. In this case, the size and perception of crowding might be related to (1) the number of contributions generated by the crowd, and (2) the ability of the organization to handle the contributions of the crowd, in terms of the number of data scientists, the availability and storage capacity of database management systems, as well as the availability of analytical tools. If the contributions of the crowd exceed the ability of the firm to evaluate the outcomes (e.g., the BP oil spill, as discussed by Alexy et al., 2012), the perception the organization might have could be an "out of control" crowd:

> There's [sic] so many ideas you become numb to them. (Coast Guard speaking of the suggestions from BP's crowd, cited by Alexy et al., 2012: 117)

Thus, high density together with the other characteristics previously mentioned, in particular seriality, distinguishes a crowd from groups or communities (von Hippel, 2005), with a consequent difference for their management and planning of related initiatives (see also West & Sims, 2018).

Consequently, an interesting definition of crowd can be the one provided by the 2009 report from the UK Cabinet Office as *"a sizeable gathering of people in a given location, with a sufficient density distribution, who have come together for a specific purpose over a measurable period of time and who, despite being predominantly strangers or in an unfamiliar situation, feel united by a common identity and are, therefore, able to act in a socially coherent manner"* (Challenger et al., 2009: 129). However, it is worth noting, that such a definition seems to emphasize the closed crowd as the subject and target of crowd management, preventing the eruption of an open crowd and its unpredictable consequences. This is also true for current perspectives on crowdsourcing; despite some initiatives counting a hundred thousand participants, they are nonetheless bounded in nature, preventing the loss of institutional control consequent from a change in the crowd towards a more open form. Besides the structural characteristics mentioned, others related to organizational facets are worth considering (see also Berlonghi, 1995). Table 3.1 shows characteristics worth considering when answering the key questions, for an effective understanding and management of crowds in crowdsourcing initiatives.

Table 3.1. Behavioral and structural characteristics and key questions for crowd management in crowdsourcing (adapted from Canetti, 1962; Berlonghi, 1995; Challenger et al., 2009; Viscusi & Tucci, 2015).

Behavioral characteristics of the crowd	Structural characteristics of the crowd	Key questions
Complexity	Seriality	How organized and structured is the crowd?
Leadership	Goal orientation	How established or spontaneous is the leadership among the members of the crowd? How much may they deviate from the crowdsourcing goals?
Acquaintance	Density	To what degree have members of the crowd connected with one another prior to the initiative?
Psychological unity	Equality	How psychologically united are the members of the crowd, thus avoiding antagonism altering the competition or the collaboration?
Emotional intensity	Seriality	How emotionally engaged is the crowd?
Volatility	Growth	To what degree are the crowd's boundaries changing, disrupting the established competition or collaboration boundaries?
Concentration of influence	Seriality	To what degree are crowd members influenced or dominated by one or more groups?
Degree of accountability	Equality	How much "lurking" and similar behaviors are taking place?

Table 3.1 shows the structural characteristics suitable for supporting the definition of evaluation measures and control parameters for each theme. These are worth considering when an organization aims to develop initiatives to solve their internal information gaps or to look for new ideas for product/ service development.

CROWD AS A SOLUTION TO DISTANT SEARCH: WHEN IS THE RIGHT TIME?

Solving problems and having the right information for the right product or service development remains a challenge for many top managers (Afuah & Tucci, 2013). Indeed, the unprecedented growth in available information through digital infrastructures makes such information a relevant asset for reducing uncertainty in decision making (*The Economist*, 2010; Viscusi & Batini, 2014). Consequently, the information industry is continuously expanding, encompassing media such as newspapers and television, credit rating agencies, market research firms, financial analysts, social media such as Youtube, Facebook, Linkedin, and Twitter, but also small companies and individual experts, e.g., in finance, law, engineering, and medicine (Sarvary, 2012). Its focus is actually on selling information products, that is, products that can be codified and "digitized," used in decision making, and paid for by decision makers (Shapiro & Varian, 1998; Sarvary, 2012). In this scenario, crowdsourcing can be a valuable alternative under certain conditions highlighted by Afuah & Tucci (2012), questioning, "when might crowdsourcing be a better mechanism for solving problems than the alternatives of either solving them internally or designating an exclusive contractor to solve them?"

The Internet and available digital platforms (Gawer & Cusumano, 2014) enable better performance of tasks through crowdsourcing, involving more arm's length transactions than traditional outsourcing to a designated contractor. Thus, Afuah & Tucci (2012) opened the black box of the current market configuration, arguing that:

(i) the market today actually includes crowdsourcing as a relevant actor;

(ii) crowdsourcing may be able to transform distant into local search, without the costs usually associated with distant search by the information market.

However, crowdsourcing adoption and the consequent transformation can happen under certain circumstances, as shown in Table 3.2.

Information technology (IT) platforms may also be suitable for moderating the core structural characteristics of a crowd, such as seriality, equality among members through self-selection, density as a quality of the closed crowd with a

Table 3.2. Variables and characteristics related to crowdsourcing adoption in distant search (Afuah & Tucci, 2012).

Variable	Characteristics	Description
Problem	Ease of delineation Ease of transmission Modularizability	The problem is easy to delineate and transmit, having a low degree of associated tacitness and complexity. Furthermore, the problem can be easily separated into components.
Knowledge	Effective distance Tacitness Complexity	The knowledge required to solve a problem is neither from the company's area of expertise nor in its possession, having a high degree of tacitness and complexity, likewise.
Crowd	Pervasiveness of know-how	The more pervasive the problem-solving know-how in a crowd, the higher the likelihood of self-selectors to solve the problem.
Solution	Experience orientation	The solution requires an evaluation after its use.
Evaluator	Experience orientation	The solution requires a high number of users for the evaluation.
Information technology (IT)	Pervasiveness Low cost	IT has a moderating effect on the other characteristics, when its diffusion is high and adoption costs are low.

controlled growth and appropriate search neighborhoods (ensuring again equality as self-selection). Modularity is also relevant to equality as self-selection, considering that more modular problems increase crowd members' incentives to self-select and engage in solving the problems (Baldwin & Clark, 2006; Afuah & Tucci, 2012).

Taking the above issues into account, while crowdsourcing problem solving and exploratory activities may be related to what we have called the closed crowd under the control of a given company as simply another form of outsourcing, today we can actually observe crowdsourcing as the symptom of the emergence of new forms of organizations and entrepreneurship. Thus, in contrast with the concept of an open crowd as a "disturbance" or "erratic," an open crowd may actually propose something completely new, which means that an open crowd also has value to the organization.

IDEAS COME NEXT: THE RISE OF CROWD-DRIVEN ENTREPRENEURSHIP

Many current technology startups are actually the symptoms of a new breed of entrepreneur exhibiting a set of characteristics that we have identified as supporting the definition of *what a crowd is* and *when crowdsourcing is worth adopting*. Indeed, they have been considered as devoted to "combinatorial innovation" (McKinsey, 2009), applying known techniques to new problems through continuous experimental activity on available digital platforms, providing open-source software or cheap pay-as-you-go services (*The Economist*, 2014), thus combining *seriality* of interactions and *modularity* of problems enabled by pervasive and low cost information technology (see Table 3.2). Other characteristics bringing crowd activity and today's entrepreneurs are *goal orientation* as well as *growth orientation*, due to their tendency to seek out business models leading to fast and profitable growth (*The Economist*, 2014). Furthermore, the organizational structure of tech startups is made by a small group of "executives" who are usually the founders of the business, with complementary skills (for example, the computer scientist Mark Zuckerberg and his economist roommate Eduardo Luiz Saverin).

Contrary to past practices, in many cases the team develops a new product or service only after working on several ideas through design thinking, rapid prototyping, and A/B testing (*The Economist*, 2014). Here, idea competitions and crowdfunding appear to be the main *interfaces* supporting interfirm modularity (cf., Staudenmayer et al., 2005) at the startup level, thus providing a virtual and flexible way towards a *semiformal* organization (Biancani et al., 2014), whose identity is characterized by *multiplicity* rather than the monolithic shape of traditional formal organizations. Multiplicity here does not refer to a dominant player plus periphery within a business ecosystem, but an organization that belongs to the many (DeLanda, 2002) such as the open crowd, and where the new company can be seen as what we earlier called a *crowd crystal*. The crowd-driven entrepreneurs exploit open crowd resources (for example, made up by participating in several closed crowd initiatives, such as those by Innocentive) as continuously generating their virtual organizational form from the actual different crowdsourcing processes in which the technology startup participates. This process of constant actualization of a virtual organization encompasses the need for business model *reconfiguration* rather than *design* (cf., Massa & Tucci, 2014). However, it is worth noting that crowd crystals may evolve or participate in less serialized forms of collectives, such as traditional online communities (Armstrong & Hagel, 1996), where people form personal relationships through maintained discussion (Rheingold, 2000) rather than anonymous goal orientation. The two forms have a similar growth orientation to open crowds. However, online communities, lacking seriality and equality as self-selection, may not create a virtual organizational form for technology startups, but rather are a starting point for new team building that may eventually lead to new technology startups.

KEY QUESTIONS FOR THE CROWD-ORIENTED ORGANIZATION

Crowdsourcing today is not only an alternative—and often an efficient one—to problem solving and collaboration activities for formal organizations exploiting what we have called the *closed crowd*, but also and most importantly, the interface for new kinds of organizational forms relying on what we have called the *open crowd*, enabling and reinforcing boundary spanning (Levina & Fayard, 2018). To provide an improved understanding of crowd-driven innovation initiatives actually managed by a given company or entrepreneurs, Figure 3.1 shows a typology according to their growth tendency (vertical axis of Figure 3.1) and degree of seriality (horizontal axis of Figure 3.1).

In what follows, we briefly analyze the crowd-driven initiatives in Figure 3.1, providing examples of platforms supporting them and discussing their plusses and minuses.

In the lower left quadrant, we have the *crowd crystal*. To understand its plusses and minuses, we consider the business-oriented social networking platform LinkedIn groups. LinkedIn groups can either be *external* (with a different degree of restriction to access), mainly targeting individual employees or managers, or else *internal*, that is, designed for the specific internal needs of a given company. This service has several plusses. First, it is relatively easy to set up and monitor activity in the group. Second, it can be used to analyze what kinds of expertise one's company has in the area(s) represented by the group. For example, in both external and internal groups on a certain topic, one can ascertain quickly who from the company is participating and what sorts of expertise they have, along with a social

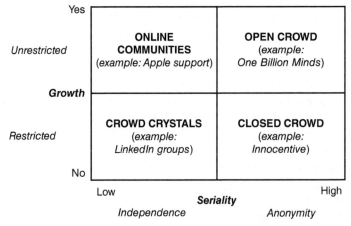

Figure 3.1. Types of crowds with regard to growth tendency and degree of seriality.

network structure within the company itself on that topic. This knowledge could also be used to launch other types of crowd-driven initiatives, such as idea competitions. In addition, internal LinkedIn groups can also result from former community projects, starting from one of the teams created to work on a certain topic, such as changes in work practices, human resource management, or technology trend identification for the years to come. However, external LinkedIn groups allow for both monitoring of specific competences and skills of employees or managers and identifying a connected population with similar characteristics outside the organization's boundaries. Also, the company's presence in these external LinkedIn groups may be managed or coordinated with an eye toward external relations and branding with regard to crowd-driven initiatives promoted by the company for different purposes.

Although both kinds of LinkedIn groups represent crowd crystals, this type of crowd has minuses in terms of lack of scale, fewer ideas, as well as less input, in addition to a low degree of seriality due to the topical rather than goal orientation, thus making them close to an online community. However, LinkedIn groups can also evolve towards either open or closed crowd types, but they nonetheless require a stronger, more specific goal orientation as well as analytics and storage capacity that are typical of platforms such as Innocentive, which is discussed in what follows for the *closed crowd* type in the lower right quadrant.

Innocentive is actually an innovation intermediary used by companies to solve highly defined technical problems via challenges in ways that often do not reveal the company's identity (Peters et al., 2013). The resulting *closed crowd* (see the lower right quadrant of Figure 3.1) has massive access to the state of the art for the subject of the competition, with a lower probability of leaking information. However, the minuses of Innocentive-like crowds are related to their being outsourcing- and narrow goal-oriented, thus neither building nor recognizing, and consequently keeping in house, the capabilities emerging from the crowd. The narrow outsourcing orientation of this kind of approach to a closed crowd may prevent R&D from understanding the participants and social structure of the crowd itself, in contrast with the crowd crystal case. For example, there may be potential "dealmakers" (Feldman & Zoller, 2012) acting in multiple crowds for their own business development, but the company will be unaware of the presence of the same parties across competitions. A company could perform an internal crowdsourcing exercise (Afuah, 2018); however, the company may lack external expertise (not to mention potential leakage of sensitive information, although certainly lower than a completely open call). In a sense, in the closed crowd as implemented through the fixed boundaries of platforms such as Innocentive, the firm is forced to modularize the problem (Schilling, 2000; Afuah & Tucci, 2012); whereas the open crowd is characterized by "generativity" (ability to evolve digitally without pre-planning the design or usage (cf. Yoo, 2013)) typical of large, varied, and uncoordinated audiences (Zittrain, 2006). Thus, the open crowd can be considered under the lens of the concept of *multitude*, which according to Tampio (2009: 387) "designates a social body in which singularities are not required to shed their differences in order to form a common notion," or according to Hardt & Negri (2000: 103) "plane of singularities," an open set of relations neither homogeneous nor identical with itself, bearing indistinct and inclusive relation to those outside of it. The concept of multitude is particularly relevant for crowdsourcing, as a form of organizing the productive process, thus for its connection with the Marxian concept of *general intellect* as the key force of production (Virno, 2004), combining technological expertise and general social knowledge or, as we would define it today, collective intelligence in a cognitive cultural economy (Vercellone, 2007) and the increasing relevance of cognitive computing and big data analytics for the full exploitation of open crowd enabled data (e.g., from runners' apps to twitter opinion mining and bot use for political campaigns).

Before moving to the open crowd, we discuss *online communities* in the upper left quadrant. Examples of these span from communities built on platforms such as Socious, Apple support communities (from the point of view of an end-user), or the Academy of Management (the main global association of management scholars) division communities. Apple support communities show how a crowd crystal may grow in an unrestricted fashion, losing the seriality character of the crowd, thus becoming no longer anonymous, and finally reaching "community" status, sharing the characteristics previously identified for groups. Communities have the plusses of being a well-known knowledge and innovation management topic for both practitioners and academics (West & Lakhani, 2008). However, they may present drawbacks due to the role of identity and beliefs in their cohesiveness, making them not easily adaptable to different, conflicting, and heterogeneous goals, and thus not very flexible. Large academic associations provide an interesting example of the difference between online communities and crowd crystals. Consider divisions within the Academy of Management. They can actually be considered communities in which academics and practitioners can discuss, share ideas, etc. on a specific topic (for example, technology and innovation management or organizational communications and information systems). However, they could evolve in different directions. In one direction, members could create smaller groups to discuss more narrow topics or as a support to a physical meeting, which could then be monitored by external parties. Because of their initial delimitation, constancy of membership, and skills self-selection, this could give rise to what we have previously defined as a crowd crystal. In another direction, members could potentially nurture a much bigger open crowd, without restriction to membership in the division, as well as a different very large online community (depending on its degree of seriality and anonymity).

Finally, in the upper right quadrant of Figure 3.1, we have the *open crowd*. Some examples of the open crowd are One Billion Minds (a platform connecting people who would like to create or participate in high-impact social projects) and Threadless, the creative e-commerce platform, initially for T-shirt design. These companies provide a nice illustration of how an online community can evolve towards an open crowd. Recall that an open crowd is appropriate when problem-solving couples with creativity or social needs. Threadless, for example, receives input from a crowd, but in reality is mainly learning about customers and marketing directly to the crowd as customers. Thus, an open crowd has among its plusses, access to a wider range of ideas, including crazy ideas (this is both a plus and a minus, depending on the analytics and storage capacity of the company). Also, when originating from online communities, it can reduce the costs of providing incentives and motivation, often related to crowdsourcing initiatives. Therefore, an open crowd is suitable as a strategic instrument for R&D, for understanding which ideas for new products and services could be viable, as well as the kind of business model innovation required (business model design or reconfiguration, see Massa & Tucci, 2014). Accordingly, an open crowd coupled with the right storage and analytic infrastructure can make businesses more aware of a disruptive change emerging in the competitive environment. As a consequence, the main minuses of an open crowd are related to the need for investments in big data and analytics to get the right information capacity as the current stock of understandings informed by a given installed base (Viscusi & Batini, 2014). Other disadvantages are related to misalignment between the volume of ideas and preferences, and return on investment, considering that, e.g. there is no deterministic connection between what people endorse and what people actually buy; actually, as the Threadless case has shown the vote is only a necessary but not sufficient part alone of a business model related to dealing with a parallel and self-reinforcing growth of an online community of users, that is at the same time part of a crowd of voters and consumers (Ogawa & Piller 2006; Lakhani & Panetta, 2007; Poetz & Schreier, 2012; Kavaliova et al., 2016; Bal et al., 2017).

CONCLUSIONS AND FUTURE RESEARCH

Considering the previously mentioned plusses and minuses, managers may want to position themselves to solve their crowd-driven innovation problems. However, certain pathways may be easier to move along than others. As shown in Figure 3.2, a crowd crystal can lead to either an online or a closed

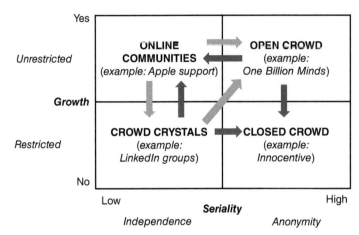

Figure 3.2. Dynamics and movement between quadrants.

crowd (not necessarily leading to an open crowd, as shown by the black arrows in Figure 3.2), or an open crowd (thus being really a key starting point for crowd-driven innovation). However, as previously mentioned, a crowd crystal can also emerge from an online community, leading to an open crowd (the path represented by the light gray arrows in Figure 3.2). Finally, an open crowd could move toward online communities and closed crowds, but closed crowds may not give rise to crowd crystals (the path represented by the black arrows in Figure 3.2).

Taking these issues into account, the majority of crowdsourcing initiatives sponsored by organizations actually seem to be more like crowd crystals or closed crowds, in which there is a control orientation with regard to crowd boundaries, density, and goals. However, these initiatives could be shifted toward different forms, depending on the goals of the organization. Business model design for effective exploitation and execution of the outputs of the diverse crowdsourcing initiatives will be key.

In terms of innovation, while there are many innovation outcomes possible in each of the quadrants, it is clear that firms may find it difficult to cross the "frontier" between closed and open crowds, due as previously discussed to the fact that a third party controls access to the crowd, which may impede knowledge flows across organizational boundaries after the exercise is over. While the output of the closed crowd initiative may be useful as outsourcing problem solving for a specific problem, it may later on hamper "outside-in" knowledge flows (Chesbrough & Bogers, 2014). Incumbents may prefer the control of the crowd crystal or closed crowd over the chaos of the open crowd, which may be characterized by virtuality, multiplicity, and pressure for constant reconfiguration of business models.

This conclusion would also point out the need for future research on whether the previously mentioned characteristics and dynamics give rise to *crowd organizations* (Pereira et al., 2016), which, for task division and allocation, are structurally different from traditional formal organizations (cf. Puranam et al., 2014), possibly related to meta-organizations (cf. Gulati et al., 2012). Furthermore, another research stream can move from crowd organizations and their different instantiations, to questioning how these instantiations and the characteristics of the crowd may lower or increase *crowd capital,* an organizational level capability, or organizational resources acquired through crowdsourcing (Prpić et al., 2015: 80), also defined as *the total number of crowd units having a demonstrated effectiveness in idea generation or task achievement* (Tucci & Viscusi, 2017). Finally, research on crowd organizations and crowd capital is also linked to investigations on how meso-level structures support effective coordination in temporary groups (cf. Valentine & Edmondson, 2014), as well as on frameworks for dynamically assembling and managing paid experts from the crowd through "flash teams" as a sequence of modular tasks that draw on paid experts from the crowd (Retelny et al., 2014). These research avenues could expand our understanding of the crowd as an organizing agent and its impact on problem solving, knowledge creation, and diffusion, as well as trajectories of innovation (cf. Dosi, 1982; Dosi & Grazzi, 2010) driven by technology-enabled crowds.

The effect on industries and organizations of open crowds are also still to be explored in future research, possibly via the mechanism of entrepreneurs exploiting open crowds as new entrants, but also for the configuration of industries such as finance, pharmaceuticals, or even the public sector, where the value created usually comes from interpretation issues and exploratory problem solving (cf. Cordella et al., 2018). Indeed, considering crowd-driven entrepreneurs and open crowd challenges as well as insights from research on interfirm networks (Madhavan et al., 2004), the answer to the title question may well be: "Yes, three's a crowd!"

REFERENCES

Afuah A. (2018). Crowdsourcing: A primer and research framework. In C. Tucci, A. Afuah, & G. Viscusi (eds.), *Creating and Capturing Value Through Crowdsourcing.* Oxford: Oxford University Press, pp. 11–38.

Afuah, A. & Tucci, C. (2012). Crowdsourcing as a solution to distant search. *Academy of Management Review, 37*(3), 355–75.

Afuah, A. & Tucci, C. (2013). Value capture and crowdsourcing. *Academy of Management Review,* (July), *38*(3), 457–60.

Alexy, O., Criscuolo, P., & Salter, A. (2012). Managing unsolicited ideas for R&D. *California Management Review, 54*(3), 116–39.

Armstrong, A. & Hagel, J. (1996). The real value of on line communities. *Harvard Business Review, 74*(3), 134–41.

Bal, A. S., Weidner, K., Hanna, R., & Mills, A. J. (2017). Crowdsourcing and brand control. *Business Horizons, 60*(2), 219–28. doi:http://doi.org/10.1016/j.bushor.2016.11.006.

Baldwin, C. Y. & Clark, K. B. (2006). The architecture of participation: Does code architecture mitigate free riding in the open source development model? *Management Science, 52*(7), 1116–27.

Bandini, S., Manenti, L., Manzoni, L., & Manzoni, S. (2011). Dealing with crowd crystals in MAS-based crowd simulation: A proposal. *AI* IA 2011: Artificial Intelligence Around Man and Beyond*, pp. 92–103.

Batty, M., DeSyllas, J., & Duxbury, E. (2003). The discrete dynamics of small-scale spatial events: Agent-based models of mobility in carnivals and street parades. *International Journal of Geographical Information Science, 17*(7), 673–97.

Berlonghi, A. E. (1995). Understanding and planning for different spectator crowds. *Safety Science, 18*, 239–47.

Biancani, S., McFarland, D. A., & Dahlander, L. (2014). The semiformal organization. *Organization Science, 25*(5), 1306–24. http://dx.doi.org/10.1287/orsc.2013.0882

Canetti, E. (1962). *Crowds and Power*. New York: Continuum.

Challenger, W., Clegg, W. C., & Robinson, A. M. (2009). *Understanding Crowd Behaviours: Guidance and Lessons Identified*. London: UK Cabinet Office.

Chesbrough, H. & Bogers, M. (2014). Explicating open innovation: Clarifying an emerging paradigm for understanding innovation, in H. Chesbrough, W. Vanhaverbeke, & J. West (eds.). *New Frontiers in Open Innovation*. Oxford: Oxford University Press, pp. 3–28.

Cordella, A., Palletti, A., & Shaikh, M. (2018). Renegotiating public value with co-production. In C. Tucci, A. Afuah, & G. Viscusi (eds.), *Creating and Capturing Value Through Crowdsourcing*. Oxford: Oxford University Press, pp. 181–203.

DeLanda, M. (2002). *Intensive Science and Virtual Philosophy*. New York: Continuum, http://openlibrary.org/b/OL8169118M/Intensive_Science_Virtual_Philosophy_(Con tinuum_Impacts)

Dosi, G. (1982). Technological paradigms and technological trajectories: A suggested interpretation of the determinants and directions of technical change. *Research Policy 11*, 147–62.

Dosi, G. & Grazzi, M. (2010). On the nature of technologies: knowledge, procedures, artifacts and production inputs. *Cambridge Journal of Economics, 34*(1), 173–84, http://dx.doi.org/10.1093/cje/bep041

Estélles-Arolas, E. & González-Ladrón-de-Guevara, F. (2012). Towards an integrated crowdsourcing definition. *Journal of Information Science, 38*(2), 189–200.

Feldman, M. & Zoller, T. D. (2012). Dealmakers in place: Social capital connections in regional entrepreneurial economies. *Regional Studies, 46*, 23–37.

Gawer, A. & Cusumano, M. A. (2014). Industry platforms and ecosystem innovation. *Journal of Product Innovation Management, 31*(3), 417–33, http://dx.doi.org/10.1111/jpim.12105

Gulati, R., Puranam, P., & Tushman, M. (2012). Meta-organization design: Rethinking design in interorganizational and community contexts. *Strategic Management Journal*, *33*(6), 571–86. http://doi.org/10.1002/smj.1975

Hardt, M. & Negri, A. (2000). *Empire*, papers3://publication/uuid/CD1E7EAF-B87C-4878-B30F-43D302087788

Howe, J. (2006a). The rise of crowdsourcing. *Wired Magazine*, 14.06, http://www.wired.com/wired/archive/14.06/crowds.html.

Howe, J. (2006b). Crowdsourcing: A definition, from http://crowdsourcing.typepad.com/cs/2006/06/crowdsourcing_a.html

Howe, J. (2008). *Crowdsourcing: Why the Power of the Crowd is Driving the Future of Business*. New York: Crown Business.

Kavaliova, M., Virjee, F., Maehle, N., & Kleppe, I. A. (2016). Crowdsourcing innovation and product development: Gamification as a motivational driver. *Cogent Business & Management*, *3*(1), 1128132. doi:10.1080/23311975.2015.1128132.

Lakhani, K. R. & Panetta, J. A. (2007). The principles of distributed innovation. *Innovations*, *2*(3), 97–112.

Levina, N. & Fayard, A-L. (2018). Tapping into diversity through open innovation platforms: The emergence of boundary spanning practices. In C. Tucci, A. Afuah, & G. Viscusi (eds.), *Creating and Capturing Value Through Crowdsourcing*. Oxford: Oxford University Press, pp. 204–35.

Madhavan, R., Gnyawali, D. R., & Jinyu, H. E. (2004). Two's company, three's a crowd? Triads in cooperative–competitive networks. *Academy of Management Journal*, *47*(6), 918–27. doi:10.2307/20159631.

Massa, L. & Tucci, C. L. (2014). Business model innovation, in M. Dodgson, D. M. Gann, & N. Phillips (eds.). *The Oxford Handbook of Innovation Management*. Oxford: Oxford University Press.

McKinsey (2009). Hal Varian on how the Web challenges managers. *Insights & Publications*, http://www.mckinsey.com/insights/innovation/hal_varian_on_how_the_web_challenges_managers

Ogawa, S. & Piller, F. T. (2006). Reducing the risks of new product development. *MIT Sloan Management Review*, *47*(2), 65.

Pereira, R. J., Viscusi, G., & Tucci, C. (2016). "What's the frequency, Kenneth?" Defining the crowd organization. In C. Baldwin, K. Lakhani, S. Thomke, & E. von Hippel (eds.). 14th International Open and User Innovation Conference (OUI), August 1–3, 2016, Harvard Business School. Boston, MA.

Peters, T., Thiel, J., & Tucci, C. L. (2013). Protecting growth options in dynamic markets: The role of strategic disclosure in integrated intellectual property strategies. *California Management Review*, *55*(4), 121–42.

Poetz, M. K. & Schreier, M. (2012). The value of crowdsourcing: Can users really compete with professionals in generating new product ideas? *Journal of Product Innovation Management*, *29*(2), 245–56, http://10.0.4.87/j.1540-5885.2011.00893.x.

Prpić, J., Shukla, P. P., Kietzmann, J. H., & McCarthy, I. P. (2015). How to work a crowd: Developing crowd capital through crowdsourcing. *Business Horizons*, *58*(1), 77–85.

Puranam, P., Alexy, O., & Reitzig, M. (2014). What's "new" about new forms of organizing. *Academy of Management Review*, 39(2), 162–80, http://doi.org/10.5465/amr.2011.0436

Retelny, D. et al. (2014). Expert crowdsourcing with flash teams. In *Proceedings of the 27th Annual ACM Symposium on User Interface Software and Technology*. New York: ACM, pp. 75–85.

Rheingold, H. (2000). *The Virtual Community: Homesteading on the Electronic Frontier*, revised edn. Cambridge, MA: The MIT Press.

Sartre, J.-P. (1960/2004). *Critique of Dialectical Reason*, J. Ree (ed.). London: Verso. (First published as *Critique de la Raison Dialectique* by Editions Gallimard, Paris 1960.)

Sarvary, M. (2012). *Gurus and Oracles—The Marketing of Information*. Cambridge, MA: MIT Press.

Schilling, M. A. (2000). Toward a general modular systems theory and its application to interfirm product modularity. *Academy of Management Review*, 25(2), 312–34.

Shapiro, C. & Varian, H. R. (1998). *Information Rules: A Strategic Guide to the Network Economy*, C. Shapiro, (ed.). Boston, MA: Harvard Business School Press.

Staudenmayer, N. A., Tripsas, M., & Tucci, C. L. (2005). Interfirm modularity and its implications for product development. *Journal of Product Innovation Management*, 22, 303–21.

Tampio, N. (2009). Assemblages and the multitude: Deleuze, Hardt, Negri, and the Postmodern Left. *European Journal of Political Theory*, 8(3), 383–400.

The Economist (2010). Data, data everywhere. *Special Report: Managing Information*, http://www.economist.com/node/15557443 (accessed October 2017).

The Economist (2014). *A Cambrian Moment—Special Report Tech Startups*. January 18.

Tucci, C. & Viscusi, G. (2017). Crowd Dynamics and Crowd Capital in Small Teams Insights from three crowdsourcing exercises in higher education. 5th Collective Intelligence Conference. New York University's Tandon School of Engineering, New York.

Turkle, S. (2011). *Alone Together: Why We Expect More from Technology and Less from Each Other*. New York: Basic Books.

Valentine, M. A. & Edmondson, A. C. (2014). Team scaffolds: How mesolevel structures enable role-based coordination in temporary groups. *Organization Science*, 26(2), 405–22.

Vercellone, C. (2007). From formal subsumption to general intellect: Elements for a Marxist reading of the thesis of cognitive capitalism. *Historical Materialism*, 15(1), 13–36.

Virno, P. (2004). *A Grammar Of The Multitude—For an Analysis of Contemporary Forms of Life*. Cambridge, MA: Semiotext(e)/Foreign Agents—MIT Press.

Viscusi, G. & Batini, C. (2014). Digital information asset evaluation: Characteristics and dimensions, in L. Caporarello, B. Di Martino, & M. Martinez (eds.). *Smart Organizations and Smart Artifacts SE—9*. Lecture Notes in Information Systems and Organisation. New York: Springer International Publishing, pp. 77–86, http://dx.doi.org/10.1007/978-3-319-07040-7_9

Viscusi, G., & Tucci, C. L. (2015). Distinguishing *"Crowded" Organizations from Groups and Communities*: Is Three a Crowd?, June 4. SSRN, http://ssrn.com/abstract=2446129

Von Hippel, E. (2005). Innovation communities. In *Democratizing Innovation*. Cambridge, MA: MIT Press, pp. 93–106.

West, J. & Lakhani, K. R. (2008). Getting clear about communities in open innovation. *Industry and Innovation*, *15*(2), 223–31, http://dx.doi.org/10.1080/13662710802033734

West, J. & Sims, J. (2018). How firms leverage crowds and communities for open innovation. In C. Tucci, A. Afuah, & G. Viscusi (eds.), *Creating and Capturing Value Through Crowdsourcing*. Oxford: Oxford University Press, pp. 58–96.

Wexler, M. N. (2011). Reconfiguring the sociology of the crowd: Exploring crowdsourcing. *International Journal of Sociology and Social Policy*, *31*(1/2), 6–20.

Yoo, Y. (2013). The tables have turned: How can the information systems field contribute to technology and innovation management research? *Journal of the Association for Information Systems*, *14*, 227–36.

Young, I. M. (1994). Gender as seriality: Thinking about women as a social collective. *Signs: Journal of Women in Culture and Society*, *19*(3), 713–38.

Zittrain, J. L. (2006). The generative Internet. *Harvard Law Review*, *119*, 1974–2040.

4

How Firms Leverage Crowds and Communities for Open Innovation

Joel West and Jonathan Sims

Abstract
There are many similarities in how firms pursuing an open innovation strategy can utilize crowds and communities as sources of external innovation. At the same time, the differences between these two network forms of collaboration have previously been blurred or overlooked. In this chapter, we integrate research on crowds and communities, identifying a third form—a crowd–community hybrid—that combines attributes of both. We compare examples of each of these three network forms, such as open source software communities, gated contests, crowdsourcing tournaments, user-generated content, and crowd science. We then summarize the intrinsic, extrinsic, and structural factors that enable individual and organizational participation in these collaborations. Finally, we contrast how these collaborative forms differ regarding their degree of innovativeness and relevance to firm goals. From this, we identify opportunities for future research on these topics.

INTRODUCTION

Historically, firms have had two ways of obtaining new technological innovations. One is to develop them internally, an approach that led to the dominant vertically integrated firms of the twentieth century (Chandler, 1977; Freeman & Soete, 1997). The other has been to source innovations through cooperation with other firms, through outsourcing, alliances, contracting, and markets for technology, as part of a process that more recently has been dubbed "open innovation" (Teece, 1986, 1992; Arora et al., 2001; Chesbrough, 2003).

Open innovation reflects firms using "purposive inflows and outflows of knowledge to accelerate internal innovation, and expand the markets for external use of innovation" (Chesbrough, 2006: 1). Most often, researchers (and managers) have focused on the inbound flows that firms commercialize to supplement or replace internal R&D (West & Bogers, 2014). Although open innovation typically involves monetary or other economic incentives for cooperation, firms can also access flows based on non-economic motivations (West & Gallagher, 2006; Dahlander & Gann, 2010; Piller & West, 2014).

In the past two decades, there has been increasing interest in how firms work with external communities—those outside the boundary of any firm (O'Mahony & Lakhani, 2011). In some cases, the community provides a common infrastructure that is prerequisite to each firms' products (Rosenkopf & Tushman, 1998). In other case, firms practicing open innovation leverage communities as an important source of external innovations, such as those that produce open source software (Dahlander & Magnusson, 2008; West & Lakhani, 2008). Research and popular interest have focused on new forms of virtual community made possible through the Internet (Rheingold, 2000). However, face to face interaction remains crucial for voluntary communities formed around users of physical goods such as sporting goods or 3D printers (Franke & Shah, 2003; West & Greul, 2016).

More recently, open innovation has turned towards externally sourcing ideas by tapping into the so-called "wisdom of crowds" (Surowiecki, 2005). Various forms of external innovation sourcing strategies—including tournaments, collaboration, open calls, and an open search for partners—have been lumped under the title of "crowdsourcing" (Afuah & Tucci, 2012; Boudreau & Lakhani, 2013; Diener & Piller, 2013). Crowdsourcing is an important new area in both applying and extending the principles of open innovation (Tucci et al., 2016).

There are important overlaps between these two forms of external collaboration: some crowdsourcing has been conducted within existing communities, while other crowdsourcing efforts have created new communities. Both forms of collaboration typically fit within the "coupled" mode of open innovation, in that they involve both inbound and outbound knowledge flows between the firm and its external collaborators (Piller & West, 2014).

There are many phenomena that can be classified under both categories, even if others are clearly from one or the other. For example, many crowdsourced activities (such as tournaments) clearly fit the definition of a crowd but not a community. These cases involve a firm working with a network of potential contributors, but without peer to peer interactions that would foster a sense of belonging or identity and thus community (e.g. Jeppesen & Lakhani, 2010). Conversely, many communities—such as trade associations and consortia involving firms—lack any of the attributes of a crowd in that they are working cooperatively towards a shared goal. Some forms combine both, such as communities engaged in social production (Benkler, 2006). This is illustrated in Figure 4.1, which classifies phenomena on two dimensions—degree of crowd

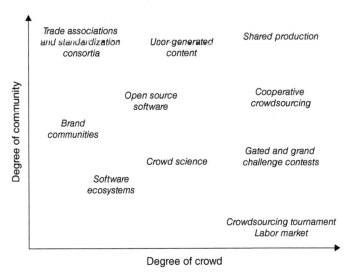

Figure 4.1. Community and crowds as phenomena.

and degree of community—illustrating those network collaborations that are crowds, communities, both, or neither.

In this chapter, we are interested in communities and crowds external to the firm, and collaborations that either directly or indirectly impact commercial activity. While communities and crowds have been utilized by firms within firm boundaries, consistent with our focus on open innovation, this chapter examines only three types of external collaborations: communities, crowds, or hybrids that combine elements of both.

As a potential source of innovations for firms, these collaborations have important similarities. All are external networks of multiple actors that can share knowledge and other information to produce an innovation or other output that can support a firm's open innovation strategy (Piller & West, 2014; West, 2014). At the same time, not all communities or crowds are organized in a way that benefits firms (West & O'Mahony, 2008). Some are organized for the benefit of individual members and have interests that are indifferent (or even antithetical) to companies (Muñiz & Schau, 2005; O'Mahony & Lakhani, 2011); the utility of others may depend upon the stage of the technological lifecycle (Seidel et al., 2016). Similarly, while innovation researchers have driven much of the research on these external collaborations, communities or crowds often produce results that do not fit a standard definition of technological innovation—including brand communities (Muniz & O'Guinn, 2001) and crowds that produce complementary assets to support an innovation (Jeppesen & Frederiksen, 2006).

This chapter seeks to contrast recent research on these three forms of network collaborations—communities, crowds, and hybrids—and examines the degree to which each form of collaboration produces technological innovation that benefits firms. It begins by reviewing definitions of each, considering where they overlap, and where they do not. It then considers variation in firm involvement—with communities, crowds, and hybrid crowds—and the role these groups play in producing innovation. Finally, it concludes with a discussion of implications and future research.

COMMUNITIES, CROWDS, AND COLLABORATION

Here we consider two specific forms of collaboration outside firm boundaries— the community and the crowd—and how the members of these efforts collaborate with each other and potentially with one or more firms. Both have elements of network organization (Howe, 2006b; West, 2014), but both also have characteristics beyond the network form identified by Powell (1990). Because there is often considerable overlap between these forms—and often the boundaries are fuzzy—researchers have tended to ignore the distinctions between these constructs.

Because community and crowd attributes may be measured by degrees, this can create overlap and confusion over terms. At the same time, communities can learn from the behavior and practices of crowds, and vice versa. As Figure 4.1 illustrates, many network forms—such as open source software, user generated content, and cooperative contests—include characteristics of both communities and crowds.

In this section, we summarize and synthesize definitions of communities and crowds as used in prior research. From this, we identify a new hybrid case that combines elements of both communities and crowds (Table 4.1).

Communities

Definition. The community form is a distinct approach for organizing human interaction (O'Mahony & Lakhani, 2011). We draw two distinctions between our definition of "virtual community" and other uses of "community" in the social sciences (Putnam, 1995; Brint, 2001; O'Mahony & Lakhani, 2011). First, here we consider "virtual communities" that include both purely online communities as well as those communities that combine online and physical interaction. The past two decades have seen the rise of geographically dispersed

Table 4.1. Contrasting communities and crowds.

	Communities	Hybrid crowd	Crowds
Reason for existing	Collaboration	Collaboration	Problem solving
Key attributes	Repeated interaction Shared goal or identity Shared governance	Repeated interaction Shared production goal Common identity or governance	Self-selected participants Competition Produce a deliverable Organized by a sponsor
Typical participants	Individuals Firms	Individuals	Individuals Ad hoc teams
Motivation	Intrinsic Personal utility Economic gain	Intrinsic or extrinsic	Economic or other incentives
Identity	Shared	A common purpose or goal	Individual
Interaction between actors	Collaborative	Collaborative	Collaborative, competitive, or both
Locus of activity	Online Face to face Both virtual and physical	Usually online; occasionally face to face meetings	Usually online
Output	Knowledge, information, or tangible goods	Usually information or information goods	Usually information or information goods
Related phenomena	Communities of practice	Crowd science	Internal crowdsourcing Crowdfunding

virtual communities, enabled by online electronic technologies (Rheingold, 2000). We define virtual communities as voluntary associations of individuals or organizations united by a common goal regardless of geographic proximity (West & Lakhani, 2008; O'Mahony & Lakhani, 2011). While many scholars (e.g. Rheingold, 2000; Brint, 2001) limit the term "virtual communities" to those that are exclusively online, economically significant work of such virtual communities often depends on episodic face to face meetings that build social ties and enable rapid resolution of complex challenges (Rosenkopf et al., 2001; Crowston et al., 2007; Leiponen, 2008, Waguespack & Fleming, 2009). Even the community that made online collaboration possible, the Internet Engineering Task Force, has been organized around regular face to face meetings for more than 25 years (Fleming & Waguespack, 2007).

Second, we are interested in virtual communities (henceforth labeled "communities") that are external to the firm, even if (e.g., Henkel, 2006; Dahlander & Wallin, 2006) they may include employees of the focal firm. This is consistent with a decision process that "takes place independently from the employment structure that guides the workplace" (O'Mahony, 2007: 144). In contrast, much of the research on communities of practice focuses on leveraging community ties between employees of a common employer who share a common identity through shared vocation (Brown & Duguid, 1991; Wenger, 2000; Bechky, 2006; O'Mahony & Lakhani, 2011).

The communities studied in open innovation share attributes of both organizations and networks (West, 2014), but they are distinct from both forms (Demil & Lecocq, 2006; O'Mahony & Ferraro, 2007; von Hippel, 2007; West & Lakhani, 2008). In particular, communities (like other voluntary associations) typically demonstrate repeated interactions, common identity, and shared purpose among their members (cf. Galacziewicz, 1985; Brint, 2001; Wellman et al., 2002b). Towards this end, von Hippel (2007: 294) writes:

> User innovation networks also may, but need not, incorporate the qualities of user "communities" for participants, where these are defined as " . . . networks of interpersonal ties that provide sociability, support, information, a sense of belonging, and social identity." (Wellman et al., 2002a: 4)

This shared identity is often associated with achieving one or more shared goals, such as producing a shared artifact or collection of artifacts.

These characteristics—particularly the impact of repeated interaction between members of a virtual community who are connected by identity but separated by geography—necessitate some form of governance. Governance provides an agreed-upon process by which communities can maintain their independence while effectively managing members' participation and contributions and facilitating predictable interactions with external parties (de Laat, 2007). Appropriately, governance has been a topic of broad academic interest for community researchers. Markus (2007: 154) notes that the literature "exhibits a wide range of views about what constitutes governance," and O'Mahony (2007) concludes that differences—in organizational form, objectives, and sponsors—will lead to different modes of governance.

Two broad community attributes are likely to affect the governance choices: the degree to which a community is more open or closed, and whether or not the community is sponsored by a firm or other organization. Communities that are open but not sponsored are more likely to adopt governance that promotes four of O'Mahony's (2007) five principles of community governance: pluralism, representation, decentralized decision-making, and autonomous participation. Closed and sponsored communities face a potentially challenging balancing act—the need to adopt governance that protects the organizers' or the sponsors' interests, while at the same time attracting external contributions (West & O'Mahony, 2008).

Levina & Fayard (2018) conclude that few boundary spanners succeed in managing their multiple commitments to different groups: explicitly designed and articulated governance may help boundary spanners to understand and manage their conflicting roles within the community. Similarly, Curto-Millet & Nisar (2018) find that codified governance practices can also clarify the roles of stakeholder groups in communities.

Our definition of community thus describes networks with repeated interaction among community members, a shared identity or purpose, and whose actions are guided by a governance process that perpetuates the community's existence. In practice, there are varying degrees of community such that some networks demonstrate some (but not all) of these attributes. While a community without shared identity would not meet von Hippel's definition, realistically, communities have degrees of identification or other attributes, just as West & O'Mahony (2008) found they had degrees of openness.

Types of communities and members. A number of different forms of community have been identified in the literature (Table 4.2).

As discussed further, many modern communities have a high degree of firm involvement (cf. West & O'Mahony, 2008). In some cases, the members of the community are firms themselves; examples of such communities include industrial collaborations organized by and for the benefit of firms, such as trade associations (Rosenkopf & Tushman, 1998) and standardization consortia (Keil, 2002), that seek to overcome collective action obstacles to achieve shared purpose. Firms within these communities agree to abide by shared goals and policies in order to influence cooperative agreements (such as technological standards) to align them with the firm's interests (Crowston et al., 2007; Fleming & Waguespack, 2007; Isaak, 2007; Leiponen, 2008). Involvement in these types of communities may be critical to both the firm's ability to innovate and their longstanding ability to favorably shape their environment.

In other cases, such as when communities support a software ecosystem, a network of firms seeks to advance its own interests by producing complementary goods (West, 2014). In the case of open source communities, the members may be either individuals or firms represented by their employees (West & Lakhani, 2008).

Communities can also connect firms with customers. A prominent example is the firm-sponsored brand community organized by firms to influence consumer perceptions of a product or group of products (Füller et al., 2008). Brand communities provide firms with an opportunity to interact with supportive customers who share an affinity for the company's brand or product. At other times, individual enthusiasts may organize their own brand communities, independent of any firm sponsorship or involvement. One example is the brand community that promoted the Apple Newton, even after the firm's abandonment of the product line (Muñiz & Schau, 2005).

Table 4.2. Contrasting forms of external communities.

Category	Participants	Production Process	Output	Control	Prior Research
User and other enthusiast communities	Individuals	Cooperative	Information	Community	Franke & Shah (2003); Hienerth (2006)
Brand communities	Consumers	Cooperative	Information	Firm	Algesheimer et al. (2005); Muñiz & Schau (2005); Füller et al. (2008)
Open source communities	Firm employees and other individuals	Cooperative	Software	Firm or community	Dahlander & Magnusson (2008); West & O'Mahony (2008); Garriga et al. (2011)
Software ecosystems	Firms or potential†	Competitive	Software	Firm	Iansiti & Levien (2004); West (2014)
Trade associations	Firms	Cooperative	Agreement (*collective action*)	Firms	Rosenkopf & Tushman (1998); Keil (2002); Dokko & Rosenkopf (2010)

† Includes established firms, new firms, unincorporated firms and nascent entrepreneurs.

Crowds

Definition. To develop a definition of a crowd first requires a definition of crowdsourcing. Crowdsourcing builds upon two postulates from the social sciences—that a large group of individuals has better information than any one individual (Surowiecki, 2005) and that many people performing small tasks can collectively perform a large task (Benkler, 2006). The process usually includes a contributor (the crowd), a sponsoring[1] organization (or other actor) soliciting these contributions, and some form of sourcing process.

There are many definitions of crowdsourcing.[2] For example, Brabham (2013: 3) defines crowdsourcing in terms of an organization that solicits a

---

[1] While prior research has not adopted consistent terminology for naming the firm, by analogy to research on open source software communities (Shah, 2006; West & O'Mahony, 2008) we adopt the term "sponsor" to refer to the organization that benefits from a crowdsourcing effort.

[2] See Estellés-Arolas & González (2012) for excerpts and an integration of forty-seven previous definitions.

crowd of volunteers to perform a task for "the mutual benefit" of both sides.[3] Perhaps the most comprehensive definition is provided by Estellés-Arolas & González (2012: 197):

> Crowdsourcing is a type of participative online activity in which an individual, an institution, a non-profit organization, or company proposes to a group of individuals of varying knowledge, heterogeneity, and number, via a flexible open call, the voluntary undertaking of a task. The undertaking of the task, of variable complexity and modularity, and in which the crowd should participate bringing their work, money, knowledge and/or experience, always entails mutual benefit. The user will receive the satisfaction of a given type of need, be it economic, social recognition, self-esteem, or the development of individual skills, while the crowd-sourcer will obtain and utilize to their advantage what the user has brought to the venture, whose form will depend on the type of activity undertaken.

However, describing the process of crowdsourcing begs the question: what is a "crowd"? Researchers have identified common attributes:

- *Large network.* Consistent with Surowiecki (2005), Howe (2006b) refers to an "undefined (and generally large) network of people."
- *Unknown potential contributors.* Poetz & Schreier (2012: 246) refer to "a potentially large and unknown population."
- *Self-selected actual contributors.* Like many others, Afuah & Tucci (2012) emphasize that within a large pool of potential contributors, individuals "self-select" to volunteer to provide information or otherwise solve the problem.
- *Open versus closed crowd.* Viscusi & Tucci (2018) argue that there are really two different types of crowds: an "open crowd" that is permeable to new members, and a "closed crowd" with well-defined boundaries that limit the crowd to existing participants and exclude potential participants.

The common thread across these definitions—one that we adopt in this chapter—is that a crowdsourcing crowd leverages the "wisdom of crowds" and incorporates two or more[4] of the following attributes:

- self-selected participants
- that explicitly or implicitly compete
- to produce a measurable deliverable (such as an answer to a question or an information good)
- as organized by and benefitting a sponsoring organization.

---

[3] Some research on crowdsourcing has blurred the distinction between crowds and communities, as when Brabham (2013: 117) defines a "crowd" as an "online community" used for crowdsourcing.

[4] We recognize that this is more expansive than some previous definitions, but believe it is an accurate summary of the crowdsourcing research to date. As with communities, it seems more realistic to define crowds in terms of degrees than to strictly bifurcate between crowd and non-crowd.

The rapid growth in practice and research on crowdsourcing is tied to new forms of collaboration enabled by the Internet—which today is by far the most common way of organizing crowdsourcing. However, contests to produce innovation, knowledge, or other antecedents to innovation[5]—solicited via an open call—date back to at least the seventeenth century, and include many famed examples such as measuring longitude or detecting radio waves (Scotchmer, 2004; Afuah & Tucci, 2012).

Types of crowds and crowdsourcing efforts. Within crowdsourcing processes and institutional forms, there are different variants (Table 4.3).

Crowdsourcing contests. These efforts enable explicit (or implicit) competition between self-selected, self-identified contributors. The earliest definitions emphasized the open call, and thus some limit "crowdsourcing" to that particular form. Perhaps the earliest attempt to define the term—by the journalist who coined it—says that "crowdsourcing represents the act of a company or institution taking a function once performed by employees and outsourcing it to an undefined (and generally large) network of people in the form of an open call" (Howe, 2006b).

While the explicit competition means a clearly defined winner, in other cases the competition is implicit. Some idea contests allow for multiple winners, and so while there is a limit to the number of ideas that will be selected—as with Threadless t-shirt designs (Brabham, 2008)—the contest may be more of a competition for attention than for designation as the single winner.

Although the idea of such contests dates back centuries, today's use of information technology can help to increase the number of participants and reduce the time needed for completion (Savage, 2012). In such contests, the firm establishes guidelines and invites outside others to participate. Compared to other methods, contests tend to focus on complex problems that may best be solved by novel or creative approaches (Boudreau & Lakhani, 2013). In the end, the winners are often those whose expertise is distant from the nature of the problem (Jeppesen & Lakhani, 2010).

Labor markets. In these cases, the competition is before the work is performed rather than afterwards: the firm puts out an open call for labor, selects one (or more) individual(s) based on skills and/or price, and then that individual performs the task for pay. Examples include Amazon Mechanical Turk, Freelancer.com, and Turkit (Howe, 2006a; Doan et al., 2011).

---

[5] While information, knowledge, and antecedents to innovation are distinct from technological innovations (West & Bogers, 2014), and not all information goods count as information, for this definition we do not draw distinctions between these different possible outputs of the crowdsourcing process.

Table 4.3. Contrasting forms of crowdsourcing.

Category	Participants	Production process	Benefits	Degree of community	Prior research
Crowdsourcing contests	Self-selected individuals	Explicitly or implicitly competitive	Sponsoring firm	Low	Idea competition (Leimeister et al., 2009), Broadcast search (Jeppesen & Lakhani, 2010), Tournament-based crowdsourcing (Afuah & Tucci, 2012), contests (Boudreau & Lakhani, 2013)
Labor markets	Individual bidder selected by firm	Individual	Sponsoring firm	Low	Outsourcing commoditized tasks (Howe, 2006a; Doan et al., 2011)
Gated contests	Individuals selected by firm	Competitive	Sponsoring firm	Low	Selective call (Diener & Piller, 2013); selective open call (Piller & West, 2014)
Grand challenge contests	Self-selected individuals or organizations	Competitive	Sponsor, winners	Low	Incentivizing major breakthrough innovation through prizes (Murray et al., 2012)
Personal problem solving	Self-selected individuals	Individual	Individual, then ecosystem	Medium	Lead user (Jeppesen & Frederiksen, 2006, Poetz & Prügl 2010), user communities (von Hippel, 2005)

Gated contests. Some crowdsourcing contests are not open to all contenders, but instead the sponsor pre-selects specific external participants to participate in the contest in a selective open call. Typically, this is done when the sponsor wants to improve the quality of the submissions, e.g. when it lacks the time needed to evaluate all possible submissions or it must expend its own resources to collaborate with each potential contributor (Diener & Piller, 2013; Piller & West, 2014). This corresponds with Shah's (2006) earlier definition of "gated" open source communities with participants selected by the sponsor—or the closed crowd of Viscusi & Tucci (2018) with participants selected by the sponsor or crowd.

Grand challenge contests are crowds organized to solve a sizable problem, often scientific in nature, whose solution would spur further technological progress. Examples include the 1714 Longitude Prize offered by an act of the English Parliament, the 1927 prize for transatlantic flight claimed by Charles Lindbergh, and the X Prize, a $10 million prize offered in 1996 for private space flight (Scotchmer, 2004). Since then, the X-Prize Foundation has sponsored a series of prizes, as have government agencies that conduct R&D, such as DARPA and NASA. These contests tend to offer large prizes (millions of dollars in today's terms) that attract large teams to make a multi-year effort: for example, the original X Prize took eight years to award. These contests may be winner take all, or reward multiple (or cooperative) contributions, but generally tend to be offered in hopes of attracting private investment to solve problems that have broader economic or societal benefits (Lampel et al., 2012; Murray et al., 2012). In the case of winner take all, the losing contributors may receive no direct benefit from their efforts, but hope to benefit after the contest ends from learning or publicity gained during the contest.

Personal problem solving. Some crowds engaged in producing decentralized solutions to their own problems. As such, this is often outside the classic definition of crowdsourcing. However, if these solutions are later shared or otherwise disseminated with others, collectively, the crowd produces a range of solutions that might parallel those generated in response to a central call. User innovation and user toolkits provide examples of such processes (von Hippel, 2005; Poetz & Prügel, 2010), as do firm-sponsored communities to organize individual complement providers (Jeppesen & Frederiksen, 2006).

Other forms of crowds—such as *cooperative crowdsourcing* and *social production*—often possess attributes of communities and thus are more accurately classified as crowd–community hybrids, as will be discussed further.

Other phenomena do not fit the above definition of crowdsourcing, but leverage crowd contributions in other ways. For example, there has been some managerial interest in how firms can crowdsource from internal contributors—harnessing the knowledge of employees (Andriole 2010; Byrén 2013)—but there has been little empirical research on it to date. The process of crowdfunding (cf. Mollick, 2014) leverages the money of external crowds but not their wisdom.

Hybrid Crowds: When Crowds are Like Communities

Definition. Regardless of their origins, some crowds share the characteristics of communities, as the two forms are often complementary. Existing communities can provide the participants in a crowd-based problem solving (e.g. DARPA, Local Motors) while, over time, crowd participants may form ties that allow them to form communities. For example, some crowds and crowdsourcing efforts include repeated peer-to-peer interactions (Afuah & Tucci, 2012; Boudreau & Lakhani, 2013). Put another way, firms can manage the contributions of crowds either through communities or contests (Lakhani, 2016).

Here we define a "hybrid crowd" as a network form that combines attributes of both crowds and communities. Typically, "hybrid crowds" include a network of contributors who have some form of shared purpose or governance, and produce a deliverable for a sponsoring organization.

Types of crowd–community hybrids. Prior research has identified numerous examples that might be classified as overlapping both communities and crowds. We now provide examples that include attributes of each form (Table 4.4).

Cooperative contests are an example of crowds that often have attributes of communities. This form of crowdsourcing allows for collaboration between members of the crowd to produce a solution (Howe, 2006b; Afuah & Tucci, 2012; Franzoni & Sauermann, 2014). Typically organized by a sponsor, these include elements of both crowd-based competition (the "contest") and community-based collaboration. These are crowdsourcing contests augmented with ongoing community collaboration, used to design and promote products. The Threadless T-shirt design community is the best known example, but Local Motors—an automotive crowdsourcing site—provides another example (Brabham, 2008; Langner & Seidel, 2014). In such cooperative contests, the organization(s) creates a community of passionate contributors to participate in both design competitions and play a role in more mundane (but important) contributions to the firm and its goals. The maintenance of such a community clearly requires a strong shared identity—and presumably a shared purpose for limiting the crowd membership—and thus most are likely to correspond with the definition of a community rather than typical open-call contests (cf. Jeppesen & Lakhani, 2010). Community members can also cooperate in contests, when firms crowdsource to the community the task of filtering and prioritizing individual contributions (Jensen et al., 2014).

Table 4.4. Attributes of crowd–community hybrids.

Category	Community attributes			Crowd attributes			
	Repeated interaction	Shared identity/ purpose	Governance	Self-selected participatnts	Competition	Production	Benefitting a sponsor
Open source software	++++	Both	By community	√	Implicit	√	+
User generated content	+++	Purpose	By Sponsor	√	Implicit	√	+
Cooperative contests	++	Purpose	By sponsor	√	Explicit	√	+++
Crowd science		Purpose	By Sponsor	√	Explicit	√	++

Social production. Crowdsourcing shares many attributes of the social production of Benkler (2006), in which a group of individuals cooperate to produce a shared good. Some researchers define crowdsourcing as including the self-organized social production of information goods—notably Wikipedia (Doan et al., 2011)—but because of a lack of sponsor, some would not consider it as such (Estellés-Arolas & González, 2012). Such social production by an independent self-organizing group shares many of the attributes common to all definitions of crowdsourcing, but lacks a sponsoring beneficiary firm (or organization). In spite of this distinction, we believe that such production should be classified as crowdsourcing for both factual and theoretical reasons[6]—just as open source software communities may be firm sponsored or autonomous (West & O'Mahony, 2008). We identify three examples of such social production.

Open source software communities are well-researched examples of crowds working with an existing community. These groups demonstrate—and in fact often depend on—the shared identity and purpose of communities (Weber, 2004; Feller et al., 2008) in addition to the practice—common in crowdsourcing—of soliciting and incorporating contributions by self-selected participants (Afuah & Tucci, 2012). In many (but not all) cases, their work is orchestrated for the benefit of a firm (West & O'Mahony, 2008).

User-generated content is a more general example of the open source process. Wikipedia challenged the dominance of established encyclopedias by using attributes of both crowds and communities (Forte et al., 2009). While a crowd of disconnected volunteers can contribute to or edit Wikipedia pages, like other communities this crowd shares a common purpose, and it has a formal self-governance system that resolves disputes by acting as editors and fact-checkers (Nov, 2007; Forte et al., 2009). Most UGC initiatives would qualify as crowdsourcing when a firm makes an open call for contributions. However, when these firms encourage (or the contributors independently engage in) repeated interactions, the resulting sociability between contributors can shape both the outcome of the content and their motivation to participate (Ghose et al., 2012).

Crowd science. In some cases, firms or other sponsors of crowdsourcing end up creating a new community to support their cause. Initiatives in "crowd science," such as Foldit and Galaxy Zoo, attract individuals to a crowd to solve a common problem, after which a community forms around the common goal and the dissemination of data (Franzoni & Sauermann, 2014).

---

[6] From a factual standpoint, the work of Wikipedia is done under the supervision and control of a non-profit organization—the Wikimedia Foundation (Ciffolilli, 2003)—and thus fits the original definition. However, from studies of independent open source communities (e.g. West & O'Mahony, 2008), the existence of such foundations is not directly related to the governance or openness of such communities, suggesting that the existence of a foundation as a crowdsourcing sponsor is not a theoretically meaningful distinction for classifying crowds.

MOTIVATING NETWORK COLLABORATORS

There are numerous motives behind firms engaging these three forms of external network collaborators, including the pursuit of new technologies, reducing costs, enhancing reputation, or seeking support for their own technologies (Dahlander & Magnusson, 2005; Henkel, 2006; Jeppesen & Frederiksen, 2006; Isaak, 2007; West & Lakhani, 2008; von Krogh et al., 2012).

Firms face two broad challenges of motivating external community and crowd participants to achieve their own objectives. The first is the necessity for understanding the community or crowd in question—namely its governance system and social norms. One potentially useful perspective is the idea that communities and crowds may represent "loosely coupled" organizational systems (Weick, 1976) which firms must both understand and adapt to if they hope to profit from interaction.

Secondly, firms must understand the nature of *individual* participation in these groups, and how to leverage it. Participation is driven by a combination of co-existing extrinsic and intrinsic motives (e.g., Hars & Ou, 2002; Dahlander & Magnusson, 2005; Lakhani & Wolf, 2005; West & Gallagher, 2006; Markus, 2007). If managers wish to harness the benefits of these external groups, they must understand both the motivations of such individual participation, and the various ways their firm might be able to capitalize on it.

Structural Forms of Participation Architecture

Firms seeking to structure a collaboration network to attract contributions need to create an architecture of participation, which West & O'Mahony (2008: 146) define as a "socio-technical framework that extends participation opportunities to external parties and integrates their contributions." One key element of this architecture—determining the size of participation effort that is valued by the contributor and the firm—is the degree of divisibility (and thus accessibility) of the externally contributed tasks.

We identify three levels of task divisibility:

Incremental. This would include making a single small contribution that has value to the sponsoring organization. This could include making a suggestion (Dahlander & Piezunka 2014), updating a Wikipedia article (Nov, 2007), or making a bug fix to open source software (Crowston & Howison, 2005).

Modular. These collaborations have a modular design with well-defined interfaces (Sanchez & Mahoney, 1996), which allows external contributors to add value in ways not anticipated by the original content designer. The original definition focused on contributing new modules to software systems, such as a new project in Apache or Eclipse or a new procedure in the GPL library (Baldwin & Clark, 2006). However, it also includes contributing entire articles to a blog or online newspaper. In many cases, a modular architecture makes incremental contributions easier because it limits the complexity that an external contributor must understand (MacCormack et al., 2006). However, not all modular architectures allow incremental contributions: Google's failed Knol encyclopedia crowdsourced entire articles, rather than Wikipedia's policy of allowing the crowd to modify any previously submitted article.

Indivisible. Most pure crowdsourcing contests seek entire completed solutions to a single well-defined problem. These include the familiar innovation tournaments such as those mediated by intermediaries such as InnoCentive and NineSigma (Howe, 2006a), and even some forms of cooperative crowdsourcing. In these contests, most contributions are submitted by individual "solvers" (Boudreau & Lakhani, 2009). On the other hand, the scale of grand challenge contests usually requires contributions to be made by groups: for example, twenty-six teams spent $100 million over eight years seeking the original $10 million X-Prize award for manned space flight (Murray et al., 2012).

Who are the participants in these network collaborations? Individuals are a core part of both communities and crowds. Communities often include firms or other organizations (West & Lakhani, 2008). Meanwhile, crowdsourcing efforts—both grand challenges and larger private contests such as the $1 million Netflix Prize—attract teams of individuals or organizations (Murray et al., 2012; King & Lakhani, 2013).

How Firms Tap into Motivation

We identify four distinct pathways firms use for influence: directly motivating the group, motivating other firms who also participate, motivating individual members, and motivating employees who are also members (Table 4.5). Each pathway presents firms with distinct challenges for aligning the goals of the firm, the external group, and its members.

Working directly with communities, crowds, and hybrid crowds. In many cases, firms identify an external group whose motivations and objectives are aligned with its own (Bonaccorsi et al., 2006; Leiponen, 2008) and proceed to work directly with that group (e.g., Keil, 2002; West, 2003; Stam, 2009; Snow et al., 2011). In these cases, one of the firm's greatest challenges is aligning the goals of the community with their own.

Given that such alignment is not established a priori, a firm must decide the degree to which they will accept the community's goals, or to determine whether—and how—they will take action to influence those objectives. When

Table 4.5. Motivational issues of firms working with communities and their members.

Firm interaction	Firm motivational goals	Prior research
With overall community	Identifying communities whose goals align to firm objectives	Bonaccorsi et al. (2006), Leiponen (2008)
	Influencing community goals to match those of the firm	Dahlander & Magnusson (2008)
Alongside other firms who are community members	Working with other firms to achieve shared community goals	Bekkers et al. (2002)
	How firms leverage intermediaries to motivate a community	Antikainen & Vaataja (2010)
With individual community members	Motivating individual community participants	Jeppesen & Frederiksen (2006), Wiertz & de Ruyter (2007), Porter & Donthu (2008), Langner & Seidel (2014)
	Assuring the quality of their contributions	Spaeth et al. (2010)
With own employees who are also community members	Reinforcing employee-member alignment with community and firm goals	Isaak (2007), Dokko & Rosenkopf (2010)
	Addressing/resolving conflict between employee-member and community goals	O'Mahony (2005), Henkel (2006), Rolandsson et al. (2011)

working with external communities, firms should look to the group's governance structure. These rules leverage culture, shared norms, and intrinsic motivations to align participation. However, when compared to firm governance, communities in particular are more likely to emphasize self-governance and democratic processes (de Laat 2007; Markus, 2007; O'Mahony, 2007; O'Mahony & Ferraro, 2007; Dahlander et al., 2008). Community governance is often designed to encourage individual (not firm) participation by providing recognition and increased responsibilities (O'Mahony & Ferraro, 2007; West & O'Mahony, 2008).

Working with other firms. Two or more firms often work collectively to tap into the motivations of community members. One of the best examples is the cooperation that unfolds between companies who share membership in a standardization group or trade association. Here, firms are motivated to work together through these communities to achieve a common objective (Bekkers et al., 2002; Keil, 2002; Hallström, 2004). We know that these firms benefit in various ways through their common participation, such as gaining access to alliance partners (Rosenkopf et al., 2001), but these firms must monitor both their relationships to their peers as well as to the community.

Working With individual members. Here, firms motivate individual members who are unaffiliated with the firm, rather than the community itself. Studies in this vein examine how firms can either motivate (e.g., Jeppesen & Frederiksen, 2006; Wiertz & de Ruyter 2007; Porter & Donthu 2008), or access the contributions of individuals (Spaeth et al., 2010). Once again a central challenge is identifying and aligning common interests, but in this setting, a firm must assess the degree to which they can motivate individual members to provide value, either by themselves or by influencing the policies of the community in a way that is favorable to the firm. One approach is to work with the leaders of the group who can motivate and coordinate the voluntary contributions of others (Markus, 2007; Dahlander et al., 2008). For communities and hybrid crowds, the motivation issues apply to two different stages of participation: first to joining the community, and then to contributing to a given collaboration (Lakhani, 2016).

Working with employees who are also members. Firms can also support their own employees' participation in an external group. These individuals can act as boundary spanners to align the interests of the firm and the community (Schweisfurth & Herstatt, 2016). Studies of this topic often focus on how employees approach the goals of the community (Isaak, 2007) alongside those of their own employer (Dokko & Rosenkopf, 2010). Here, firms must confront their employees' dual allegiances, which may force a firm to address agency issues and possibly role conflict (O'Mahony, 2005; Henkel, 2008; Rolandsson et al., 2011).

Helping government and other not-for-profit organizations. Originally conceived as a strategy for profit-maximizing firms, the principles of open innovation can also be applied to benefit government (public) agencies as well as not-for-profit organizations. The process of identifying and sorting innovations from external crowds and communities parallels that of firms; with two major differences. First, the success of the sponsoring organization—whether national government, local government, academic, or other non-profit—is measured by achieving its mission rather than profit goals. Second, participants tend to be motivated by intrinsic support for that mission (or non-monetary extrinsic rewards such as recognition) rather than by monetary rewards (Hilgers & Ihl, 2010; Chesbrough & Di Minin, 2014; Franzoni & Sauermann, 2014; Cordella et al., 2018).

Intrinsic Motivations Driving Participation in Communities and Crowds

Intrinsic motives are present in both communities (Lakhani & Wolf, 2005) and crowds (Boudreau & Lakhani, 2013). Research on user innovation has emphasized the importance of "scratching an itch," where the community member works to address his or her individual need (Baldwin et al., 2006; Franke et al., 2006; West & Lakhani, 2008). Also common to both is motivation related to improving one's career prospects by gaining skills or visibility (Hars & Ou, 2002; Lakhani & von Hippel, 2003; von Krogh et al., 2003; Lakhani & Wolf, 2005; West & Gallagher, 2006).

Communities provide a form of social interaction that can itself be a form of motivation. Personal identification with the community and its goals can be a powerful motivator (Hertel et al. 2003; Lakhani & Wolf, 2005; von Hippel, 2007). For example, the Stallman (1985) manifesto, which perceived that software should be "free," has attracted many (von Krogh et al., 2003; Shah, 2006; Stewart & Gosain, 2006; Nov, 2007). However, motivation can differ depending on the degree of involvement, as Budhathoki & Haythornthwaite (2013) found among OpenStreetMap contributors: those who contributed the most were motivated more by their affiliation to the community and learning, while less frequent contributors were motivated more by the idea that mapping data should be free.

Compared with communities, crowds exhibit fewer (if any) interactions between members. Crowdsourcing efforts are also more likely to ask for a one-time effort, while community engagement is ongoing. Thus intrinsic motives to participate in crowds are more likely to be driven by a desire to make an individual contribution (i.e., provide user-generated content or participate in the contest) than it is to develop social ties with other like-minded individuals.

Extrinsic Motivations Driving Participation in Communities and Crowds

Because participation in these external groups is typically voluntary and often uncompensated, it makes sense that most of the research on motivations has focused on those that are intrinsic. That said, there are extrinsic motivations provided by communities and crowds. The most unambiguous is monetary payment, whether for those who are paid by their employer to work in a community (Hertel et al., 2003; Fleming & Waguespack, 2007), or for user entrepreneurs forming their own companies (Hienerth, 2006). Similarly, for crowd participants, the motivation of winning a prize can be compelling. Other extrinsic motivations include career signaling, the desire to access other contributions, and the related expectation of reciprocity (e.g., Franke & Shah, 2003; Lakhani & von Hippel, 2003; O'Mahony, 2003). At the same time, individual (particularly extrinsic) motivations must be weighed against the cost of participation.

DEGREES OF COLLABORATIVE INNOVATIVENESS

As noted earlier, the efforts of most crowds and some communities directly benefit firms (Howe, 2006b; West & O'Mahony, 2008). At the same time, the goals of a few crowds (and many communities) are indifferent—or even hostile—to those of firms (Lih, 2009; O'Mahony & Lakhani, 2011). Thus, these network forms vary considerably in the degree to which they benefit firms and their open innovation strategies.

At the same time, there is wide variation in the role that communities and crowds play in providing innovations to others. At times, the nature of the innovative challenge itself may influence the process by which organizations choose to engage communities, crowds, or hybrid crowds. As suggested by Viscusi & Tucci (2018), the characteristics of different types of crowds and communities lend themselves to helping to solve different types of innovative challenges.

Here, we define innovation broadly, as either new products or services or changes to process (Dahlander & Gann, 2010). At one end of a spectrum (see Table 4.3), communities and crowds do provide innovations, whether to firms, their members, or society at large. In the middle are communities and crowds that do not play a direct role in providing innovation, but facilitate its diffusion, adoption, and use by complementing innovation. At the other end of the spectrum are those communities or crowds whose roles are clearly unrelated to innovation, but may provide other benefits (such as symbolic meaning) to their members.

Thus, we can classify various examples of these network forms across these two dimensions: the degree to which they benefit firms, and the degree to which they create technological innovations (Figure 4.2). Consistent with our focus, here we examine those cases where these networks contribute to the benefit of a firm or other organization, and consider the differing degrees of innovativeness in those contributions.

Direct Contributions to Open Innovation

Both communities (West & Lakhani, 2008) and crowds (Boudreau & Lakhani, 2013) can potentially contribute to a firm's open innovation strategies. Such contributions may take the form of innovations, or other antecedents or components of innovation such as inventions and technical or market knowledge; after sourcing such innovations, firms face the subsequent challenge of integrating and bringing them to market (West & Bogers, 2014).

Communities. Many communities play an important role in creating technological innovations. This may be by directly providing those innovations, or by

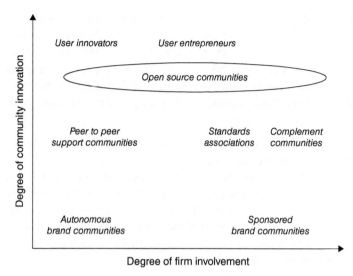

Figure 4.2. Dimensions of firm–community interaction.

directly providing knowledge that enables innovation by firms or other parties. Communities provide access to several forms of knowledge, extending techno-logical innovation beyond the limits of their own resources (e.g., Lee & Cole, 2003). Community knowledge may come from lead users (Jeppesen & Frederiksen, 2006; Hienerth, 2006), from other firms in the community (Wade, 1995), or from the community itself (Henkel, 2006). At best, newly acquired community knowledge can form the basis of collective development (Snow et al., 2011) that enables firms to overcome technological problems. It can also increase the demand (and thus the supply) of innovative comple-mentary products and services produced by community members (Henkel, 2006: 955).

Hybrid crowds. Outside groups that combine attributes of communities and crowds can also provide direct contributions to firm innovations. As men-tioned previously, open source software can be seen as both a community (of programmers and active contributors) and a crowd (of users and infrequent contributors). These hybrid crowds can directly contribute to both radical and incremental innovation, depending on how the firm interacts with the com-munity (Sims & Seidel, 2016).

Customer groups and lead users can also take the form of either commu-nities or crowds. Consumer groups have contributed a significant number of innovation opportunities across various industries (Terwiesch & Ulrich, 2009), and lead users are able to develop innovations that build on the work of pre-existing designs and products (Hienerth, 2006).

New technologies are firms sourcing innovations from crowd–community hybrids in novel ways. One example is the collaborative contest, where contributors who may not know each other (an attribute that would be more common in a community), work together in hopes of solving a common problem. For example, the computer game FoldIT uses non-experts to assist in examining and rearranging proteins, often surpassing the abilities of dedicated computers (Savage, 2012).

Crowds. Many firms are now using contests to source innovations directly from the crowd. While the ideas generated may not be as feasible as those developed internally, they are often more novel (Jeppesen & Lakhani, 2010; Poetz & Schreier 2012; Franke et al., 2014). That said, an increase in contributors does not equal more (or even better) ideas; increased productivity is not always associated with the growth of the crowd (Boudreau & Jeppesen, 2015), and repeat contributors to the crowd may propose incremental changes to ideas already implemented (Bayus, 2013).

Indirect Contributions to Open Innovation

In many cases, firms do not use communities as a source of direct innovations, but to complement internal development efforts, by reducing costs or gaining new insights (Bonaccorsi et al., 2006; Samuelson, 2006; West & Gallagher, 2006; Piva et al., 2012). This is consistent with the decades-old finding that technical inventions require many complementary assets—such as marketing, distribution, support, or add-on products—to realize their full value (Teece, 1986).

Communities. Indirect contributions to firm innovation often come from communities who can provide unique insights on the limitations of alternatives (Jeppesen & Frederiksen, 2006; Shah & Tripsas, 2007; Baldwin & von Hippel, 2011; Mahr & Lievens, 2012).

Some communities also create frameworks and processes that enable firms to better access user ideas, as the research on toolkits has illustrated (von Hippel & Katz, 2002; Piller & Walcher, 2006).

Communities also support innovation by providing infrastructure or resources that help these firms to commercialize their own innovations. Examples include standard-setting organizations and trade associations. By developing a common set of standards, firms can create innovations internally with confidence that they will be compatible with others (e.g., Rosenkopf et al., 2001; Keil, 2002).

Similarly, firms bringing a new technology to market require validation to provide legitimacy (Garud et al., 2002). Communities can provide such legitimation. These may be external groups such as trade associations, or communities created by the firms themselves to legitimate a new product category (Snow et al., 2011).

Finally, communities can help to diffuse and disseminate firm innovations (Dahlander & Magnusson, 2005) by providing support (Lakhani & von Hippel, 2003; Henkel, 2008) and complementary goods (Jeppesen & Frederiksen, 2006).

Hybrid crowds. Crowd–community hybrids also play a role in indirectly contributing to firm innovation. In many cases, these contributions are complementary goods and capabilities (as defined by Teece, 1986) that support such innovation. For example, Propellerhead Software crowdsourced to an external community the provision of customized sounds that made its Reason software more valuable (Jeppesen & Frederiksen, 2006), and Dell crowdsourced product design ideas to their IdeaStorm community to improve or create new product ideas (Di Gangi & Wasko, 2009; Bayus, 2013).

Open source software is again perhaps the most prominent example. Using open source software allows a firm to rely on the support of an entire community of volunteer contributors for assistance. The low cost and traditionally high quality software saves firms from having to devote resources (capital or human) to maintaining the software, allowing them to spend more time developing their own innovations (e.g. Bonaccorsi et al., 2006).

User-generated content also provides a platform on which firms can build their own innovations. For example, those contributing to OpenStreetMap provided firms with a high quality and low cost mapping solution (Budhathoki & Haythornthwaite, 2013). Similarly, firms can now augment their own internal efforts by working with cooperative crowds to analyze "big data" in ways that have provided insight beyond what the firm was able to develop on their own (Martinez & Walton, 2014).

Crowds. Firms could conceivably crowdsource support or other user-generated content to support their innovation efforts. The degree to which crowds contribute indirectly to innovation is influenced by various crowd characteristics. The typology introduced by Viscusi & Tucci (2018) suggests that the use of "closed crowds"—such as those managed by an innovation intermediary such as Innocentive—forces a company to conceptualize and even modularize its innovation challenges, making it more appropriate for outsourcing problem solving. In contrast, the contributions to firm innovation from "open crowds" (which similar to our concept of hybrid crowds) can be more difficult to specify a priori due to their flexibility and fluidity of membership.

Contributions Beyond Innovations

Communities. Some communities simply do not contribute to firm innovation, but may still create value for firms and their members by providing symbolic meaning (Dahlander et al., 2008). Sponsored brand communities are a common example. They allow firms to reinforce their brands, promote products, and solicit feedback from enthusiastic customers and lead users (e.g., Jeppesen & Frederiksen, 2006; Füller et al., 2008; Porter & Donthu, 2008; Marchi et al., 2011). For firms, the end result is often higher customer loyalty, engagement, or identification with the firm's products (e.g. Algesheimer et al., 2005; Harrison & Waluszewski, 2008). They can also leverage the collective insight of the community to access tacit knowledge and insights held by the community (Schau et al., 2009).

Other communities are independent of any particular firm interests, as when patients with similar medical conditions share information and provide mutual support (Jayanti & Singh, 2010; Laing et al., 2011). In rare cases, customers create their own brand communities without firm involvement, as when owners of the handheld Newton tablet organized after Apple had canceled the product line (Muñiz & Schau, 2005).

Hybrid crowds. At times, hybrid crowds contribute to firms in ways beyond innovations. For example, the research on open source contributions shows that many of these contributions are motivated by reputational and intrinsic (as opposed to monetary) incentives (Shah, 2006). For firms who employ developers who are "boundary spanners" with an open source community, these communities can act as a means for firms to promote themselves to gain market traction in the form of referrals. In a similar way, firms that solicit user-generated content (e.g. Threadless or Local Motors) can use those same users to promote their brand.

Crowds. Crowd-based tournaments and contests may provide benefits beyond the actual innovations sourced. This might include connecting to a larger pool of enthusiasts, winning publicity and goodwill that comes with sponsoring such challenges.

Beyond their use in innovation contests, crowds are also used to source content or other contributions unrelated to any innovation, such as providing content supporting a firm's daily operations. For example, online retailers such as Amazon.com rely on individual users to provide product ratings to help other users (Shen et al., 2015), while Yelp depends upon detailed customer reviews of popular destinations. Uber uses rankings by all ridesharing passengers to monitor customer satisfaction. In these examples, the voluntary feedback from individual contributors provides a critical complement to the firm's core product or service.

DISCUSSION, CONCLUSIONS, AND FUTURE RESEARCH

Since Rheingold (1993), researchers have learned a great deal about the nature of communities, their governance, and the activities of their constituent members. Researchers have studied a variety of different communities and community–firm interactions, while firms have identified communities as an important source of external innovations for firms practicing open innovation. More recently, researchers have identified crowds as a potential source of external innovations, as well as hybrid forms of communities and crowds that combine elements of each.

Contribution

This chapter has three main contributions. First, by reviewing prior research on crowds and communities, it identifies and contrasts three network forms of external collaborations that, potentially, firms can join. A community is a network of individuals or organizations that have repeated interaction and shared goals or identity; a crowd is a network of individuals that utilizes the wisdom of crowds with some (if not all) of the previously identified attributes. The chapter also introduces the community/crowd hybrid construct and discusses the characteristics, activities, and use of these hybrid crowds.

Secondly, it offers two dimensions of classifying all three types of networked external collaborations. The first is the degree of firm involvement—whether the network is controlled by a single firm, shared control by multiple firms, or independent of any firm control. The second is the degree of innovation produced by the network: whether creating (or directly contributing to) an innovation strategy, producing complementary products needed to support an innovation strategy, or providing other benefits such as marketing and support.

Finally, it considers how firms leverage these external collaborations to support their open innovation strategies, and how these strategies are similar and different based on these three attributes—the form of collaboration, the degree of community innovativeness, and the degree of firm involvement. In particular, because motivation is essential to assuring a supply of external innovations (West & Gallagher, 2006), it focuses on what motivates the participants in these collaborations and what firms can do to increase that motivation.

Future Research

Here we suggest future research opportunities related to the three forms of external collaborations. We also suggest research ideas for the two dimensions of firm involvement and network innovativeness, with particular focus on how this would help firms leverage collaborations to support open innovation.

Communities. Our review identifies some gaps in the literature. At the level of the phenomenon, we know a lot about how firms work with brand and open source communities. But what are the limits of these insights of how motiv-ation, cooperation, and integration work in other settings? For example, which of the open source governance mechanisms translate to other types of com-munities (cf. Raasch et al., 2009)? Similarly, are the benefits of brand engage-ment the same in pure brand communities as in those used to provide support, product ideas, or even complementary goods? And while an increasing body of work has examined how firms run innovation contests, we know less about the role of community in influencing the interactions between solvers—or how communities run by intermediaries are different from those run directly by the firm itself.

Although open innovation researchers have conceptualized communities and crowds as two distinct forms of collaboration, this chapter has sought to demonstrate how they play similar roles in a firm's external sourcing strategies. Some research (West, 2014; Viscusi & Tucci, 2018) has focused on the structural similarity of communities and crowds as network forms of organization, but both differ from Powell's (1990) network form and from each other.

Hybrid crowds. While the community/crowd hybrids share many of the attributes of their two elemental antecedents, future research could examine how these hybrid crowds are different from these antecedents.

A crucial (but still nascent) area of research for such hybrid forms is the relative importance and interaction effects (i.e. synergies) between the success factors for each of these component forms. Research on crowdsourcing contests often focuses on attracting contributors with the right knowledge and motivating them to develop and share such knowledge (Jeppesen & Lakhani, 2010; Franke et al., 2014). Meanwhile, research on communities tends to emphasize governance and other aspects of coordinating and organ-izing these individual contributions (Markus, 2007; West & O'Mahony, 2008; Lakhani et al., 2013). For hybrid forms such as cooperative crowdsourcing or social production (e.g., Franzoni & Sauermann, 2014; Langner & Seidel, 2014), this raises several questions. Should improving success focus more on struc-turing the cooperation or attracting the right crowd? What are the interaction effects between the nature of the crowd and how it is organized?

At the same time, historically, they have distinct processes and cultures. For example, communities (as suggested by von Hippel, 2007) tend to be very relational, whereas many forms of firm-sponsored crowdsourcing (such as tournaments) are highly transactional, focused on achieving a specific out-come; this suggests a number of research opportunities as to how (and to what degree) a given network adopts the attributes of either. Similarly, these hybrids differ on a number of easily identified dimensions (such as those listed in Table 4.4), but do these differences correlate with the processes these crowd–communities use, the nature of their collaborations, or the conditions under which they are successful? And for crowd–community hybrids that combine key elements of these transaction and relational extremes—such as winner-take-all tournaments and attempts to build shared identity—how are (or can) these tensions be managed to improve the success of the hybrid network?

We are also interested in path-dependent differences between hybrid crowds of differing origins. Once stable, is a community that adopted crowd-sourcing demonstrably different from crowds onto which community-like shared purpose has been grafted? Similarly, since the latter hybrids differ in their degree of shared purpose or identity, is there a threshold (or tipping point) that marks the transition between a crowd and a community/crowd hybrid?

Crowds. Sponsors of crowdsourcing initiatives have the opportunity to graft community-like attributes or mechanisms onto them, such as repeated inter-action or internal governance, and in fact sponsors are beginning to do so—including repeated interactions (Brabham, 2008) or shared identity (Levina & Fayard, 2018). What are the real costs and benefits to sponsors of including these mechanisms? What are the moderators of these benefits? These might be internal factors such as the nature or size of the crowd, the demographics of the members, or the duration or complexity of the challenge. Or the moderators might be factors external to the crowd, such as attributes of the sponsor (reputation, organizational slack, corporate culture, crowdsourcing experience), the industry (industry concentration, rate of technological change), or attributes of potential or actual participants (expertise, demographics, personality traits, opportunity cost).

At the other extreme, some forms of network collaboration involve a zero-sum allocation of value capture between sponsoring firms and network participants. Both the process and outcomes of this allocation have implications for perception of fairness and the motivation of participants (Afuah & Tucci, 2013; Franke et al., 2013). However, much more research needs to be done on how these processes, outcomes, and perceptions impact the results of such collaborations.

We are particularly struck by the emphasis on the hybrid (rather than pure) crowd form for providing support or other innovation complements, such as user-generated content and other support. Is the pure crowd an unstable form for this requirement? Did the hybrid forms arise via path dependencies? Or have firms found that utilizing hybrid forms is a more effective way of achieving these goals?

Degrees of firm involvement. As we have shown, these collaborations differ in their degree of firm involvement. In terms of motivation and governance, we have significant research on how independent communities work with their members (e.g., Franke & Shah, 2003; Lakhani & Wolf, 2005; Markus, 2007;

O'Mahony, 2007; O'Mahony & Ferraro, 2007). However, we rarely (e.g., O'Mahony, 2003) see what happens to the governance or individual motivation within such communities when they interact with firms, let alone the internal community dynamics of communities controlled by a single firm. Similarly, we understand the community contributions and role conflicts of sponsored employees, but less about their interpersonal interactions with community members (or fellow employees). We also have only fragmentary research on the interaction effects of multiple motivations, whether complementary (and thus additive) in their effects (Raasch & von Hippel, 2013), or crowding out (Alexy & Leitner, 2011).

Finally, we need to know more about the conditions under which firms are able to benefit from their engagement with these collaborations. Is successful engagement a unique skill, a commodity, or merely contingent upon the firm's market or technological position versus its rivals? While we have general measures of the benefits of such engagement, we know less about when (or if) those benefits exceed the cost of engagement.

Degrees of network innovativeness. These collaborations also differ in their degree of innovativeness. In terms of output from the external collaboration, some firms manage collaborations that produce complements (such as apps) in a way similar to brand or support communities—as a marketing function to improve the perception of the product rather than its actual content. What are the similarities and differences between these two uses, and with those collaborations that more directly impact the innovativeness of a firm's offerings? For collaborations that combine multiple goals (e.g., complements and brand development), does one set of goals tend to dominate the culture and norms of the collaborators? How is this different between collaborations that feature strong community identification and those that have little or no elements of community identity or shared purpose (such as contests or labor markets)?

While we have sought to classify collaborations assuming they are optimized for a particular type of output (and degree of innovativeness)—and this seems realistic for a transactional crowdsourcing initiative, this may be an oversimplification of communities and hybrid forms of collaboration. For example, the members of a typical open source software community (a crowd–community hybrid) not only produce innovation, but also provide peer-to-peer support and other goods and services complementary to such innovation (e.g., Spaeth et al., 2010). Therefore, it could be useful to think about the way a given network collaborates across a range of value-creating tasks or activities—much as Du et al. (2014) looked at open innovation success at the level of individual projects—and the degree to which the collaboration, the sponsor or member interactions, and success vary between these differing activities.

CONCLUSION

With the ongoing creation and diffusion of Internet collaboration technologies by firms and individuals, these three external forms of networked collaborations will become even more important going forward. Researchers on crowdsourcing and communities will continue to benefit by collaborating with each other, and drawing insights from their respective scientific and managerial research.

ACKNOWLEDGMENTS

We gratefully acknowledge feedback from Oliver Alexy, Teppo Felin, Marion Poetz, Christina Raasch, Ammon Salter, and Sebastian Spaeth, as well as the editors and authors of this volume. Earlier versions were presented at RWTH Aachen, University of Bath, the 2012 Open and User Innovation Workshop, and the 2014 Academy of Management annual meeting. The usual disclaimers apply.

REFERENCES

Afuah, A. & Tucci, C. (2012). Crowdsourcing as a solution to distant search. *Academy of Management Review, 37*(3), 355–75.

Afuah, A. & Tucci, C. (2013). Value capture and crowdsourcing. *Academy of Management Review, 38*(3), 457–60.

Alexy, O. & Leitner, M. (2011). A fistful of dollars: Are financial rewards a suitable management practice for distributed models of innovation? *European Management Review, 8*(3), 165–85.

Algesheimer, R., Dholakia, U., & Herrmann, A. (2005). The social influence of brand community: Evidence from European car clubs. *Journal of Marketing, 69*(3), 19–34.

Andriole, S. (2010). Business impact of Web 2.0 technologies. *Communications of the ACM 53*(12), 67–79.

Antikainen, M. & Vaataja, H. (2010). Rewarding in open innovation communities–how to motivate members. *International Journal of Entrepreneurship and Innovation Management, 11*(4), 440–56.

Arora, A., Fosfuri, A., & Gambardella, A. (2001). Markets for technology and their implications for corporate strategy. *Industrial and Corporate Change 10*(2), 419–51.

Baldwin, C. & Clark, K. (2006). The architecture of participation: Does code architecture mitigate free riding in the open source development model? *Management Science, 52*(7), 1116–27.

Baldwin, C. & von Hippel, E. (2011). Modeling a paradigm shift: from producer innovation to user and open collaborative innovation. *Organization Science, 22*(6), 1399–417.

Baldwin, C., Hienerth, C., & von Hippel, E. (2006). How user innovations become commercial products: A theoretical investigation and case study. *Research Policy* 35(9), 1291–313.

Bayus, B. (2013). Crowdsourcing new product ideas over time: An analysis of the Dell IdeaStorm community. *Management Science, 59*(1), 226–44.

Bechky, B. (2006). Gaffers, gofers, and grips: Role-based coordination in temporary organizations. *Organization Science, 17*(1), 3–21.

Bekkers, R., Duysters, G., & Verspagen, B. (2002). Intellectual property rights, strategic technology agreements and market structure: The case of GSM. *Research Policy, 31*(7), 1141–61.

Benkler, Y. (2006). *The Wealth of Networks: How Social Production Transforms Markets and Freedom*. New Haven, CT: Yale University Press.

Bonaccorsi, A., Giannangeli, S., & Rossi, C. (2006). Entry strategies under competing standards: Hybrid business models in the open source software industry, *Management Science, 52*(7), 1085–98.

Boudreau, K. & Jeppesen, L. (2015). Unpaid crowd complementors: The platform network effect mirage. *Strategic Management Journal, 36*, 1761–77.

Boudreau, K. J. & Lakhani, K. R. (2009). How to manage outside innovation. *MIT Sloan Management Review, 50*(4), 69–76.

Boudreau, K. J. & Lakhani, K. R. (2013). Using the crowd as an innovation partner. *Harvard Business Review, 91*(4), 60–9.

Brabham, D. (2008). Crowdsourcing as a model for problem solving an introduction and cases. *Convergence: The International Journal of Research into New Media Technologies, 14*(1), 75–90.

Brabham, D. (2013). *Crowdsourcing*. Cambridge, MA: MIT Press.

Brint, S. (2001). Gemeinschaft revisited: A critique and reconstruction of the community concept. *Sociological Theory, 19*(1), 1–23.

Brown, J. & Duguid, P. (1991). Organizational learning and communities-of-practice: Toward a unified view of working, learning, and innovating. *Organization Science, 2*(1), 40–57.

Byrén, E. (2013). Internal crowdsourcing for innovation development: How multinational companies can obtain the advantages of crowdsourcing utilizing internal resources. M.Sc. thesis, Department of Technology Management and Economics, Chalmers University of Technology, Report No. E2013:091.

Budhathoki, N. & Haythornthwaite, C. (2013). Motivation for open collaboration: Crowd and community models and the case of OpenStreetMap. *American Behavioral Scientist, 57*(5), 548–75.

Chandler, A. (1977). *The Visible Hand: The Managerial Revolution in American Business*. Cambridge, MA: Belknap Press.

Chesbrough, H. (2003). *Open Innovation: The New Imperative for Creating and Profiting from Technology*. Boston, MA: Harvard Business School Press.

Chesbrough, H. (2006). Open innovation: A new paradigm for understanding industrial innovation, in H. Chesbrough, W. Vanhaverbeke, and J. West (eds.). *Open Innovation: Researching a New Paradigm*. Oxford: Oxford University Press, pp. 1–12.

Chesbrough, H. & Di Minin, A. (2014). Open social innovation, in H. Chesbrough, W. Vanhaverbeke, and J. West (eds.). *New Frontiers in Open Innovation.* Oxford: Oxford University Press, pp. 169–88.

Ciffolilli, A. (2003). Phantom authority, self-selective recruitment and retention of members in virtual communities: The case of Wikipedia. *First Monday, 8,* 12.

Cordella, A., Palletti, A., & Shaikh, M. (2018). Renegotiating public value with co-production. In C. Tucci, A. Afuah, & G. Viscusi (eds.), *Creating and Capturing Value Through Crowdsourcing.* Oxford: Oxford University Press, pp. 181–203.

Crowston, K., Li, Q., Wei, U., Eseryel, Y., & Howison, J. (2007). Self-organization of teams for free/libre open source software development, *Information and Software Technology, 49*(6), 564–75.

Crowston, K. & Howison, J. (2005). The social structure of free and open source software development. *First Monday, 10*(2), http://firstmonday.org/article/view/1207/1127

Curto-Millet, D. & Nisar, A. (2018). Ethics in crowdsourcing: Revisiting and revising the role of stakeholder theory. In C. Tucci, A. Afuah, & G. Viscusi (eds.), *Creating and Capturing Value Through Crowdsourcing.* Oxford: Oxford University Press, pp. 310–34.

Dahlander, L. & Gann, D. (2010). How open is innovation? *Research Policy, 39*(6), 699–709.

Dahlander, L. & Magnusson, M. (2005). Relationships between open source software companies and communities: Observations from Nordic firms, *Research Policy, 34*(4), 481–93.

Dahlander, L. & Magnusson, M. (2008). How do firms make use of open source communities? *Long Range Planning, 41*(6), 629–49.

Dahlander, L. & Piezunka, H. (2014). Open to suggestions: How organizations elicit suggestions through proactive and reactive attention, *Research Policy, 43*(5), 812–27.

Dahlander, L. & Wallin, M. (2006). A man on the inside: unlocking communities as complementary assets, *Research Policy, 35*(8), 1243–59.

Dahlander, L., Frederiksen, L., & Rullani, F. (2008). Online communities and open innovation. *Industry and Innovation, 15*(2), 115–23.

de Laat, P. (2007). Governance of open source software: State of the art. *Journal of Management and Governance, 11*(2), 165–77.

Demil, B. & Lecocq, X. (2006). Neither market nor hierarchy nor network: The emergence of bazaar governance, *Organization Studies, 27*(10), 1447–66.

Di Gangi, P. & Wasko, M. (2009). Steal my idea! Organizational adoption of user innovations from a user innovation community: A case study of Dell Ideastorm. *Decision Support Systems, 48*(1), 303–12.

Diener, K. & Piller, F. (2013). *The Market for Open Innovation: A Survey of Open Innovation Accelerators,* 2nd edn. Raleigh, NC: Lulu.

Doan, A., Ramakrishnan, R., & Halevy, A. (2011). Crowdsourcing systems on the world-wide web. *Communications of the ACM, 54*(4), 86–96.

Dokko, G. & Rosenkopf, R. (2010). Social capital for hire? Mobility of technical professionals and firm influence in wireless standards committees. *Organization Science, 21*(3), 677–95.

Du, J., Leten, B., & Vanhaverbeke, W. (2014). Managing open innovation projects with science-based and market-based partners. *Research Policy, 43*(5), 828–40.

Estellés-Arolas, E. & González-Ladrón-de-Guevara, F. (2012). Towards an integrated crowdsourcing definition. *Journal of Information Science, 38*(2), 189–200.

Feller, J, Finnegan P., Fitzgerald, B., & Hayes, J. (2008). From peer production to productization: A study of socially enabled business exchanges in open source service networks. *Information Systems Research, 19*(4), 475–93.

Fleming, L. & Waguespack, D. (2007). Brokerage, boundary spanning, and leadership in open innovation communities. *Organization Science, 18*(2), 165–80.

Forte, A., Larco, V., & Bruckman, A. (2009). Decentralization in Wikipedia governance. *Journal of Management Information Systems, 26*(1), 49–72.

Franke, N. & Shah S. (2003). How communities support innovative activities: An exploration of assistance and sharing among end-users, *Research Policy, 32*(1), 157.

Franke, N., von Hippel, E., & Schreier, M. (2006). Finding commercially attractive user innovations: A test of lead-user theory. *Journal of Product Innovation Management, 23*(4), 301–15.

Franke, N., Keinz, P., & Klausberger, K. (2013). Does this sound like a fair deal? Antecedents and consequences of fairness expectations in the individual's decision to participate in firm innovation. *Organization Science, 24*(4), 1495–516.

Franke, N., Poetz, M., & Schreier, M. (2014). Integrating problem solvers from analogous markets in new product ideation. *Management Science, 60*(4), 1063–81.

Franzoni, C. & Sauermann, H. (2014). Crowd science: The organization of scientific research in open collaborative projects. *Research Policy, 43*(1), 1–20.

Freeman, C. & Soete, L. (1997). *The Economics of Industrial Innovation.* Cambridge, MA: MIT Press.

Füller, J., Matzler M., & Hoppe, M. (2008). Brand community members as a source of innovation. *Journal of Product Innovation Management, 25*(6), 608–19.

Galacziewicz, J. (1985). Interorganizational relations. *Annual Review of Sociology, 11,* 281–304.

Garriga, H., Spaeth, S., & von Krogh, G. (2011). Open source software development: Communities' impact on public good. *Social Computing, Behavioral–Cultural Modeling and Prediction.* Berlin: Springer, pp. 69–77.

Garud, R., Jain, S., & Kumaraswamy, A. (2002). Institutional entrepreneurship in the sponsorship of common technological standards: The case of Sun Microsystems and Java. *Academy of Management Journal, 45*(1), 196–214.

Ghose, A., Ipeirotis, P., & Li, B. (2012). Designing ranking systems for hotels on travel search engines by mining user-generated and crowdsourced content. *Marketing Science, 31*(3), 493–520.

Hallström, K. (2004). *Organizing International Standardization: ISO and the IASC in Quest of Authority.* Cheltenham, UK: Edward Elgar.

Harrison, D. & Waluszewski, A. (2008). The development of a user network as a way to re-launch an unwanted product. *Research Policy, 37*(1), 115–30.

Hars, A. & Ou, S. (2002). Working for free? Motivations for participating in open-source projects. *International Journal of Electronic Commerce, 6*(3), 25–39.

Henkel, J. (2006). Selective revealing in open innovation processes: The case of embedded linux. *Research Policy, 35*(7), 953–69.

Henkel, J. (2008). Champions of revealing—the role of open source developers in commercial firms. *Industrial & Corporate Change, 18*(3), 435–71.

Hertel, G., Niedner, S., & Herrmann, S. (2003). Motivation of software developers in open source projects: An Internet-based survey of contributors to the Linux kernel. *Research Policy, 32*(7), 1159.

Hienerth, C. (2006). The commercialization of user innovations: The development of the Rodeo kayak industry. *R&D Management, 36*(3), 273–94.

Hilgers, D. & Ihl, C. (2010). Citizensourcing: Applying the concept of open innovation to the public sector. *International Journal of Public Participation, 4*(1), 67–88.

Howe, J. (2006a). The rise of crowdsourcing, *Wired, 14,* 6(June), 1–4.

Howe, J. (2006b). Crowdsourcing: A definition. Crowdsourcing weblog, June 2, http://crowdsourcing.typepad.com/cs/2006/06/crowdsourcing_a.html

Iansiti, M. & Levien, R. (2004). Strategy as ecology. *Harvard Business Review, 82*(2), 68–81.

Isaak, J. (2007). The role of individuals & social capital in POSIX standardization. *International Journal of IT Standards and Standardization Research, 4*(1), 1–23.

Jayanti, R. & Singh, J. (2010). Pragmatic learning theory: An inquiry–action framework for distributed consumer learning in online communities. *Journal of Consumer Research, 36*(6), 1058–81.

Jensen, M. B., Hienerth, C., & Lettl, C. (2014). Forecasting the commercial attractiveness of user-generated designs using online data: An empirical study within the LEGO user community. *Journal of Product Innovation Management, 31*(S1), 75–93.

Jeppesen, L. & Frederiksen, L. (2006). Why do users contribute to firm-hosted user communities? The case of computer-controlled music instruments. *Organization Science, 17*(1), 45–63.

Jeppesen, L. B. & Lakhani, K. R. (2010). Marginality and problem-solving effectiveness in broadcast search. *Organization Science, 21*(5), 1016–33.

Keil, T. (2002). De-facto standardization through alliances—lessons from Bluetooth, *Telecommunications Policy, 26*(3), 205–13.

King, A. & Lakhani, K. R. (2013). Using open innovation to identify the best ideas. *Sloan Management Review, 55*(1), 41–8.

Laing, A., Keeling, D., & Newholm, T. (2011). Virtual communities come of age: Parallel service, value, and propositions offered in communal online space. *Journal of Marketing Management, 27*(3–4), 291–315.

Lakhani, K. R. (2016). Managing communities and contests to innovate with crowds, in Harhoff, D., & Lakhani, K. R. (eds.). *Revolutionizing Innovation: Users, Communities, and Open Innovation.* Cambridge, MA: MIT Press, pp. 109–34.

Lakhani, K. R. & von Hippel, E. (2003). How open source software works: "Free" user-to-user assistance. *Research Policy, 32*(6), 923–43.

Lakhani, K. R. & Wolf, R. G. (2005). Why hackers do what they do: Understanding motivation and effort in free/open source software projects, in J. Feller, B. Fitzgerald, S. Hissam, & K. R. Lakhani (eds.). *Perspectives on Free and Open Source Software.* Cambridge, MA: MIT Press, pp. 3–22.

Lakhani, K. R., Lifshitz-Assaf, H., & Tushman, M. (2013). Open innovation and organizational boundaries: Task decomposition, knowledge distribution and the locus of innovation, in A. Grandori (ed.). *Handbook of Economic Organization: Integrating Economic and Organization Theory*. Cheltenham, UK: Edward Elgar, pp. 355–82.

Lampel, J., Jha, P., & Bhalla, A. (2012). Test-driving the future: How design competitions are changing innovation, *Academy of Management Perspectives, 26*(2), 71–85.

Langner, B. & Seidel, V. (2014). Sustaining the flow of external ideas: The role of dual social identity across communities and organizations. *Journal of Product Innovation Management, 32*(4), 522–38.

Lee, G. & Cole, R. (2003). From a firm-based to a community-based model of knowledge creation: The case of the Linux kernel development. *Organization Science, 14*(6), 633–49.

Leimeister, J., Huber, M., Bretschneider, U., & Krcmar, H. (2009). Leveraging crowdsourcing: activation-supporting components for IT-based ideas competition, *Journal of Management Information Systems, 26*(1), 197–224.

Leiponen, A. (2008). Competing through cooperation: The organization of standard setting in wireless telecommunications, *Management Science, 54*(11), 1904–19.

Levina, N. & Fayard, A-L. (2018). Tapping into diversity through open innovation platforms: The emergence of boundary-spanning practices. In C. Tucci, A. Afuah, & G. Viscusi (eds.), *Creating and Capturing Value Through Crowdsourcing*. Oxford: Oxford University Press, pp. 204–35.

Lih, A. (2009). *The Wikipedia Revolution: How a Bunch of Nobodies Created the World's Greatest Encyclopedia*. New York: Hyperion.

MacCormack, A., Rusnak, J., & Baldwin, C. Y. (2006). Exploring the structure of complex software designs: An empirical study of open source and proprietary code. *Management Science, 52*(7), 1015–30.

Mahr, D. & Lievens, A. (2012). Virtual lead user communities: Drivers of knowledge creation for innovation. *Research Policy, 41*(1), 167–77.

Majchrzak, A., & Malhotra, A. 2013. Towards an information systems perspective and research agenda on crowdsourcing for innovation, *Journal of Strategic Information Systems, 22*(4), 257–68.

Marchi, G., Giachetti, C., & de Gennaro, P. (2011). Extending lead-user theory to online brand communities: The case of the community Ducati. *Technovation, 31*(8), 350–61.

Markus, M. (2007). The governance of free/open source software projects: Monolithic, multidimensional, or configurational? *Journal of Management & Governance, 11*(2), 151–63.

Martinez, M. & Walton, G. (2014). The wisdom of crowds: The potential of online communities as a tool for data analysis. *Technovation, 34*(4), 203–14.

Mollick, E. (2014). The dynamics of crowdfunding: An exploratory study. *Journal of Business Venturing, 29*(1), 1–16.

Muñiz, A. & Schau, H. (2005). Religiosity in the abandoned Apple Newton brand community. *Journal of Consumer Research, 31*(4), 737–47.

Muniz, A. M., Jr. & O'Guinn, T. C. (2001). Brand community. *Journal of Consumer Research, 27*(4), 412–32.

Murray, F., Stern, S., Campbell, G., & MacCormack, A. (2012). Grand innovation prizes: A theoretical, normative, and empirical evaluation. *Research Policy, 41*(10), 1779–92.

Nov, O. (2007). What motivates Wikipedians? *Communications of the ACM, 50*(11), 60–4.

O'Mahony, S. (2003). Guarding the commons: How community managed software projects protect their work. *Research Policy, 32*(7), 1179.

O'Mahony, S. (2005). Non-profit foundations and their role in community-firm software collaboration, in J. Feller, B. Fitzgerald, S. Hissam, & K. R. Lakhani (eds.). *Perspectives on Free and Open Source Software.* Cambridge, MA: MIT Press, pp. 393–413.

O'Mahony, S. (2007). The governance of open source initiatives: What does it mean to be community managed? *Journal of Management & Governance, 11*(2), 139–50.

O'Mahony, S. & Ferraro, F. (2007). The emergence of governance in an open source community. *Academy of Management Journal, 50*(5), 1079–106.

O'Mahony, S. & Lakhani, K. R. (2011). Organizations in the shadow of communities. *Research in the Sociology of Organizations, 33,* 3–36.

Piller, F. & Walcher, D. (2006). Toolkits for idea competitions: A novel method to integrate users in new product development. *R&D Management, 36*(3), 307–18.

Piller, F. & West, J. (2014). Firms, users, and innovation: An interactive model of coupled open innovation, in H. Chesbrough, W. Vanhaverbeke, and J. West (eds.). *New Frontiers in Open Innovation.* Oxford: Oxford University Press, pp. 29–49.

Piva, E., Rentocchini, F., & Rossi-Lamastra, C. (2012). Is open source software about innovation? Collaborations with the open source community and innovation performance of software entrepreneurial ventures. *Journal of Small Business Management, 50*(2), 340–64.

Poetz, M. & Prügl, R. (2010). Crossing domain-specific boundaries in search of innovation: Exploring the potential of pyramiding. *Journal of Product Innovation Management, 27*(6), 897–914.

Poetz, M. & Schreier, M. (2012). The value of crowdsourcing: Can users really compete with professionals in generating new product ideas? *Journal of Product Innovation Management, 29*(2), 245–56.

Porter, C. & Donthu, N. (2008). Cultivating trust and harvesting value in virtual communities. *Management Science, 54*(1), 113–28.

Powell, W. (1990). Neither market nor hierarchy: Network forms of organization. *Research in Organizational Behavior, 12,* 295–336.

Putnam, R. (1995). Bowling alone: America's declining social capital. *Journal of Democracy, 6*(1), 65–78.

Raasch, C. & von Hippel, E. (2013). Innovation process benefits: the journey as reward. *Sloan Management Review, 55*(1), 33–9.

Raasch, C., Herstatt, C., & Balka, K. (2009). On the open design of tangible goods. *R&D Management, 39*(4), 382–93.

Rheingold, H. (1993). *The Virtual Community: Homesteading on the Electronic Frontier.* Reading, MA: Addison Wesley.

Rheingold, H. (2000). *The Virtual Community: Homesteading on the Electronic Frontier*, revised edn. Cambridge, MA: MIT Press.

Rolandsson, B., Bergquist M., & Ljungberg, J. (2011). Open source in the firm: Opening up professional practices of software development. *Research Policy, 40*(4), 576–87.

Rosenkopf, L. & Tushman, M. (1998). The coevolution of community networks and technology: Lessons from the flight simulation industry. *Industrial & Corporate Change, 7*(2), 311–46.

Rosenkopf, L., Metiu, A., & George, V. P. (2001). From the bottom up? Technical committee activity and alliance formation. *Administrative Science Quarterly, 46*(4), 748–72.

Samuelson, P. (2006). Pragmatic embrace of open source. *Communications of the ACM, 49*(10), 21–25.

Sanchez, R. & Mahoney, J. (1996). Modularity, flexibility, and knowledge management in product & organization design. *Strategic Management Journal, 17*(S2), 63–76.

Savage, N. (2012). Gaining wisdom from crowds. *Communications of the ACM, 55*(3), 13–15.

Schau, H., Muñiz, A. Jr, & Arnould, E. (2009). How brand community practices create value. *Journal of Marketing, 73*(5), 30–51.

Schweisfurth, T. & Herstatt, C. (2016). How internal users contribute to corporate product innovation: The case of embedded users. *R&D Management, 46*(S1), 107–26.

Scotchmer, S. (2004). *Innovation and Incentives.* Cambridge, MA: MIT Press.

Seidel, V., Langner, B., & Sims, J. (2016). Dominant communities and dominant designs: Community-based innovation in the context of the technology life cycle. *Strategic Organization, 14*(4). (Published June 17, 2016 as Articles in advance of print, 1–22.)

Shah, S. (2006). Motivation, governance, and the viability of hybrid forms in open source software development. *Management Science, 52*(7), 1000–14.

Shah, S. & Tripsas, M. (2007). The accidental entrepreneur: The emergent and collective process of user entrepreneurship. *Strategic Entrepreneurship Journal, 1* (1–2), 123–40.

Shen, W., Hu, Y. J., & Rees Ulmer, J. (2015). Competing for attention: An empirical study of online reviewers' strategic behavior. *MIS Quarterly, 39*(3), 683–96.

Sims, J. & Seidel, V. (2016). Organizations coupled with communities: The strategic effects on firms engaged in community-coupled open innovation. *Industrial and Corporate Change, 26*(4), 647–65.

Snow, C., Fjeldstad, Ø., Lettl C., & Miles, R. (2011). Organizing continuous product development and commercialization: The collaborative community of firms model. *Journal of Product Innovation Management, 28*(1), 3–16.

Spaeth, S., Stuermer M., & von Krogh, G. (2010). Enabling knowledge creation through outsiders: Towards a push model of open innovation. *International Journal of Technology Management, 52*(3–4), 411–31.

Stallman, R. (1985). The GNU manifesto. *Dr. Dobbs Journal, 10*(3), 30–1.

Stam, W. (2009). When does community participation enhance the performance of open source software companies? *Research Policy, 38*(8), 1288–99.

Stewart, K. & Gosain, S. (2006). The impact of ideology on effectiveness in open source software development teams. *MIS Quarterly*, *30*(2), 291–314.

Surowiecki, J. (2005). *The Wisdom of Crowds*. New York: Anchor.

Teece, D. (1986). Profiting from technological innovation: Implications for integration, collaboration, licensing and public policy. *Research Policy*, *15*(6), 285–305.

Teece, D. (1992). Competition, cooperation, and innovation: Organizational arrangements for regimes of rapid technological progress. *Journal of Economic Behavior & Organization*, *18*(1), 1–25.

Terwiesch, C. & Ulrich, K. (2009). *Innovation Tournaments: Creating and Selecting Exceptional Opportunities*. Boston: Harvard Business Press.

Tucci, C. L., Chesbrough, H., Piller, F., & West, J. (2016). When do firms undertake open, collaborative activities? Introduction to the special section on open innovation and open business models. *Industrial and Corporate Change*, *25*(2), 283–8.

Viscusi, G. & Tucci, C. (2018). Three's a crowd? In C. Tucci, A. Afuah, & G. Viscusi (eds.), *Creating and Capturing Value Through Crowdsourcing*. Oxford: Oxford University Press, pp. 39–57.

von Hippel, E. (2005). *Democratizing Innovation*. Cambridge, MA: MIT Press.

von Hippel, E. (2007). Horizontal innovation networks—by and for users. *Industrial & Corporate Change*, *16*(2), 293–315.

von Hippel, E. & Katz, R. (2002). Shifting innovation to users via toolkits. *Management Science*, *48*(7), 821–33.

von Krogh, G., Haefliger, S., Spaeth, S., & Wallin, M. W. (2012). Carrots and rainbows: Motivation and social practice in open source software development. *MIS Quarterly*, *36*(2), 649–76.

von Krogh, G., Spaeth, S., & Lakhani, K. R. (2003). Community, joining, and specialization in open source software innovation: A case study. *Research Policy*, *32*(7), 1217–41.

Waguespack, D. M. & Fleming, L. (2009). Scanning the commons? Evidence on the benefits to startups participating in open standards development. *Management Science*, *55*(2), 210–23.

Wade, J. (1995). Dynamics of organizational communities and technological bandwagons: An empirical investigation of community evolution in the microprocessor market. *Strategic Management Journal*, *16*(S1), 111–33.

Weber, S. (2004). *The Success of Open Source*. Cambridge, MA: Harvard University Press.

Weick, K. (1976). Educational organizations as loosely coupled systems. *Administrative Science Quarterly*, *21*(1), 1–19.

Wellman, B., Boase, J., & Chen, W. (2002a). The networked nature of community on and off the Internet, working paper. Centre for Urban & Community Studies, University of Toronto.

Wellman, B., Boase, J., & Chen, W. (2002b). The networked nature of community: Online and offline. *IT & Society*, *1*(1), 151–65.

Wenger, E. (2000). Communities of practice & social learning systems. *Organization*, *7*(2), 225–46.

West, J. (2003). How open is open enough? Melding proprietary & open source platform strategies. *Research Policy, 32*(7), 1259–85.

West, J. (2014). Challenges of funding open innovation platforms: Lessons from Symbian Ltd., in H. Chesbrough, W. Vanhaverbeke, & J. West (eds.). *New Frontiers in Open Innovation*. Oxford: Oxford University Press, pp. 71–93.

West, J. & Bogers, M. (2014). Profiting from external innovation: A review of research on open innovation. *Journal of Product Innovation Management, 31*(4), 814–31.

West, J. & Gallagher, S. (2006). Challenges of open innovation: The paradox of firm investment in open-source software. *R&D Management, 36*(3), 319–31.

West, J. & Greul, A. (2016). Atoms matter: The role of local makerspaces in the coming digital economy, in F. Xavier Olleros and Majlinda Zhegu (eds.). *Research Handbook on Digital Transformations*. Cheltenham, UK: Elgar, pp. 182–202.

West, J. & Lakhani, K. R. (2008). Getting clear about communities in open innovation. *Industry & Innovation, 15*(2), 223–31.

West, J. & O'Mahony, S. (2008). The role of participation architecture in growing sponsored open source communities. *Industry & Innovation, 15*(2), 145–68.

Wiertz, C. & de Ruyter, K. (2007). Beyond the call of duty: Why customers contribute to firm-hosted commercial online communities. *Organization Studies, 28*(3), 347–76.

5

The Road to Crowdfunding Success:
A Review of the Extant Literature

Vincenzo Butticè, Chiara Franzoni, Cristina Rossi-Lamastra, and Paola Rovelli

Abstract

The literature on crowdfunding, the practice of collecting money (fundraising) from a "crowd" of Internet users, has devoted the bulk of its attention to identifying the determinants of success of crowdfunding campaigns. Thanks to the support of the crowd, crowdfunding helps people to enact their projects and entrepreneurial ideas, being particularly important for those who have typically encountered problems accessing traditional sources of finance. Nevertheless, the benefits of crowdfunding are not just limited to raising money. In this chapter, we review the literature on this research and we highlight the main empirical results that have emerged on the topic. We describe the elements and characteristics of crowdfunding campaigns and we discuss how they relate to crowdfunding success. We show that the debate is still in its infancy with several areas in need of further investigation. In the conclusion, we call readers' attention to some existing gaps.

INTRODUCTION

Crowdfunding, the practice of collecting small amounts of money from the crowd of Internet users (Belleflamme et al., 2013), is gaining more and more resonance worldwide (*The Economist*, 2013). Although it is difficult to measure the real magnitude of the phenomenon, it is fair to say that it involves huge amounts of projects and capital. Only in 2014, technology projects raised a total of $139.8 million on Kickstarter, which corresponds to 13.7 percent of the total amount collected on the platform (Colombo et al., 2015a).

The term crowdfunding appeared for the first time in Wired Magazine in 2006 (Howe, 2006)[1] and it relates to the earlier concepts of crowdsourcing (Afhua & Tucci, 2012) and microfinance (Robinson, 2001; Harrison, 2013). Thanks to the support of the crowd, crowdfunding helps people to enact their projects and entrepreneurial ideas (Beaulieu & Sarker, 2013), this being particularly important for those who have typically encountered problems accessing traditional sources of finance (e.g., Dushnitsky & Marom, 2013; Mollick & Robb, 2016). Nevertheless, the benefits of crowdfunding are not just limited to raising money. Indeed, in accordance with the essence of crowdsourcing, crowdfunders often provide valuable feedback and ideas that *fundraisers* (i.e., those who publish projects and collect money through crowdfunding) can exploit to develop further their projects and entrepreneurial ideas (e.g., Riedl, 2013; Colombo et al., 2015b; Skirnevskiy et al., 2017).

The large resonance of crowdfunding in the popular press has gone hand in hand with a growing scholarly research effort (Gerber & Hui, 2013), with many researchers from multiple fields investigating this novel phenomenon. Moreover, several panels on crowdfunding have been organized during important conferences at the Academy of Management or the Strategic Management Society, and dedicated special issues have been published by several journals (California Management Review, Entrepreneurship Theory and Practice, Venture Capital, etc.).

In particular, the growing literature on crowdfunding has devoted the bulk of its attention to identifying the *determinants of success of crowdfunding campaigns*[2] (Short et al., 2017). Accordingly, for the sake of relevance, in this chapter, we review and systematize this literature strand. Specifically, our review offers a quick gateway to crowdfunding research for scholars who intend to enter this new and fascinating area, thus serving as a starting point for their future studies. Moreover, the review attempts to provide a summary useful to practitioners, who wish to learn more on what makes a successful campaign.

To ensure the comprehensiveness of the literature review, we conducted a systematic search in the main publication databases for the keyword "crowdfunding" in the title, abstract, and keywords of papers. First, we used the Scopus database (http://www.scopus.com) to collect all articles already published or in press in scientific journals as of March 2017. Second, we searched the SSRN (http://www.ssrn.com) and Google Scholar (http://www.scholar.com) databases to gather very recent contributions that have not yet appeared in press. The search process resulted in 702 articles. After a first screening of the abstracts (or papers when the abstract was absent), we

---

[1] Synonymous are crowdfinancing or crowdinvesting (Tomczak & Brem, 2013).

[2] For example, the literature on reward-based crowdfunding studies how the likelihood of success relates to the conditions offered by the fundraiser (e.g., the quality of the project, the range of rewards that they will provide to crowdfunders in exchange for their support, the duration of the campaign, etc.).

reduced our sample to 179 relevant articles, considering only those which were in line with the aim of this review. As we explain in the following paragraph, we focus on a few specific models of crowdfunding, and consequently we excluded all papers that fall beyond these models.

We chose to organize the review as follows. In the next section (Crowdfunding: Its Features and Definitions), we provide a general overview of the crowdfunding phenomenon. First, we discuss its origins and main characteristics, presenting the diverse models of crowdfunding and the actors involved, and specifying the rationales behind selection of the models considered in the review. Moreover, we discuss the multifaceted nature of crowdfunding and the related definitions that exist of this phenomenon. We discuss alternative definitions and, more interestingly, we integrate these into a novel and more comprehensive definition.

In the subsequent section (Achieving Crowdfunding Success), we introduce the concept of success of a crowdfunding campaign. Specifically, we show that crowdfunding success has a multi-dimensional nature (Ahlers et al., 2015), being responsive to both monetary and non-monetary benefits (Dushnitsky & Marom, 2013; Gerber & Hui, 2013). We then define the entities involved in a crowdfunding campaign, distinguishing the project, the fundraiser, and the crowdfunders (i.e., those who finance fundraisers' projects) and discuss how they relate to the probability of success, also considering the interaction among fundraisers and their crowdfunders. Then, we further describe the features of a crowdfunding projects like the project category (e.g., design, music, technology, etc.), the target capital, the duration, the rewards, and more generally the information provided by the fundraisers. We synthetize state-of-the-art findings about the impact of the choices regarding project features on the likelihood of campaign success. Following this, we move on to consider the characteristics of fundraisers and crowdfunders and examine the answers that current studies have provided to the following questions: Who are they? What are their individual characteristics? Why do they decide to post crowdfunding projects or to fund them? How do crowdfunders' characteristics influence crowdfunding success? Then, we focus on contributions that have examined how interactions among the fundraisers and their crowdfunders affect the success of crowdfunding campaigns (e.g., Colombo et al., 2015b). Lastly, we draw conclusions and highlight avenues for future research.

CROWDFUNDING: ITS FEATURES
AND DEFINITIONS

In this paragraph, we summarize the main features of crowdfunding and clarify the terminology used in this literature and in this chapter. To this end, we discuss the multiple definitions of crowdfunding currently adopted by the literature and we integrate them to propose an updated and more general definition than those used before.

Crowdfunding is a novel phenomenon, which still lacks a widely accepted definition. Currently, many definitions coexist, which are often specific to the context of the study (Tomczak & Brem, 2013). Nevertheless, we believe that providing a general definition is fundamental for tracing the boundaries of a phenomenon, which is one of the crucial steps towards its analysis (von Krogh et al., 2012). For instance, financial studies conceive crowdfunding as a method of raising funds for projects by simultaneously addressing a large pool of potential investors (Tirdatov, 2014), while innovation scholars view this funding method as a new way to finance innovative projects and connect innovative ideas to the crowd of Internet users (Riedl, 2013). Of course, attempts have been made to bridge these different views. Among them, the most popular is the definition by Schwienbacher & Larralde (2010: 4), who describe crowd-funding as *an open call, essentially through the Internet, for the provision of financial resources either in form of donation or in exchange for some form of reward and/or voting rights in order to support initiatives for specific purposes.* This definition is an insightful starting point, however in our opinion it requires fine tuning to mirror the recent development of the literature. To this end, we describe crowdfunding and its characteristics with the purpose of proposing here an updated and comprehensive definition of the phenomenon.

In essence, crowdfunding is a combination of microfinance (Robinson, 2001) and crowdsourcing (Howe, 2006; Harrison, 2013). Akin to microfinance, crowdfunding entails the provision of relatively small amounts of money (Harrison, 2013) and helps people to acquire financial resources for their projects and entrepreneurial ideas (Beaulieu & Sarker, 2013). Like in microfinance, many of those who raise money with crowdfunding are those who would normally encounter difficulties in obtaining financial resources from banks and other traditional financial operators. Likewise, crowdfunding has elements that are typical of crowdsourcing. Similar to crowdsourcing, crowdfunding involves an open call through the Internet and necessitates the voluntary participation of a distributed network of individuals (Belleflamme et al., 2013). Similarities with crowdsourcing are however not limited to use of the Internet and to open participation. An important similarity is that crowd-funding facilitates the interaction with a crowd of potential future users and customers (Ordanini et al., 2011) and offers the opportunity of collecting feedback and suggestions from the crowd of the Internet users (Colombo et al., 2015b). These inputs favor the emergence of a collaborative design (Gerber & Hui, 2013) and, ultimately, the development of better products (Riedl, 2013), in ways that are common to other crowdsourcing initiatives (Afuah, 2018; Šundić & Leitner, 2018). What makes crowdfunding unique is the fact that Internet users provide both the capital necessary to enact ideas and entrepreneurial projects (Burkett, 2011) and the knowledge to improve the quality of these projects (Gerber & Hui, 2013). Hence, in outlining a definition of crowdfunding, it is important to remember that crowdfunding does not only relate to collecting money, but it also relates to collecting feedback and suggestions.

Furthermore, a comprehensive definition should not overlook that there are *diverse participants* in any crowdfunding campaign and that several *crowdfunding models* do exist.

Main participants in a crowdfunding campaign. The nascent literature on crowdfunding has evidenced three kinds of players: the fundraisers, the crowdfunders, and the managers of crowdfunding platforms. *Fundraisers* are those who propose the ideas and/or projects to be funded (Mollick, 2014). The *crowdfunders* are those who support the crowdfunding campaigns by providing financial backing to the fundraisers. Typically, crowdfunders are proactive and are a source of feedback and new ideas in addition to financial resources. It is worth observing that many individuals operate both as fundraisers and crowdfunders of different projects (Hardy, 2013) and that there are even self-ruled open calls for successful fundraisers to become active sponsors of other crowdfunders (e.g., the "Kicking it Forward" initiative).[3] Finally, the *crowdfunding platforms* are intermediaries that work to enable transactions between the fundraisers and the crowdfunders. These intermediaries own and manage the websites, serve as matchmakers, and earn a fee or share on the transactions (Burkett, 2011; Koch & Cheng, 2016). The platforms manage the search engines, check the legal requirements, provide online payment mechanisms, and, in some cases, perform an initial screening aimed at filtering out low quality projects (Löher, 2017). In so doing, crowdfunding platforms reduce search costs (Agrawal et al., 2014) and coordination costs (Crosetto & Regner, 2014) between the fundraiser and the crowdfunders, lowering the potential for opportunistic behaviors (Löher, 2017).

As a result of the low entry costs, the number of platforms in operation has seen dramatic growth over time, although different countries have different growth rates (Dushnitsky et al., 2016). At the end of 2016, about 500 platforms were estimated to be operating worldwide (Ramos & González, 2016).

Crowdfunding models. Since 2012, several scholars have proposed taxonomies of crowdfunding models. A popular classification (e.g., Griffin, 2012; Lehner, 2012; Mitra, 2012; Ahlers et al., 2015) revolves around what crowdfunders receive in exchange for their contributions. Following this classification, crowdfunding models are generally broken down into four types: *donation-based, reward-based, equity-based,* and *lending-based*. Belleflamme et al. (2014) have compared these diverse crowdfunding models and found that fundraisers prefer to opt for a reward-based campaign when the capital requirement is small in

---

[3] http://kickingitforward.org (accessed October 28, 2015).

comparison with the market size, otherwise, fundraisers would choose an equity-based crowdfunding model. Selecting equity-based crowdfunding is highly recommended when fundraisers are highly interested in receiving feedback from the crowd (Miglo, 2016); moreover, Cholakova & Clarysse (2015) find that only the financial motives related to equity crowdfunding play a role for individuals.

Let us focus in greater depth on these models. The donation-based model entails no remuneration in exchange for the money pledged by the crowdfunders. On the contrary, in other models of crowdfunding the crowdfunders receive a specific return. In the reward-based model, crowdfunders pledge money in exchange for a product, a gadget, or a service chosen from a list. Sometimes the reward is merely symbolic (e.g., "a grateful thank you from the proponent"), such that the distinction between reward and donation-based crowdfunding can often be blurred. In other cases, the reward involves the pre-purchase of a product or a service. Reward-based crowdfunding is gaining increasing popularity among fundraisers, who typically use it to finance projects in the cultural and creative fields (Kuppuswamy & Bayus, 2017). A third model is equity-based crowdfunding, where crowdfunders provide money in exchange for a share of the risk capital of a firm. In this case, they acquire ownership and voting rights, with the intention of participating in the distribution of future profits. This crowdfunding model is highly regulated due to a risk profile and liabilities typical of other seed financing activities, such as business angeling, venture capital, and IPOs (Lasrado & Lugmayr, 2013). The public offering of equity shares on the Internet further exacerbates these liabilities.

In peer-to-peer-lending, the fundraisers seek to borrow certain amounts of money from the crowd in the form of loans, at the cost of an interest rate. The interest rate is flexible and typically regulated by an algorithm that lowers the interest rate when more lenders place bids. Some scholars consider peer-to-peer lending as a crowdfunding model, while other scholars view it as a partially different model.

In respect of this taxonomy, it is worth highlighting that in this review, we consider only papers focusing on donation, reward, and equity crowdfunding. Here, we exclude contributions referring to the lending model because it differs from the other crowdfunding models in several respects. First, lending-based crowdfunding entails a limited interaction with the crowd and thus it generates limited advantages in terms of collection of feedback and suggestions ascribable to the phenomenon of crowdsourcing, which is the core of this book. Second, microcredit lending has existed for a long time offline, and its coupling with Internet media has not qualitatively altered its essence, such that peer-to-peer lending can arguably be considered the online version of a pre-existing funding mechanism, rather than a new funding channel. For these reasons, contributions on lending-based crowdfunding strongly relate to the partly separated literature of microcredit, and share limited analogies with the emerging crowdfunding literature, which largely focuses on donation, reward, and equity crowdfunding.

Other (less known) taxonomies do not consider the reward type and rather propose alternative criteria of classification. These are the *timing* of the campaign with respect to the state of the project (Kappel, 2008), the *money collection scheme* implemented in the platform (Cumming & Johan, 2013), and the presence or absence of an *intermediary* that facilitates the matching between the parties of the transaction (Kaufman et al., 2013). The first taxonomy distinguishes between *ex-ante crowdfunding*, when the campaign precedes the starting of the project, and *ex-post crowdfunding*, when the campaign takes place only once the project has been realized. The second taxonomy distinguishes between *all or nothing*, in which the fundraisers receive the funds only if they reach the threshold set at the launch of the crowdfunding campaign, and *keep it all*, where the fundraisers can retain money only when at least the target amount was collected at the day of closure. A study by Wash & Solomon (2011) provided evidence that the *all or nothing* scheme helps fundraisers to collect money for risky projects and allows collection of a greater amount of capital compared to the keep it all. Finally, scholars differentiate *indirect crowdfunding*, which involves a third party that works as intermediary between fundraiser and crowdfunders, and *direct crowdfunding*. However, to date, indirect crowdfunding, intermediated by a crowdfunding platform active on the web, represents the standard and overwhelming majority of the market, making this taxonomy of relatively little use.[4]

This brief survey has highlighted three aspects that a comprehensive definition of crowdfunding should include: the provision of feedbacks from crowdfunders, the crucial role of crowdfunding platforms, and the existence of several crowdfunding models. Accordingly, we propose the following definition that we consider appropriate to grasp the recent evolution of crowdfunding:

> *Crowdfunding is the act of collecting monetary contributions together with feedback and suggestions from a crowd of contributors (in the form either of donation or in exchange for some forms of reward) through an open call on enabling web platforms.*

ACHIEVING CROWDFUNDING SUCCESS

A fundraiser can achieve several benefits by running a crowdfunding campaign. As previously mentioned, the first and most straightforward one is raising

---

[4] Some relatively rare exceptions are the funding of political campaigns (e.g., Barack Obama's presidential campaign in 2008) or other popular causes.

money needed to support a project or an entrepreneurial idea (e.g., Gerber & Hui, 2013; Mollick, 2014; Mollick & Kuppuswamy, 2014). However, looking closer, several non-monetary benefits exist and these are often the primary motive for engaging in crowdfunding (Dushnitsky & Marom, 2013; Gerber & Hui, 2013). Specifically, the main non-monetary benefit of crowdfunding for a fundraiser consists in accessing quickly and without intermediaries a source of customers who are often willing and ready to experiment with new products. Very much in line with the users' innovation and crowdsourcing literature (West & Sims, 2018), crowdfunding allows a fundraiser to develop a virtual community of followers (Butticè et al., 2017), which provides a valuable source of information for those who are in the process of testing and improving early versions of innovative products. This holds true for both reward-based and donation-based campaigns (Dushnitsky & Marom, 2013; Hui et al., 2014) and for equity-based campaigns (Agrawal et al., 2014; Di Pietro et al., 2017). Users typically highlight defects, suggest product improvements, and provide feedback that reduce the development time and costs and eventually take the product to a higher quality level, thus making it ready for the mass market. In reward-based crowdfunding, sometimes fundraisers even ask the crowdfunders to participate in the development of products/services after the end of the campaign, but before actual product shipment, eventually becoming co-creators of the product. Even when the involvement of the customer base is minimal, the campaign proves useful as a means of marketing (Belleflamme et al., 2013; Gerber & Hui, 2013), and to test customers' willingness to pay (Belleflamme et al., 2013, 2014). In equity-based crowdfunding, it has been proved that fundraisers can use campaigns to gain information about the size of the potential demand (Agrawal et al., 2014) and that crowdfunders can occasionally become involved in the management of the firm (Di Pietro et al., 2017), but this does not appear to be the norm. Collectively, a successful crowdfunding campaign can serve as a means to help start-ups and entrepreneurs to achieve legitimacy (Frydrych et al., 2014), learn about the market, and improve the attractiveness in the eyes of other potential funders, like venture capitalists or business angels.

In terms of measuring crowdfunding success, one main metric is meeting the target amount within the project duration, i.e., raising at least the amount of money stated as the campaign goal within the time span of the campaign (Colombo et al., 2015b). However, this definition of success applies only to *all or nothing* campaigns. As these campaigns have a clear-cut definition of success, scholars have devoted to them the bulk of their research effort. Virtually all of the empirical papers studying the determinants of crowdfunding success included in this review adopt a notion of success based on meeting the target amount (e.g., Boeuf et al., 2014; Agrawal et al., 2015). To the best of our knowledge, only a few scholars make a step forward to consider other dimensions of success. These include (i) the total amount of capital raised (e.g., Belleflamme et al., 2013; Colombo et al., 2015b), (ii) the total number of crowdfunders (e.g., Colombo et al., 2015b), and (iii) the speed of investments (specifically the equity-based study by Ahlers et al., 2015). Nonetheless, these metrics would be incapable of measuring success in terms of the feedback and overall legitimacy that a campaign might bring. Consequently, we encourage scholars to identify measures of success capable of representing non-monetary benefits. Based on the nature of existing studies, in the remainder of this paragraph, we review these studies referring to the basic definition of success: reaching the target capital.

It is worth stressing that, so far, few studies have looked at equity-based crowdfunding. Those that did[5] produced results consistent with the literature on donation- and reward-based crowdfunding. For these reasons in the remainder of the chapter, we refer directly to the literature on donation- and reward-based crowdfunding and highlight, whenever available, whether the results would also extend to equity-based crowdfunding.

The Main Features of a Crowdfunding Campaign

Crowdfunding campaigns encompass several features. In this following, we introduce five main features, which have been shown to correlate with campaign success: (i) *typology of project content*, (ii) *target capital*, (iii) *duration of the campaign*, (iv) *rewards* (when present), and (v) *information made available*.

In terms of project content, crowdfunding spans a large number of categories and sectors. A significant number of projects are aimed at developing a product with a technological core (Colombo et al., 2015a; Mollick, 2016). Among these projects, the chances of being funded appears to depend in part on the type of innovation that is being developed (Chan & Parhankangas, 2017). Projects aimed at developing incremental innovations usually have favorable funding outcomes, possibly because their content is more directly understandable by the average crowdfunder. By contrast, projects that feature radical innovations have less favorable funding outcomes, possibly because they are riskier or because their content is more difficult to communicate to the crowd. Aside from technological projects, many projects have an orientation to sustainability. Calic & Mosakowski (2016) found that these projects have a higher chance of receiving funds. Finally, many crowdfunding campaigns aim at supporting *artistic works* (Galuszka & Bystrov, 2014), like for instance theatre (Beaulieu & Sarker, 2013; Bœuf et al., 2014; Josefy et al., 2017), dance, photography, movies (including documentary movies, Sørensen, 2012), and

---

[5] In our systematic search for crowdfunding papers, we found only fifteen papers specific to equity-based crowdfunding campaigns.

videogames. Other projects are about design (e.g., Beaulieu & Sarker, 2013), fashion and crafts, agriculture (Liao et al., 2015), food, and journalism (Jian & Usher, 2014; Jian & Shin, 2015). At the same time, many donation-based crowdfunding projects aim at covering personal medical expenses (Sisler, 2012) or at financing scientific research (Marshall, 2013; Marlett, 2015). An important criterion of distinction that has proved useful is whether the project is *non-profit* versus *for profit*, the former being found more likely to succeed than the latter (Pitschner & Pitschner-Finn, 2014; Liao et al., 2015).

Two further features of the campaign are the *target capital* and the *duration*, which consists in the time span over which the project is open for money collection. Scholars unanimously consider the setting of the right target capital as a crucial determinant of the success of the campaign. Indeed, consistent evidence exists that the target capital has a negative impact on a project's success, namely, the higher the target capital, the lower the probability of success (see e.g., Gleasure & Feller, 2014; Mollick, 2014; Zheng et al., 2014; Colombo et al., 2015b; Liao et al., 2015 among others). More specifically, the target capital influences the number of crowdfunders and the amount of money that these would pledge. Colombo et al. (2015b) have noted that crowdfunders increase with the target capital, but they provide smaller amounts of money. In addition, Frydrych et al. (2014) find that projects with higher target capital experience great difficulty in achieving legitimacy and their fundraisers have to make more effort to obtain funds. If we shift our attention to *duration*, we notice that scholars have come to opposite findings. Namely, Frydrych et al. (2014) and Mollick (2014) have found a negative relation between duration and the probability of success, while Liao et al. (2015) affirm that longer campaigns favor achievement of the target capital. This difference in results may depend on the country of analysis: United States for Frydrych and colleagues (2014) and for Mollick (2014), China for Liao and colleagues (2015). As confirmation of this, when comparing Chinese and United States contexts, Zheng et al. (2014) find a positive relation between duration and success in China, and a negative relation in the USA.

Rewards are another important feature of crowdfunding campaigns when they allow crowdfunders to choose from a menu of alternative rewards. According to prior empirical works (Gerber & Hui, 2013; Boeuf et al, 2014), the number and types of rewards seems to influence the success of a campaign. Bœuf and colleagues (2014) distinguish between two types of reward: *symbolic* rewards and *material* rewards. The former consist in acknowledging the crowdfunders for the support received. Acknowledgment can be given privately, for instance in the form of a thank-you email, or publicly, for instance by listing the crowdfunder's name on a website or in the credits of a movie (Butticè & Colombo, 2017). The latter consist in gadgets and gifts, or in a product, which is often the outcome of the project for which funding is sought.

Thürridl & Kamleitner (2016) recognize that projects aimed at financing social causes tend to offer symbolic rewards. By comparison, projects aimed at financing market products offer mainly material rewards (e.g., a product). Concerning the degree to which these two kinds of rewards could be a substitute for one another, Bœuf and colleagues (2014) find that the use of symbolic rewards in crowdfunding campaigns intended to finance theatre plays is valuable only in the case where the fundraiser offers no other material reward.

A fifth important feature for the success of a crowdfunding campaign consists in the amount and quality of the *information* made available by the fundraiser to potential crowdfunders. Several contributions have documented empirically that the amount and quality of information provided by fundraisers have a positive correlation with the probability of success (Gleasure & Feller, 2014; Burtch et al., 2015). For example, the odds of success are higher when fundraisers include links to external webpages and resources (Colombo et al., 2015b; Butticè et al., 2017), and provide frequent project updates throughout the duration of the campaign (Gleasure & Feller, 2014; Xu et al., 2014). These results hold also for equity-based campaigns (Block et al., 2016; Beckwith, 2016). Another strong predictor of success is the provision of videos (Mollick, 2014; Zvilichosky et al., 2015) and images in the project description (Colombo et al., 2015b). Dushnitsky & Marom (2013) note that effective videos tend to be short, smart, and targeted to potential crowdfunders and their motivations. Parhankangas & Renko (2017) show that using a simple and easily understandable language in the videos that pitch campaigns increases the probability of success for projects intended to support social causes, while this positive effect of videos tends to disappear in *for-profit* projects. The probability of success increases also when displaying the contributions already received (Colombo et al., 2015b). Finally, having comments posted in the project page correlates positively with crowdfunding success, but in this case the relation becomes negative if the number of comments becomes too large (Gleasure & Feller, 2014). To sum up, as noted by Ahlers and colleagues (2015), the positive relation between providing information and the probability of success depends on the reduction of information asymmetries between the fundraiser and the crowdfunders allowed by the disclosure of information. However, quite interestingly, the information provided might have drawbacks. For instance, an overly long text (Xu et al., 2014) and the existence of spelling errors relate negatively to success (Mollick, 2014). Finally, several recent studies also focus on linguistic cues as a factor that can potentially influence success, given the importance of the so-called *entrepreneurial narrative* in the judgement formation of the crowdfunders (Kim et al., 2016). Manning & Bejarano (2017) maintain that there are two basic narrative styles, which they call "ongoing journeys" and "results-in-progress," and that successful project pitches often combine both these styles. The "ongoing journey" style centers around a long-term bold vision. The "results-in-progress" style is anchored to the present reality and describes the technological

merit of the project. Mitra & Gilbert (2014) focus on a different textual charac-
teristic and highlight the importance of language as a means to persuade and to
generate a sense of reciprocity in crowdfunding projects. In this respect, Tirdatov
(2014) identifies twenty-one categories of rhetorical appeals frequently reported
in successful projects. These rhetorical appeals are ascribable to the three Aris-
toteles' means of persuasion: *ethos* (i.e., the way to achieve credibility), *pathos*
(i.e., the way to produce emotions in the audience), and *logos* (i.e., logical
arguments to support the claims).

Fundraiser Motivations and Characteristics

Fundraisers have a key role in crowdfunding, being those who give rise to
crowdfunding campaigns. In the following, we review the studies that have
analyzed fundraisers' motivations and characteristics, highlighting how these
affect the success of crowdfunding campaigns.

The literature has discussed several reasons for using crowdfunding instead
of traditional ways of funding. First, fundraisers see crowdfunding as a way
of overcoming difficulties in accessing traditional sources of financing.
Crowdfunding is indeed an (apparently) easy, safe, and well-organized way
to raise money and thus it is extremely valuable for those who are not able
to obtain funds from banks, venture capitalists, or business angels (Gerber &
Hui, 2013; Kim & Hann, 2014; Mollick, 2014; Mollick & Kuppuswamy, 2014;
Fleming & Sorenson, 2016). Through crowdfunding, fundraisers can reduce
the cost of capital (Agrawal et al., 2016) since they can search for finance on a
global scale, sell on the crowdfunding platform products for which traditional
markets are difficult to penetrate, and provide a greater amount of information to crowdfunders, thus increasing their willingness to pay (Agrawal et al.,
2015). Moreover, with crowdfunding, fundraisers can maintain control over
their product (Gerber & Hui, 2013) and simultaneously show to the traditional
financial operators that there is demand for their products (Hornuf &
Schwienbacher, 2014; Mollick, 2014; Colombo & Shafi, 2016). Second,
crowdfunding is a way of sharing creative ideas (Kuo & Gerber, 2012) and
obtaining feedback about products from the crowd of users of the Internet
(Dushnitsky & Marom, 2013). Third, crowdfunding is particularly valuable
for marketing purposes (Mollick, 2014; Mollick & Kuppuswamy, 2014). It
allows access to public attention (Lambert & Schwienbacher, 2010; Gerber &
Hui, 2013; Belleflame et al., 2014) and increases awareness around the
project. Through crowdfunding, fundraisers can obtain approval for themselves and their work (see again Gerber & Hui, 2013). They can learn new
communication skills, get in contact with other people, establish long-term
interactions (Kuo & Gerber, 2012; Gerber & Hui, 2013), and enlarge their
personal, business network (Schwienbacher & Larralde, 2010) and their fan

base (Gerber & Hui, 2013). However, in spite of all the aforementioned advantages, crowdfunding has some disadvantages, which may reduce fundraisers' willingness to resort to its use. For instance, fundraisers may fear public failure, or an inability to attract enough crowdfunders, and they may be scared by the time and effort required to attract a large crowd (Gerber & Hui, 2013). Even when they succeed in attracting this large crowd, fundraisers face high costs in managing their numerous crowdfunders, who (usually) provide only small amounts of money (Gerber & Hui, 2013).

Apart from studying their motivation, the literature has also devoted attention to the different kinds of fundraisers, noting that they may be individuals, teams, or organizations. Many fundraisers describe themselves as would-be entrepreneurs, aiming to collect funds to develop their business ideas (Jian & Shin, 2015), startups (Meer, 2014), corporations (Dushnitsky & Marom, 2013), charitable organizations (Meer, 2014), or other non-profit entities. Various studies exist on the diverse types of fundraisers, analyzing whether and how they have different likelihoods of success. Specifically, scholars have mainly investigated three features: the profit versus non-profit organizations, fundraiser gender (male versus female), and the role of fundraisers' social capital (Kim & Hann, 2014; Mollick, 2014).

Profit versus non-profit. In line with what has been highlighted previously, non-profit organizations usually tend to be more successful than for-profit ones (Belleflamme et al., 2013, 2014; Pitschner & Pitschner-Finn, 2014; Liao et al., 2015). One possible explanation is that non-profit organizations and projects are of broader interest or could potentially affect a larger share of society (Marshall, 2013; Belleflame et al., 2014). Another possible explanation is that non-profit organizations are usually more oriented towards the quality of their project, rather than purely on the collection of money. In so doing, they can attract a large share of crowdfunders who are not primarily motivated by monetary rewards, but by the social impact of the project (Belleflamme et al., 2014). However, in spite of achieving the target more easily, on average, non-profit projects appear to attract comparatively fewer crowdfunders and a lower amount of capital, compared with for-profit projects (Pitschner & Pitschner-Finn, 2014).

Male versus female. A growing stream of research has investigated gender issues in the crowdfunding realm. The topic is especially relevant in light of the known difficulties that women experience in raising finance through traditional sources (Kuppuswamy & Mollick, 2015; Greenberg & Mollick, 2017). Overall, studies on crowdfunding support the view that the gender of fundraisers matters in determining the outcome of a crowdfunding campaign (Frydrych et al., 2014; Kuppuswamy & Mollick, 2015; Greenberg & Mollick, 2017). Specifically, individual female fundraisers have higher success rates than their male counterparts (Frydrych et al., 2014; Colombo et al., 2015b; Greenberg & Mollick, 2017). Further works have looked at cases in which a team with or without women proposes a crowdfunding project (e.g., Greenberg & Mollick, 2017). It emerges that projects with at least one woman in the team of fundraisers perform better than projects proposed only by men. Specifically, the former have higher success rates and attract more female crowdfunders, especially in the case of technological projects (Greenberg & Mollick, 2017). The authors explain this result using what they term *activist choice homophily*. In areas where women are under-represented (e.g. technology), female crowdfunders would have a strong tendency to fund the few projects led by female fundraisers, making females comparatively more successful. This dynamic seems to exist also in equity crowdfunding (Vismara et al., 2016). However, scholars also notice that women are on average less likely to start and fund projects than men (Kuppuswamy & Mollick, 2015), and attribute this to lower confidence and hubris of women compared with men. These characteristics would contribute to reducing women's overall entrepreneurial activity. Specifically, low confidence prevents women from pursuing low-quality opportunities, while low hubris leads women to pursue fewer high-quality opportunities. Moreover, women are less likely than men to be serial fundraisers and rarely launch more than one campaign, irrespective of whether or not their prior campaigns were successful. These gender-associated differences hold consistently across different studies. The only exception is work by Radford (2016), which shows that in donation-based crowdfunding women are penalized when they have male-stereotypical job roles (e.g. college professors).

Fundraisers' social capital. A well-established stylized fact in the crowdfunding literature is that social capital, i.e. *networks, norms and social trust that facilitate coordination and cooperation for mutual benefit* (Putnam, 1995: 1), helps fundraisers to achieve success (Mollick, 2014; Zheng et al., 2014; Colombo et al., 2015b; Butticè et al., 2017). Contributions to this stream of research have looked at several different notions of social capital. Butticè and colleagues (2017) focus on social capital that accrues to serial crowdfunders from past campaigns and show that this social capital helps fundraisers to achieve funding, but the effect is short-lived and disappears quickly. By contrast, Colombo et al. (2015b) and Liao et al. (2015) distinguish between external and internal social capital, depending on whether the fundraisers have developed social capital outside or within the crowdfunding platform. Liao et al. (2015) find positive effects on success for both types of social capital, with the type of project moderating both of these effects. Conversely, Colombo et al. (2015b) do not find any direct effect from external social capital and show that higher internal social capital allows more crowdfunders to be obtained in the early stages of the campaign, which in turn is a strong predictor of success. These results are consistent in the literature on equity-based crowdfunding (Vismara, 2016b), the only exception being work by Ahlers et al. (2015) which shows that social capital has little or no impact on crowdfunding success.

Recent studies have turned their attention to a broader set of variables. A few new studies look at fundraisers' prior history (Polzin et al., 2017) and show that having prior experience within the crowdfunding platform (Butticè et al., 2017; Skirnevskiy et al., 2017) and in the entrepreneurial ecosystem (Courtney et al., 2017; Ralcheva & Roosenboom, 2017) eases the way to collection of funding. Two studies focus on the personality traits of fundraisers and how these relate to the odds of success. They find that success is more likely when the fundraiser shows openness (Thies et al., 2016) and conscientiousness (Bernardino & Santos, 2016). One study looks at fundraisers' race/ethnicity and points to a disadvantage for African-American fundraisers (Younkin & Kuppuswamy, 2017). Another study looked at the location of fundraisers in the USA and found that these reside also in locations that have traditionally being deserted by professional investors such as venture capitals (Sorenson et al., 2016).

THE ROLE OF CROWDFUNDERS

Crowdfunders are the engine behind crowdfunding campaigns and are a critical element of crowdfunding during and after the collection of financial resources (Hardy, 2013). However, only a few studies have examined crowdfunders and their relation with project success.

We have stressed before that the crowdfunder's role goes beyond the offering of financial contributions and extends to the provision of ideas (Gambardella, 2012) and feedback (Martin, 2012). In many cases, crowdfunders offer the initial customers' base to the fundraisers for testing completely new products (Ordanini et al., 2011), and sometimes they contribute to product design by becoming real co-developers (Gerber & Hui, 2013). In addition, those crowdfunders that back a project in the early days of a campaign work as predictors that reduce uncertainty (Burtch et al., 2013) and facilitate the attraction of further contributions (Colombo et al., 2015b). This effect depends on three different mechanisms: observational learning, word-of-mouth, and uncertainty reduction through extensive feedback. Observational learning occurs when the crowdfunders are unclear about the quality of a project and take the observation of large support from others as a signal of confidence in the quality of the project (Mohammadi & Shafi, 2015). Second, early crowdfunders trigger information cascades that generate word-of-mouth (Colombo et al., 2015b; Hornuf & Neuenkirch, 2016; Vismara, 2016a) around the project thanks also to social networks (Mollick, 2014). Finally, early contributions make immediately available suggestions and feedback that fundraisers use to modify their projects and meet the needs of a broader audience (Colombo et al., 2015b). These three mechanisms concur to explain why early crowdfunders are of crucial importance (Ordanini et al., 2011), and several studies have noted that they are closely associated with the overall success of a crowdfunding campaign. In this regard, Colombo et al. (2015b) document that, in the context of reward-based crowdfunding, contributions collected in the early days of a campaign have a strong positive effect on the probability of reaching the target capital. Vismara (2016a, b) obtains a similar result using data on equity-based crowdfunding. In addition, scholars in computer sciences have investigated the role of early crowdfunders on project success, finding results consistent with the managerial literature. Rao and colleagues (2014) build a metric based on the contributions collected in the first five days of the campaign and show that this correctly predicts 84% of successful campaigns. Similarly, Etter et al. (2013) propose a method for predicting the success of reward-based crowdfunding campaigns by utilizing the initial 15% of money inflows raised.

Researchers who have investigated patterns of contributions over the entire duration of crowdfunding campaigns typically report the existence of three distinct phases (Ordanini et al., 2011; Walsh, 2014; Kuppuswamy & Bayus, 2017). In the first phase, there is a quick and significant flow of contributions from crowdfunders, who often have kinship and friendship relationships with the fundraiser (Agrawal et al., 2015). In the same phase, additional support may come from other fundraisers from the same platform, drawn by feelings of reciprocity (Colombo et al., 2015b). In the second phase of the process, there are often fewer contributions and slow progress (Ordanini et al., 2011; Kuppuswamy & Bayus, 2015). This is a critical phase and only a minority of projects are able to avoid being stuck at this point (Ordanini et al., 2011). Those that succeed eventually enter the third and final phase, where there may be a rapid growth of contributions and the target is reached (Ordanini et al., 2011; Crosetto & Regner, 2014; Kuppuswamy & Bayus, 2017).

The emerging literature on crowdfunding calls for more research on the motivations that drive crowdfunders to support a campaign. At present, scholars have singled out five main possible motivations: *economic rewards, philanthropy, sense of community belonging, social recognition,* and *formalization of contracts.* These motivations seem to drive participation in both reward- (Gerber & Hui, 2013) and equity-based crowdfunding (Agrawal et al., 2014) but, to the best of our knowledge, no study has yet quantified their relative importance. In the following, we discuss the five motivations in detail.

Economic rewards. The first and possibly most obvious motivation for participating in a crowdfunding campaign is the desire to obtain an economic return. This motivation is relevant in the reward-based model, where crowdfunders obtain rewards in exchange for their contributions, and in equity-based, where crowdfunders become shareholders of the company (Ordanini et al., 2011).

Philanthropy. Many studies of online communities, such as those on the Open Source community (see von Krogh et al., 2012, for a comprehensive discussion), have reported that individuals contribute because of altruism and a desire to help others. It seems likewise plausible that altruism and philanthropy would play a role in crowdfunding, especially for projects supporting social causes and for donation-based crowdfunding (Agrawal et al., 2014). Philanthropy has thus an intrinsic nature (Deci, 1980) and has much in common with the psychological factors that influence decisions on charitable giving (Agrawal et al., 2014). Interviews with crowdfunders indicate that they report feelings of satisfaction and pleasure from the realization of the projects they have supported (Hemer, 2011), especially when they have actively contributed to the success by sharing their knowledge with the fundraisers (Zheng et al., 2014). Philanthropy appears to be important especially when support is sought by fundraisers with whom the crowdfunder feel they have some connection (Hemer, 2011), and when support is sought for social causes that are perceived to be aligned with their own identity (Gerber & Hui, 2013). Interestingly enough, preliminary results also seem to confirm the importance of philanthropic motivations in the case of equity crowdfunding. Indeed, crowdfunders, driven by the intent of contributing to the diffusion of innovations are especially committed to the funding of innovative products (Agrawal et al., 2014).

Sense of community belonging. Gerber & Hui (2013) report that many crowdfunders contribute to crowdfunding campaigns for the sake of feeling part of a community. For these individuals, contributing is a way to express feelings of belonging to or membership of a group (Ordanini et al., 2011). The prominence of these motivations is evidenced when several crowdfunders publish the logo of a project on their Facebook profile (Harms, 2007) or buy gadgets or apparel (e.g. a T-shirt or hat) that display the logo (Colombo et al., 2015b).

Social recognition. Several studies have suggested that aiming to improve one's social position among crowdfunding users may contribute to driving participation in a campaign. Crowdfunders may indeed envisage the campaign as a means of obtaining reputational gain (Burtch et al., 2015) and social recognition (Agrawal et al., 2014). For example, some could be driven by the desire to be part of the elite of pioneer early adopters of a new product or new technology (Hemer, 2011). Along this line of reasoning, Burtch et al. (2013) have noted that the visibility of contributions to peers increases the level of satisfaction of some crowdfunders.

Formalization of contracts. This motivation is an important driver in supporting the participation of fundraisers' families and friends (Agrawal et al., 2015). In this respect, crowdfunding is one way of transforming a liberality or an act of friendship into a legal obligation (Frydrych et al., 2014). This helps to mitigate concerns of crowdfunders and fundraisers that participation would jeopardize friendship (Agrawal et al., 2014).

Fundraiser–Crowdfunder Interactions

Here we describe how relations between the fundraiser and crowdfunders influence the likelihood of obtaining sufficient money to fund a project.

We start by looking at the proximity of the two parties and we then conclude considering other forms of fundraiser/crowdfunder relationships.

A large literature has shown that the geographical proximity of the parties of a transaction influences the transaction itself. This also seems to hold in the case of crowdfunding, despite the omnipresent reach of the Internet. Specifically, evidence exists that local crowdfunders contribute earlier in campaigns and, when making their funding decisions, they attach less importance to the amount that fundraisers have already collected. However, the debate on the role of geography in crowdfunding is still ongoing. Agrawal and colleagues (2015) argue that crowdfunding reduces distance-related economic frictions, such as monitoring and due diligence, and observe that the effect of geographical proximity depends on crowdfunders who have personal connections with the fundraisers and live close to them. In their study of funding dynamics in Brazil, Mendes-Da-Silva and colleagues (2015) highlight a negative association between fundraiser/crowdfunder geographical distance and the value of contributions. They find that long-distance crowdfunders contribute smaller sums to projects. Hornuf & Schmitt (2016) obtain a similar result in the context of equity-based crowdfunding. Furthermore, Günther and colleagues (2016) note that geographical distance is negatively correlated with investments within the home country of the fundraiser, while potential investors that are in a different country are no longer sensitive to geographic distance. Originally, Giudici et al. (2017) focus on the role of the characteristics of the local area where crowdfunders reside. Focusing on entrepreneurial projects posted on reward-based platforms, the authors find that fundraisers who reside in areas where people have high levels of altruism are more likely to succeed; thus supporting the view that geography matters in crowdfunding.

Research on relationships between fundraisers and crowdfunders does not take into account only the geographical dimension. Social proximity or homophily appears to matter. Evidence exist that fundraising is easier when fundraisers and crowdfunders have similar occupational and/or educational backgrounds (Jian & Shin, 2015). Results on gender homophily are less clear. Greenberg & Mollick (2017) find that women outperform men in fields that are largely male-dominated. This result stands in stark contrast to expectations concerning homophily, but could likewise be explained by female crowdfunders funding female fundraisers (Greenberg & Mollick, 2017). Contrary to this argument, the work of Mohammadi & Shafi (2015) highlights the tendency of women to invest in equity-based projects in which the proportion of male investors is comparatively higher.

Finally, fundraiser–crowdfunder interactions that occur within crowdfunding platforms may also affect the probability of success. Colombo and colleagues (2015b) show that fundraisers with a track record of support for prior projects have a comparatively greater chance of success net of their prior experience on the platform. The authors propose that this effect likely depends on feelings of direct or indirect reciprocity. Similarly, Xu et al. (2014) highlight that fundraisers that interact with crowdfunders by providing reminders and updates on the progress of the projects have a greater chance of success in collecting funds.

CONCLUSIONS AND FUTURE RESEARCH

Moving from an updated definition of crowdfunding, which incorporates the latest insights of scholarly research on the topic, this chapter offers a comprehensive review of the existing literature on the drivers of success of crowdfunding projects. The review shows that the debate on this topic is still in its infancy. Many studies end in opposite results and adopt diverse conceptual lenses, methodologies, and test-beds, thus raising concern about their generalizability.

As with any research, this work has limitations, which open up avenues for future research. First, in identifying articles to be included in our literature review, we used only the keyword "crowdfunding." It is the broadest possible keyword and additional keywords might also be relevant. Specifically, there might be articles belonging to different streams of literature and referring to neighboring phenomena, which could be of help in understanding how crowdfunding works. Second, we focus attention on the determinants of crowdfunding project success in terms of their achievement of the target capital. In so doing, we disregard other kinds of crowdfunding success, such as, for instance, the success of the crowdfunding platforms or of the projects in terms of market acceptance. Therefore, we welcome future research that extends this work in this direction and takes in to account other success dimensions. In spite of these limitations, this chapter also highlights several areas in need of further investigation. Accordingly, we sketch here a research agenda that serves as a starting point for identifying new lines of inquiry. To this end, we highlight factors influencing funding success that scholars have so far largely neglected. Then, we stress the importance of inquiring about what happens after the end of the crowdfunding campaign. Providing an exhaustive list of research topics is beyond our scope, we only wish to call readers' attention to some existing gaps.

Extant literature on the determinants of the success of crowdfunding projects has mainly focused on understanding the role of the main actors involved during a crowdfunding campaign. In so doing, it has broadly under-remarked the role of the rewards. Although initial contributions have addressed this aspect (Bœuf et al., 2014; Frydrych et al., 2014), at present, the relative importance of various kinds of rewards has never taken central stage in the debate. We believe that a deeper empirical investigation of rewards can significantly advance the debate. This is especially true in reward-based crowdfunding, wherein fundraisers are encouraged by platforms to propose a variety of rewards to push crowdfunders' participation. As of now only a few, if any, studies have distinguished reward types. These studies hint that offering rewards that facilitate social interactions and social identification (e.g. official merchandising) correlate with the likelihood of success (Colombo et al., 2015b; Butticè & Colombo, 2017).

A second area of importance for future investigations relates to the post-campaign outcomes. The fact that crowdfunding provides a viable way to raise money for those who usually cannot raise money from traditional sources does not tell us much about the efficiency of crowdfunding in financing valuable projects. A related question is: would fundraisers be able accomplish the projects that they commit to? We know from the literature that fundraisers in reward-based crowdfunding deliver with large delays (Mollick, 2014; Kim et al., 2017), but we need to learn more in this regard.

Finally, it would be interesting to understand whether crowdfunding would be comparatively more likely than other sources of finance to support innovative or high-risk projects. As we have stressed in this chapter, crowd-funding seems a powerful financing mechanism for innovative projects because it provides a quick and effective means for testing and receiving feedback (Dushnitsky & Marom, 2013; Gerber & Hui, 2013). Industry experts and the popular press have stressed widely the claim that many of the most important projects—including novel 3-D printers, electronic watches, video game consoles, and computer hardware—were initially fund-ed by the crowd (Jeffries, 2013). Although this argument is plausible, few if any contributions have tried to confront this anecdotal evidence with rigorous empirical data.

We hope that this review of the literature will serve as a stimulus for continuing research in this interesting and relevant field.

REFERENCES

Afuah, A. (2018). Co-opetition in crowdsourcing: When simultaneous cooperation and competition deliver superior solutions. In C. Tucci, A. Afuah, & G. Viscusi (eds.), *Creating and Capturing Value Through Crowdsourcing*. Oxford: Oxford University Press, pp. 271–91.

Afuah, A. & Tucci, C. L. (2012). Crowdsourcing as a solution to distant search. *Academy of Management Review*, 37(3), 355–75.

Agrawal, A., Catalini, C., & Goldfarb, A. (2014). Some simple economics of crowd-funding. *Innovation Policy and the Economy*, 14(1), 63–97.

Agrawal, A., Catalini, C., & Goldfarb, A. (2015). Crowdfunding: Geography, social networks, and the timing of investment decisions. *Journal of Economics & Management Strategy*, 24(2), 253–74.

Agrawal, A., Catalini, C., & Goldfarb, A. (2016). Are syndicates the killer app of equity crowdfunding? *California Management Review, 58*(2), 111–24.

Ahlers, G. K., Cumming, D., Günther, C., & Schweizer, D. (2015). Signaling in equity crowdfunding. *Entrepreneurship Theory and Practice, 39*(4), 955–80.

Beaulieu, T. & Sarker, S. (2013). Discursive meaning creation in crowdfunding: A socio-material perspective, http://aisel.aisnet.org/icis2013/proceedings/ResearchInProgress/80

Beckwith, J. J. (2016). Predicting success in equity crowdfunding, http://repository.upenn.edu/joseph_wharton_scholars/25

Belleflamme, P., Lambert, T., & Schwienbacher, A. (2010). Crowdfunding: An industrial organization perspective. In preliminary paper prepared for the workshop, Digital Business Models: Understanding Strategies, Paris, June 25–26.

Belleflamme, P., Lambert, T., & Schwienbacher, A. (2013). Individual crowdfunding practices. *Venture Capital, 15*(4), 313–33.

Belleflamme, P., Lambert, T., & Schwienbacher, A. (2014). Crowdfunding: Tapping the right crowd. *Journal of Business Venturing, 29*(5), 585–609.

Bernardino, S. & Santos, J. F. (2016). Financing social ventures by crowdfunding: The influence of entrepreneurs' personality traits. *The International Journal of Entrepreneurship and Innovation, 17*(3), 173–83.

Block, J. H., Hornuf, L., & Moritz, A. (2016). Which updates during an equity crowdfunding campaign increase crowd participation? https://ssrn.com/abstract=2781715

Bœuf, B., Darveau, J., & Legoux, R. (2014). Financing creativity: Crowdfunding as a new approach for theatre projects. *International Journal of Arts, 16*(3), 33–48.

Burkett, E. (2011). A crowdfunding exemption-online investment crowdfunding and US securities regulation. *Transactions: Tenn. J. Bus. L., 13*(1), 63–106.

Burtch, G., Ghose, A., & Wattal, S. (2013). An empirical examination of the antecedents and consequences of contribution patterns in crowd-funded markets. *Information Systems Research, 24*(3), 499–519.

Burtch, G., Ghose, A., & Wattal, S. (2015). The hidden cost of accommodating crowdfunder privacy preferences: A randomized field experiment. *Management Science, 61*(5), 949–62.

Butticè, V. & Colombo, M. G. (2017). Industry specificity and the effect of internal social capital in reward-based crowdfunding, in S. Alvarez, G. Carayannis, E. G., Dagnino, G. B., & Faraci, R. (eds.). *Entrepreneurial Ecosystems and the Diffusion of Startups.* Cheltenham (UK): Edward Elgar.

Butticè, V., Colombo, M. G., & Wright, M. (2017). Serial crowdfunding, social capital, and project success. *Entrepreneurship Theory and Practice, 41*(2), 183–207.

Calic, G. & Mosakowski, E. (2016). Kicking off social entrepreneurship: How a sustainability orientation influences crowdfunding success. *Journal of Management Studies, 53*(5), 738–67.

Chan, C. S. & Parhankangas, A. (2017). Crowdfunding innovative ideas: How incremental and radical innovativeness influence funding outcomes. *Entrepreneurship Theory and Practice, 41*(2), 237–63.

Cholakova, M. & Clarysse, B. (2015). Does the possibility to make equity investments in crowdfunding projects crowd out reward-based investments? *Entrepreneurship Theory and Practice, 39*(1), 145–72.

Colombo, M. & Shafi, K. (2016). When does reward-based crowdfunding help firms obtain venture capital and angel finance? SSRN working paper, http://dx.doi.org/10.2139/ssrn.2785538

Colombo, M. G., Franzoni, C., & Rossi-Lamastra, C. (2015a). Cash from the crowd. *Science, 348*(6240), 1201.

Colombo, M. G., Franzoni, C., & Rossi-Lamastra, C. (2015b). Internal social capital and the attraction of early contributions in crowdfunding. *Entrepreneurship Theory and Practice, 39*(1), 75–100.

Courtney, C., Dutta, S., & Li, Y. (2017). Resolving information asymmetry: Signaling, endorsement, and crowdfunding success. *Entrepreneurship Theory and Practice, 41*(2), 265–90.

Crosetto, P. & Regner, T. (2014). Crowdfunding: Determinants of success and funding dynamics, http://www.econstor.eu/handle/10419/108542

Cumming, D. & Johan, S. (2013). Demand-driven securities regulation: Evidence from crowdfunding. *Venture Capital, 15*(4), 361–79.

Deci, E. L. (1980). *The Psychology of Self-Determination.* New York: Free Press.

Di Pietro, F., Prencipe, A., & Majchrzak, A. (2017). Crowd equity investors: An underutilized asset for open innovation in startups. *California Management Review,* 0008125617738260. ISO 690.

Dushnitsky, G. & Marom, D. (2013). Crowd monogamy. *Business Strategy Review, 24*(4), 24–6.

Dushnitsky, G., Guerini, M., Piva, E., & Rossi-Lamastra, C. (2016). Crowdfunding in Europe: Determinants of platform creation across countries. *California Management Review, 58*(2), 44–71.

Etter, V., Grossglauser, M., & Thiran, P. (2013). Launch hard or go home!: predicting the success of Kickstarter campaigns. *Proceeding COSN '13: Proceedings of the first ACM conference on Online social networks,* pp.177–82. Boston, MA, October 07–08, 2013, ACM, New York, NY. doi: 10.1145/2512938.2512957.

Fleming, L. & Sorenson, O. (2016). Financing by and for the masses. *California Management Review, 58*(2), 5–19.

Frydrych, D., Bock, A. J., Kinder, T., & Koeck, B. (2014). Exploring entrepreneurial legitimacy in reward-based crowdfunding. *Venture Capital, 16*(3), 247–69.

Galuszka, P. & Bystrov, V. (2014). The rise of fanvestors: A study of a crowdfunding community. *First Monday, 19*(5).

Gambardella, M. (2012). How to (crowd-) fund and manage the (user-) innovation: the case of Big Buck Bunny. *Proceeding OSDOC '12: Proceedings of the Workshop on Open Source and Design of Communication,* Lisboa, Portugal, June 11, 2012, ACM, New York, NY, pp. 51–6. doi: 10.1145/2316936.2316946.

Gerber, E. M. & Hui, J. (2013). Crowdfunding: Motivations and deterrents for participation. *ACM Transactions on Computer–Human Interaction (TOCHI), 20*(6), 1–31.

Giudici, G., Guerini, M., & Rossi-Lamastra, C. (2017). Reward-based crowdfunding of entrepreneurial projects: the effect of local altruism and localized social capital on proponents' success. *Small Business Economics,* pp.1–18, https://doi.org/10.1007/s11187-016-9830-x.

Gleasure, R. & Feller, J. (2014). Observations of non-linear information consumption in crowdfunding, in R. Prasath, P. O'Reilly, & T. Kathirvalavakumar (eds.). *Mining*

Intelligence and Knowledge Exploration. Cham ZG, Switzerland: Springer International Publishing, pp. 372–81.

Greenberg, J. & Mollick, E. R. (2017). Activist choice homophily and the crowdfunding of female founders. *Administrative Science Quarterly*, 62(2), 341–74.

Griffin, Z. J. (2012). Crowdfunding: Fleecing the American masses. *Case W. Res. JL Tech. & Internet*, 4(2), 375–403.

Günther, C., Johan, S., & Schweizer, D. (2016). Is the crowd sensitive to distance? How investment decisions differ by investor type, https://ssrn.com/abstract=2725463

Hardy, W. (2013). How to perfectly discriminate in a crowd? A theoretical model of crowdfunding, https://ideas.repec.org/p/war/wpaper/2013-16.html (accessed October 25, 2017).

Harms, M. (2007). What drives motivation to participate financially in a crowdfunding community? http://papers.ssrn.com/sol3/papers.cfm?abstract_id=2269242

Harrison, R. (2013). Crowdfunding and the revitalization of the early stage risk capital market: Catalyst or chimera? *Venture Capital*, 15(4), 283–7.

Hemer, J. (2011). A snapshot on crowdfunding, https://www.econstor.eu/handle/10419/52302

Hornuf, L. & Neuenkirch, M. (2016). Pricing shares in equity crowdfunding. *Small Business Economics*, 48(4): 795–811.

Hornuf, L. & Schmitt, M. (2016). Does a local bias exist in equity crowdfunding? The impact of investor types and portal design, https://ssrn.com/abstract=2801170

Hornuf, L. & Schwienbacher, A. (2014). Crowdinvesting—angel investing for the masses? https://ssrn.com/abstract=2401515

Howe, J. (2006). The rise of crowdsourcing. *Wired*, 14(6), 1–4.

Hui, J. S., Greenberg, M. D., & Gerber, E. M. (2014). Understanding the role of community in crowdfunding work. *Proceedings of the 17th ACM conference on Computer supported cooperative work & social computing*, CSCW, 62–74.

Jeffries, A. (2013). How Kickstarter stole CES: The rise of the indie hardware developer. *The Verge*, https://www.theverge.com/2013/1/10/3861406/kickstarter-at-ces (accessed October 25, 2017).

Jian, L. & Shin, J. (2015). Motivations behind donors' contributions to crowdfunded journalism. *Mass Communication and Society*, 18(2), 165–85.

Jian, L. & Usher, N. (2014). Crowd-funded journalism. *Journal of Computer-Mediated Communication*, 19(2), 155–70.

Josefy, M., Dean, T. J., Albert, L. S., & Fitza, M. A. (2017). The role of community in crowdfunding success: Evidence on cultural attributes in funding campaigns to "save the local theater." *Entrepreneurship Theory and Practice*, 41(2), 161–82.

Kappel, T. (2008). Ex ante crowdfunding and the recording industry: A model for the US. *Loy. LA Ent. L. Rev.*, 29, 375.

Kaufman, Z. D., Kassinger, T. W., & Traeger, H. L. (2013). Democratizing entrepreneurship: An overview of the past, present, and future of crowdfunding. *Bloomberg BNA Securities Regulation & Law Report*, 45(5), 208–17.

Kim, K. & Hann, I. H. (2014). Crowdfunding and the democratization of access to capital: A geographical analysis, http://papers.ssrn.com/sol3/papers.cfm?abstract_id=2334590

Kim, P. H., Buffart, M., & Croidieu, G. (2016). TMI: Signaling credible claims in crowdfunding campaign narratives. *Group & Organization Management, 41*(6), 717–50.

Kim, Y., Shaw, A., Zhang, H., & Gerber, E. (2017). Understanding trust amid delays in crowdfunding. *Proceeding CSCW '17: Proceedings of the 2017 ACM Conference on Computer Supported Cooperative Work and Social Computing*, Portland, OR, February 25–March 1, ACM New York, NY, pp. 1982–96, doi: 10.1145/2998181.2998207.

Koch, J. A. & Cheng, Q. (2016). The role of qualitative success factors in the analysis of crowdfunding success: Evidence from Kickstarter, https://ssrn.com/abstract=2808428

Kuo, P. Y. & Gerber, E. (2012). Design principles: Crowdfunding as a creativity support tool. In *CHI'12 Extended Abstracts on Human Factors in Computing Systems*, pp.1601–6, ACM (2012).

Kuppuswamy, V. & Bayus, B. L. (2015). Crowdfunding creative ideas: The dynamics of project backers in Kickstarter, https://papers.ssrn.com/sol3/papers.cfm?abstract_id=2234765

Kuppuswamy, V. & Bayus, B. L. (2017). Does my contribution to your crowdfunding project matter? *Journal of Business Venturing, 32*(1), 72–89.

Kuppuswamy, V. & Mollick, E. (2015). Hubris and humility: Gender differences in serial founding rates, http://papers.ssrn.com/sol3/papers.cfm?abstract_id=2623746

Lasrado, L. & Lugmayr, A. (2013). Crowdfunding in Finland a new alternative disruptive funding instrument for business. *Proceedings of International Conference on Making Sense of Converging Media*, October, pp. 194–207.

Lehner, O. M. (2012). A literature review and research agenda for crowdfunding of social ventures. In *Research Colloquium on Social Entrepreneurship*. Oxford: University of Oxford, Skoll Center of SAID Business School.

Liao, C., Zhu, Y., & Liao, X. (2015). The role of internal and external social capital in crowdfunding: Evidence from China. *Revista de Cercetare si Interventie Sociala, 49*, 187–204.

Löher, J. (2017). The interaction of equity crowdfunding platforms and ventures: An analysis of the preselection process. *Venture Capital, 19*(1–2), 51–74.

Manning, S. & Bejarano, T. A. (2017). Convincing the crowd: Entrepreneurial storytelling in crowdfunding campaigns. *Strategic Organization, 15*(2), 194–219.

Marlett, D. (2015). Crowdfunding art, science and technology: A quick survey of the burgeoning new landscape. *Leonardo, 48*(1), 104–5.

Marshall, J. (2013). Kickstart your research. *Proceedings of the National Academy of Sciences, 110*(13), 4857–9.

Martin, T. A. (2012). The JOBS Act of 2012: Balancing fundamental securities law principles with the demands of the crowd, http://papers.ssrn.com/sol3/Papers.cfm?abstract_id=2040953

Meer, J. (2014). Effects of the price of charitable giving: Evidence from an online crowdfunding platform. *Journal of Economic Behavior & Organization, 103*, 113–24.

Mendes-Da-Silva, W., Rossoni, L., Conte, B. S., Gattaz, C. C., & Francisco, E. R. (2015). The impacts of fundraising periods and geographic distance on financing music production via crowdfunding in Brazil. *Journal of Cultural Economics*, *39*(2), 1–25.

Miglo, A. (2016). Crowdfunding: Balancing imperfect information and moral hazard considerations, https://ssrn.com/abstract=2793631

Mitra, D. (2012). The role of crowdfunding in entrepreneurial finance. *Delhi Business Review*, *13*(2), 67–72.

Mitra, T. & Gilbert, E. (2014). The language that gets people to give: Phrases that predict success on Kickstarter. *Proceeding CSCW '14: Proceedings of the 17th ACM Conference on computer Supported Cooperative Work & Social Computing*, pp. 49–61. Baltimore, MD, February 15–19, ACM, New York, NY doi: 10.1145/2531602.2531656.

Mohammadi, A. & Shafi, K. (2015). The contribution patterns of equity-crowdfunding investors: Gender, risk aversion and observational learning, https://static.sys.kth.se/itm/wp/cesis/cesiswp419.pdf

Mollick, E. (2014). The dynamics of crowdfunding: An exploratory study. *Journal of Business Venturing*, *29*(1), 1–16.

Mollick, E. (2016). Containing multitudes: The many impacts of Kickstarter funding, https://ssrn.com/abstract=2808000

Mollick, E. & Kuppuswamy, V. (2014). After the campaign: Outcomes of crowdfunding, https://ssrn.com/abstract=2376997

Mollick, E. & Robb, A. (2016). Democratizing innovation and capital access. *California Management Review*, *58*(2), 72–87.

Ordanini, A., Miceli, L., Pizzetti, M., & Parasuraman, A. (2011). Crowd-funding: Transforming customers into investors through innovative service platforms. *Journal of Service Management*, *22*(4), 443–70.

Parhankangas, A. & Renko, M. (2017). Linguistic style and crowdfunding success among social and commercial entrepreneurs. *Journal of Business Venturing*, *32*(2), 215–36.

Pitschner, S. & Pitschner-Finn, S. (2014). Non-profit differentials in crowd-based financing: Evidence from 50,000 campaigns. *Economics Letters*, *123*(3), 391–4.

Polzin, F., Toxopeus, H., & Stam, E. (2017). The wisdom of the crowd in funding: Information heterogeneity and social networks of crowdfunders. *Small Business Economics*, https://link.springer.com/article/10.1007/s11187-016-9829-3

Putnam, R. D. (1995). Bowling alone: America's declining social capital. *Journal of Democracy*, *6*(1), 65–78.

Radford, J. S. (2016). The emergence of gender inequality in a crowdfunding market: An experimental test of gender system theory, https://ssrn.com/abstract=2804265

Ralcheva, A. & Roosenboom, P. (2016). On the road to success in equity crowdfunding, https://ssrn.com/abstract=2727742

Ramos, J. & González, B. (2016). Crowdfunding and employment: An analysis of the employment effects of crowdfunding in Spain, in D. Brüntje & O. Gajda (eds.). *Crowdfunding in Europe: State of the Art in Theory and Practice*. Cham ZG, Switzerland: Springer International Publishing.

Rao, H., Xu, A., Yang, X., & Fu, W. T. (2014). Emerging dynamics in crowdfunding campaigns, in W. G. Kennedy, N. Agarwal & S. J. Yang (eds). *Social Computing*,

Behavioral-Cultural Modeling and Prediction. SBP. Lecture Notes in Computer Science, vol. 8393. Cham, Switzerland: Springer International Publishing, pp. 333–40

Riedl, J. (2013). Crowdfunding technology innovation. *Computer, 46*(3), 100–3.

Robinson, M. S. (2001). *The Microfinance Resolution: Suitable Finance for the Poor.* Washington, DC: World Bank.

Schwienbacher, A. & Larralde, B. (2010). Crowdfunding of small entrepreneurial ventures, https://ssrn.com/abstract=1699183

Short, J. C., Ketchen, D. J., McKenny, A. F., Allison, T. H., & Ireland, R. D. (2017). Research on crowdfunding: Reviewing the (very recent) past and celebrating the present. *Entrepreneurship Theory and Practice, 41*(2), 149–60.

Sisler, J. (2012). Crowdfunding for medical expenses. *Canadian Medical Association Journal, 184*(2), E123–4.

Skirnevskiy, V., Bendig, D., & Brettel, M. (2017). The influence of internal social capital on serial creators' success in crowdfunding. *Entrepreneurship Theory and Practice, 41*(2), 209–36.

Sørensen, I. E. (2012). Crowdsourcing and outsourcing: The impact of online funding and distribution on the documentary film industry in the UK. *Media, Culture & Society, 34*(6), 726–43.

Sorenson, O., Assenova, V., Li, G-C., Boada, J., & Fleming, L. (2016). Expand innovation finance via crowdfunding. *Science, 354*(6319), 1526–8.

Šundić, M. & Leitner, K-H. (2018). Co-creation from a telecommunication provider's perspective: A comparative study on innovation with customers and employees. In C. Tucci, A. Afuah, & G. Viscusi (eds.), *Creating and Capturing Value Through Crowdsourcing*. Oxford: Oxford University Press, pp. 236–70.

The Economist (2013). Winning over the crowd: What works, and what doesn't, on the biggest crowdfunding site, http://www.economist.com/blogs/graphicdetail/2013/01/daily-chart-12

Thies, F., Wessel, M., Rudolph, J., & Benlian, A. (2016). Personality matters: How signaling personality traits can influence the adoption and diffusion of crowdfunding campaigns, http://aisel.aisnet.org/ecis2016_rp/36

Thürridl, C. & Kamleitner, B. (2016). What goes around comes around? *California Management Review, 58*(2), 88–110.

Tirdatov, I. (2014). Web-based crowd funding: Rhetoric of success. *Technical Communication, 61*(1), 3–24.

Tomczak, A. & Brem, A. (2013). A conceptualized investment model of crowdfunding. *Venture Capital, 15*(4), 335–59.

Vismara, S. (2016a). Equity retention and social network theory in equity crowdfunding. *Small Business Economics, 46*(4), 579–90.

Vismara, S. (2016b). Information cascades among investors in equity crowdfunding. *Entrepreneurship Theory and Practice*, http://onlinelibrary.wiley.com/doi/10.1111/etap.12261/full

Vismara, S., Benaroio, D., & Carne, F. (2016). Gender in entrepreneurial finance: Matching investors and entrepreneurs in equity crowdfunding, in A. Link (ed.). *Gender and Entrepreneurial Activity*. Cheltenham, UK: Edward Elgar.

von Krogh, G., Rossi-Lamastra, C., & Haefliger, S. (2012). Phenomenon-based research in management and organization science: When is it rigorous and does it matter? *Long Range Planning, 45*(4), 277–98.

Walsh, A. (2014). Seek! Creating and crowdfunding a game-based open educational resource to improve information literacy. *Insights: the UKSG Journal, 27*(1), 63–7.

Wash, R. & Solomon, J. (2011). Crowdfunding and the return rule: Reducing risk but increasing spread. Working paper, Michigan State University.

West, J. & Sims, J. (2018). How firms leverage crowds and communities for open innovation. In C. Tucci, A. Afuah, & G. Viscusi (eds.), *Creating and Capturing Value Through Crowdsourcing*. Oxford: Oxford University Press, pp. 58–96.

Xu, A., Yang, X., Rao, H., Fu, W. T., Huang, S. W., & Bailey, B. P. (2014). Show me the money! An analysis of project updates during crowdfunding campaigns. *Proceeding, CHI '14: Proceedings of the SIGCHI Conference on Human Factors in Computing Systems*, pp. 591–600. Toronto, ON, April 26–May 1, ACM, New York, NY. doi: 10.1145/2556288.2557045.

Younkin, P. & Kuppuswamy, V. (2017). Is the crowd colorblind? Founder race and performance in crowdfunding. *Management Science*, http://pubsonline.informs.org/doi/abs/10.1287/mnsc.2017.2774

Zheng, H., Li, D., Wu, J., & Xu, Y. (2014). The role of multidimensional social capital in crowdfunding: A comparative study in China and US. *Information & Management, 51*(4), 488–96.

Zvilichovsky, D., Inbar, Y., & Barzilay, O. (2015). Playing both sides of the market: Success and reciprocity on crowdfunding platforms, https://ssrn.com/abstract=2304101

Part II

Tournament-Based Crowdsourcing

6

A Problem in the Making: How Firms Formulate Sharable Problems for Open Innovation Contests

Martin W. Wallin, Georg von Krogh, and Jan Henrik Sieg

Abstract

Crowdsourcing in the form of innovation contests stimulates knowledge creation external to the firm by distributing technical, innovation-related problems to external solvers and by proposing a fixed monetary reward for solutions. While prior work demonstrates that innovation contests can generate solutions of value to the firm, little is known about how problems are formulated for such contests. We investigate problem formulation in a multiple exploratory case study of seven firms and inductively develop a theoretical framework that explains the mechanisms of formulating sharable problems for innovation contests. The chapter contributes to the literatures on crowdsourcing and open innovation by providing a rare account of the intra-organizational implications of engaging in innovation contests and by providing initial clues to problem formulation—a critical antecedent to firms' ability to leverage external sources of innovation.

INTRODUCTION

During new product development, firms must solve numerous technical, innovation-related problems such as design flaws, glitches in pilot-production, and process or performance shortcomings in product upgrades. As a result, innovation has often been characterized as a problem-solving process (see e.g. Allen, 1966; Iansiti & Clark, 1994; Pisano, 1996; Thomke, 2003; Terwiesch, 2008; Foss et al., 2016). In the post World War II period, firms relied heavily on their own capabilities to solve innovation-related problems (Chandler,

1977; Langlois, 2003). Today, firms increasingly solve problems through engaging with knowledgeable outsiders, such as customers, suppliers, and technical experts. Indeed, the appeal of crowdsourcing very much rests on the idea of "tap[ping] the latent talent of the crowd" (Howe, 2006). However, in this chapter we will develop an argument that successful crowdsourcing is less about *tapping* latent talent and more about *enticing* outside talent to solve a particular problem. In particular, we will demonstrate that problem formulation may be a critical antecedent to successful crowdsourcing.

Crowdsourcing is a means of solving problems by outsourcing a task to a crowd through an open call (Howe, 2006, 2008; Jeppesen & Lakhani, 2010; Afuah & Tucci, 2012). This "open innovation" process (Chesbrough, 2003; Langlois, 2003; von Hippel, 2005; Laursen & Salter, 2006; Chesbrough et al., 2008; Mowery, 2009; Dahlander & Gann, 2010) entails "finding creative ways to exploit internal innovation, incorporating external innovation into internal development, and motivating outsiders to supply an ongoing stream of external innovations" (West & Gallagher, 2006: 319). "Open innovation contests" (hereafter "innovation contests") is a form of crowdsourcing where firms stimulate problem solving by "broadcasting" (Lakhani et al., 2007; Jeppesen & Lakhani, 2010) a problem statement to a very large pool of self-selecting outside solvers and by proposing a monetary reward for solutions (Terwiesch & Xu, 2008; Jeppesen & Lakhani, 2010; Sieg et al., 2010; Boudreau et al., 2011; Afuah, 2018).

Innovation contests are currently making successful inroads into private as well as public sectors (Tapscott & Williams, 2006; National Research Council, 2007; McKinsey & Company, 2009; White House, 2010). For example, the X Prize Foundation offered $10 million for the first flight to an altitude of 100 kilometers, Netflix awarded $1 million to the team of researchers that managed to substantially improve the accuracy of the company's movie recommendation algorithm, and the DARPA Grand Challenges encourage the development of autonomous robotic vehicles. Publicly known examples of leading firms using contests to address pressing issues are Eli Lilly, Dow AgroSciences, Audi, Shell, and Pepsi.[1] The trend towards outside problem solving has also given rise to specialized intermediaries such as InnoCentive, NineSigma, and Idea Crossing, that provide platforms, support, and consultation for innovation contests.[2]

While prior research has contributed greatly to the understanding of design and effectiveness of innovation contests (e.g. Taylor, 1995; Che & Gale, 2003; Schottner, 2008; Terwiesch & Xu, 2008; Jeppesen & Lakhani, 2010; Boudreau

---

[1] See e.g. http://www.xprize.org http://www.darpa.mil/news-events/2014-03-13 http://www.ideaconnection.com/contests/contest (accessed May 29, 2017).

[2] http://www.innocentive.com   http://www.ninesigma.com   http://www.ideacrossing.org (accessed May 29, 2017).

et al., 2011), surprisingly little is known about how firms formulate the problems that set them off. This is an important gap considering that problem statements are "sine qua non" of innovation contests (Jeppesen & Lakhani, 2010: 1018). Similarly, received literature on how firms leverage external sources of innovation largely omits problem formulation and jumps to the question of how firms search, source, incentivize, and contract for innovation (see West & Bogers, 2014 for a review). As we will show, since neither the existing literature on innovation contests nor the encompassing open innovation literature offer a theoretical basis for approaching problem formulation for innovation contests, we briefly review two literature streams in organization theory that explicitly deal with innovation-related problem formulation and explore to what degree they can account for problem formulation for innovation contests.

LITERATURE REVIEW

Innovation Contests

Innovation contests are a form of crowdsourcing where a firm (the seeker) "broadcasts" (Jeppesen & Lakhani, 2010) a written problem statement to self-selecting external problem solvers and proposes a fixed monetary reward for solutions meeting pre-specified criteria (Taylor, 1995; Che & Gale, 2003; Schottner, 2008; Terwiesch & Xu, 2008). Innovation contests have mostly been used to solve "technical, innovation-related" problems (von Hippel, 1994), such as the need for a novel method to ensure the authenticity of a recycled PET polymer for fabric uses; the need for a computer algorithm to simulate insect behavior in response to a new pesticide used on wheat; and the specification of a new synthesis route for a chemical compound that satisfies specific criteria in terms of yield, purity, and cost. Innovation contests for such problems use "targeted prizes" posted ex ante, as opposed to "blue-sky prizes" which provide ex post rewards to innovation (Scotchmer, 2004); this chapter is only concerned with the former, which requires a written problem statement to run. Another central feature is that seekers either organize innovation contests themselves (as in the case of P&G's Connect and Develop program, see Huston & Sakkab, 2006), or employ an innovation intermediary that maintains a large network of external problem solvers and consults seeker firms on how to effectively leverage innovation contests (Jeppesen & Lakhani, 2010; Sieg et al., 2010).

Innovation contests may offer significant rewards for firms (Green & Stokey, 1983; Taylor, 1995; Fullerton & McAfee, 1999; Che & Gale, 2003; Maurer & Scotchmer, 2004; Schottner, 2008; Terwiesch & Xu, 2008; Jeppesen & Lakhani, 2010; Boudreau et al., 2011): (a) The seeker only pays for solutions meeting its performance criteria and thus shifts the cost of failures (e.g. the sunk costs of problem-solving efforts) to external problem solvers; (b) the seeker stimulates external problem solvers, who often outnumber internal staff by far, to exert massively parallel problem solving efforts and thus potentially decreasing the time to find a solution; (c) the seeker stimulates problem solvers with heterogeneous knowledge sets and may thus profit from more diverse solutions than could be generated internally.

Critical to our analysis, innovation contests imply a split of the seeker firm's innovation process into problem formulation inside the firm and problem solving outside the firm by external solvers. The internal problem formulation process needs to generate problem statements, indicating what problems the seeker wants solved, i.e. written descriptions of the problems and criteria for the desired solutions (Lakhani et al., 2007; Terwiesch & Xu, 2008). The statements are the "sine qua non" (Jeppesen & Lakhani, 2010: 1018) of innovation contests since solvers rely on them when developing solutions and since the statements are usually the only piece of information solvers receive from seekers (see e.g. Terwiesch & Xu, 2008; Jeppesen & Lakhani, 2010; Sieg et al., 2010). Existing research on contest design has largely adopted an economic perspective, addressing issues such as the optimal number of problem solvers (Fullerton & McAfee, 1999; Che & Gale, 2003; Terwiesch & Xu, 2008; Boudreau et al., 2011;), award structure (Taylor, 1995; Terwiesch & Xu, 2008), and the relative benefits of contests as incentive mechanisms (McLaughlin, 1988; Glazer & Hassin, 1988; Maurer & Scotchmer, 2004). Recently, researchers have also investigated innovation contests from an organizational perspective, shedding light on questions such as the problem solving effectiveness of innovation contests (Jeppesen & Lakhani, 2010) and managerial challenges for seeker firms (Sieg et al., 2010). However, to our knowledge, existing theory and research has not yet addressed the issue of problem formulation for innovation contests.

Cognizing Problems or Constructing Problems?

Two streams of literature on organization theory provide competing perspectives on problem formulation for innovation contests: the cognitivist perspective (e.g. March & Simon, 1958/1993; Cyert & March, 1963; Simon, 1996; Nickerson & Zenger, 2004; Felin & Zenger, 2012); and the constructionist perspective (e.g. Nonaka, 1994; von Hippel & Tyre, 1995; Carlile, 2002; Bechky, 2003; Nonaka & von Krogh, 2009). The cognitivist perspective holds that problems are abstract, universal, and objective cognitive representations by problem solvers, and views problem formulation as a by-product of problem solving. Managers deliberately select or stumble upon problems and subsequently organize the search for solutions (Cohen et al., 1972; Nickerson & Zenger, 2004; Hsieh et al., 2007). In contrast, the constructionist perspective views problems as

pieces of subjectively held knowledge (Landry, 1995) that are actively formulated by applying, integrating, and creating knowledge.

Cognizing problems is a powerful image when problems have clear solution
criteria and a given set of permissible solution moves within a solution space
(Newell & Simon, 1972; Kotovsky et al., 1985), or when problem solvers start
with an initial problem representation, develop a first solution, generate additional information about the problem by testing the solution, and adapt
representations based on new information (Simon, 1977; Kulkarni & Simon,
1988; Fernandes & Simon, 1999; Klahr & Simon, 1999). The problem statement
is here a cognitive or symbolic "representation" of a solution space (Fernandes
& Simon, 1999). The cognitivist perspective can under certain conditions
account for solving both simple puzzles such as "Missionaries and Cannibals"
and complex and "ill-structured" problems (Simon, 1973). Indeed, decades of
work on problem solving in innovation rests upon this basic perspective (e.g.
Nelson & Winter, 1977; Nelson, 1982; Loch et al., 2001; Thomke & Bell, 2001).
However, the perspective may be less useful when accounting for problem
formulation as separate and precursory to problem solving, as the two processes
are assumed to co-evolve.

Constructing problems is an alternative image that does not assume problems to be abstract, universal, and objective representations. The constructionist
perspective on problem formulation can be traced back to the knowledge-based
view of the firm (Kogut & Zander, 1992; Grant, 1996; Spender, 1996; Tsoukas,
1996), research on adaptive learning (von Hippel & Tyre, 1995; Tyre & von
Hippel, 1997), the concept of communities of practice (Brown & Duguid, 1991,
2001), and organizational knowledge creation theory (Nonaka, 1994; Nonaka &
von Krogh, 2009). In sum, problem-related knowledge depends on the physical,
social, and technical context in which the problem is encountered (Dougherty,
1992; von Hippel & Tyre, 1995; Carlile, 2002; Bechky, 2003). Tyre & von Hippel
(1997) stress that different physical contexts provide individuals with clues
about the problem and opportunities to use their tacit problem-solving
skills. Problem-related knowledge is therefore tacit or "sticky." What an individual tacitly knows about a problem in one context cannot be shared with
individuals in another context without effort; knowledge is less "universal or
objective" than often assumed (Dougherty, 1992; von Hippel, 1994; Carlile,
2004). Efforts to share problem-related knowledge include social activities such
as discussions, experiments, joint physical demonstrations, and face-to-face
conversations (Knorr-Cetina, 1981; Carlile, 2002; Bechky, 2003; Hargadon &
Bechky, 2006). Moreover, in order to formulate innovation-related problems,
individuals must share tacit problem-related knowledge (Nonaka, 1994;
Nonaka & von Krogh, 2009) through close face-to-face dialogue. These
dialogues allow teams to create concepts that externalize tacit problem-
related knowledge encoded in writing (Nonaka & Konno, 1998). Problem
formulation for innovation contests may thus be understood as knowledge

externalization. However, the existing literature considers externalization within a team where knowledge can be shared and justified through intense interactions. As explained later, such interactions are severely limited in innovation contests. The constructionist perspective, therefore, highlights two challenges for seeker firms: encoding tacit knowledge in written problem statements and making problem-related knowledge sharable with external solvers in different contexts. Armed with these insights, we use the rest of the chapter to explore how firms formulate sharable problems for innovation contests.

RESEARCH DESIGN

Research Setting and Case Selection

We adopted a multiple case study design (Yin, 2003; Eisenhardt & Graebner, 2007) involving a method of constant comparison, cycling between data collection, data analysis, and further data collection based on emergent themes (Corbin & Strauss, 2008).

We employed a two-step theoretical sampling strategy. First, we identified "typical cases" (Miles & Huberman, 1994; Yin, 2003) by selecting firms that had worked with InnoCentive (representing a closed crowd, as discussed in Chapter 3 by Viscusi & Tucci, 2018), an innovation intermediary that specializes in organizing innovation contests for its clients (for a discussion about the role of intermediaries in innovation, see Howells, 2006). Second, final case selection followed the logic of replication (Yin, 2003). From the population of typical cases (N ~ 60) we selected six firms constituting "polar types" (Eisenhardt, 1989; Eisenhardt & Graebner, 2007) representing successful and unsuccessful cases. The underlying logic is to select cases that either predict similar results (a "literal replication," here a successful outcome) or predict contrasting results for reasons that the generated theory can explain (a "theoretical replication," here a non-successful outcome) (Yin, 2003). Three cases were deemed successful based on the firm's ability to formulate a stream of problems for innovation contests, meaning that the firm made a long-term commitment to the innovation contest that over time yielded several submitted problems. The remaining three cases were classified as unsuccessful as none of these firms was able to formulate a stream of problems (i.e. either only a few problems submitted in total or several in a few "bursts," thus not representing a stream of problems) and subsequently quit working with InnoCentive after a few contests. Table 6.1 provides overviews of the case firms. To protect their anonymity, we have labeled the successful cases Sbrinz, Appenzeller, and Schabziger, and the unsuccessful cases Baer, Tomme, and Flada.

Table 6.1. Overview of case companies.

	Sbrinz	Appenzeller	Schabziger	Baer	Tomme	Flada
Industry	Consumer goods	Agro chemicals	Pharma	Specialty chemicals	Chemicals	Specialty chemicals
Location of headquarters	Europe	USA	Europe	Europe	USA	Europe
Number of problems submitted to innovation contests	12	80	25	6	30	12
Continued to run innovation contests?	Yes	Yes	Yes	No	No	No

Data Collection

We collected data from four sources, between October 2007 and September 2010. First, we interviewed a total of eighteen (senior) managers and (senior) scientists from the selected six InnoCentive client firms (several informants were interviewed repeatedly). The interviews followed semi-structured, open-ended guidelines and took the form of "guided conversations" (Yin, 2003: 89). We asked managers about their activities in the ongoing collaboration with InnoCentive and the activities of their staff in formulating problems. Second, we were granted deep access to InnoCentive. We conducted formal interviews with eighteen InnoCentive staff (senior managers, scientists, and salespeople). In these interviews, we asked questions about InnoCentive's relationship with the case firms. Similar to the seeker interviews, we focused both on individual problem formulation processes and on capturing InnoCentive employees' sense of how problem formulation "works." Interviews with informants at seeker firms and InnoCentive were partially conducted in person and partially by telephone. The interviews lasted between fifty minutes and two hours; all of them were recorded and subsequently transcribed verbatim (resulting in about 600 pages of text). We also visited the InnoCentive headquarters for a three-day visit. During that time, we were granted free access to all InnoCentive premises. We held numerous informal conversations, observed the daily work in the building, and were invited to internal meetings. We took detailed notes of our observations and wrote them up within twenty-four hours. Third, we collected data from archival sources such as InnoCentive press releases and published problem statements. Data from archival sources totaled about 300 pages of text. Fourth, during the course of the research project we conducted eleven supplementary interviews with managers and engineers/scientists at other seeker firms from various industries, such as engineering products, consumer products, and chemical products. The purpose of these validation interviews was to crosscheck data points and interview statements and to solicit broader feedback on emerging ideas, constructs, and relationships. In all, we conducted forty-seven interviews and transcribed them verbatim. Appendix 6.1 provides examples of informants' quotes.

FINDINGS

Towards a Framework for Formulating Sharable Problems for Innovation Contests

The framework for formulating sharable problems for innovation contests consists of two dimensions—the problem formulation *process* and organizational *roles* within this process–captured as the horizontal and vertical dimensions of Figure 6.1. The framework is developed inductively from literal and theoretical replications of successful and unsuccessful cases (cf. Yin, 2003). In the successful cases, firms were able to formulate a stream of problems for innovation contests, while in the unsuccessful cases they were not able to do so. First, we detail the necessary process elements and roles and provide examples from the successful cases. We then present evidence *ex negativo* that *all* the generative process elements and organizational roles are conditions for seekers to formulate sharable problems for innovation contests.

	Problem generation	Problem separation	Problem publication
Sponsor	–Activating scientists with problems		
Coordinator	–Activating scientists with problems –Selecting suitable problems		–Managing legal risks –Controlling competitive implications
Advisor	–Drafting problem statements	–Giving solvers' perspective	
Developer	–Drafting problem statements	–Taking solvers' perspective	–Managing legal risks –Controlling competitive implications

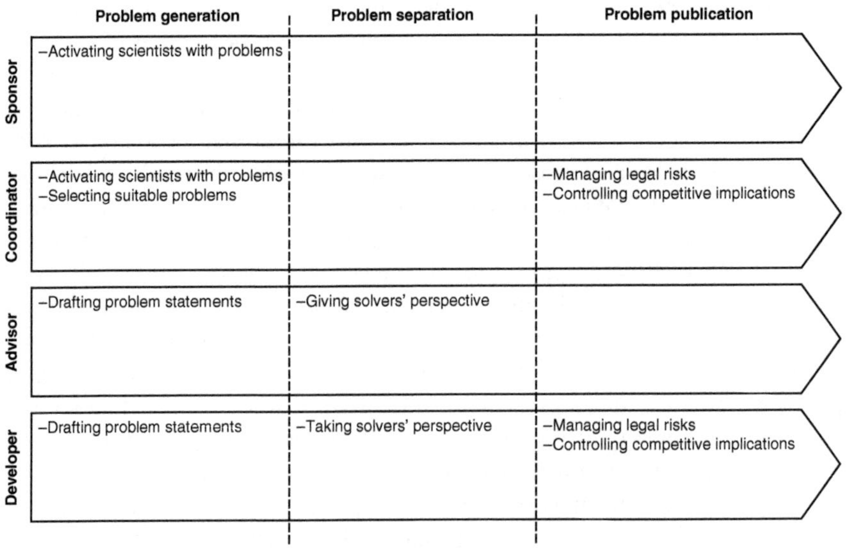

Figure 6.1. A model of problem formulation for innovation contests.

The problem formulation process for innovation contests comprises three generative elements: *problem generation*, activities to motivate scientists to draft precise written statements of problems suitable for innovation contests; *problem separation*, activities to disentangle problems from their internal context by incorporating the perspective of solvers in drafting problem statements; and *problem publication*, activities to manage legal risks and control competitive implications.

The tasks within the three generative process elements are distributed among four organizational roles: *developers*, scientists/engineers who take ownership of problems and have the lead in generating, separating, and publishing specific problems; *advisors*, experienced scientists/engineers who assist developers in problem generation and separation; *coordinators*, R&D managers who motivate scientists to generate problems and are partially responsible for problem publication; and *sponsors*, senior managers who take the budgetary responsibility for innovation contests and help to generate problems by promoting innovation contests towards scientists. Developer, advisor, coordinator, and sponsor are our own labels for these roles and do not represent the job titles of seeker employees.

Generative Process Elements in Formulating Sharable Problems

Problem generation: Activating scientists and drafting problem statements. Problem generation for innovation contests involves activating scientists who hold problems, selecting suitable problems, and drafting problem statements. Since innovation contests represent a "new way of working," as the research director of Sbrinz said, many scientists in the three case firms tended to focus on the risks entailed in innovation contests and were, therefore, not immediately prone to using innovation contests in order to solve one of their own problems. At Sbrinz, the research director therefore sought to promote a "dare-to-try attitude" by making scientists aware that innovation contests were a "calculated risk" (and thus acceptable) for the firm. In parallel, a mid-level R&D manager at Sbrinz was engaged in "internal marketing," i.e. she held formal and informal meetings in which she promoted innovation contests as an opportunity for scientists to leverage external knowledge for solving their problems. These meetings also sought to make scientists feel comfortable with the legal and competitive risks inherent in innovation contests. Similarly, at Schabziger, several R&D managers activated scientists by "walking around" and asking about specific problems that could benefit from external resources.

Scientists as well as R&D managers in the three case companies were well aware of the costs of an innovation contest—the posting fee as well as the proposed reward. They sought a "rational" approach, by only attempting to generate "suitable" problems, i.e. only selecting those problems where an innovation contest would be "worth it" or cost effective. To assess the cost and benefits of innovation contests for certain problems, seeker employees engaged in several activities. First, multiple informants stressed that they tried to "make sure that you reached all the internal brain capacity before you go out" (quote), for instance, by tapping into personal networks and presenting the problem in different meetings within the R&D function. Second, R&D managers prioritized problems for submission by discussing the potential of problem candidates to advance various research projects. Third, seeker scientists also tried to ensure that the seeker organization would have a "real need" for the solution.

When seeker scientists become motivated to submit a suitable problem to an innovation contest, they need to draft a problem statement. However, as one informant put it, "...when you have a problem normally you don't define the problem; normally the problem arises in the lab." Seeker scientists, therefore, do not have a problem statement available; they rather need to draft problem statements by "put[ting] the problem on paper." The writing process itself resembles a "mental simulation" in which the scientist tries to imagine a situation when she/he receives the solution. An informant said, "...we do try and think about what information we need to have to know if this really is a solution." Scientists, thus, try to think upfront about technical requirements and often "end up working with the list of requirements" (scientist at Sbrinz). Sometimes, these requirements are framed negatively in terms of exclusion criteria and seeker scientists "think about what kind of solutions we don't want to have," as another informant put it.

In many cases, a crucial step to defining precise, scientifically valid solution criteria is to determine a problem's causes, i.e. to trace observed problem manifestations back to a more fundamental scientific phenomenon. For example, if the absorption capacity of a diaper needs to be improved, this problem can be tracked back to the absorption capacity of different polymers in the diaper and ultimately to certain aspects of ion condensation that need to be controlled to improve the absorption capacity. In many instances, seeker and intermediary scientists facilitated the search for problem causes by asking questions, as described by one informant from InnoCentive:

The first three questions are "What's the problem?" and then "What's the underlying problem?" and then the third one says, "No, really, what's the problem?" And... most people know what they want, right, they say we need this or we need that. And that's not the problem, that's a solution. [...] So what I usually ask them is "Why don't you just do it?" They say, "Well, we need this, you know, this part, you know, or we need this piece of equipment that does that, analyzes this." And I will say, "Why don't you just make one?" And they say, "We can't" and so then I keep beating them going "Why not?" Because eventually you get to why we can't because we don't have this or we don't know how to do that and then you start getting to what the actual problem is, right. And it's probably only a small piece.

Other informants referred to this questioning process as "finding the endpoint," getting to the "bottom of the problem," "finding the underlying problem," or "getting to the root cause."

Problem separation: Giving and taking the solver's perspective. Problems are entangled in their specific context through taken-for-granted assumptions held by scientists and others. At Sbrinz, for instance, "requirements that are kind of part of the culture everybody knows" comprised an environmental policy excluding a long list of chemical compounds from possible solutions. Separating problems from the internal seeker context requires the seeker to uncover such contextual assumptions. To this end, seeker scientists either cognitively *take* the perspective of external problem solvers or encourage others to *give* their perspective, e.g. by interacting with internal colleagues and inter- mediary scientists who attempt to simulate the perspective of a potential solver.

Our informants told us that taking the perspective of solvers or "putting yourself in the shoes of the solver" enables them to better understand how the problem is entangled in the specific seeker context. For instance, seeker scientists often took technical equipment for granted but recognized it as an important part of the problem's context when they imagined that they were in the position of a solver. Imagining being a university student or retired engineer, seeker scientists realized that these solvers would "of course" have little equipment available to conduct experiments. Such mental simulations also allow seeker scientists to surface solvers' time constraints and limitations regarding solvers' ability to test potential solutions, as an informant's reflec- tion on the outcome of such a simulation makes clear:

> You can't say that it [the solution] can't be something we know because then they [the solvers] don't know if they are wasting their time. They can't make a judgment. And you can't say something like it shouldn't be patented in the patent literature at large because that's, it's too much, it takes too long to do that search.

Putting oneself in the solver's shoes does not only reveal solver constraints but also their problem-solving capabilities. For instance, one informant said that when writing a problem statement "...I assume that most of the people who are reading it are scientists or engineers." Seeker scientists thus (sometimes) assume that problem solvers have had similar scientific training and under- stand the same concepts as seeker scientists. Using these concepts to describe a problem enables seeker scientists to disentangle the problem from the seeker's specific context and to make it understandable for external solvers.

While taking the solver's perspective was often an important first step for seeker scientists in problem separation, seeker scientists also found it helpful to discuss with internal colleagues or intermediary scientists to surface add- itional contextual assumptions. In these discussions, seeker colleagues and intermediary scientists "took" the perspective of problem solvers and "gave" it to seeker scientists. In other words, seeker colleagues and intermediary scientists represent the voice and interests of solvers in the discourse around drafting problem statements. Seeker colleagues, for instance, ask "naïve questions" that external problem solvers may pose such as: "Would this be an acceptable solution for you?" or "Is this parameter measurable, does a solver know when they're done?" A seeker scientist who had run several innovation contests said that he often reminded colleagues that solvers typically work alone and, thus, have difficulty solving problems that require multiple skill sets.

Intermediary scientists attempt to make the perspective of solvers explicit by voicing concerns that the solvers may have, or describing their likely reaction to information in the problem statements. Through these interactions, seeker scientists often uncover hidden assumptions. For instance, one intermediary scientist described a typical interaction with a seeker scientist who had implicitly assumed that solvers' technical capabilities could be ignored when defining solution parameters:

> And then, if there are things that you [seeker scientist] would prefer, you say, you know, we'd like to be able to measure that [. . .] at, let's say, 100 ppm or something, but it would be really nice if we can measure it down at 10 ppm. And then solvers know, "Hey, if I can go even lower, mine has a better chance of winning." [. . .] They're [solvers] not stupid, right, they all know to go lower. But what happens is, if you set it at 1 ppm even though you'd take 25 ppm, probably the smartest guys, the two guys that know the most about the problem look at one and go, "That's impossible. I'm not even going to waste my time. I can get it to, let's say, twenty but there's no way I can get it to one" and they may just walk away.

Such "walking away" from problems that cannot be solved with existing skills is an important market feature, ensuring that those who stay are also those who are the most competent to solve the problem. However, by literally raising the "voice of solvers" and describing how the most competent solvers would react to the seeker scientist's proposed solution parameters, the intermediary scientist demonstrated that the seeker scientist had implicitly focused on the internally most desirable solution parameters and, thereby, ignored many sufficiently competent solvers with feasible solutions to hand.

Several informants from seekers and the intermediary similarly reported that seeker scientists often (wrongly) assumed that solvers had the same access to data that they themselves enjoyed. For instance, an intermediary scientist reported that when discussing a modeling problem that required extensive time-series data, he told seeker scientists, "You know what, do me a favor, you go get it [data] and we'll put it in the challenge. I don't want the solvers having to do it." By advocating solvers' interests, the intermediary scientist made explicit for seeker scientists how much their problem statement relied on access to their specific data source. In several cases, seeker scientists also made an incorrect assumption that solvers could take on the same amount of risk as could seeker employees. To correct this flawed assumption, one intermediary scientist described solvers' risk-taking propensity to a seeker scientist as follows:

> *If I have to spend $1,000 to try to make $20,000 and I don't know if I'm going to get it or not I'm probably not going to do that, right? There's, no guarantee. [...] actually they'll put in a tremendous number of hours, but if they have to, you know, pull $500 of their own money out then they're like "maybe this isn't worth the effort".*

Exposed to a large network of solvers, the intermediary scientist here performs a valuable function. By voicing solvers' potential concerns, the intermediary scientist has made explicit that seeker scientists had assumed that solvers could spend the same resources on experiments that they could themselves. In hindsight, the seeker scientist described this interaction with the intermediary scientist: "We wanted the solvers to do some experiments, but then [after discussing with the intermediary scientist] we understood that probably it was too risky for the solvers."

Problem publication: Managing legal risks and controlling competitive implications. Problem publication involves managing legal risks and controlling competitive implications of information to be published in the problem statement. For instance, according to an informant, publishing a problem might "alert competitors" and "lead them to our ground" which "can block us" if competitors were developing intellectual property rights (IPR-) protected solutions to the problem. To evaluate the severity of such competitive implications, seeker employees tried to guess competitors' current state of knowledge. Seekers sometimes developed a work-around, for instance, by not asking for a novel synthesis route to the desired chemical compound, but to a structurally similar one.

Making problem-related information public can also jeopardize future patenting activities, as publicized information can no longer be part of a patent application. The seeker organizations, thus, gauged the sensitivity of information by first discussing it internally. Both Appenzeller and Schabziger, for instance, defined a contact person within the legal/IP department who was responsible for assessing the legal and competitive risks and then clearing each problem statement. At Sbrinz, seeker lawyers were involved in negotiating a master services agreement, but individual scientists were entrusted with evaluating whether a specific piece of information was publishable. The seeker organization then either decided to accept the risk that some sensitive information would be published, on the grounds that any innovation contest involves some level of legal risks or disguised sensitive information. For instance, the seeker organizations had been working on problems to be submitted to innovation contests internally and, thus, knew about many partial solutions. Seekers did not want to pay for these known partial solutions but faced the risk that solvers might sue them if these solutions were later part of a patent application. In light of this risk, seekers either excluded whole solution approaches (e.g. any synthesis route involving a particular compound) or defined a "filter." In the latter case, seeker employees set up criteria according to which the innovation intermediary would filter out submitted solutions before forwarding solutions to the seeker. Seekers also prepared documentation of internal work on the problem to be able to prove that these partial solutions had actually been generated internally.

Organizational roles in problem formulation for innovation contests. The developer is a technical/scientific role that is usually filled by bench scientists or engineers within the seeker organization. Developers are essential to the problem formulation process: they carry out most operational tasks, i.e. they write and rewrite the problem statement and, thus, spend more time and resources on formulating a specific problem than any other role. In other words, while all roles are necessary, most work in innovation contest problem formulation falls onto the developer. Because of their investment in time and resources, developers usually have a strong and genuine interest in getting the problem resolved.

The advisor is also a technical/scientific role often filled by senior and well-respected scientists/engineers from the seeker organization and the innovation intermediary. Compared with developers, advisors remain more passive during problem generation. Advisors typically wait to act until called in by developers or coordinators to help to draft a problem statement. Advisors are also involved in problem separation. During problem separation, advisors support developers by drawing on experience from the problem context, and from having participated in previous innovation contests where they have familiarized themselves with the specific problem formulation requirements as well as knowledge of the problem itself.

In contrast with developers and advisors, the coordinator is a management role involved in both problem generation and problem publication. In problem generation, coordinators serve as a "spokesperson" or "ambassador... who carries the flag" of innovation contests, according to one informant. Coordinators also play an important role in problem publication. They do so by providing managerial approval to select a particular problem (over other problems) and a specific problem statement (over alternative statements), thereby removing much uncertainty and anxiety from developers regarding priorities and the release of potentially sensitive information.

The sponsor is a senior management role filled by a person within the seeker organization who is ultimately responsible for innovation contests. Sponsors are crucial for problem generation since they have the internal clout to build awareness for and legitimacy of innovation contests among scientists and mid-level R&D managers.

Theoretical Replications of Unsuccessful Cases

In this section, findings from three theoretical replications of unsuccessful cases (Yin, 2003) demonstrate how deviations from the three generative process elements and four organizational roles hinder seekers from formulating streams of problems for innovation contests.

Deviations in problem generation and the coordinator and sponsor roles. Innovation contests were introduced "top-down" in all three cases. After senior R&D managers who assumed the sponsor roles had decided to use innovation contests, scientists were given the opportunity to submit problems. However, many scientists were worried about shouldering the work load of a problem formulation process, alerting competitors by publishing "good" problems, and running into patenting problems if solvers submitted solutions touching on current patenting activities. As sponsors did not anticipate these concerns, they focused on promoting the economic rationale behind innovation contests and did not activate scientists with problems. At Baer and Flada, sponsors thus "extracted" problems by selecting the most "visible" problems and assigning individual scientists or research groups to submit these problems to innovation contests. At Tomme, the sponsor remained rather passive and waited for research groups to approach him with problems. Given these introductions of innovation contests to the firm, there were two similar implications in all three cases. First, at none of the firms did the sponsors perceive the need for an R&D manager to assume a coordinator role, working with scientists to select suitable problems that would have a good chance of being solved. Second, seekers instead selected "holy grail" or "crapshoot" problems—long-standing, relatively complex problems with low solution chances.

In all three cases, innovation contests met with negative feedback from seeker scientists and yielded an "objectively low" solution rate. These were two major factors that contributed to the reported perception of failure and the decision to quit running innovation contests. The findings show that the formulation of problems for innovation contests requires careful attention to problem generation. The findings also underscore that the construct of "problem generation" does not correspond to the identification or extraction of the most visible problems (as in the case of Baer, Tomme, and Flada), but to "activation" of scientists with problems and thereafter selection of suitable problems. Sponsors and coordinators play a vital role in activating scientists and selecting problems by discussing with developers which problems they are motivated to formulate *and* which they perceive as having a good chance of being solved.

Deviations in problem separation and the advisor role. At Baer, Tomme, and Flada, we observe that sponsors did not associate problem formulation for innovation contests with problem separation. Instead, sponsors approached problem formulation as the technical task of writing down the problem. Sponsors at these three case firms expected the innovation intermediary to perform this technical task in return for the intermediary's fee. However, developers gradually learned about the challenges of problem separation as they received feedback from the intermediary scientists and then realized that the problem formulation process would require significant allocation of time and effort. Since sponsors did not approach the challenge of problem separation, they also did not designate internal advisors, who would have assisted developers in problem separation. In retrospect, as Flada's CTO remarked, this created a difficult situation in which "the scientists were very much exposed to the InnoCentive people, so they had to do a lot on their own with little support within Flada." A lack of internal support meant that problem separation was less effective, since internal advisors did not explain to developers how to turn a problem description into a document that fits with InnoCentive guidelines and would be understandable for external solvers. Intermediary scientists did assist developers with these challenges but, as outsiders, they were less capable of explaining how a separated problem statement would differ from standard internal problem descriptions. Developers also lacked informal "sparring partners" who were well acquainted with their specific research problems. In sum, the lack of an internal advisor role made problem separation more cumbersome for internal scientists and thus undermined the formulation of problems for innovation contests. The three cases provide evidence that problem separation should involve an internal advisor role.

Deviations in problem publication and the coordinator role. At Baer, Tomme, and Flada, scientists drafting problem statements reported that controlling sensitive information in the problem statements and evaluating the commercial effectiveness of innovation contests fell under their individual responsibilities. Scientists, in other words, did not perceive the competitive and legal risks of innovation contests to be of a magnitude that would affect the whole organization and that would need its overall commitment, but rather as risks facing them individually. Scientists sought to minimize their personal risks to the detriment of innovation contest effectiveness in the seeker organizations. For instance, rather than controlling information and appraising the sensitivity of the problem, scientists reported minimizing sensitive information in problem statements. At Baer, Tomme, and Flada, we observed that many problems came from areas where the firms had long research histories and, thus, knew about many solution approaches. Since the firms were patenting some of these approaches, developers had to define a filter, i.e. exclude some solution approaches in the problem statement, to avoid solvers submitting solutions the firms already knew about. Such known but not IP-protected solutions could have caused the firm to pay royalties for IP in a known solution. According to the CTO of Flada, "The pressure on scientists was such that they felt that if they don't define that filter right they will look stupid because sooner or later we might run into some difficulties [in patenting processes]." Scientists, thus, defined very narrow filters that excluded many solution approaches. Since there was no coordinator role at Flada, no one counteracted the scientists' tendency to be overly conservative in avoiding patenting risks. Moreover, senior R&D management was too far removed from individual scientists' work on technical problem formulation to sense and address these concerns quickly enough. In sum, the three cases provide evidence that problem publication needs to involve control of sensitive information and appraisal of the value of external knowledge. Coordinators should support scientists in these activities because scientists will otherwise resort to minimizing instead of controlling sensitive information, thus appraising external knowledge extremely conservatively and undermining the chances of obtaining solutions from external solvers.

DISCUSSION, CONCLUSIONS, AND FUTURE RESEARCH

Implications for Crowdsourcing

The study demonstrates how crowdsourcing in the form of innovation contests stirs up "encrusted routines" of innovation, how problem formulation enters as a critical challenge, and how managerial actions facilitate effective problem formulation. First, innovation contests tend to—primarily—disrupt the work of scientists and engineers. People who were previously working within insulated functions and roles were suddenly exposed to new challenges and risks. These findings are in line with Alexy et al.'s (2013) findings that the adoption of open source software development influenced different job roles quite differently. Here, the importance of desk scientists is underscored by the fact that they are involved in all elements of problem formulation.

Second, our research demonstrated that problem formulation consists of three elements: problem generation, problem separation, and problem formulation. Failure to recognize any of these elements will invariably lead to failure. The challenge to formulate problems is underscored by the fact that in the practice of engineers and bench scientists, continuous streams of problems, solutions, decisions, and actors make innovation more similar to a garbage-can process with stochastic properties than a linear and rational process of separable problem formulation and solving. This image is mirrored in the literature as well (e.g. March & Simon, 1958/1993; Cyert & March, 1963; Cohen et al., 1972; Simon, 1996; Nickerson & Zenger, 2004; Felin & Zenger, 2012; von Hippel & von Krogh, 2016). However, innovation contests turn this image of innovation on its head. Now problems are exposed to radical incisions; formulation and solution are partitioned in content, time, and space as they are allocated to external and often unknown solvers. To mitigate the challenge of problem generation, management could encourage, support, and activate engineers and scientists who already have possible issues and problems in mind—rather than just telling them to draft problem statements. Our findings on problem separation complement those in the recent literature on innovation contests. For example, Boudreau et al. (2011) found that problems requiring solutions from multiple knowledge domains benefited from large numbers of solvers, whereas restricting entry to the contest is better for single-domain problems. Their result dovetails our finding to build solver representations through perspective giving and perspective taking. Seeker firm personnel need to understand the nature of the problem, how solvers perceive it, and who potential solvers may be, for example, whether they are "marginal" solvers or not (Jeppesen & Lakhani, 2010). In this regard, innovation intermediaries may play a crucial role.

Implications for Open Innovation

The current study adds to the fast-growing literature on open innovation. First, our research demonstrated that problem formulation is a critical antecedent to successfully solving technical problems through innovation contests. Yet, problem formulation is largely inconspicuous in received open innovation literature. For example, in their extensive review West & Bogers (2014) develop a process model of how firms leverage external sources of innovation. Their four-phase linear model includes (1) obtaining, (2) integrating, (3) commercializing, and (4) interactions between the firm and its collaborators. Our study suggests a step zero (0) that precedes obtaining solutions: formulating the problem. Indeed, West & Bogers write that is was impossible to separate search from acquisition—a testament to how intertwined problem solving and problem formulation are in theory as well as in practice. However, as we have demonstrated, under some circumstances they need to be separated.

Second, we expand and explain how problem formulation may impact other forms and aspects of open innovation. For example, recent work has explored how seeker firms initiate collaboration through selective revealing (Alexy et al., 2011). The seeker firm moves beyond building absorptive capacity to exploit external knowledge (Cohen & Levinthal, 1990) to *stimulating* external problem solvers who next *create* knowledge. Our model adds that the seeker firm's capacity to stimulate solvers relies on specific mechanisms of problem formulation. For example, open innovation that stimulates know-ledge creation through contract research (e.g. Howells, 1999) or R&D alliances (e.g. Oxley & Sampson, 2004) requires a formulation of the prob-lem being solved. Accordingly, problem formulation research provides an entrée to analyzing how firms adapt and change when they innovate with external partners. Analogous to building and maintaining absorptive cap-acity for open innovation (Harison & Koski, 2010; Robertson et al., 2012), firms may need to build a "problem formulation capacity" by overcoming Laursen & Salter's (2014) "paradox of openness." The capacity for formu-lating problems needs to mitigate perceived risks, such as the limits to IPR protection (as most knowledge does not meet the bar for patentability). It may also be that problem formulation capacity is more fundamental to the boundary of the firm than problem solving capability. Clearly, firms can draw on outside expertise to solve a problem, when the problem is well defined—but formulating the problem properly is a necessary condition for solving it. We are reminded that problems are partly solved when they are well defined. Indeed, when the problem is well defined, finding a solution becomes a task that can be broken down into assignments, automated to some degree, and managed through project management principles. Problem formulation for innovation contests is a different story altogether.

Third, our work also shows the limitations of innovation contests as an effective "organizational design" for innovation (Felin & Zenger, 2012). The lack of seeker–solver interaction excludes certain problems from being effect-ively defined. This is the case with a rapid increase in the cost of building solver representation, for example when solvers, their resources, and their capabilities are entirely unknown at the outset, forcing the firm to gather infor-mation about potential solvers (e.g. a problem akin to market research for a new product) (see Chapter 7, by Ranade & Vershney, 2007, on the advantages of crowdsourcing when the seeker is unsure about solver strength). Alternatively, the contest method can only solve problems when the scale of solver commu-nities offsets the negative effect of a problem that lacks important information. By broadcasting the problem to a very large group of potential solvers, the seeker can increase the probability that some solvers will find the problem rewarding—and therefore that a desired solution can be found. Yet broadcast-ing problem statements to solvers is costly (and risky), such as having to evaluate many solution candidates or setting up communication infrastruc-tures. When building solver representation is too costly (or even impossible) or when scale advantages cannot be reached at a reasonable cost, other organiza-tional forms that allow for greater interaction between seekers and solvers may be more effective.

Implications for Innovation Intermediation

Our chapter also contributes to the literature on innovation intermediation (Howells, 2006; Sieg et al., 2010). First, the study underscores the importance of innovation intermediary alignment. The innovation intermediary needs to align the interests of the seekers and solvers, and to do so it must have better access to and knowledge of the solver community than the seeker firm. By serving multiple seeker firm clients, the intermediary maintains a greater diversity in its solver community than any seeker firm is likely to. Such diversity is good for innovation contest methods (Jeppesen & Lakhani, 2010) and is likely to require scale in the number of contests to be upheld. The innovation intermediary achieves alignment by helping the seeker firm's management to mitigate perceived risks in the contests and by building solver representations. We found that InnoCentive's deep understanding of its solver community guided the seeker firm's management to strike a fine balance between protecting proprietary knowledge and releasing effective problem statements to the solvers. The innovation intermediary often represented the "voice of the solver" and reminded seekers firm's personnel of solvers' resources and capabilities.

Second, drawing on these observations, we contend that for seeker firms, not knowing the "potential" solver could jeopardize the outcome of innovation contests. Firms that want competitively or legally sensitive problems to be solved should not simply release statements into the public. Accessing a community understood and supported by an intermediary is a better approach, because it allows protection and enables the seeker firm to formulate a problem attuned to expert solvers. Innovation intermediation enables the seeker firm to remain anonymous, if needed. While sometimes beneficial, anonymity also creates new challenges for the intermediary. The name and industry of seeker firms could provide important cues to solvers and when they are not published, the intermediary needs to find ways of extracting other relevant information from the firm and channeling this to the community. Not surprisingly, our interviews with managers indicated that innovation intermediation is considered a safe and cost-effective way of gaining access to a large pool of outside talent.

Limitations and Future Research

Our study faces limitations. The sample includes firms of different size and from different industries, and it tilts towards relatively large chemical, pharmaceutical, and consumer products firms. The sample firms primarily submitted chemical and biological problems to innovation contests. Future research should explore effective problem formulation for innovation contests in other industries and contexts. Our work focused on seeker firms, and the intermediary's relationship with seeker firms and solvers. Henry Chesbrough has remarked that a challenge for innovation intermediaries is to scale operations to effectively assist a large number of firms in innovation contests.[3] The research issue deserves extensive attention in future work. The current work suggests that managers consider the innovation contest a successful open innovation method when it solves a technical problem that has been effectively formulated with the help of an intermediary. An intriguing theme for future work is how the intermediary's assistance in problem formulation across seeker firms can be standardized and scaled.

CONCLUSION

Drawing on rich empirical cases, we inductively develop a theoretical framework outlining mechanisms for seeker firms' formulation of sharable problems in innovation contests. The framework consists of three generative process elements ("problem generation," "problem separation," and "problem publication") and four organizational roles ("developer," "advisor," "coordinator," and "sponsor"). The chapter responds to recent calls to investigate the intra-organizational implications of open innovation by illuminating the organizational processes and roles necessary to stimulate external knowledge creation in successful innovation contests. The study shows that open innovation in general, and innovation contests in particular, hold strong implications for organization theory by questioning the orthodoxy of problem solving.

ACKNOWLEDGMENTS

The authors would like to thank Joel West and Linus Dahlander, conference attendees at Imperial College London, and seminar attendees at Bocconi University for their valuable comments. We appreciate the advice and encouragement from the editors and gratefully acknowledge the support from respondents in numerous case companies.

[3] Comment at Imperial College London conference, June 26, 2012.

APPENDIX A6.1

Examples of informants quotes.

Process elements	First-order concept	Second-order theme
Process elements		
Example: "The way we chose was to involve the scientists from the start very much to let them come up with the problems. So we don't say you should have a challenge, we more ask them and that's the way we have been working all along and I think that's one thing that's important. You couldn't order somebody to make a challenge." *Sbrinz manager*	Asking employees for potentially suitable problems	Activating scientists with problems
Example: "You have to know what you're going to do with the answers and what things you're going to be looking for to know which one [solutions] you like." *Sbrinz scientist (I)*	Determining the need for a solution	Selecting suitable problems
Example: "We do spend quite a bit of time in determining what the strict criteria are that we would use to judge our solutions in terms of precision, if it's in terms of compounds, purity, the amount, things like that." *Appenzeller manager (I)*	Determining the parameters necessary to evaluate solutions	Drafting problem statements
Problem separation		
Example: "I think it's an attempt really to help the solvers not waste their time either, because if there is a situation where we have tried it and it doesn't worked, we would tell the solver that." *Appenzeller manager (II)*	Estimating the requirements for solvers	Taking the solvers' perspective
Example: "I thought a lot about this and talked to a lot of people in-house, how to overcome the problem that, I mean, this is our main competence. We know so much about this and how to produce a question that gets new insights in an area that we already know so much about." *Sbrinz scientist (II)*	Discussing the problem with internal colleagues	Giving the solvers' perspective
Problem publication		
Example: "It could be that we are working on some technique that hasn't been used for that purpose before, and if we then say, and perhaps we don't even want to mention that because we see that we want to patent that and then we need also to keep it as confidential as possible to be able to patent it. I can't give you really a very good example, but there are cases that we don't want to reveal things that we are, because we are in the process of patenting or so." *Sbrinz manager*	Disguising legally sensitive information in the problem statement	Managing legal risks
Example: "The hard part is knowing what exactly is it that I want and how much of that I can tell on this site and if I can't tell enough it doesn't make any sense what I'm asking you all and as an example there's this order challenge and I'm sure you'll hear about that because I haven't helped to write it, but I heard about it, I've been participating in the discussions because it was an early one and they had a lot of discussions that they don't want to say it's a [name of product category] because it's a little too much." *Sbrinz scientist (I)*	Deleting competitively sensitive information in problem statements	Controlling competitive implications

REFERENCES

Afuah, A. (2018). Crowdsourcing: A primer and research framework. In C. Tucci, A. Afuah, & G. Viscusi (eds.), *Creating and Capturing Value Through Crowdsourcing*. Oxford: Oxford University Press, pp. 11–38.

Afuah, A. & Tucci, C. L. (2012). Crowdsourcing as a solution to distant search. *Academy of Management Review, 37*(3), 355–75.

Alexy, O., George, G., & Salter, A. (2011). From sensing shape to shaping sense: A dynamic model of absorptive capacity and selective revealing. *Proceedings of the 2011 DRUID Conference*. London: Imperial College Business School.

Alexy, O., Henkel, J., & Wallin, M. W. (2013). From closed to open: Job role changes, individual predispositions, and the adoption of commercial open source software development. *Research Policy, 42*(8), 1325–40.

Allen, T. J. (1966). Studies of problem-solving in engineering design. *IEEE Transactions on Engineering Management, EM13*(2), 72–83.

Bechky, B. A. (2003). Sharing meaning across occupational communities: The transformation of understanding on a production floor. *Organization Science, 14*(3), 312–30.

Boudreau, K. J., Lacetera, N., & Lakhani, K. R. (2011). Incentives and problem uncertainty in innovation contests: An empirical analysis. *Management Science, 57*(5), 843–63.

Brown, J. S. & Duguid, P. (1991). Organizational learning and communities-of-practice: Toward a unified view of working, learning, and innovation. *Organization Science, 2*(1), 40–57.

Brown, J. S. & Duguid, P. (2001). Knowledge and organization: A social-practice perspective. *Organization Science, 12*(2), 198–213.

Carlile, P. R. (2002). A pragmatic view of knowledge and boundaries: Boundary objects in new product development. *Organization Science, 13*(4), 442–55.

Carlile, P. R. (2004). Transferring, translating, and transforming: An integrative framework for managing knowledge across boundaries. *Organization Science, 15*(5), 555.

Chandler, A. D. (1977). *The Visible Hand: The Managerial Revolution in American Business*. Cambridge, MA: Harvard University Press.

Che, Y. K. & Gale, I. (2003). Optimal design of research contests. *American Economic Review, 93*(3), 646–71.

Chesbrough, H. W. (2003). The era of open innovation. *MIT Sloan Management Review, 44*(3), 35–41.

Chesbrough, H. W., Vanhaverbeke, W., & West, J. (2008). *Open Innovation: Researching a New Paradigm*. Oxford: Oxford University Press.

Cohen, W. M. & Levinthal, D. A. (1990). Absorptive capacity: A new perspective on learning and innovation. *Administrative Science Quarterly, 35*, 128–52.

Cohen, M. D., March, J. G., & Olsen, J. P. (1972). A garbage can model of organizational choice. *Administrative Science Quarterly, 17*(1), 1–25.

Corbin, J. & Strauss, A. (2008). *Basics of Qualitative Research*, 3rd ednd. Thousand Oaks: Sage.

Cyert, R. M. & March, J. G. (1963). *A Behavioral Theory of the Firm*. Englewood Cliffs, NJ: Prentice-Hall.

Dahlander, L. & Gann, D. M. (2010). How open is innovation? *Research Policy, 39*(6), 699–709.

Dougherty, D. (1992). Interpretive barriers to successful product innovation in large firms. *Organization Science*, 3(2), 179–202.

Eisenhardt, K. M. (1989). Building theories from case study research. *The Academy of Management Review*, 14(4), 532–50.

Eisenhardt, K. M. & Graebner, M. E. (2007). Theory building from cases: Opportunities and challenges. *Academy of Management Journal*, 50(1), 25–32.

Felin, T. & Zenger, T. R. (2012). Open innovation, problem solving and the theory of the firm. Open Innovation: New Insights and Evidence conference, London, June 25.

Fernandes, R. & Simon, H. A. (1999). A study of how individuals solve complex and ill-structured problems. *Policy Sciences*, 32(3), 225–44.

Foss, N. J., Frederiksen, L., & Rullani, F. (2016). Problem-formulation and problem-solving in self-organized communities: How modes of communication shape project behaviors in the free open-source software community. *Strategic Management Journal*, 37, 2589–610.

Fullerton, R. L. & McAfee, R. P. (1999). Auctioning entry into tournaments. *Journal of Political Economy*, 107(3), 573–605.

Glazer, A. & Hassin, R. (1988). Optimal contests. *Economic Inquiry*, 26(1), 133–43.

Grant, R. M. (1996). Toward a knowledge-based theory of the firm. *Strategic Management Journal*, 17(Winter Special issue), 109–22.

Green, J. R. & Stokey, N. L. (1983). A comparison of tournaments and contracts. *Journal of Political Economy*, 91(3), 349–64.

Hargadon, A. & Bechky, B. A. (2006). When collections of creatives become creative collectives: A field study of problem solving at work. *Organization Science*, 17(4), 484–500.

Harison, E. & Koski, H. (2010). Applying open innovation in business strategies: Evidence from Finnish software firms. *Research Policy*, 39(3), 351–9.

Howe, J. (2006). The rise of crowdsourcing. *Wired*, 14(6), 1–4.

Howe, J. (2008). *Crowdsourcing: How the Power of the Crowd is Driving the Future of Business*. New York: Crown Business.

Howells, J. (1999). Research and technology outsourcing. *Technology Analysis & Strategic Management*, 11(1), 17–29.

Howells, J. (2006). Intermediation and the role of intermediaries in innovation. *Research Policy*, 35(5), 715–28.

Hsieh, C., Nickerson, J. A., & Zenger, T. R. (2007). Opportunity discovery, problem solving and a theory of the entrepreneurial firm. *Journal of Management Studies*, 44(7), 1255–77.

Huston, L. & Sakkab, N. (2006). Connect and develop. *Harvard Business Review*, 84(3), 58–66.

Iansiti, M. & Clark, K. B. (1994). Integration and dynamic capability: Evidence from product development in automobiles and mainframe computers. *Industrial & Corporate Change*, 3(3), 557–605.

Jeppesen, L. B. & Lakhani, K. R. (2010). Marginality and problem-solving effectiveness in broadcast search. *Organization Science*, 21(5), 1016–33.

Klahr, D. & Simon, H. A. (1999). Studies of scientific discovery: Complementary approaches and convergent findings. *Psychological Bulletin*, 125(5), 524–43.

Knorr-Cetina, K. (1981). *The Manufacture of Knowledge. An Essay on the Constructivist and Contextual Nature of Science*. Oxford: Pergamon Press.

Kogut, B. & Zander, U. (1992). Knowledge of the firm, combinative capabilities, and the replication of technology. *Organization Science*, 3(3), 383–97.

Kotovsky, K., Hayes, J. R., & Simon, H. A. (1985). Why are some problems hard—evidence from Tower of Hanoi. *Cognitive Psychology*, 17(2), 248–94.

Kulkarni, D. & Simon, H. A. (1988). The processes of scientific discovery—the strategy of experimentation. *Cognitive Science*, 12(2), 139–75.

Lakhani, K. R., Jeppesen, L. B., Lohse, P. A., & Panetta, J. A. (2007). *The Value of Openness in Scientific Problem Solving*. Cambridge, MA: Harvard Business School.

Landry, M. (1995). A note on the concept of "problem." *Organization Studies*, 16(2), 315–43.

Langlois, R. N. (2003). The vanishing hand: The changing dynamics of industrial capitalism. *Industrial and Corporate Change*, 12(1), 351–85.

Laursen, K. & Salter, A. J. (2006). Open for innovation: The role of openness in explaining innovation performance among UK manufacturing firms. *Strategic Management Journal*, 27, 131–50.

Laursen, K. & Salter, A. J. (2014). The paradox of openness: Appropriability, external search and collaboration. *Research Policy*, 43(5), 867–78.

Loch, C. H., Terwiesch, C., & Thomke, S. (2001). Parallel and sequential testing of design alternatives. *Management Science*, 47(5), 663–78.

March, J. G. & Simon, H. A. (1958/1993). *Organizations*, 2nd edn. Cambridge, MA: Blackwell.

Maurer, S. & Scotchmer, S. (2004). *Innovation and Incentives*. Boston, MA: MIT Press.

McKinsey & Company (2009). And the winner is: Capturing the power of philanthropic prizes, http://mckinseyonsociety.com/downloads/reports/Social-Innovation/And_the_winner_is.pdf (accessed August 29, 2012).

McLaughlin, K. J. (1988). Aspects of tournament models: A survey. *Research in Labor Economics*, 9, 225–56.

Miles, M. B. & Huberman, A. M. (1994). *Qualitative Data Analysis: An Expanded Sourcebook*, 2nd edn. Thousand Oaks: SAGE Publications.

Mowery, D. C. (2009). *Plus ca change*: Industrial R&D in the "third industrial revolution." *Industrial & Corporate Change*, 18(1), 1–50.

National Research Council (2007). *Innovation Inducement Prizes at the National Science Foundation*. Washington, DC: The National Academies Press.

Nelson, R. R. (1982). The role of knowledge in R-and-D efficiency. *Quarterly Journal of Economics*, 97(3), 453–70.

Nelson, R. R. & Winter, S. G. (1977). In search of useful theory of innovation. *Research Policy*, 6(1), 36–76.

Newell, A. & Simon, H. A. (1972). *Human Problem Solving*. Englewood Cliffs: Prentice-Hall.

Nickerson, J. A. & Zenger, T. R. (2004). A knowledge-based theory of the firm: the problem solving perspective. *Organization Science*, 15, 617–22.

Nonaka, I. (1994). A dynamic theory of organizational knowledge creation. *Organization Science*, 5(1), 14–37.

Nonaka, I. & Konno, N. (1998). The concept of "Ba": Building a foundation for knowledge creation. *California Management Review*, 40(3), 40–54.

Nonaka, I. & von Krogh, G. (2009). Tacit knowledge and knowledge conversion: Controversy and advancement in organizational knowledge creation theory. *Organization Science, 20*(3), 635–52.

Oxley, J. E. & Sampson, R. C. (2004). The scope and governance of international R&D alliances. *Strategic Management Journal, 25*(8–9), 723–49.

Pisano, G. (1996). Learning-before-doing in the development of new process technology. *Research Policy, 25*, 1097–119.

Ranade, G. & Varshney, L. (2018). The role of information patterns in designing crowdsourcing contests. In C. Tucci, A. Afuah, & G. Viscusi (eds.), *Creating and Capturing Value Through Crowdsourcing*. Oxford: Oxford University Press, pp. 154–80.

Robertson, P. L., Casali, G. L., & Jacobson, D. (2012). Managing open incremental process innovation: Absorptive capacity and distributed learning. *Research Policy, 41*(5), 822–32.

Scotchmer, S. (2004). *Innovation and Incentives*. Chicago: MIT press.

Schottner, A. (2008). Fixed-prize tournaments versus first-price auctions in innovation contests. *Economic Theory, 35*(1), 57–71.

Sieg, J. H., Wallin, M. W., & von Krogh, G. (2010). Managerial challenges in open innovation: A study of innovation intermediation in the chemical industry. *R & D Management, 40*(3), 281–91.

Simon, H. (1973). Structure of ill-structured problems. *Artificial Intelligence, 4*(3–4), 181–201.

Simon, H. (1977). *Models of Discovery and Other Topics in the Methods of Science*. Dordrecht and Boston, MA: D. Reidel.

Simon, H. (1996). *The Sciences of the Artificial*, 3rd edn. Cambridge, MA: MIT Press.

Spender, J. C. (1996). Making knowledge the basis of a dynamic theory of the firm. *Strategic Management Journal, 17*, 45–62.

Tapscott, D. & Williams, A. D. (2006). *Wikinomics: How Mass Collaboration Changes Everything*. New York: Penguin.

Taylor, C. R. (1995). Digging for golden carrots—an analysis of research tournaments. *American Economic Review, 85*(4), 872–90.

Terwiesch, C. (2008). Product development as a problem-solving process, in S. Shane (ed.), *Handbook of Technology and Innovation Management*. New York, NY: John Wiley & Sons, pp. 143–71.

Terwiesch, C. & Xu, Y. (2008). Innovation contests, open innovation, and multiagent problem solving. *Management Science, 54*(9), 1529–43.

Thomke, S. (2003). *Experimentation Matters*. Cambridge, MA: Harvard Business School Press.

Thomke, S. & Bell, D. E. (2001). Sequential testing in product development. *Management Science, 47*(2), 308–23.

Tsoukas, H. (1996). The firm as a distributed knowledge system: A constructionist approach. *Strategic Management Journal, 17*, 11–25.

Tyre, M. J. & von Hippel, E. (1997). The situated nature of adaptive learning in organizations. *Organization Science, 8*(1), 71–83.

Viscusi, G. & Tucci, C. (2018). Three's a crowd? In C. Tucci, A. Afuah, & G. Viscusi (eds.), *Creating and Capturing Value Through Crowdsourcing*. Oxford: Oxford University Press, pp. 39–57.

von Hippel, E. (1994). "Sticky information" and the locus of problem solving: Implications for innovation. *Management Science*, *40*(4), 429–39.

von Hippel, E. (2005). *Democratizing Innovation*. Cambridge, MA: The MIT Press.

von Hippel, E. & Tyre, M. J. (1995). How learning by doing is done—Problem identification in novel process equipment. *Research Policy*, *24*(1), 1–12.

von Hippel, E. & von Krogh, G. (2016). Identifying viable "need–solution pairs": Problem solving without problem formulation. *Organization Science*, *27*(1): 207–21.

West, J. & Bogers, M. (2014). Leveraging external sources of innovation: A review of research on open innovation. *Journal of Product Innovation Management*, *31*(4), 814–31.

West, J. & Gallagher, S. (2006). Challenges of open innovation: The paradox of firm investment in open-source software. *R&D Management*, *36*(3): 319–31.

White House (2010). Guidance on the use of challenges and prizes to promote open government. Memorandum for the Heads of Executive Departments and Agencies, Office of Management and Budget, Washington, DC, http://www.whitehouse.gov/omb/assets/memoranda_2010/m10-11.pdf (accessed August 29, 2012).

Yin, R. K. (2003). *Case Study Research: Design and Methods*, 3rd edn. Thousand Oaks: SAGE Publications.

7

The Role of Information Patterns in Designing Crowdsourcing Contests

Gireeja V. Ranade and Lav R. Varshney

Abstracts

Crowdsourcing contests are used widely by organizations as a means of accomplishing tasks. These organizations would like to maximize the utility obtained through worker submissions to the contest. If this utility is greater than that obtained through alternative means of completing the task (e.g. hiring someone), the task should be crowdsourced. We analyze the utility generated for different types of tasks and provide a rule of thumb for crowdsourcing contest design. Knowledge about the relative strengths of the workers participating in the contest is an important factor in contest design. When the contest organizer is unsure about the strength of the workers, crowdsourcing contests deliver higher utility than would hiring or assignment. Disseminating worker strength information acts as a lever to influence participation and increase utility in the contest. Finally, while crowdsourcing is a good option for generic tasks, it might perform poorly for highly specialized tasks.

INTRODUCTION

Information technologies that provide lightning-speed communication at low cost have changed the nature of work. Organizations can now leverage networks, communities, and ecosystems of people to perform tasks. Workforces are globally distributed and diverse. Large projects are broken up into smaller encapsulated pieces. In fact, the millennial generation shows a cultural preference for project-based rather than jobs-based work (Bollier, 2011). Within this environment, methods of collective intelligence have emerged as key business tools (Malone et al., 2010), and are now used by all major companies (Cuenin, 2015). A fundamental understanding of this evolution of work is essential to shape its future form.

A notable example of the decentralized organization of work is crowdsourcing. Crowdpower has been harnessed to design everything from T-shirts to software to artificial intelligence algorithms, by soliciting contributions via open calls (Tapscott & Williams, 2006; Boudreau et al., 2011). The ability to reach a large crowd of skilled workers quickly and inexpensively gives firms an alternative means for accomplishing tasks. As such, it is important to understand the pros and cons of a fluid, crowd-based labor force. To quote the management scientist Thomas Malone, "There is this misconception that you can sprinkle crowd wisdom on something and things will turn out for the best. That's not true. It's not magic" (Lohr, 2009). Similarly, Viscusi & Tucci (2018) raise the question of the "right time" for crowdsourcing, and the role that information can play in crowdsourcing. Afuah (2018) also discusses how the makeup of the crowd, and the goals of the seeker (manager) can affect crowdsourcing outcomes. We delve into these questions in this chapter, and focus on the design of crowdsourcing contests based on:

1. the type of task, in terms of what is to be accomplished,
2. the types of players participating, and
3. the information pattern, i.e. the availability of information regarding the skills and strengths of these players.

First, we provide a mathematically oriented taxonomy for tasks based on the optimal solution method. This ties in closely with the various forms of crowdsourcing discussed by West & Sims (2017). Our classification gives specific conditions for whether crowdsourcing can generate revenue for the employer for a particular task. A challenge in digital crowdsourcing markets is how to incentivize workers and improve the quality of the work done (Afuah & Tucci, 2012). We take an informational perspective on answering this question with regard to the skill levels of workers. Of course, task formulation is another important aspect for incentivizing workers as well as identifying the appropriate workers for a given task, as discussed by Wallin et al. (2017). We do not consider this aspect here.

In particular, crowdsourcing has been thought of as a good tool for skills identification (Malone et al., 2010). There are two important considerations in choosing a person for a task. The first is the skill-level/strength and ability of the person to perform the task. However, a second and important consideration is the amount of effort the person will put into the task, since this will affect the final utility to the organization. Our theoretical framework provides a heuristic for an organization to find the best person for a job and further incentivize him or her to attain peak performance through crowdsourcing or otherwise. After all, it is human motivation modulating cognitive energy that makes crowd systems go (Varshney, 2012; Chandler & Kapelner, 2013; Ghosh, 2013; West & Sims, 2017).

Our theoretical framework takes a first step towards determining the optimal work structure for a given task: labor-based, division into microtasks, a crowdsourcing contest (internal or external), or something else entirely, as depicted in Figure 7.1. Knowing how to organize work with minimum friction (Varshney, 2012) is critical for the efficient design of the knowledge economy.

The chapter focuses on crowdsourcing contests, where monetary or otherwise tangible rewards are provided to the winners of competitive events. These are also referred to as crowdsourcing tournaments in the remainder of this book. We focus on the case where there is only one winner for each task. This is different from other forms of crowdsourcing where crowd workers do not receive direct extrinsic rewards, such as in social production (e.g. Wikipedia or citizen science initiatives (Benkler, 2006; Howe, 2008)), and is also different from paid microtask forums (e.g. Amazon Mechanical Turk or freelance markets like Upwork) (Chatterjee et al., forthcoming) where there is no contest. Contests may be internal, with competition only among the employees of the organization, or external and open to the public (e.g. Kaggle or TopCoder). Our results apply to both of these types of crowdsourcing.

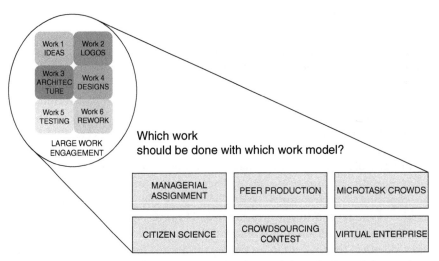

Figure 7.1. With the zoo of organizational design possibilities for knowledge work, it is important to know when each is most effective.

PREVIOUS WORK

There has been extensive previous work on the design of crowdsourcing contests. This work has spanned the theoretical space using game-theoretic and statistical models and has also involved experiments and data collection. For example, Archak & Sundararajan (2009) provide a rule of thumb for the prize structure for optimal participation in crowdsourcing contests using a game-theoretic model, whereas Cavallo & Jain (2012) use a model to examine the design of payment mechanisms to workers from the perspective of achieving a socially optimal outcome. Different types of judging in contests, whether cardinal or ordinal, have also been discussed in the context of contest design by Ghosh & Hummel (2015). A recent survey gives a detailed overview of the factors influencing the decision to crowdsource (Thuan et al., 2016).

Certain prior works have focused on the impact of the skill level of workers on contest outcomes. Experiments conducted on Taskcn showed that highly skilled (experienced) players have the most influence on the contest designer's revenue and drive aggregate reward and reserve-price effects, effectively setting a baseline on submission quality (Liu et al., 2011); an early high-quality submission deters other high-quality players from competing. An all-pay auction model of how players with different skills choose different contests to enter, and a comparison with experiments on Taskcn, demonstrate that as the players get more experienced, the model predictions are close to the empirical data (DiPalantino & Vojnović, 2009).

More broadly, previous work has found that game-theoretic models can serve as good predictors of the outcome in real games. For instance, Boudreau et al. (2016) examined the response of players to increased participation in contests using data from 755 different contests. They found that the response to added participants conformed precisely with the theoretical predictions from Moldovanu & Sela (2001, 2006): while most participants responded negatively, the highest-skilled participants responded positively to the increased participation.

Our work takes an informational perspective on many of these aspects that arise in the design of crowdsourcing contests. Work in decentralized control, game theory, and team theory has traditionally focused on the information pattern or information structure that is available to agents in the game and/or control problem (Ho et al., 1978; Ho et al., 1981). This information pattern essentially captures the notion of "who knows what" in the given setup. For instance, it might capture different parameters regarding a game that various players are aware of—players with more information can be in an advantageous position.

It is well known that these information structures and player reputations affect player participation and game outcomes (Kreps & Wilson, 1982;

Rasmusen, 1994). We bring this informational perspective to the story of crowdsourcing and discuss how the "informational lever" of player skills can be used in crowdsourcing contest design. Previous experimental work that studied reputation systems in crowdsourcing has shown that "cheap talk" might indeed influence player behavior and this can have a positive impact on organizer revenues (Archak, 2010).

There has also been empirical work exploring the impact of information in crowdsourcing contests. An examination of event structure empirically found that dyadic contests do not improve performance compared with a single piece rate for simple and short tasks (Straub et al., 2015). Further, empirical investigation of the informational aspect of contest design led to the conclusion that giving feedback on the competitive position in contests tends to be negatively related to workers' performance: if workers are playing against strong competitors, feedback on their competitive position is associated with workers quitting the task. If the competitors are weak, workers tend to compete with lower effort. Results presented in this chapter provide a theoretical counterpoint to the empirical results from Straub et al. (2015).

Our theoretical development relies heavily on game-theoretic analysis of all-pay auctions (Hillman & Riley, 1989; Amann & Leininger, 1996).

CONTRIBUTIONS AND MAIN RESULTS

The main contributions of the chapter are as follows. First, this work compares the efficacy of crowdsourcing contests to task assignment by a manager. Task assignment is meant to capture the situation where a manager chooses a particular worker for the task. This worker then chooses an effort level with which to complete the task and then completes it. The quality of the result depends on the effort the player puts in, and the manager must accept this outcome regardless of the quality. This is roughly the model used in freelance markets (Chatterjee et al., forthcoming), though reputation systems are used there to ensure high-quality performance.

Clearly, the specific map of skill level to players is very important for targeted assignment of tasks—the manager (or task assigner) must have an estimate of the skills for each worker. Highly skilled players can provide high quality outcomes while putting in a lower effort.

Uncertainty regarding skill. The first set of results focuses on modeling the uncertainty a manager has about worker skills. How does this limit the manager's ability to accurately assign tasks and incentivize people? When and how can crowdsourcing help?

We find that if the manager is uncertain about the skills of the workers involved, crowdsourcing contests are better for single tasks if:

- managers are very uncertain about the resources and skills of workers;
- the pool of workers is diverse in its ability to perform the given task; and
- workers have a low default base effort.

Previous work by Malone et al. (2010) had claimed that the first condition is sufficient, but we see here that it need not be.

Information pattern of worker skills. The second set of results focuses on the information pattern of skill levels among workers. The theoretical results here complement empirical results of Straub et al. (2015) and highlight the impact of varying information sets between workers. Workers may have information about other workers participating in the contest through participation lists and reputation based on statistics or leaderboards (commonly employed by crowdsourcing platforms such as TopCoder and Kaggle). These digital reputations and public rankings provide players with good estimates of the strengths of other players in a contest. This information affects participation and effort levels from the workers.

We find that a weak player is incentivized to put in a very low effort (i.e. quit) if he or she finds out that the other player in the game is very strong. On the other hand, when all the workers in the pool are weak, disseminating this information can increase utility to the organizer. In a pool with strong workers, it is advantageous to keep this information hidden, since this incentivizes the strong players to put in more effort. An obvious informational lever to control the crowd will emerge via participant lists.

Multiple Tasks and Multiple Workers

When organizations may have multiple different tasks and diverse workers, as in crowdsourcing platforms like TopCoder or Kaggle, we find that:

- crowdsourcing can perform as well as optimal assignment of workers to tasks, if the tasks do not require special skills and most workers have similar skill levels with regard to the task;
- crowdsourcing contests can be suboptimal even if there is just one weak player in the pool; and
- crowdsourcing contests can perform badly for highly specialized tasks. Instead of pulling out highly skilled workers from a crowd, it might lead to mediocre performance by everyone.

This is a much more complicated set of conditions than described by Malone et al. (2010).

Taxonomy

Another question that is often raised is should we invoke collective intelligence to perform a task? Should this be via collection, contest (tournament), or collaboration (Malone et al., 2010; Afuah et al., 2018)? Within this framework, contests can be thought of as a subtype of collection, where certain contributions are awarded prizes. For collection (e.g. microtasks or contests) to be the appropriate choice, it is claimed that it must be possible to divide the overall activity into small pieces that can be done independently by different members of the crowd. Malone et al. (2010) assert that contests are a useful way of doing collection when only one or a few good solutions are needed. In contrast to this claim, our final multiple-task model demonstrates that under certain conditions, tasks where many solutions are useful to the contest designer are more suitable to be solved using crowdsourcing contests than tasks where only a few good solutions are needed. This turns out to be true because when a large number of qualified players are available, multiple tasks will most effectively mobilize them.

CROWDSOURCING CONTESTS AS ALL-PAY AUCTIONS

Our work builds on previous ideas to model crowdsourcing contests as all-pay auctions (DiPalantino & Vojnović, 2009; Archak & Sundararajan, 2009; Liu et al., 2011). Here, we use the terms workers, contestants, players, and bidders interchangeably.

Our goal is to identify the best worker for a given task and incentivize him/her to do his/her best. Crowdsourcing forums such as TopCoder and Kaggle make heavy use of leader boards and public participation records, and we will see herein that such mechanisms for changing information patterns will be critical. The models used here build on these ideas where all players have distinct, public costs. We show that weaker players are deterred from entering when they know strong players are already participating.

We limit attention to auction models with complete information to distill the salient aspects of this comparison. We assume that all players know the skill levels of all other players. High skills implies low costs per unit effort.

Economists have studied first-price all-pay auctions extensively (Hillman & Riley, 1989; Baye et al., 1996). The parallel with crowdsourcing is as follows. A contest designer proposes a task to a pool of players. The players then choose whether to enter the contest. Entering the contest involves submitting a solution (bid) for the task. The contest designer chooses the best solution as the winner and awards the announced prize. A player only gets paid if they are selected as the winner of the contest. However, they forfeit their bid (effort, opportunity cost, etc.) regardless of whether they win, just as in an all-pay auction.

THE MODEL

Consider a crowdsourcing contest with n players (denoted P_1 to P_n) and prize value $A > 0$. To capture the idea that players may have different skill sets and abilities to perform the given task, we introduce costs per unit effort c_i, $1 \leq i \leq n$, for each player. For instance, an expert may only need a few hours to complete a task and would have a low cost per unit effort, whereas a novice might have a much higher cost. Each player submits a bid x_i that represents the quality of their submission, at cost $c_i x_i$. The prize is awarded to the best submission, i.e. the highest bid x_i. The valuation of a player, $v_i = \frac{A}{c_i}$ is the ratio of the prize value to the cost per unit effort for the player.

Consider a two-player contest with players P_1 and P_2. Then the expected utilities of the players, $E[U_1]$ and $E[U_1]$, for their respective bids, are given by

$$E[U_1] = A \cdot \Pr[x_1 > x_2] - x_1 c_1 \tag{7.1}$$

$$E[U_2] = A \cdot \Pr[x_2 > x_1] - x_2 c_2. \tag{7.2}$$

Complete Information Case

First, we consider the complete information setting, where the prize value and players costs, c_i, are publicly known. Player bidding strategies depend on the other player costs, but only as a multiset. The specific mapping of costs to players is irrelevant in determining bidding strategies.

Consider the case where $c_1 < c_2$, i.e. P_1 is the stronger player. In this case, the all-pay auction has been studied previously and we restate the results below, adapted to our setting.

Theorem 1 (Hillman & Riley (1989)). *The two-player contest described above admits a unique Nash equilibrium. At equilibrium, P_1 bids uniformly at random on $[0, \frac{A}{c_2}]$. P_2 bids 0 with probability $\frac{c_2 - c_1}{c_2}$, and with the remaining probability, $\frac{c_1}{c_2}$, bids uniformly on $[0, \frac{A}{c_2}]$.*

Theorem 2 (Hillman & Riley (1989)). *If $n \geq 3$ players are involved with strictly increasing costs for P_1, P_2, P_3, i.e. $(c_1 < c_2 < c_3 < c_4 \leq \cdots \leq c_n)$, and they act as if there were no other agents, then P_3 to P_n do not enter the contest at all and submit bids 0 with probability 1.*

From Theorem 2, we can see that our model is inaccurate in that it is well known that more than just two players tend to participate in crowdsourcing contests. This might be because the assumption of rational players breaks down, or because players underestimate the competition, or player skill levels are sufficiently similar that it is in fact rational for many to enter. When one considers an all-pay auction with n players, where there is a set of $m \geq 3$ players of identical skill levels, there arc many asymmetric Nash equilibria, with more than two players entering the competition (Baye et al., 1996).

We know from empirical studies (Liu et al., 2011) that the strong players in a contest are the most influential for contest outcomes. Hence, we focus on the two-player case here for simplicity, since this allows us to focus on the player skill levels and information pattern of the game very clearly. Building on this, next we consider a model with incomplete information, where players are unaware of the strengths of the competition.

For simplicity, we consider the model with a unique Nash equilibrium, with distinct player costs. Ideas and insights from this model can be extended to the model of Baye et al. (1996).

Asymmetric Information Case

In the asymmetric information case, the prize A is publicly known, but the player costs c_i are private and known only to the individuals. Players have a prior belief about other players' valuations. In the two-player case P_1 knows their own cost c_1, and also knows that the second player's valuation, $v_2 = A/c_2$, is distributed according to $v_2 = \text{Uniform}[0, 1]$. The same is true for P_2. This is the setting considered by Amann & Leininger (1996), and the following theorem follows for the symmetric case that we consider.

Theorem 3 (Amann & Leininger (1996)). *The two-player contest with incomplete information admits a unique Nash equilibrium. At equilibrium, player P_i, who observes his private valuation $v_i = \frac{A}{c_i} \leq 1$, bids $x_i = \int_0^{v_i} w \cdot f_W(w)dw$, where W represents the player P_i's belief about the other player, and $f_W(w)$ is the probability density function of a uniform random variable on $[0, 1]$.*

Note here that the equilibrium bid of a player x_i is a deterministic function of their valuation v_i. This is unlike the case with complete public information about player costs, where players randomize their strategies.

The next section builds on the all-pay auction formalism and game-theoretic characterization we have developed here and categorizes tasks that can be completed on a crowdsourcing contest platform.

A TAXONOMY OF TASKS

An all-pay auction traditionally assumes that all submitted bids serve as revenue to the auctioneer. However, in a crowdsourcing contest, this might not be the case. Some events may have synergy while others have redundancy across entries (Bettencourt, 2009). The utility that the contest designer derives from a task depends on its nature: we denote contest returns by the function $f(\vec{x})$, where $\vec{x}$ is the vector of the worker bids. Depending on f, the designer may want to change the parameters of the contest or decide whether it is even worthwhile to hold an event. The utility derived by the contest designer is:

$$U_{task} = f(\vec{x}) - A_x, \tag{7.3}$$

where $\vec{x}$ represents the vector of n bids $x_1, x_2, \ldots, x_n$.

The function f can provide a mathematically oriented classification of potential crowdsourcing tasks. Tasks may be:

- selective, e.g. software component design;
- integrative, e.g. information aggregation or idea generation; or
- market creation, e.g. the XPRIZE (Bhushan, 2010).

We carry the terms selective and integrative from Schenk & Guittard (2011), which is one among many recent taxonomies for crowdsourcing. Contests that derive utility from the top-k entries interpolate between the extremes of selective and integrative tasks (Archak & Sundararajan, 2009).

In a selective task, only one working solution is useful to the designer. In this case, the designer typically derives utility from the maximum, and the utility function would be

$$f(\vec{x}) = max(x_1, x_2, \ldots, x_n). \tag{7.4}$$

On the other hand, an integrative idea generation contest might provide an additive or even super-additive utility to the designer, but might be subject to a coordination cost per player ($\gamma > 0$) and have

$$f(\vec{x}) = a\sum\nolimits_{i=1}^{n} x_i, a > 0. \tag{7.5}$$

However, these tasks might also be subject to coordination costs per player, as in

$$f(\vec{x}) = a\sum\nolimits_{i=1}^{n} x_i - \gamma n, a > 0. \tag{7.6}$$

Modeling *market creation* though a function is more challenging. The XPRIZE Foundation notes that their goal is "about launching new industries that attract capital, that get the public excited, that create new markets" (Tapscott & Williams, 2010: 131). Thus, independent of the quality of bids, the sheer number of entries provides utility. We model this as

$$f(\vec{x}) = an + \beta, \tag{7.7}$$

where n is the number of players.

One may further desire the f function to be upper-bounded by some maximum value. Here, we use f to characterize which tasks are best suited to crowdsourcing contests. As a minimum requirement, we would like to ensure that the contest designer's utility $\mathbb{E}[U_{task}]$ is positive, so that no losses are incurred by running a contest. This idea extends to ensuring against some minimum profit.

We consider four examples below. More than just mathematical derivation within the model, our point is to show that the parameters of the player pool influence how a particular task should be solved.

Example 1. *In a two-player selective winner-take-all contest, (7.4), the expected utility under equilibrium can be calculated using Theorem 1. Drawing on the theory of order statistics, we take the expected value of the maximum of the bids to get:*

$$\mathbb{E}[f(\vec{x}) - A] = \mathbb{E}[U_{task}] = \frac{A}{6}\left(\frac{3c_2 + c_1}{c_2^2}\right) - A. \tag{7.8}$$

Thus, $\mathbb{E}[U_{task}]$ is positive if and only if $\frac{3c_2-c_1}{6c_2^2} - 1 > 0$. The player strengths c_1 and c_2 determine whether the contest designer's utility is positive. If $c_2 \gg c_1$, i.e. the second player is much weaker than the first, then the condition reduces to $c_2 < \frac{1}{2}$. On the other hand, if $3c_2 - c_1 = \varepsilon$ is small, then $c_2^2 < \frac{\varepsilon}{6}$ is a strong enough condition to ensure positive utility.

Example 2. *For an integrative task with super-additive f as in (7.5), even a weak player pool can provide positive utility, as below.*

$$\mathbb{E}[U_{task}] = a\left(\frac{A}{2c_2} + \frac{c_1 A}{2c_2^2}\right) - A. \tag{7.9}$$

Therefore, $\mathbb{E}[U_{task}] > 0$ if and only if $a > \frac{2c_2^2}{c_1+c_2}$. If $c_2 \gg c_1$, this reduces to $\frac{a}{2} > c_2$, while if $c_2 - c_1 = \varepsilon$ is small, then a sufficient condition for positive $\mathbb{E}[U_{task}]$ is given by $a > c_2$, since $\frac{a}{2} > \frac{c_2^2}{2c_2} + \varepsilon > \frac{c_2}{2}$. In the case where $a = 1$, we see that the positive utility conditions for integrative tasks are weaker than those for selective tasks.

Example 3. *Consider (7.4) with n players who have strictly decreasing valuations. We noted earlier that in this case, $x_3, \ldots, x_n = 0$ almost surely, and hence, $\mathbb{E}[U_{task}]$ for the contest designer is exactly as (7.8). Clearly, with added coordination costs, as in (7.6), a winner-take-all contest would be exactly the wrong structure.*

Example 4. *In the case of an event where the objective is market creation, the designer's utility does not even depend on the effort of the players.*

In closing, we observe that if $f_1(\vec{x}) \geq f_2(\vec{x})$ for all $\vec{x}$, $\mathbb{E}[U_{task}](f_2) > 0$ implies that $\mathbb{E}[U_{task}](f_1) > 0$, since player bidding strategies are independent of the designer's valuation function f. Even with approximate functions, this provides contest designers with a simple rule of thumb to order potential f functions.

CROWDSOURCING VERSUS ASSIGNMENT

Crowdsourcing can be a powerful way of reaching a large pool of workers inexpensively. Further, workers can self-select tasks they want to work on and fluidly move from one task of their choosing to another. The fluidity of the crowdsourcing model allows a player to self-select tasks and the right model might increase the labor force of the future (Bollier, 2011). With this agency, workers will likely choose tasks that they are good at and enjoy. However, it is important not to think of crowdsourcing as a catch-all solution and we should note that sometimes players may not know themselves perfectly.

On the other hand, the assignment of tasks by a manager to a worker requires detailed information about player skill sets. Since different tasks require different skills, it is important that a manager assigns to each worker a task that he or she will be good at. For instance, one software development project may require knowledge of Java, whereas another might require use of DB2. How useful is crowdsourcing for skills identification?

The winner-take-all format provides natural performance incentives without the cost of organizational frameworks. Quite clearly, such a model comes with the benefits and pitfalls of an outcome-based reward structure which have been extensively studied in the literature (e.g. Dixit, 2002). How important are these competitive incentive factors?

Our model addresses the tradeoff between endogenous incentives offered by a contest-based solution versus externally provided incentives, and the effect of observation noise when a manager assigns a task to a player for a selective task with two players. Similar models can easily be developed for integrative or market creation tasks. A second model looks at a multi-task, multi-player setting and captures the potential of crowdsourcing contests in solving hard matching problems and yielding higher utility for both designers and players.

Of course, completion of the task at hand with maximum utility may be only one among many objectives desired by the contest designer. A longer-term perspective may necessitate consideration of completion of many (similar or dissimilar) tasks over time, which may require workforce evolution and retention. Further, it has been observed empirically that crowdsourcing contests may be inefficient, since they are prone to over-effort; in aggregate, players may exert more than fifteen times the effort required to complete the task (Varshney et al., 2011). Direct assignment of tasks to players minimizes such over-effort and can offer training benefits. These issues are not addressed in the models here but are discussed elsewhere (Varshney et al., 2011; Singla et al., 2014).

Crowdsourcing a Single Task

The key model we use in this chapter involves modeling the skills of players, the skills required to complete a certain task. Let each task be represented by a k-bit binary number. This binary representation of the task corresponds to the skills required to complete that task. Thus if two tasks have exactly the same k-bit binary representation, they require exactly the same skills. Tasks that require very different skills have binary representations that are very far away from each other.

Similarly, we think of each player being represented by a k-bit string that represents his or her skill level. This model is similar to the model used by Hong & Page (2001). The objective of a manager is then to assign to each task a person who is "closest" in the skill space to the task.

To model this, we examine the Hamming distance between tasks and worker. If this distance is low, then the worker has a good skill set for the task and if the Hamming distance is large, the worker has a poor skill set for the task. Thus the Hamming distance serves as a proxy for the overall skill level of a worker with respect to a task.

The key point of this model is that we can now quantitatively model the imperfect worker information of a manager, as a noisy observation on the binary skill vector of the work. Say the manager observes each skill vector with a bit flip probability, σ. Using only this observation, the manager is now required to assign a player to a task. Naturally, the manager chooses that player that appears to be closest to the task in Hamming distance.

Complete information case. Now consider a two-player setup with complete information. Thus all the player/worker strengths/skill levels are known to all the other players entering the contest, though the manager may have a noisy observation. Let player 1 be the stronger player for the task, i.e. let P_1 be the Player who is closest in Hamming distance to the task. Let d_i, where $i = 1, 2$, represent the distances of Players 1 and 2 from the task, which serve as a proxy for the costs incurred for the players. As per our assumption, $d_1 < d_2$.

Let $\vec{S_1}$ and $\vec{S_2}$ represent the length-k skill vectors of the two players, and $\vec{Z_1}, \vec{Z_2}$ be the two independent noise vectors ~Bernoulli(σ). The manager observes $\vec{S_1} + \vec{Z_1}$ and $\vec{S_2} + \vec{Z_2}$, which are at distances e_1 and e_2 from the task.

First, let us calculate the utility achieved with noiseless perfect assignment. The stronger player, player 1, will at best exert $x_1 = A/d_1$ effort to complete the task, since any extra effort would lead to a negative expected utility for the player. Let θ be the base fraction of effort exerted by players through external (non-competition-based) incentives. If v is the base utility obtained by the contest-designer, then with optimal assignment the expected utility is given by

$$\mathbb{E}[U_{opt}] = v + \theta \frac{A}{d_1} - A = v + A\left(\frac{\theta}{d_1} - 1\right). \tag{7.10}$$

Theorem 4. *The expected utility achieved by targeted assignment,* $\mathbb{E}[U_{man}]$, *and crowdsourcing contest mechanisms with public valuations,* $v_1 = \frac{A}{c_1}$ *and,* $v_2 = \frac{A}{c_2}$, $\mathbb{E}[U_{cs}]$, *are given as*

$$\mathbb{E}[U_{man}] = v + A\left[\Pr(\mathrm{r})\frac{\theta}{d_1} + (1 - \Pr(\mathrm{r}))\frac{\theta}{d_2} - 1\right] \tag{7.11}$$

$$\mathbb{E}[U_{cs}] = v + \frac{2A}{3d_2}\frac{d_2 - d_1}{d_1} - A \tag{7.12}$$

respectively, where $\Pr(r)$ *is the probability that the task is assigned to the correct player, and can be calculated as below.*

Proof. It is a straightforward expectation that gives $\mathbb{E}[U_{man}]$ as (7.11), once we have $\Pr(r)$. To calculate $\Pr(r)$, we note that an error will be made by the manager if they observe that P_2 is closer to the task than P_1, i.e. $e_1 > e_2$ even though $d_1 < d_2$. Hence, $\Pr(\mathrm{r}) = \Pr(e_1 < e_2 | d_1 < d_2)$. Hence, we are interested in the change in $e_1 - e_2$ compared to $d_1 - d_2$. This probability is the same as that if $\vec{s}_1$ were perturbed by noise $\vec{z} \sim \mathrm{Bernoulli}(\phi)$, where $\phi = 2\sigma - 2\sigma^2$, with $\vec{s}_2$ unchanged. Let d_{ch} be the change in $\vec{s}_1$ due to the noise $\vec{z}$. Then,

$$\Pr(r) = \sum_{l=0}^{d_2 - d_1} \Pr(d_{ch} = l) \tag{7.13}$$

$$\Pr(d_{ch} = l) = \sum_{k=0}^{k_1} \binom{n - d_1}{l + k}\binom{d_1}{k}\phi^{l+2k}(1 - \phi)^{n-l-2k}, \tag{7.14}$$

where $k_1 = \min(d_1, n - d_1 - l)$. The remaining calculations are omitted for brevity.

Since a crowdsourcing mechanism picks out the maximum bidder, we can calculate the distribution of the expected utility under equilibrium as the $\mathbb{E}[\max(x_1, x_2)]$, where bids x_1 and x_2 have distributions as specified by Theorem 1. This gives (7.12).

Asymmetric information case. Now, consider the case of asymmetric information, where players do not know each other's distances d_1 and d_2. At most they might have some distributional information about their competitors. We assume each player knows his or her own distance from the task perfectly.

Theorem 5.   *Consider the two-player game with private valuations v_1 and v_2. Let a player's belief about their opponent's strategy (i.e. the bid they expect the opponent to play) be Uniform[0, 1]. Then, the expected utility achieved with crowdsourcing contest mechanisms, $\mathbb{E}[U_{csa}]$, is given as*

$$\mathbb{E}[U_{csa}] = v + \frac{1}{2}\left(\frac{A}{d_1}\right)^2 - A. \qquad (7.15)$$

Proof. From Theorem 3, we know that if the player valuation is v_1, then at equilibrium a player will submit the bid where $f_W(w) = 1$ if $w\varepsilon[0, 1]$ and $f_W(w) = 0$ otherwise. Then, $x_i(v_i)$ is given by

$$x_i(v_i) = \int_0^{v_i} w \cdot f_w(w)dw = \int_0^{v_i} w \cdot 1 \cdot dw = \frac{v_i^2}{2}. \qquad (7.16)$$

Since the higher bid will come from the stronger player, Player 1, we use v_1 in the expression above to give the result.

Discussion.   To gain more insight into the theorems, Figures 7.2, 7.3, and 7.4 show the relative utility obtained by the task designer with different values of the managerial noise and base level of effort. Since empirical productivity estimates

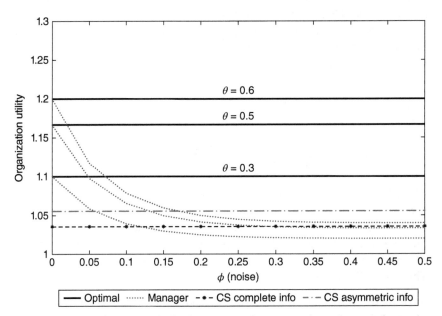

Figure 7.2. One strong one weak player. Since the strong player does not know that the other player is weak, they exert more effort and the asymmetric information setup has higher revenue than the complete information setup.

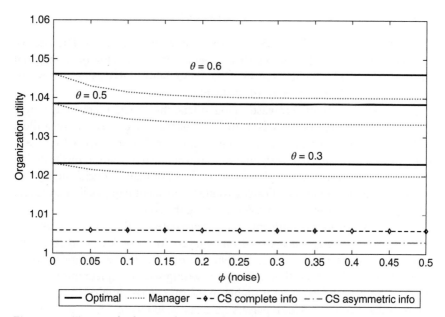

Figure 7.3. Two weak players. Player 1, who is weak, does not know that Player 2 is also weak and vice versa, and so neither exerts much effort (since their own valuation is low they have reason to believe the other player is stronger). They do not even exert the level of effort that would be exerted in the complete information case and the manager utility obtained with asymmetric information is lower than that with complete information.

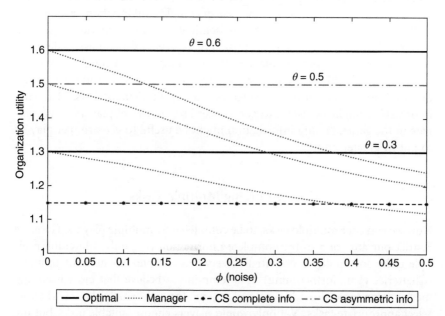

Figure 7.4. Two strong players. With two strong players, both bid strongly based on their own valuation since each has reason to believe they are the stronger player, and asymmetric information does better than complete information.

show that θ might be about 0.5, we vary θ between 0.3 and 0.6. The relative strengths of the two players can affect whether crowdsourcing or managerial assignment provides higher returns. Note these figures serve as examples and changes to θ, ϕ, d_1, and d_2 may affect the plots.

As Figure 7.2 shows, crowdsourcing offers the greatest advantage over assignment when the skill levels in the pool of players are diverse, regardless of the information workers have about each other. We see that with a weak pool of players, targeted assignment performs better than crowdsourcing (Figure 7.3). With two strong players, noise does not matter much, and crowdsourcing does not offer significant advantages in identifying skill (Figure 7.4) when players are aware of who else is entering the contest.

Now let us consider the information pattern between the workers. Consider first Figure 7.2. Here, since the strong player does not know whether the second player is stronger or weaker than thems. Hence, they are incentivized to exert more effort than they would in a setting with complete information, and the utility to the manager is higher in the case of asymmetric information. On the other hand, when both players are weak, as in Figure 7.3, the asymmetric information setup extracts less utility than does the complete information setup. This is because both players believe they are the weaker of the two players. Neither person thinks they have a significant chance of winning and neither exert much effort. Finally, in the case where the whole pool is made of strong players, as in Figure 7.4, each assumes they have a high chance of winning and places a relatively high bid. Unlike the complete information case, the effort levels are not bottlenecked by the strength of the weaker player, and the effective utility to the manager is much higher than in the case of complete information.

These observations suggest that dissemination of information regarding player skills can be used as an "informational lever" by a contest designer to elicit higher effort from the players. If the manager has a rough idea about the multiset of skills in the player pool, they can use this to tune the release of this information through leader boards or participant lists. Releasing information might be useful to get weaker and mid-level players to participate in the game. Hiding information might be useful to get stronger players to put in greater effort.

Crowdsourcing Multiple Tasks

Now we consider multiple tasks, to be completed by multiple players. Here, we restrict our attention to the complete information case only. Matching multiple tasks and multiple potential solvers is a complex assignment problem (Chatterjee et al., forthcoming). It is tempting to believe that crowdsourcing mechanisms could provide a natural scheme through which players will self-select appropriate tasks. Not only would players choose suitable tasks, but the competition could provide performance incentives. This section explores a simple multi-player, multi-task model.

We would like to explore a setting with $2n$ tasks of two types each. One set of n tasks might be dependent on Java programming skill and, say, the other set of skills is dependent on graphic design. The players are also categorized into these two types and there are n players for each type. Players of a given type are better at tasks of the same type. A Java programmer (or graphic artist) can complete a Java task (or graphic design task) at a low cost (c_l), whereas hey have a high cost (c_h) for a graphic design task (or Java task).

We find that:

- for generic tasks with many skilled players, crowdsourcing can easily achieve close to optimal utility for a task;
- surprisingly, crowdsourcing contests can provide utility close to zero even with a pool of many strong players and just one weak player; and
- crowdsourcing contests perform badly for highly specialized tasks, which only few experts might be qualified to perform. In fact, these experts might get buried under the crowd.

We introduce some new notation to set up the framework. Consider a setting with $2n$ tasks denoted by $(E_J(1), \ldots, E_J(n))$ and $(E_G(1), \ldots, E_G(n))$ and $2m$ players denoted by $(P_J(1), \ldots, PJ(m))$ and $(P_G(1), \ldots, P_G(m))$, with $m \geq n$. There are n tasks of each of two types: Java-based (type J) or graphic design-based (type G), and similarly, m players of each type.

Players of a given type are better at tasks of the same type. A Java programmer (or graphic artist) can complete a Java task (or graphic design task) at a low cost (c_l), whereas they have a high cost (c_h) for a graphic design task (or Java task). $P_J(i)$ has cost $c_{JJ}(i) = c_i + \varepsilon(i)$ for tasks $E_J(1)$ to $E_J(n)$, and cost $c_{JG}(i) = c_h + \varepsilon(i)$ for $E_G(1)$ to $E_G(n)$. Costs for $P_G(i)$, i.e. $c_{GG}(i)$ and $c_{GJ}(i)$, are defined similarly. The $\varepsilon(i)$ are to be thought of as error terms: $\varepsilon(i) \lll c_i \ll c_h$. Base effort θ is as defined earlier. Without loss of generality, assume that the player costs are ordered:

$$c_{JJ}(1) < c_{JJ}(2) < \ldots < c_{JJ}(m) \lll c_{GJ}(1) < c_{GJ}(2) < \ldots < c_{GJ}(m), \text{ and}$$
$$c_{GG}(1) < c_{GG}(2) < \ldots < c_{GG}(m) \lll c_{JG}(1) < c_{JG}(2) < \ldots < c_{JG}(m).$$

The optimal utility, U_{opt}, is achieved when each player is matched to a task of his or her type. This total utility is the sum of utilities of the events less the reward paid out, and acts as our baseline. This is given by

$$\mathbb{E}[U_{opt}] = 2nA\left(\frac{\theta}{c_l} - 1\right). \tag{7.17}$$

However, doing this matching manually is difficult, which motivates the use of crowdsourcing.

Theorem 6.   *In the framework described above, if the manager observes an incorrect player type with probability ϕ, then the expected contest designer utility, U_{man}, is*

$$\mathbb{E}[U_{man}] = 2nA\left(\frac{(1-\phi)\theta}{c_l} + \frac{\phi.\theta}{c_h} - 1\right). \tag{7.18}$$

Proof. An expectation calculation gives

$$\mathbb{E}[U_{man}] = (1-\phi)\sum_{i=1}^{n}\theta\frac{A}{c_{JJ}} + \phi\sum_{i=1}^{n}\theta\frac{A}{c_{JG}} + (1-\phi)\sum_{i=1}^{n}\theta\frac{A}{c_{GG}} + \phi\sum_{i=1}^{n}\theta\frac{A}{c_{GJ}} - 2nA. \tag{7.19}$$

Substituting values of the costs gives the desired (7.18).

Now consider the crowdsourcing scenario. Each player can submit entries for any task, however, finally only one player will be picked per task and each player can only win one contest. Note that with enough skilled competitors, crowdsourcing can yield higher utility than even optimal assignment (7.17), since $0 \leq \theta \leq 1$, and is often close to 0.5.

Theorem 7.   *In a crowdsourcing contest, as described above, when $m \geq n+1$, the expected utility from crowdsourcing is*

$$\mathbb{E}[U_{cs}] = 2nA\left(\frac{1}{c_l} - 1\right), \tag{7.20}$$

as $n \to \infty$.

Proof. First, consider all tasks of the type. For notational ease, let $v_{JJ}(i) = \frac{A}{c_{JJ}(i)}$.

This problem essentially boils down to an all-pay auction, with n identical goods $E_1, ..., E_n$, and 2_n, and players. The n highest bidders will be assigned the n tasks. Such auctions with multiple goods and players have been extensively studied (Barut & Kovenock, 1998; Clark & Riis, 1998), and we build on this work here.

When all the players have unequal valuations, this game has a unique Nash equilibrium, in which only the strongest $n+1$ players actively bid, while the rest almost surely bid 0. Thus, only players $P_J(1)$ to $P_J(n+1)$ with values $v_{JJ}(1)$ to $v_{JJ}(n+1)$ will actively submit entries for tasks of type J.

From Clark & Riis (1998), we know that $P_J(1)$ to $P_J(n)$ will randomize over the interval $[\ell(i), v_{GJ}(1)]$, where

$$\ell(i) = \left(1 - \prod_{k=i}^{n}\frac{v_{JJ}(k)}{v_{JJ}(i)}\right)v_{JJ}(n+1), i = 1, 2, ..., n. \tag{7.21}$$

$P_J(n+1)$ randomizes uniformly over $[0, v_{JJ}(n+1)]$.

Let r be a parameter such that $r = 1$ if $\ell(1) \leq x \leq v_{JJ}(n+1)$, else $r = s$ if $\ell(s) \leq x < \ell(s-1)$. Then, the distribution of the bidding strategy (Clark & Riis, 1998) $F_{J,i}(x)$, for $i = 1, 2, \ldots, n$ is given by

$$F_{J,i}(x) = 1 - \left(\frac{v_{JJ}(i)}{\prod_{k=r}^{n} v_{JJ}(k)^{\frac{1}{n+1-r}}} \right) \left(1 - \frac{x}{v_{JJ}(n+1)} \right)^{\frac{1}{n+1-r}}. \tag{7.22}$$

Player $P_J(n+1)$ submits 0 with probability $\frac{v_{JJ}(n+1)}{v_{JJ}(n)}$, and otherwise randomizes according to eq. (7.22) with $v_{JJ}(n)$ in place of $v_{JJ}(i)$.

The expected utility of each player in this case is given by $v_{JJ}(i) - v_{JJ}(n+1)$. The expected payoff to the contest designer would be the sum of the n highest bids of the players.

As n becomes large, players submit entries close to the upper bound $v_{JJ}(n+1)$. Similar to the two-player all-pay auction where no players bid higher than the weaker player's valuation, the weakest player's valuation $v_{JJ}(n+1)$ is an upper bound on the bids of all players. Note that if $v_{JJ}(i) \approx v_{JJ}(k)$ for all i, k, the lower bound for the support of the mixed strategies of all players is close to 0. $r = 1$ for most x in this interval, and

$$F_{j,i}(x) \approx 1 - \left(1 - \frac{x}{v_{JJ}(n+1)} \right)^{\frac{1}{N}}. \tag{7.23}$$

Since all players adopt the same strategy, the probability of any one player winning is $\frac{n}{n+1}$. Thus, the expected bid is the difference of the expected gross surplus and the expected utility,

$$\mathbb{E}[x_i] = \frac{n}{n+1} v_{JJ}(i) - \left(v_{JJ}(i) - v_{JJ}(n+1) \right) \tag{7.24}$$

$$\approx \frac{n}{n+1} \left(\frac{A}{c_l} \right). \tag{7.25}$$

With the assumption $v_i \approx v_{n+1}$ for all i, we have that the expected bid for player i is $\frac{n}{n+1} v_i \approx \frac{n}{n+1} \frac{A}{c_l}$.

Now consider the tasks of type G. The $n+1$ strongest players for this task are the players of type G. Since these players were strictly weaker than the players of type J for the tasks of type J, none actively participated in any of those tasks. However, they will actively bid on the tasks of type G, following exactly the same patterns as the players of type J in bidding on the tasks of type J. Hence, the total expected utility to the contest designer, using crowd-sourcing in the case of approximately identical costs (or values) for all players of a type, is given by

$$\mathbb{E}[U_{cs}] \approx \sum_{i=1}^{n} \frac{n}{n+1} \left(\frac{A}{c_i} \right) + \sum_{i=1}^{n} \frac{n}{n+1} \left(\frac{A}{c_i} \right) - 2nA, \qquad (7.26)$$

$$
\begin{aligned}
&= 2n \frac{n}{n+1} \left(\frac{A}{c_i} \right) - 2nA \\
&= 2nA \left(\frac{1}{c_i} - 1 \right), \text{ as } n \to \infty.
\end{aligned} \qquad (7.27)
$$

Theorem 8. *If c_h is high enough that $\frac{A}{c_h} \approx 0$, then the expected utility from crowdsourcing $\mathbb{E}[U_{cs}] = 0$.*

Proof. This result follows just as Theorem 7. Intuitively, since there are only enough players to complete the task, each player is assured of winning a task and thus has no incentive to put in a non-zero bid.

Note that lack of competition leads to low performance by all players. Instead, in this case if tasks were assigned by a manager, albeit noisily, significant utility could be derived for at least some of the tasks. The natural thought process might lead us to believe that crowdsourcing contests are good for skill discovery—it is easy to think that expert players will clearly become obvious in a competitive setting. This setting gives a clear example where this would not be the case. Crowdsourcing may not be a good solution when the contest designer has many tasks of a specialized nature that require highly skilled players who are in short supply. This model easily extends to more than two types of events and players.

When it is possible to divide a large project into smaller tasks, the best way to harness multiple players is through multiple tasks. A first-price auction with multiple players only incentivizes the two strongest players to enter the contest. However, if contest designers are able to divide a large task into many smaller tasks of different types that are matched to the different types of players in the crowd, both the designers and the players could receive higher utilities. Our guidelines for crowdsourcing tasks both support and complement those from Malone et al. (2010).

CONCLUSIONS AND FUTURE RESEARCH

Complementing empirical work in the area of crowdsourcing contest design, we have developed a theoretical framework that may guide organizations considering crowdsourcing contests to do work. The basic idea is to find the best workers for jobs, and incentivize them to do their best, with various informational levers for crowd control. More broadly, we have tried to understand the implications, strengths, and weaknesses of more fluid task-focused labor markets.

The simple models presented here are only a first step. Models involving multiple prizes, and also those which take into account repeated game effects such as player learning and retention costs, are necessary future work. Our larger goal is to understand the best ways in which to organize work when there are many design possibilities for different types of tasks and information patterns.

ACKNOWLEDGMENTS

We thank Eric Bokelberg, Ankur Mani, Anshul Sheopuri, and Lada Adamic for helpful discussions.

REFERENCES

Afuah, A. (2018). Co-opetition in crowdsourcing: When simultaneous cooperation and competition deliver superior solutions. In C. Tucci, A. Afuah, & G. Viscusi (eds.), *Creating and Capturing Value Through Crowdsourcing*. Oxford: Oxford University Press, pp. 271–91.

Afuah, A. & Tucci, C. L. (2012). Crowdsourcing as a solution to distant search. *Academy of Management Review, 37*(3), 355–75.

Afuah, A., Tucci, C. L., and Viscusi, G. (2018). Introduction to creating and capturing value through crowdsourcing, in C. Tucci, A. Afuah, and G. Viscusi (eds), *Creating and Capturing Value Through Crowdsourcing*. Oxford: Oxford University Press, pp. 1–8.

Amann, E. & Leininger, W. (1996). Asymmetric all-pay auctions with incomplete information: The two-player case. *Games and Economic Behavior, 14*(1), 1–18.

Archak, N. (2010). Money, glory and cheap talk: Analyzing strategic behavior of contestants in simultaneous crowdsourcing contests on TopCoder.com. In *Proceeding WWW' 10: Proceedings of the 19th International World Wide Web (WWW'10)*, pp. 21–30, pp. 21–30. Raleigh, NC, April 26–30, ACM New York, NY. doi: 10.1145/1772690.1772694.

Archak, N. & Sundararajan, A. (2009). Optimal design of crowdsourcing contests. *Proceedings of the International Conference on Information Systems* (ICIS), p. 200, https://aisel.aisnet.org/icis2009/200 (accessed October 26, 2017).

Barut, Y. & Kovenock, D. (1998). The symmetric multiple prize all-pay auction with complete information. *European Journal of Political Economy, 14*(4), 627–44.

Baye, M. R., Kovenock, D., & de Vries, C. G. (1996). The all-pay auction with complete information. *Economic Theory, 8*(2), 291–305.

Benkler, Y. (2006). *The Wealth of Networks: How Social Production Transforms Markets and Freedom*. New Haven, CT: Yale University Press.

Bettencourt, L. M. A. (2009). The rules of information aggregation and emergence of collective intelligent behavior. *Topics in Cognitive Science, 1*(4), 598–620.

Bhushan, B. (2010). The incentives and disincentives of innovation prizes: A survey of the dropout teams from Progressive Insurance Automotive X PRIZE. S.M. thesis, Massachusetts Institute of Technology.

Bollier, D. (2011). *The Future of Work: What It Means for Individuals, Businesses, Markets and Governments.* Washington DC: The Aspen Institute.

Boudreau, K. J., Lacetera, N., & Lakhani, K. R. (2011). Incentives and problem uncertainty in innovation contests: An empirical analysis. *Management Science*, 57(5), 843–63.

Boudreau, K. J., Lakhani, K. R., & Menietti, M. (2016). Performance responses to competition across skill levels in rank-order tournaments: Field evidence and implications for tournament design. *The Rand Journal of Economics*, 47(1), 140–65.

Cavallo, R. & Jain, S. (2012). Efficient crowdsourcing contests. In *Proceedings of the 11th International Conference on Autonomous Agents and Multiagent Systems*, (AAMAS' 12) Vol. 2, pp. 677–86. Valencia, Spain, June 04–08, International Foundation for Autonomous Agents and Multiagent Systems Richland, SC.

Chandler, D. & Kapelner, A. (2013). Breaking monotony with meaning: Motivation in crowdsourcing markets. *Journal of Economic Behavior & Organization*, 90, 123–33.

Chatterjee, A., Varshney, L. R., & Vishwananth, S. (2017). Work capacity of freelance markets: Fundamental limits and decentralized schemes. *IEEE/ACM Transactions on Networking*, 25(6), 3641–54.

Clark, D. J. & Riis, C. (1998). Competition over more than one prize. *American Economic Review*, 88(1), 276–89.

Cuenin, A. (2015). Each of the top 25 best global brands has used crowdsourcing, http://www.crowdsourcing.org/editorial/each-of-the-top-25-best-global-brands-has-used-crowdsourcing/50145 (accessed October 26, 2017).

DiPalantino, D. & Vojnović, M. (2009). Crowdsourcing and all-pay auctions. In *Proceedings of the 10th ACM Conference on Electronic Commerce (EC'09)*, pp. 119–28 Stanford, CA, July 6–10, ACM New York, NY, doi:10.1145/1566374.1566392.

Dixit, A. (2002). Incentives and organizations in the public sector. *Journal of Human Resources*, 37(4), 696–727.

Ghosh, A. (2013). Game theory and incentives in human computation systems, in P. Michelucci (ed.), *Handbook of Human Computation*. New York: Springer, pp. 725–42.

Ghosh, A. & Hummel, P. (2015). Cardinal contests. In *Proceedings of the 24th International Conference on World Wide Web (WWW'15)*, pp. 377–87. Florence, Italy, May 18–22, International World Wide Web Conferences, Geneva, Switzerland. doi:10.1145/2736277.2741652.

Hillman, A. L. & Riley, J. G. (1989). Politically contestable rents and transfers. *Economics & Politics*, 1(1), 17–39.

Ho, Y.-C., Kastner, M. P., & Wong, E. (1978). Teams, signaling, and information theory. *IEEE Transactions on Automatic Control, AC-23*(2), 305–12.

Ho, Y.-C., Luh, P. B., & Muralidharan, R. (1981). Information structure, Stackelberg games, and incentive controllability. *IEEE Transactions on Automatic Control, AC-26*(2), 454–60.

Hong, L. & Page, S. E. (2001). Problem solving by heterogeneous agents. *Journal of Economic Theory*, 97(1), 123–63.

Howe, J. (2008). *Crowdsourcing: Why the Power of the Crowd is Driving the Future of Business*. New York: Three Rivers Press.

Kreps, D. M. & Wilson, R. (1982). Reputation and imperfect information. *Journal of Economic Theory*, *27*(2), 253–79.

Liu, T. X., Yang, J., Adamic, L. A., & Chen, Y. (2011). Crowdsourcing with all-pay auctions: A field experiment on Taskcn. *Management Science*, *60*(8), 2020–37.

Lohr, S. (2009). The crowd is wise (when it's focused). *New York Times*, July 18.

Malone, T. W., Laubacher, R., & Dellarocas, C. (2010). The collective intelligence genome. *MIT Sloan Management Review*, *51*(3), 21–31.

Moldovanu, B. & Sela, A. (2001). The optimal allocation of prizes in contests.*American Economic Review*, *91*(3), 542–58.

Moldovanu, B. & Sela, A. (2006). Contest architecture. *Journal of Economic Theory*, *126*(1), 70–96.

Rasmusen, E. (1994). *Games and Information: An Introduction to Game Theory*, 4th edn. Malden, MA: Blackwell Publishing.

Schenk, E. & Guittard, C. (2011). Towards a characterization of crowdsourcing Practices. *Journal of Innovation Economics*, *1*(7), 93–107.

Singla, A., Bogunovic, I., Bartók, G., Karbasi, A., & Krause, A. (2014). Near-optimally teaching the crowd to classify. In *Proceedings of the 31st International Conference on Machine Learning (ICML 2014)*, pp. 154–62.

Straub, T., Gimpel, H., Teschner, F., & Weinhardt, C. (2015). How (not) to incent crowd workers. *Business & Information Systems Engineering*, *57*(3), 167–79.

Tapscott, D. & Williams, A. D. (2006). *Wikinomics: How Mass Collaboration Changes Everything*, expanded edn. New York: Portfolio Penguin.

Tapscott, D. & Williams, A. D. (2010). *Macrowikinomics: Rebooting Business and the World*. New York: Portfolio Penguin.

Thuan, N. H., Antunes, P., & Johnstone, D. (2016). Factors influencing the decision to crowdsource: A systematic literature review. *Information Systems Frontiers*, *18*(1), 47–68.

Tucci, C., Afuah, A., and Viscusi, G. (2018). Introduction to creating and capturing value through crowdsourcing. In C. Tucci, A. Afuah, and G. Viscusi (eds), *Creating and Capturing Value Through Crowdsourcing*, Oxford: Oxford University Press.

Varshney, L. R. (2012). Participation in crowd systems. In *Proceedings of the 50th Annual Allerton Conference on Communication, Control, and Computing*, pp. 996–1001), http://ieeexplore.ieee.org/abstract/document/6483327/ (accessed October 26, 2017).

Viscusi, G. & Tucci, C. (2018). Three's a crowd? In C. Tucci, A. Afuah, & G. Viscusi (eds.), *Creating and Capturing Value Through Crowdsourcing*. Oxford: Oxford University Press, pp. 39–57.

Wallin, M., von Krogh, G., & Sieg, J. (2017). A problem in the making: How firms formulate sharable problems for open innovation contests. In C. Tucci, A. Afuah, & G. Viscusi (eds.), *Creating and Capturing Value Through Crowdsourcing*. Oxford: Oxford University Press, pp. 39–57.

West, J. & Sims, J. (2018). How firms leverage crowds and communities for open innovation. In C. Tucci, A. Afuah, & G. Viscusi (eds.), *Creating and Capturing Value Through Crowdsourcing*. Oxford: Oxford University Press, pp. 58–96.

Part III

Collaboration-Based Crowdsourcing

8

Renegotiating Public Value with Co-Production

Antonio Cordella, Andrea Paletti, and Maha Shaikh

Abstract

In the context of public sector organizations, the governance model for co-production could help to deliver better public services that fulfill the expectations of citizens, via crowdsourcing. This chapter considers how and why co-production is a valuable solution for producing public services, but also highlights the challenges that public sector organizations face when co-production is adopted without being customized for public sector service delivery. In the context of the public sector, co-production needs to be focused on public value creation and not on public service production processes. This subtle shift in focus allows us to discuss how and why adopting co-production models that are successful in the private sector cannot be applied directly to public sector organizations; instead they need to be tailored in the light of a better understanding of the requirements of public value creation.

INTRODUCTION

In current public management and e-government literatures crowdsourcing, and co-production more generally, is a key concept in describing public participation in government mediated by e-petitioning, e-participation, or e-democracy (Berry & Moss, 2006; Boulos et al., 2011; Linders, 2012; Harrison & Sayogo, 2014). In this chapter we analyze different forms of co-production as possible mechanisms that can be adopted by public organizations to increase their ability to produce and provide services that better match citizens' expectations. In the context of public sector organizations, co-production should account for specificities that are not common in the private sector context. The most relevant of these specificities lies in the public value that public sector organizations need to consider when service production and delivery is concerned (Benington & Moore, 2010). This chapter compares different modes of co-production that can be employed to deliver public services, and highlights both the potential and limitations of innersourcing (Kratzer et al., 2017), crowdsourcing (Afuah, 2018b), and opensourcing (West & Sims, 2018) in different situations. Our theoretical discussion highlights how different co-production modes can expand the operational capabilities needed by public sector organizations to increase the value they produce and deliver to citizens via public services.

Over the years, public management studies have developed a rich set of theories to frame the best production configuration to optimize the value they create and provide useful solutions. Within this debate increasing interest is to be found in public management literature concerning the notion of public value to help frame new approaches to public sector management (O'Flynn, 2007; Bryson et al., 2014). These new approaches aim to respond to the questionable results of public management theories, mainly focused on efficiency and rationalization in public sector services production and delivery (Verbeeten & Speklé, 2015). Public value approaches to public sector management reframe public management theories, shifting the focus from cost efficiency to fulfillment of broader socially expected outcomes (Osborne et al., 2013). This shift in focus reflects the struggle that public sector organizations and hence management face when their activities are judged by the society as a collective entity that uses, benefits, and not least, contributes to the production of these services. Public sector organizations have in fact been mostly concerned with how to increase efficiency and hence reduce the costs of producing what they have traditionally delivered. For such organizations the belief is that the only value perceived by the society of relevance is one of cost efficiency. Public administrations are indeed criticized not only for their production costs—often referred to as inefficient—but also for what they produce and deliver i.e. the nature of their activities.

To deliver what is expected by society, public administrations have to better understand what is socially expected and to dynamically respond to changes in social expectations. Information and communication technologies (ICTs), as a more networked world, as well as a more informed and aware society are changing the landscape within which public sector organizations produce and deliver their services and the way in which these services are valued (Linders, 2012).

In this chapter we will analyze the role of co-production in public sector services and discuss how co-production can help public sector organizations to produce and perform services that are better valued by contemporary society and therefore help public administration to more effectively produce public value. We conclude that public sector organizations concerned with public value production will shift their services' production process into co-production models that have already shown their value in the development of open source software and other products and services.

We claim that co-production can help to overcome many of the limitations associated with bureaucracy where public value creation is concerned. Co-production does indeed offer the operational capacity needed to produce public value when this value is produced by a dynamic, networked, and socially more aware society. Our analysis will also highlight how, and why, it is difficult to design co-production frameworks able to produce public value.

The remaininder of the chapter is structured as follows: the second section introduces the notion of public value; the third section discusses the relationships between public value creation and bureaucracy; the fourth section presents the main ideas of co-production; the fifth section focuses on how co-production could help public value creation; and lastly, the sixth section concludes our chapter.

VALUE CREATION IN THE PUBLIC SECTOR

Benington & Moore (2010) propose the strategic triangle as a framework for depicting the public value creation process. We will build on this framework to discuss how and why co-production is more valuable than bureaucracy when public value creation is concerned. The strategic triangle of public value consists of three main dimensions: the *authorizing environment, operational capacity,* and *public value outcomes.*

The authorizing environment consists of multiple stakeholders pursuing their own interests but also communal interests from short, medium, and long-term perspectives with regard to their broad social and political expectations. It is the domain within which public value is framed. The operational capacity reflects the organizational configuration and capacity used by the public administration to deliver what multiple stakeholders expect to fulfill both their individual and communal interests. The outcomes of this process, such as public services and regulations, are valued by citizens on the basis of their preferences, and the latter is framed and defined by the authorizing environment.

BUREAUCRACY AND VALUE CREATION

Historically, bureaucracy and the bureaucratic logic are the organizational configurations within which public sector organizations produce and deliver public sector services. Bureaucracies therefore define the operational capacity of most public sector organizations and shape the value that these organizations deliver. The reason why bureaucracies are chosen to coordinate activities within public sector organizations is because of their capacity to increase efficiency in organizational practices and procedures while preserving the values of equality and fairness of public sector actions.

The operational capacity of bureaucratic organizations consists of their ability to add value to public services by making the action of public sector organizations more standardized and hence efficient, and by so doing guarantee the values of impartiality, fairness, and equality in delivering public services. When these values are at the center of the interests shaping the authorizing environments, bureaucracy produces outcomes that fulfill public value.

The operational capacity of bureaucracy acts both as enabler and constrainer of the value generation processes enabled by this organizational configuration. The operational capacity of bureaucracy is the result of the application of technical knowledge and calculation in order to meet efficiency needs. Weber (1946) identifies bureaucracies as the ideal response that rationalization—in this context meaning the "use of calculation to master phenomena and things through the domination of rules and instrumental systems" (Clegg, 2007)—can offer to help an organization to reach its goals efficiently.

The historical logic underpinning the design of bureaucratic organizations, i.e. the search for rationalization and efficiency—is also very similar to that which has dominated new public management (NPM). NPM in fact, like the Weberian theorization of bureaucracy, is driven by the goal of designing the optimal organizational setting for the efficient production and delivery for the public sector. Even if the two theorizations propose alternative solutions, they share the same efficiency drivers and result in organizational configurations that have a very similar operational capacity. They both search for organizational configurations that optimize the production and delivery of public services. Both "theories" build on the assumption that value is closely associated with the production process and that, as in the industrial economy, increasing the efficiency of the production process will add value to the produced products.

The operational capacity of bureaucracy and of NPM redesigned organizations fails to produce value in the contemporary landscape, where value is increasingly produced by those who consume the products/services rather than by those who produce them (Moore, 1995; Zuboff & Maxmin, 2002). When the value of products and services is not produced inside the organization but defined and shaped by those who use and consume the products, it is clear that the search for optimal internal organizational solutions simply by rationalizing the production process would make for a useless endeavor.

Alternative solutions are needed to help public and private sector organizations to acquire the operational capacity needed to better generate value when they are no longer in control of the processes that generate value.

Co-production is an emerging production paradigm that accounts for the need of involving those who produce value by consuming the products *into* the production process. In this chapter, we discuss how public sector organizations concerned with public value production can learn from co-production experiences in the private sector that have helped to increase the value generated, in situations where the internal rationalization of the production processes has had no major effects on the value generating processes of the product/service.

BUREAUCRACY AND PUBLIC VALUE

Bureaucracies are organizational arrangements designed to increase the efficiency of organizational practices and procedures. It is therefore not surprising that the bureaucratic logic, as the main driver for organizing of public sector bodies, has a very long tradition and roots in history. Graeber (2015) found the first example of bureaucratic rationalization in the organization of the postal system of the Holy Roman Empire. The highly rationalized and standardized procedures of the Roman postal system, which allocated each worker to a fixed task in order to guarantee an efficient service, is indeed one of the first examples of bureaucratic order in the organization of public offices (Graeber, 2015). Two thousand years after the first adoption of the bureaucratic logic in public sector organizations Weber's theorization of bureaucracy (Weber, 1946) provides a scientific foundation to the design of bureaucratic organization, applying technical knowledge to predict and plan each aspect of the organization's procedures and hence increase its performance. Weber's approach to bureaucratic rationalization takes a very similar approach to Taylor's theorization of the organization of industrial production processes (Taylor, 1911). Weber and Taylor share the view that the application of technical knowledge to rationalize administrative and production processes will provide the operational capacity needed to increase the value generated by every organization. They both propose technical based approaches to the analysis and redesign of organizational processes. Accordingly, a standardized and hence technically structured work flow would add value by increasing the operational efficiency of the production and administrative processes. Following this prescription, managerial theories were developed to offer solutions to help public and private organizations to increase their efficiency and hence to reduce the costs of production (and accordingly increase profits).

   In the context of public sector organizations, the search for administrative efficiency has made operational capacity of paramount importance, not only to better deliver services, but also to respond to the challenges imposed by budget and investment cuts. To fulfill these needs, public sector organizations have increasingly relied on managerial approaches typical of private organizations as structured in new public management (NPM) frameworks (Hood, 1991; Cordella & Bonina, 2012). As in the case of technical rationalization, NPM deals with problem of organizational performances by looking at the mechanisms used to coordinate work-flow activities and by designing a set of solutions aimed at leveraging operational efficiency and effectiveness of organizational performances—such as six-sigma and BPR.

From Weber's theorization of bureaucracy to the more modern models of public management (Osborne & Gaebler, 1992; Osborne & Plastrik, 1997; Dunleavy et al., 2006; Hood & Lodge, 2006), scholars have always considered value generation processes the pillar of public administration of an organization. Accordingly they have focused on the search for optimal organizational designs to increase the value produced by public administrations.

Many public sector services cannot however be produced without the inputs and contributions of external agents, not least citizens. Air pollution provides us with a neat and simple example to make our point. Public sector agencies monitor, design, and enforce policies to reduce air pollution to provide a better and healthier environment for citizens. It is certainly important to increase the efficiency and effectiveness of administrative procedures undertaken to achieve these goals. However, the value of these policies is not solely shaped by the efficiency of the administrative procedure governing the policies, but rather by the actions that citizens put in place to fulfill the goals of the policy. So it takes both the individual and collective contributions to reduce pollution.

There are indeed many situations where citizens do not consume public services produced by their public administration, as depicted in the citizens-custom rhetoric. Very often citizens co-produce public services and hence contribute to the value creation process delivered by these services, over and above any action of a public sector office. Efficient health care systems require citizens not to abuse access to health care services: if every citizen goes unnecessarily to the Accident and Emergency (A&E) hospital department, the system will be overloaded and not all patients needing this care will be able to receive it; ultimately reducing the effectiveness of the service. A better use of existing resources needs to handle any overwhelming demand for the system with a reasoned and careful approach by citizens. Such an approach by citizens will go much farther in using the system efficiently than any rationalization of the production model by the public sector. At a more macro level, it is reasonable to argue that without the input of citizens it is impossible for governments to design and implement public policies that aim to fulfill public expectations and generate public value (Bovaird, 2007).

The concept of public value explains why the operational capacity offered by technical approaches to administrative rationalization, which still drive much of public management theories and models, often fails to add value to public service production and delivery. These models in fact assume that value is produced within the organization and not by those who consume the services produced by the administration.

Public Value: Beyond Bureaucracy

Citizens are not only mere customers of public administration; they evaluate public services and goods not only according to the benefits they receive as individuals, but also according to the value these services generate for society at large (O'Flynn, 2007; Bovaird & Loeffler, 2012; Cordella & Bonina, 2012). Citizens not only value the public services they use and benefit from individually, but also place real value on public services that help to fulfill their personal social expectations and visions. Similarly, they not only contribute to the production of services they value and consume, but also to services they do not consume or value (for the most part). What makes things yet more interesting is that citizens may inadvertently facilitate the collective value production. For instance, an individual can choose to cycle or walk to work to keep themselves fit, however by doing so they are at the same time reducing pollution. Environmental ideas may not be a strong value incentive for their decision, yet they are able to appreciate that they are creating public value indirectly.

The challenge of public sector organizations is not simply to deliver the services citizens want and need in order to fulfill their individual needs (in Hobbes' terms, feeding the wolf's needs), but rather it is twofold. They must do the former while providing the social and economic environment that citizens want and need so to achieve both their individual *and* social expectations and aspirations. Public management's focus on efficiency and rationalization is driven by the assumption that citizens need more of scarce resources, and hence the search for a better production process that will be able to deliver as much as possible to as many as possible. This approach to public sector management clearly segments those who produce—public agencies—from those who consume services: citizens. On the contrary, a public value approach to public sector management would necessitate the design of organizations that have the operational capacity needed to satisfy the collective vision and which do not necessarily overlap with individual consumption of services.

This difference can be described with a simple example. Citizens value ambulance services even if they do not need to use the service. Citizens are willing to pay to have the services available, not only to benefit from them individually, but also to provide access to the services to all those who might need an ambulance. Citizens pay for many services that they do not benefit from immediately or even in the near future but are, in many cases, happy to do so because they do not place value solely on their individual access to the service, but rather to its social availability. Governments, in order to fulfill these expectations, have to take a different approach to public service management and find suitable necessary operational capacity to produce as much value as possible in an environment where they do not have control over the resources needed to frame value and to produce it.

The bureaucratic organization and all the managerial approaches to public management and value creation that focus on the standalone value creation process and on its technical efficiency fail to generate and deliver public value, which is the outcome of collective actions and inputs. To produce and deliver public value is not easy because it requires an operational capacity able to deliver outcomes that match the expectations of a multitude of individuals. These expectations also change over time (Alford & Hughes, 2008; Cordella & Bonina, 2012). For example after the accident at the Fukushima nuclear plant, a radical change in the public opinion of Japan and Germany made former nuclear policies employed by governments to frame their actions obsolete, where only a few years before the tragic event there was uncontroversial support by the public (Huenteler et al., 2012). This is the reason why it is difficult to provide services that fulfill public value, since this value changes over time and is shaped by many goals and expectations that may be even conflictual. For example, many people value public services but most of them do not appreciate contributing with taxation for their provision.

To solve this issue and produce public services that are able to fulfill public value, it becomes necessary to elaborate an alternative approach to public management from that implicit in the bureaucratic model, NMP, and all their ramifications. The latter models, as argued by Zuboff & Maxmin (2002), do not provide the operational capacity needed to produce services that meet the needs of people. These organizational models fail to provide the operational capacity needed to collect the inputs necessary to create products and services that support and enable clients and citizens to reach their particular aspirations and goals. Organizations that aim to fulfill the requirements of customers and citizens will need to reconsider the value-making proposition and become more open to alternative production models, based on co-production and crowdsourcing (Levina & Fayard, 2018) platforms that allow production and delivery of customer expectations.

Co-production would help to meet the needs of changing public values and offer more effective and efficient public services (Joshi & Moore, 2004; Vamstad, 2012; Verschuere et al., 2012). Although co-production was theorized more than a decade ago (Ostrom, 1996), the failure of the dominant theories of public management and the introduction of ICT technologies make co-production today a more valid and easy alternative for delivering public services and goods (Crozier, 1964; Collins, 2001).

In the following sections, we explain how co-production can better align public services with current public value ideas, and how ICTs are enabling citizens to deploy co-production on a large scale (Bovaird, 2007) while, at the same time, challenging the old model of public administration that still considers them simply as passive consumers (Barzelay, 2001).

CO-PRODUCTION: NEW MODES OF VALUE

The growing relevance of co-production can be traced to a company's inability to clearly identify the needs and expectations of customers. Part of this growth in recent years can be explained by the rise of a globalized economy where the Internet has generated multiple and fast changing needs and ideas that have made old marketing logics somewhat anachronistic (Zuboff & Maxmin, 2002). Since corporations are unable to anticipate what customers really want, they have instead started to provide basic services, standards, and infrastructure that customers can then configure and use to develop their own services and products (Prahalad & Ramaswamy, 2000; Vargo & Lusch, 2004). Google, for example, provides its maps as a platform available to various customers that create the service and products they need. An example of a company building on top of Google Maps is Uber. Uber has built its business on Google Maps by developing a service that Google had not considered viable to build in-house. Co-production allows the combination of dispersed knowledge that is hidden in the crowd (Viscusi & Tucci, 2018) of users to build new products and services (Vargo & Lusch, 2004) that better satisfy customers. A direct consequence of co-production is the increase in satisfaction and customer loyalty which generates competitive advantage for the company concerned (Barrutia & Echebarria, 2012; Grissemann & Stokburger-Sauer, 2012; Chathoth et al., 2013).

Drawing on the seminal definition by Ostrom (1996), co-production is "the process through which inputs used to produce a good or service are contributed by individuals who are not 'in' the same organization" (p. 1073). Understood in this manner it is clear that crowdsourcing is one way to operationalize co-production. Borrowing from one of the earliest theorizations of crowdsourcing, we draw on Afuah & Tucci's (2012) interpretation (Howe, 2006; Howe, 2008; Jeppesen & Lakhani, 2010) to define crowdsourcing as "the act of outsourcing a task to a 'crowd,' rather than to a designated 'agent' (an organization, informal or formal team, or individual), such as a contractor, in the form of an open call" (p. 355). Though more often understood in a private setting, there is growing visibility of crowdsourcing practices being implemented by governments around the world (Brudney & England, 1983; Brandsen & Pestoff, 2006; Bovaird, 2007; Riccucci et al., 2015).

Governments to date have been understood to both need and want to control and manage crowds (Wexler, 2011). It could be argued that the growing interest in crowdsourcing and other forms of co-production are yet another form of crowd control. But perhaps this does not explain the entire reality. There is an acknowledged need for cutting back costs in government, and co-production is being viewed as a potential solution. Returning to the strategic triangle (Moore, 1995; Benington & Moore, 2010), coproduction would be brought to the public sector to improve operational capacity. However, this desire to adopt co-production as a way of cutting costs by the government is not a new phenomenon—we found that it was mentioned as early as 1981 (and this was probably not even the first mention)—a time when co-production was not a phrase that carried the positive connotations it holds today (Wilson, 1981), but at the same time the ability to increase operational capacity is not direct or inevitable. It sounds attractive to be able to outsource both the problem defin-ition and problem solution to your customers, in this case citizens (Bovaird, 2007; Meijer, 2011; Jakobsen, 2012). In practice, however, both the private and public sectors have faced challenges with their engagement with co-production models (Fitzgerald et al., 2011; Bouras et al., 2014; Sieber & Johnson, 2015).

The debate between Bloodgood (2013) and Afuah & Tucci (2013) is valu-able because its draws together the issues of co-production *with* value creation (Afuah, 2018a). As Bloodgood points out, crowdsourcing does indeed need to stress the value creation elements, but this becomes less of a concern in scenarios where the risk of imitation does not lead to serious and adverse consequences. Public sector organizations might vie with each other for resources but their goal is seldom profit orientated. This could well lay the groundwork for crowdsourcing as an option over and beyond internal cre-ation of value or the option to outsource to a third-party supplier (Afuah & Tucci, 2012). And value creation and the ability to capture it are key parts of any business model, including that of public sector services production. In the private sector, value creation implies that the value created should be more than that used by the resources to create the good/service (Ye & Kankanhalli, 2013; McNamara et al., 2013; Baden-Fuller & Haefliger, 2013), and value capture usually refers to harnessing the largest portion possible of the wealth and return from the deployment of your resources (Bowman & Ambrosini, 2000; Morgan & Finnegan, 2014; McNamara et al., 2013). Somewhat dissimi-lar in public sector organizations, public value capture takes on a different role and significance, as does public value creation. Any "business model" that is employed in the public sector needs a much broader focus than private companies. Drilling down to the most basic idea, private companies work to increase their profit margin, and whether they execute this through a strategic advantage or some other mechanism, the end game is the same—increased profit. The idea of public value creation is more complex than that. To make sense of this idea it becomes necessary to step back from the premise of a supply or production of a service/good. In order to arrive at this point public sector organizations need to have made some complicated decisions about how the process of co-production will help, whom it will help, but most importantly, whether it will marginalize any group of society or have other implications on other policies being implemented. Social and public value, seen as a collective is not a direct concern for private companies, but it is for the public sector. As Jackson (2001) explains, "The performance of the public sector is not only judged in terms of efficiency – in particular the narrow concept of cost. Many public services were also judged in terms of their contribution to achievement of equity – who receives the services and in what quantity and with what effect upon the distribution of incomes (welfare)" (p. 14).

The private sector has appropriated multiple co-production strategies that are aimed at increasing their operational capabilities. Governance and hence operational capability in the private sector is concerned mainly with two issues, firstly, the search for the best coordination mechanism needed to solve a problem, and secondly, seeking help on better identifying what the problem is. Each different model of co-production entails a specific operational capability—which derives from the governance model—with some imposing a more authoritarian style of management, while others are closer to a democratic and open style. The criteria of comparison between different models of co-production are coordination and communication channels, incentives schemes embedded into the system, and property rights related to what is produced (Felin & Zenger, 2014). Co-production with authoritarian governance models are usually those that are turned inwards within an organization to reach ideas and feedback that were not possible with old structures and practices (Gaughan et al., 2007; Lindman et al., 2008). The organization in question is focused on internal use and creation of ideas from its own employees. Private sector companies such as Nokia and others have explored such techniques to some advantage. There is greater control over the ideas created as they are always clearly owned by the company employing the creator, and the coordination of work can be managed in detail as the employees are bound to the company by contract. The incentives involved are often promotion or greater control over your own projects that are offered to the creator. However, the extent of ideas and variation in solutions possible is limited with such an approach.

More complex yet undeniably productive models of governance include open structures of control and management, such as crowdsourcing, opensourcing, and plumbing user communities for ideas and solutions. In the private sector, organizations would decide on a particular technique based on how complex the problem is that they want a solution for, and how deeply hidden the information is that could help to solve the problem (Felin & Zenger, 2014). Crowdsourcing (Howe, 2006; Afuah & Tucci, 2012; Boudreau, 2012; Boudreau & Lakhani, 2013) as a model works best when the problem can be broken down into simple modules so as to ensure that the hidden knowledge can be found in an accessible manner. For instance, Amazon Turk is a straightforward way to access developers with the necessary knowledge to solve a problem. Only highly modular pieces of software are usually sourced through this method. In this scenario the problem is already clear, and it is sourcing the solution (and the best mechanism to coordinate the process).

Open sourcing (Agerfalk & Fitzgerald, 2008; Morgan & Finnegan, 2014) and working with user communities (von Hippel, 2001; Lakhani & von Hippel, 2003) would be an effective approach if the problem is complex so that it is difficult to break down into simple parts, and also when the knowledge needed to solve it is too hidden in the crowd (thus making it difficult to source directly). There are multiple examples of the private sector indulging in such practices. One of the oldest and now quite seminal examples in the field of open innovation is that of Proctor & Gamble's "Connect and Develop" scheme (Sakkab, 2002). In this example the problem was unclear and thus the solution was more hidden in the crowd than usual. Customers (both current and future) were considered to be in a better place to identify their own problems that they were wanting to be resolved. P&G then chose the solutions (and their problems) that they were keen to develop, usually on the basis, not of public value, but where monetary value was more assured and greater.

Studies of public sector organizations that engage with co-production and its various forms such as open sourcing (Hamel & Schweik, 2009; Fishenden & Thompson, 2013; van Loon & Toshkov, 2015) or crowdsourcing (Needham, 2008; Pestoff, 2013), are insightful about the challenges of such mechanisms of public participation, yet few discuss the implications that different forms of co-production have in relation to public value. We argue that the distinctive nature of public value creation requires a deeper analysis that has not been engaged with in mainstream literature on crowdsourcing and co-production, because the latter studies are mostly based in the private sector. This discussion is important and needs to be addressed to make co-production a more effective possibility for public sector use. Co-production, or its related term, participation, has been argued by some to be a possible approach to building value within a society (Jackson, 2001). Adopting an economic perspective, Jackson (2001) shows how the understanding of what is entailed by the architecture of the public sector needs expansion to include ideas promulgated by Sah & Stiglitz (1986). Improved public sector architecture needs to include distributed decision-making authority but at the same time, there must be proper incentives built into the system to use distributed information to make better decisions. Without the proper incentives for public sector officials to make better use of the information available, the *ability* to make a decision becomes less effective. And these decisions also need to deliver value, but as we argue above and which is reiterated by Jackson (2001), value is more than just a reduction of costs, in the public sector especially, it entails benefits that are equitably managed and accessible. The governance structure that would support co-production and where such decision-making authority can be distributed and value can be created is potentially a platform (Baldwin & Woodard, 2009; Fishenden & Thompson, 2013; Kim & Shin, 2016).

There is a yet more dubious role hinted at about co-production adoption by governments around the world. Proactively adopting the crowd as co-producers can at the same time serve another vital purpose for governments, control, and acceptance (parallels in the private sector would be buy-in to a product/service through ownership models) and a re-establishment of the position of the elite (Jackson, 2001; Wexler, 2011).

CO-PRODUCTION AND IN THE PUBLIC SECTOR: A NEW VALUE GENERATING PROPOSITION

Having discussed the importance of governance structures to shaping co-production processes and the value they generate, we now turn our attention to how such newer production models could be adopted by the public sector and the challenges accompanying this adoption. We are agreed that co-production could be used to produce more value in private sector production processes (Payne et al., 2008; Vargo et al., 2008), but public sector organizations have to be careful when embracing co-production, especially where public value creation is concerned. As already discussed, public value creation embraces conflicting values that are not maximized following traditional value generation processes (Cordella & Willcocks, 2010; Cordella & Bonina, 2012). Public administrations have to offer public services that are not always sustainable according to the business logic, based on revenue maximization, but that are perfectly on track with broader socio-economical goals reflected in public value ideas (Rainey et al., 1976). For example, when a public administration decides to open a school in a remote village with very few kids, it might act against the principles of cost efficiency. However, this decision can be perfectly in line with shared public value, which makes it socially expected that every child will have access to public education no matter the cost of providing the service.

When co-production is considered in public service production and provision, it is public value creation and not cost efficiency that becomes the chosen benchmark. The state has to offer many services to all citizens in its territory independent of the volume of the demand, the cost of the provision, and the value that individual citizens associate with the service. Services have to be made available in a manner that guarantees equal and fair access to all. Since different configurations in the production and delivery processes can affect the way in which these services are accessed and consumed by citizens (Cordella, 2007), the co-production model chosen to deliver these services needs to be thought through to ensure that the expected values are embedded within the service.

As discussed, co-production can be mediated by authoritarian governance, crowdsourcing, and opensourcing (see Table 8.1). Each of these governance structures has specific impacts on the value generated in public sector co-production. These values have to be benchmarked against the broader impact on public value creation, and not simply or only against the cost efficiency of the production process. Authoritarian models guide us on how to better produce and deliver existing services. In this case, value is generated by increasing efficiency and effectiveness of the production process. The adoption of these models in the public sector would follow the same logic and root as bureaucratic rationalization and/or NPM. These governance structures presuppose that the problem is known and that co-production can help to find better solutions on how to solve the given (known) problem.

Table 8.1. Implications of different governance types of co-production.

	Perspective	
Type of governance	**Private sector:** Aim to reach maximum efficiency.	**Public value:** Aim to satisfy collective expectations.
Authoritarian	Co-production is a tool to optimize single production processes.	Public value is generated when a more efficient production process for a service does not negatively impact other services and the broader public value generated by the public administration.
Crowdsourcing	Co-production is used to exploit dispersed resources and knowledge in order to have more efficient and effective production of goods and services. The company is in control of the production process. The "crowd" reduces the cost of production.	Co-production is used to allow citizens to alleviate common problems or deliver better services according to citizens' aspirations. Crowdsourcing produces services that are wanted and needed by citizens but that public administration cannot produce or serve without the support of citizens. The public administration is in control of the production process.
Opensourcing	Co-production is used to source the production process because the company does not have the knowledge and breadth of competence to control it.	Co-production is used to find the best solution and ideas to create or implement services that match current expectations. Since the production process cannot be controlled, public administration governs it to guarantee that the value that is produced does not negatively affect other sources of public value.

The focus in on process rationalization, and public value creation is not deeply considered.

The open governance structures of crowdsourcing and outsourcing enable operational capabilities that can help public sector organizations to better internalize social expectations and produce services that actually deliver public value. Crowdsourcing is very useful in supporting public service organizations in exploiting resources available in the society to deliver services that could not be delivered without the support of citizens. When public administration is able to control how social services are consumed, this affects the creation of social value, and such a phenomenon is referred to as public value crowdsourcing. Both of the cases, pollution and access to health care services, that we have discussed provide good examples of public value crowdsourcing. Public administration has control over provision of the service, but citizens using it define the value the service will generate for society. This is why we can refer to such cases as public value crowdsourcing. Opensourcing in public value creation instead, refers to all those cases where governments and public administrations have to rely on citizens' input to frame policies that might be needed to build buy-in to crowdsourcing or more traditional value production processes.

Moreover, when public administrations rely on co-production to support public value creation, they do not solely consider the value that the co-production process is adding to the production of the single service, but also the potential effects that the service might have on other services or values (Cordella & Willcocks, 2012). This further complicates public value and makes it yet more distinct with regard to value creation in a private sector business model idea. For example, allowing citizens to patrol their neighbourhood and intervene to secure it might be particularly convenient from the business logic, because it increases the level of social security and reduces the cost of the service for society. However, crowdsourcing the policing service would undermine the monopoly of the force, which is a foundation of democracy. The public value framework suggests that in this case, co-production is not the most valuable solution because there are other important legal and social-economic aspects that have to be considered when public value creation is concerned.

Consequently, the choice of co-producing public services needs to be made according to the pubic value creation framework, and not by following the private sector rationale that would drive the configuration of services. Co-production can indeed be a valuable solution to involving citizens in the production and provision of public services and hence to better account for the public value they contribute. The possibility of citizens co-producing public services would allow for a more effective account of social aspirations and expectations and hence the production and delivery of services that are more valuable because they deliver effective public value.

HOW CAN PUBLIC ADMINISTRATION BENEFIT FROM CO-PRODUCTION AND CROWDSOURCING TO BETTER PRODUCE PUBLIC VALUE?

Over the past thirty years, public administrations have been criticized for their inability to produce and deliver services that meet the expectations of citizens. Bureaucracy, in both private and public organizations, is considered the main source of the problem. The rigidity and standardization of bureaucratic procedures reduce organizational capability to adapt to dynamic and more complex social and economic environments, to deliver the expected services. Investments in co-production are often the response to this challenge. Different co-production governance structures embedded within platforms have been adopted by private sector organizations to respond to these challenges (Battistella & Nonino, 2012; Ceccagnoli et al., 2012). Therefore, a direct approach to overcoming bureaucracy would be to advise public administrations to implement an open platform that provides infrastructure and services that can be recombined by individual citizens and businesses to configure services that fulfill their needs. Although bureaucracies fail to deliver what individual citizens want, it is also true that bureaucracies are categorically more effective at delivering social expectations of fairness and equality, which are the pillars of most democratic societies. For this reason, public administration providing a platform that enables individuals to co-produce services that they want can indeed provide better services to individuals, but might at the same time fail to deliver equal and fair services to all citizens, and hence fail to increase public value which is generated by these services. If public administrations are concerned with public value production and not with individual value provision, a different approach to the evaluation of the value generated by new organizational solutions used to produce and deliver public services is needed. A different approach means a different structure and management and this implies new standards and procedures.

According to Hodgson & Cicmil (2007), the implementation of standards, infrastructures, and processes that allow co-production can potentially change how public organizations work and the value they produce. The choice of the technological and organizational setting used to support co-production should therefore consider the impact that the specific configuration has on broader political and social value. Hence, it is necessary to think about how to govern the platform that allows co-production in the public sector. In fact, as previously discussed, the literature has analyzed the governance of co-production in the private sector but there are few studies of co-production in the public sector.

In the context of public sector, the governance model for co-production has even more importance since it will not only need to guarantee the fulfillment of public value, but also deliver efficient and effective services. Co-production in the public sector demands a new level of intervention and control by the public administration and the state (O'Reily, 2011; Linders, 2012). Public administrations need to set and provide standards and regulations, frame channels of collaboration, and sponsor and mobilize the resources to facilitate co-production (Boulos et al., 2011; Fishenden & Thompson, 2013). In addition, it would be necessary to monitor how public services are delivered in order to make co-production activities align with the overall action of the public administration. This calls for new responsibilities and tasks to be undertaken by public administrations. In fact, it is necessary to pay attention to public services that are co-produced and crowdsourced (Boudreau, 2005; O'Reilly, 2011) in order to avoid a distorted deployment of co-production.

CONCLUSIONS AND FUTURE RESEARCH

The bureaucratic model generates value, focusing on the efficiency of the production process and not on the consumer and citizens' needs. In recent years, this approach to value creation has revealed itself to be obsolete and ineffective. Efficiency is no longer a competitive advantage since it is very difficult for companies to predict what consumers want and need. Public sector organizations fail to deliver public services and goods according to the current citizens' aspirations and visions. Private sector organizations adopting co-production have overcome these difficulties, providing basic platforms to involve consumers in the production process and to better produce services that fulfill customers' current needs and values. In this new model of production, end users are seen as an active part of the value chain creation process. However, any attempt to transfer co-production models and strategies from the private sector to the public sector without customization creates the risk of breaking the coordination structure. The public sector is a complex reality where each action has to consider several socio-economic and ethical issues to produce public value.

Adoption of the public value creation perspective is indeed very challenging to implement. In fact, each public administration is a delicate equilibrium of stratified political powers, and pre-defined roles and procedures (Weber, 1946), so that it is difficult to predict and assess the social and political impacts that the implementation of co-production platforms can have on social expectations and hence on public value. Co-production in the public sector might increase the value generated by a single service by negatively affecting other services, thus reducing the overall positive impact it has on public value creation. Co-production in public service production and provision should not be seen as a substitute for all other production configurations, as bureaucracy has been in the past. The challenge for public sector organizations is to find the right balance of production processes to optimize public value creation. Co-production should not be considered as an alternative to all other forms of public service production, but rather as a resource that in the right configuration with other structures could help to better produce public value.

To optimize the public value generated by these configurations, public sector organizations could become platforms that balance the effects that different production processes of public services, including co-production, bureaucracy, and others such has outsourcing, have on the challenge of producing public value. Future research could explore the changes that public sector organizations face while managing such complex public service production configurations. It is especially critical to concentrate more research effort on understanding the governance and organizational models that public organizations will need to adopt when they embrace co-production.

REFERENCES

Afuah, A. (2018a). Co-opetition in crowdsourcing: When simultaneous cooperation and competition deliver superior solutions. In C. Tucci, A. Afuah, & G. Viscusi (eds.), *Creating and Capturing Value Through Crowdsourcing*. Oxford: Oxford University Press, pp. 271–91.

Afuah, A. (2018b). Crowdsourcing: A primer and research framework. In C. Tucci, A. Afuah, & G. Viscusi (eds.), *Creating and Capturing Value Through Crowdsourcing*. Oxford: Oxford University Press, pp. 11–38.

Afuah, A. & Tucci, C. L. (2012). Crowdsourcing as a solution to distant search. *Academy of Management Review, 37*, 355–75.

Afuah, A. & Tucci, C. L. (2013). Value capture and crowdsourcing. *Academy of Management Review, 38*, 457–60.

Agerfalk, P. & Fitzgerald, B. (2008). Outsourcing to an unknown workforce: Exploring opensourcing as a global sourcing strategy. *MIS Quarterly, 32*, 385–400.

Alford, J. & Hughes, O. (2008). Public value pragmatism as the next phase of public management. *The American Review of Public Administration, 38*(2), 130–48.

Baden-Fuller, C. & Haefliger, S. (2013). Business models and technological innovation. *Long Range Planning, 46*, 419–26.

Baldwin, C. Y. & Woodard, C. J. (2009). Platforms, markets and innovation, in Gawer, A. (ed.), *The Architecture of Platforms: A Unified View*. Cheltenham, UK: Edward Elgar Publishing.

Barrutia, J. M. & Echebarria, C. (2012). Greening regions: the effect of social entrepreneurship, co-decision and co-creation on the embrace of good sustainable development practices. *Journal of Environmental Planning and Management, 55*, 1348–68.

Barzelay, M. (2001). *The New Public Management: Improving Research and Policy Dialogue*. Berkeley: University of California Press.

Battistella, C. & Nonino, F. (2012). Open innovation web-based platforms: The impact of different forms of motivation on collaboration. *Innovation, 14*, 557–75.

Benington, J. & Moore, M. H. (2010). *Public Value: Theory and Practice.* Basingstoke, UK: Palgrave Macmillan.

Berry, D. M. & Moss, G. (2006). Free and open-source software: Opening and democratising e-government's black box. *Information Polity, 11,* 21–34.

Bloodgood, J. (2013). Crowdsourcing: Useful for problem solving, but what about value capture? *Academy of Management Review, 38,* 455–7.

Boudreau, K. (2005). The boundaries of the platform: Vertical integration and economic incentives in mobile computing. Working papers from Massachusetts Institute of Technology (MIT), Sloan School of Management.

Boudreau, K. J. (2012). Let a thousand flowers bloom? An early look at large numbers of software app developers and patterns of innovation. *Organization Science, 23,* 1409–27.

Boudreau, K. J. & Lakhani, K. R. (2013). Using the crowd as an innovation partner. *Harvard Business Review, 91,* 60–8.

Boulos, M. N. K., Resch, B., Crowley, D. N., Breslin, J. G., Sohn, G., Burtner, R., Pike, W. A., Jezierski, E., & Chuang, K.-Y. S. (2011). Crowdsourcing, citizen sensing and sensor web technologies for public and environmental health surveillance and crisis management: trends, OGC standards and application examples. *International Journal of Health Geographics, 10,* 67.

Bouras, C., Filopoulos, A., Kokkinos, V., Michalopoulos, S., Papadopoulos, D., & Tseliou, G. (2014). Policy recommendations for public administrators on free and open source software usage. *Telematics and Informatics, 31,* 237–52.

Bovaird, T. (2007). Beyond engagement and participation: User and community coproduction of public services. *Public Administration Review, 67,* 846–60.

Bovaird, T. & Loeffler, E. (2012). From engagement to co-production: The contribution of users and communities to outcomes and public value. *VOLUNTAS: International Journal of Voluntary and Nonprofit Organizations, 23,* 1119–38.

Bowman, C. & Ambrosini, V. (2000). Value creation versus value capture: Towards a coherent definition of value in strategy. *British Journal of Management, 11,* 1–15.

Brandsen, T. & Pestoff, V. (2006). Co-production, the third sector and the delivery of public services. *Public Management Review, 8,* 493–501.

Brudney, J. L. & England, R. E. (1983). Toward a definition of the coproduction concept. *Public Administration Review, 43,* 59–65.

Bryson, J. M., Crosby, B. C., & Bloomberg, L. (2014). Public value governance: Moving beyond traditional public administration and the new public management. *Public Administration Review, 74,* 445–56.

Ceccagnoli, M., Forman, C., Huang, P., & Wu, D. J. (2012). Cocreation of value in a platform ecosystem: The case of enterprise software. *MIS Quarterly, 36,* 263–90.

Chathoth, P., Altinay, L., Harrington, R. J., Okumus, F., & Chan, E. S. W. (2013). Co-production versus co-creation: A process based continuum in the hotel service context. *International Journal of Hospitality Management, 32,* 11–20.

Clegg, S. (2007). Something is happening here, but you don't know what it is, do you, Mister Jones? *ICT in the Contemporary World.* Information Systems and Innovation Group, London School of Economics and Political Science.

Collins, J. C. (2001). *Good to Great: Why Some Companies Make the Leap...and Others Don't.* New York: Random House.

Cordella, A. (2007). E-government: Towards the e-bureaucratic form? *Journal of Information Technology, 22,* 265–74.

Cordella, A. & Bonina, C. M. (2012). A public value perspective for ICT enabled public sector reforms: A theoretical reflection. *Government Information Quarterly, 29,* 512–20.

Cordella, A. & Willcocks, L. (2010). Outsourcing, bureaucracy and public value: Reappraising the notion of the "contract state." *Government Information Quarterly, 27,* 82–8.

Cordella, A. & Willcocks, L. (2012). Government policy, public value and IT outsourcing: The strategic case of ASPIRE. *The Journal of Strategic Information Systems, 21,* 295–307.

Crozier, M. (1964). *The Bureaucratic Phenomenon.* Chicago: Chicago University Press.

Dunleavy, P., Margetts, H., Bastow, S., & Tinkler, J. (2006). New public management is dead—Long live digital-era governance. *Journal of Public Administration Research and Theory, 16,* 467–94.

Felin, T. & Zenger, T. R. (2014). Closed or open innovation? Problem solving and the governance choice. *Research Policy, 43,* 914–25.

Fishenden, J. & Thompson, M. (2013). Digital government, open architecture, and innovation: Why public sector IT will never be the same again. *Journal of Public Administration Research and Theory, 23,* 977–1004.

Fitzgerald, B., Kesan, J. P., Russo, B., Shaikh, M., & Succi, G. (2011). *Adopting Open Source Software: Challenges and Opportunities.* Cambridge, MA: MIT Press.

Gaughan, G., Fitzgerald, B., Morgan, L., & Shaikh, M. An Examination of the use of inner source in multinational corporations. 1st OPAALS Workshop, 26–27th November 2007, Rome, Italy.

Graeber, D. (2015). *The Utopia of Rules: On Technology, Stupidity, and the Secret Joys of Bureaucracy.* New York, Melville House.

Grissemann, U. S. & Stokburger-Sauer, N. E. (2012). Customer co-creation of travel services: The role of company support and customer satisfaction with the co-creation performance. *Tourism Management, 33,* 1483–92.

Hamel, M. & Schweik, C. M. (2009). Open-source collaboration: Two cases in the U.S. public sector. *First Monday, 14*(1), 5 January 2009.

Harrison, T. M. & Sayogo, D. S. (2014). Transparency, participation, and accountability practices in open government: A comparative study. *Government Information Quarterly, 31,* 513–25.

Hodgson, D. & Cicmil, S. (2007). The politics of standards in modern management: Making "the project" a reality. *Journal of Management Studies, 44,* 431–50.

Hood, C. (1991). A public management for all seasons. *Public Administration, 69,* 3–19.

Hood, C. & Lodge, M. (2006). *The Politics of Public Service Bargains: Reward, Competency, Loyalty—and Blame.* Oxford, Oxford University Press.

Howe, J. (2006). *The Rise of Crowdsourcing* [Online]. WIRED, http://www.wired.com/wired/archive/14.06/crowds.html

Howe, J. (2008). *Crowdsourcing: Why the Power of the Crowd is Driving the Future of Business.* New York: Crown Business.

Huenteler, J., Schmidt, T. S., & Kanie, N. (2012). Japan's post-Fukushima challenge—implications from the German experience on renewable energy policy. *Energy Policy, 45,* 6–11.

Jackson, P. M. (2001). Public sector added value: Can bureaucracy deliver? *Public Administration*, *79*, 5–28.

Jakobsen, M. (2012). Can government initiatives increase citizen coproduction? Results of a randomized field experiment. *Journal of Public Administration Research and Theory*, *23*(1), 27–54.

Jeppesen, L. B. & Lakhani, K. R. (2010). Marginality and problem-solving effectiveness in broadcast search. *Organization Science*, *21*, 1016–33.

Joshi, A. & Moore, M. (2004). Institutionalised co-production: Unorthodox public service delivery in challenging environments. *The Journal of Development Studies*, *40*, 31–49.

Kim, T. & Shin, D.-H. (2016). Social platform innovation of open source hardware in South Korea. *Telematics and Informatics*, *33*, 217–26.

Kratzer, J., Meissner, D., & Roud, V. (2017). Open innovation and company culture: Internal openness makes the difference. *Technological Forecasting and Social Change*, *119*, 128–38.

Lakhani, K. & von Hippel, E. (2003). How open source software works: "Free" user-to-user assistance. *Research Policy*, *32*, 923–43.

Levina, N. & Fayard, A-L. (2018). Tapping into diversity through open innovation platforms: The emergence of boundary-spanning practices. In C. Tucci, A. Afuah, & G. Viscusi (eds.), *Creating and Capturing Value Through Crowdsourcing*. Oxford: Oxford University Press, pp. 204–35.

Linders, D. (2012). From e-government to we-government: Defining a typology for citizen coproduction in the age of social media. *Government Information Quarterly*, *29*, 446–54.

Lindman, J., Rossi, M., & Marttiin, P. (2008). Applying open source development practices inside a company. *Open Source Development, Communities and Quality*, *275*, 381–7.

McNamara, P., Peck, S. I., & Sasson, A. (2013). Competing business models, value creation and appropriation in English football. *Long Range Planning*, *46*, 475–87.

Meijer, A. J. (2011). Networked coproduction of public services in virtual communities: From a government-centric to a community approach to public service support. *Public Administration Review*, *71*, 598–607.

Moore, M. H. (1995). *Creating Public Value: Strategic Management in Government*. Cambridge, MA: Harvard University Press.

Morgan, L. & Finnegan, P. (2014). Beyond free software: An exploration of the business value of strategic open source. *The Journal of Strategic Information Systems*, *23*, 226–38.

Needham, C. (2008). Realising the potential of co-production: Negotiating improvements in public services. *Social Policy and Society*, *7*, 221–31.

O'Flynn, J. (2007). From new public management to public value: Paradigmatic change and managerial implications. *Australian Journal of Public Administration*, *66*, 353–66.

O'Reilly, T. (2011). Government as a platform. *Innovations: Technology, Governance, Globalization*, *6*, 13–40.

Osborne, D. & Gaebler, T. (1992). *Reinventing Government: How the Entrepreneurial Spirit is Transforming Government*. Reading Mass., Adison Wesley Publishing Company.

Osborne, D. & Plastrik, P. (1997). *Banishing Bureaucracy: The Five Strategies for Reinventing Government.* Reading, MA: Addison-Wesley.

Osborne, S. P., Radnor, Z., & Nasi, G. (2013). A new theory for public service management? Toward a (public) service-dominant approach. *American Review of Public Administration, 43*, 135–58.

Ostrom, E. (1996). Crossing the great divide: Coproduction, synergy, and development. *World Development, 24*, 1073–87.

Payne, A., Storbacka, K., & Frow, P. (2008). Managing the co-creation of value. *Journal of the Academy of Marketing Science, 36*, 83–96.

Pestoff, V. (2013). Collective action and the sustainability of co-production. *Public Management Review, 16*, 383–401.

Prahalad, C. K. & Ramaswamy, V. (2000). Co-opting customer competence. *Harvard Business Review, 78*, 79–90.

Rainey, H. G., Backoff, R. W., & Levine, C. H. (1976). Comparing public and private organizations. *Public Administration Review, 36*, 233–44.

Riccucci, N. M., Van Ryzin, G. G., & Li, H. (2015). Representative bureaucracy and the willingness to coproduce: An experimental study. *Public Administration Review, 76*(1), 121–30.

Sah, R. K. & Stiglitz, J. E. (1986). The architecture of economic systems: hierarchies and polyarchies. *American Economic Review, 76*, 716–27.

Sakkab, N. (2002). Connect & develop complements research & develop at P&G. *Research—Technology Management, 45*, 38–45.

Sieber, R. E. & Johnson, P. A. (2015). Civic open data at a crossroads: Dominant models and current challenges. *Government Information Quarterly, 32*(3), 308–15.

Taylor, W. F. (1911). *The Principles of Scientific Management.* New York & London: Harper Brothers.

Vamstad, J. (2012). Co-production and service quality: The Case of cooperative childcare in Sweden. *VOLUNTAS: International Journal of Voluntary and Nonprofit Organizations, 23*, 1173–88.

Van Loon, A. & Toshkov, D. (2015). Adopting open source software in public administration: The importance of boundary spanners and political commitment. *Government Information Quarterly, 32*, 207–15.

Vargo, S. L. & Lusch, R. F. (2004). Evolving to a new dominant logic for marketing. *Journal of Marketing, 68*, 1–17.

Vargo, S. L., Maglio, P. P., & Akaka, M. A. (2008). On value and value co-creation: A service systems and service logic perspective. *European Management Journal, 26*, 145–52.

Verbeeten, F. H. M. & Speklé, R. F. (2015). Management control, results-oriented culture and public sector performance: Empirical evidence on new public management. *Organization Studies, 36*(7), 953–78.

Verschuere, B., Brandsen, T., & Pestoff, V. (2012). Co-production: The state of the art in research and the future agenda. *VOLUNTAS: International Journal of Voluntary and Nonprofit Organizations, 23*, 1083–101.

Viscusi, G. & Tucci, C. (2018). Three's a crowd? In C. Tucci, A. Afuah, & G. Viscusi (eds.), *Creating and Capturing Value Through Crowdsourcing.* Oxford: Oxford University Press, pp. 39–57.

von Hippel, E. (2001). Innovation by user communities: Learning from open-source software. *MIT Sloan Management Review, 42*, 82–6.

Weber, M. (1946). *Bureaucracy. From Max Weber: Essays in Sociology.* New York, Oxford University Press.

West, J. & Sims, J. (2018). How firms leverage crowds and communities for open innovation. In C. Tucci, A. Afuah, & G. Viscusi (eds.), *Creating and Capturing Value Through Crowdsourcing.* Oxford: Oxford University Press, pp. 58–96.

Wexler, M. N. (2011). Reconfiguring the sociology of the crowd: exploring crowdsourcing. *International Journal of Sociology and Social Policy, 31*, 6–20.

Wilson, R. K. (1981). Citizen coproduction as a mode of participation: conjectures and models. *Journal of Urban Affairs, 3*, 37–49.

Ye, H. & Kankanhalli, A. (2013). Leveraging crowdsourcing for organizational value co-creation. *Communications of the Association for Information Systems, 33*, 225–44, http://aisel.aisnet.org/cais/vol33/iss1/13

Zuboff, S. & Maxmin, J. (2002). *The Support Economy: Why Corporations are Failing Individuals and the Next Episode of Capitalism.* New York: Penguin.

9

Tapping into Diversity Through Open Innovation Platforms: The Emergence of Boundary-Spanning Practices

Natalia Levina and Anne-Laure Fayard

Abstract

Crowdsourcing for innovation is gaining critical momentum, with an increasing number of organizations engaging with digital platforms. While collecting ideas from a broad set of participants is now easier than ever, combining and deploying them in innovative ways is becoming increasingly difficult. As a result, organizations are faced with challenges in productively integrating ideas generated by the crowd. Organizations seeking to learn about and combine new perspectives have traditionally turned to consulting companies to tap into external expertise. In this chapter, we compare how consulting companies approach the problem of translating and integrating across a diversity of expertise with how external innovation is addressed in innovation-focused crowdsourcing platforms. We examine the nature of boundaries that arise in both types of endeavors and draw on boundary-spanning theories to develop an understanding of the differences between traditional ways of integrating diverse ideas compared with digitally mediated approaches.

INTRODUCTION

Crowdsourcing for innovation and ideas seems to be gaining critical momentum in today's society. Coined by Jeff Howe (2006), the term crowdsourcing refers to "the act of a company or institution taking a function once performed by employees and outsourcing it to an undefined (and generally large) network of people in the form of an open call." While in the early days, many crowdsourcing platforms were focused on rather mundane tasks, such as labeling images and text on Amazon's Mechanical Turk or posting photos into a common photo repository on iStockPhoto, today new platforms that are geared toward collecting ideas and solving innovation problems are going live at a staggering rate (Hossain, 2015). Hence, using a crowdsourcing platform to create innovative products or services has almost become synonymous with doing open innovation (Chesbrough, 2003), even though there are significant differences between these two phenomena (Afuah & Tucci, 2012; Afuah, 2018).

Crowdsourcing websites that support both "open crowds," such as Threadless, and "closed crowds," such as Innocentive (Viscusi & Tucci, 2018), promise to help organizations gain access to a great diversity of ideas and perspectives coming from multiple areas of human endeavor (Malone et al., 2010, 2011). For example, Innocentive allows companies to publicly post their innovation challenges, typically in the domain of science and engineering, and to solicit solutions from a wide variety of solvers. It has been documented that successful solutions often come from participants who have different backgrounds from those who have posted the problem (Jeppesen & Lakhani, 2010). Successful open innovation platforms, given their public nature, often have hundreds of thousands of participants. In design-oriented websites such as DesignCrowd, CrowdSpring, and Jovoto, it is not atypical for hundreds of concepts to be submitted in the initial rounds of competition. The sheer number of submissions may increase the likelihood of finding at least some innovative solutions for complex problems (Boudreau et al., 2011).

While collecting ideas from a broad set of participants is now easier than ever, sorting through them, combining them in innovating ways, and deciding which ideas are worth pursuing, is an increasingly difficult task because of the diversity and the number of ideas gathered. The possibilities offered by new technologies thus open up a series of challenges, including how to engage groups of diverse individuals most of whom have never worked together before, integrate their viewpoints, and create a productive dialogue; how participants might learn enough about the client's context to generate useful ideas; and how to evaluate, meaningfully, hundreds of ideas when they come from diverse technological, sociopolitical, and business contexts. Alternatively, if the platform limits its scope to a particular type of contributor (e.g. just architects or designers), organizations could miss the breadth of ideas that a diverse crowd is supposed to offer them. In order to facilitate the evaluation of a great number of ideas, crowdsourcing platforms could use crowd-based selection mechanisms (e.g. popular vote) for evaluating ideas, but that would assume that the public is able to take into account the context in which these ideas need to be applied—a time-consuming task that may also expose confidential company information. Finally, and perhaps most importantly, if the crowd actually develops novel and valuable ideas, it may be difficult to implement these ideas in an organization that is accustomed to its old ways of thinking and working (Lakhani et al., 2013; Levina et al., 2014).

Indeed, the knowledge-based view of the firm (Kogut & Zander, 1992, 1996) maintains that traditional organizations are stronger than markets in combining diverse ideas into meaningful and valuable products and services. Instead of boiling the ocean, organizations build combinative capabilities geared towards combining and transforming expertise coming from specific diverse domains. For example, many innovative firms have been able to successfully combine marketing and engineering capabilities (e.g. Dougherty, 1992; Carlile, 2004). These integrative capabilities usually take years to build as they involve the development of social structures that foster common interests, practices, language, and identity (Levina & Vaast, 2005). For example, Apple is known for building capabilities that combine computer design, hardware, and software, in ways that its industry competitors find hard to match. Yet, it took Apple many years to figure out how to do this (Isaacson, 2011). How can open innovation platforms enable boundary spanning across domains of expertise, as well as across organizational contexts, without making such costly investments?

While crowdsourcing of innovation is relatively recent, for many years, organizations that believed that innovative ideas can come from accessing and integrating a greater diversity of resources have turned to consulting companies to tap into expertise they were lacking in house. For example, management consultants are known for bringing diverse perspectives to "shake up" established organizational structures (Clegg et al., 2004; Kitay & Wright, 2004; Sturdy et al., 2009). Some consulting companies specialize in innovation consulting, whereby they both hire people from diverse backgrounds and develop organizational practices that enable these people to work well together and integrate diverse ideas (Hargadon & Sutton, 1996, 1997). Their consulting services range from pure ideation consulting to post-ideation product design and prototyping (e.g. IDEO, Continuum, WhatIf, or FrogDesign) or even systems development (e.g. Razorfish). These companies tend to have a greater number of boundaries that they have learned how to span, but they are still rather strategic in picking which types of people work for them and how to integrate their expertise (e.g. Kelley, 2005; Anand et al., 2007). For example, Haragadon & Sutton (1996, 1997) have shown how IDEO, one of the most famous innovation consulting firms, strategically built organizational practices aimed at brokering knowledge across diverse boundaries to enable innovation. In this way, innovation consultancies can be seen as a hybrid between closed innovation approaches and crowdsourcing platforms, as illustrated in Figure 9.1.

In this chapter, we compare how consulting companies approach the problem of translating and integrating across the diversity of expertise and

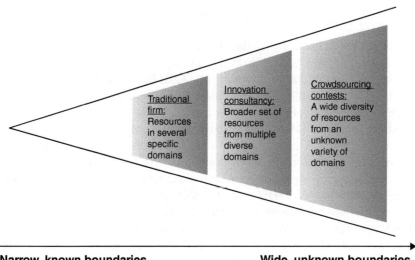

Narrow, known boundaries　　　　　　　**Wide, unknown boundaries**

Figure 9.1. Breadth of boundaries.

resources, with how distributed innovation is addressed in a crowdsourcing platform. We conducted in-depth field studies of two innovation consultancies: one has recently built a crowdsourcing platform, and the other uses a network of subcontractors to access expertise they do not have in house. Our analysis highlights the specific practices that each of these open innovation providers has developed to enable boundary spanning across diverse contexts. While many dimensions of boundary spanning are better suited for traditional organizational forms, where teams that have worked together for many years can integrate expertise by drawing on their joint practices (e.g. as described in Levina & Vaast, 2005), we found that new boundary-spanning practices have emerged online that allow participants who do not know each other well to still engage in productive collaborations.

BACKGROUND LITERATURE

In this chapter, to which the authors have contributed equally, we build upon four streams of literature: the literature on boundary spanning and boundary objects; the literature on management consultants and their role as knowledge brokers; the literature on online communities and knowledge collaboration; and the literature on crowdsourcing of innovation.

Boundary Spanning in Organizations

There is a broad literature on the notions of boundaries, boundary spanning, and boundary objects, and their role in supporting collaboration, problem solving, and innovation (e.g. Orlikowski, 2002; Levina & Vaast, 2005; Carlile, 2004; Hsiao et al., 2012). The development of information technology, globalization, and "hyperspecialization" (e.g. Malone et al., 2011) is increasing the need for communication and collaboration between individuals scattered around the world. This has led to people from diverse backgrounds working across a variety of complex, ambiguous, and often fluid boundaries to engage in boundary-spanning work in order to collaborate and produce new knowledge (Espinosa et al., 2003; Levina & Vaast, 2008; Faraj et al., 2011).

Boundary-spanning work is particularly important in the context in which actors have not interacted with each other before, as it can give rise to innovative outcomes if the challenges of dealing with diversity are successfully met (Carlile, 2004). Carlile (2004) has taken the approach of classifying knowledge boundaries into syntactic (based on differences in labeling the same information), semantic (based on differences in interpretation), and pragmatic (based on differences in practices). Based on this classification of "knowledge boundaries," he distinguishes three types of boundary-spanning outcomes, namely, knowledge transfer, translation, and transformation. Levina & Vaast (2013) have pointed out that "knowledge boundaries" are not defined deterministically before actors engage with each other and that, instead, it would be more fruitful to describe which social boundaries (e.g. organizational, professional, national, etc.) are salient in a particular boundary-spanning context and how through their actions, agents produce new outcomes or reproduce old ways of working. They have argued that agents who have never worked together before may still be able to draw on existing institutional structures such as practices in their industry, professional group, or organization to reproduce both the structure of relations and the associated knowledge, without transforming it. Thus, instead of knowledge boundaries defining what type of boundary-spanning work ensues, it is the boundary-spanning work that shapes knowledge outcomes, such as novelty.

Levina & Vaast (2013) proposed two modes of boundary spanning—transactional and collaborative boundary spanning—based on whether relations across boundaries are produced or transformed in practice. Transactional boundary spanning is based on exchanging objects (ideas, information, designs) across boundaries, often involving translational work, but eventually reproducing existing relations and knowledge. Collaborative boundary-spanning work is based on collaborating effectively across boundaries so as to transform practices and knowledge of the actors involved. Levina & Vaast (2005, 2008, 2013) have elaborated on how to recognize relevant social boundaries in boundary-spanning work using the notion of field of practice and identifying which fields and boundaries are most salient in a given situation.

Much has been written on what it takes to achieve effective collaboration across boundaries. Effective collaboration has been defined as the type of relationship among parties that "(1) leverages the differences among participants to produce innovative, synergistic solutions and (2) balances divergent stakeholder concerns" (Hardy et al., 2005: 58). Earlier work has established that developing a common identity through discourse is a crucial step for enabling effective collaboration. However, this is a necessary but not sufficient condition. It takes a particular type of practice to achieve effective collaboration. For example, in studying teams with diverse hierarchical authority, certain practices of providing feedback led to better learning across diverse team members (Van der Vegt et al., 2010). Levina & Vaast (2005) propose that for effective collaboration to take place in boundary-spanning work, it is necessary to create a joint practice that is separate from the practices of parties involved. These joint practices (or a new joint field as they called it) would enable people from diverse backgrounds to not only create a new shared identity, but also to build new joint language, objects, and practices that would eventually constitute new knowing at the boundary. Finally, in Levina & Vaast's later work (2008, 2013), they note that such joint fields may already be created for actors to tap into, and that collaborating effectively may mean transforming relations within these fields rather than creating new fields from scratch. For example, they have illustrated in their study of offshore software development, how a whole variety of institutional fields (e.g. national, organizational, professional, industrial, etc.) have given rise to boundaries that have created challenges in knowledge work, but those same fields have also been used to establish effective collaboration over time as actors have become sufficiently socialized into each of these salient fields.

The work on boundary spanning highlights two crucial elements of boundary-spanning practice: boundary spanners, people who are able to span boundaries of various fields and to establish common practices involving various groups; and boundary objects, objects that are plastic enough to adapt to the needs of diverse parties yet robust enough to maintain a common identity across sites. Boundary spanners have been studied for a long time in social theory and may be identified as ambassadors, translators, knowledge brokers, and gate-keepers (see Levina & Vaast, 2005, for a review). People are often nominated to play boundary-spanning roles (e.g. sales people, cross-functional team leaders, etc.), but very few actually succeed as such roles require participation in multiple diverse practices and having several diverse identities, without necessarily being fully accepted as central to either group. To highlight this phenomenon, Levina & Vaast (2005) propose to distinguish between nominated boundary spanners and those who actually fulfill their roles in practice (boundary spanners-in-practice), which may often be a different individual from the one nominated. Pawlowski & Robey (2005) show how IT professionals in a large enterprise served as effective boundary spanners-in-practice (or what they called brokers), because they were able to translate across multiple user groups and enable them to renegotiate their individual practices during the process of enterprise system implementation. To achieve this, boundary spanners needed to gain access to diverse practices, participate in them at least peripherally, and be seen as legitimate representatives of diverse perspectives. In other words, they had to be legitimate peripheral participants (LPP) in each practice (Levina & Vaast, 2005).

Because so few people are able to become boundary spanners-in-practice (Kane & Levina, 2017), the literature has highlighted the crucial role played by boundary objects, seeing artifacts as solutions to some of the challenges associated with nominating individuals (Star, 1989; Star & Griesemer, 1989). While earlier work, including that of Carlile (2004), has highlighted the role of boundary objects as a better substitute for boundary spanners when collaborative boundary-spanning work was desired, Levina & Vaast (2005) claim that boundary spanners-in-practice are necessary to develop boundary objects and practice surrounding their use. They argue that if certain boundaries have not been spanned before, it is first necessary for people to develop objects that represent differences among groups and to define the "common identity" of these objects (Levina & Vaast, 2005). Take an example, described by Bechky (2003), where a leading assembler was able to support the transformation of the understanding of other assemblers and engineers—by changing their views and relations—with the use of a prototype. While the object was instrumental in agents changing their views, it was the boundary spanner's use of these objects that enabled such a transformation. Boundary objects in that sense can be used not only to share meanings but also to mediate social relations and legitimize work (Bechky 2003; Ewenstein & Whyte, 2009). There has been a growing body of literature classifying boundary objects and comparing them to other types of objects involved in collaboration (e.g. Star, 1989; Ewenstein & Whyte, 2009; Barrett & Oborn, 2010; Nicolini et al., 2012). In general, the literature focuses on boundary objects as tangible, concrete artifacts. There has been increasing acknowledgment, though, that boundary objects may also be symbolic; in particular, concepts and narratives have been shown to function as boundary objects in certain types of practice (e.g. Bartel & Garud, 2009). Depending on the nature of boundary-spanning practice, agents may engage in exchanging objects within established fields reproducing established relations, or they may transform practices and engage in effective collaboration by creating new objects or giving new meaning to existing objects (Levina & Vaast, 2006, 2013).

In discussing prior research on boundary spanning, Levina & Vaast (2013) proposed that in transactive boundary-spanning work, boundary spanners act as translators and boundary objects are used to transfer or translate information from one context to another. The boundary-spanning work corresponds to reflecting and adding to the work of others, while relations among actors are reproduced (Levina & Vaast, 2013). In collaborative boundary-spanning work, boundary spanners are not only translators but also negotiators transforming and, in some cases, building new joint practices. Boundary objects are not only used to transfer information, but they also represent the differences among groups as well as the shared identities across groups. Collaborative practices involve not only reflecting on and adding to the work of others, but also, at least in some cases, challenging the work of others so as to produce new relations among agents involved (Levina 2005; Levina & Vaast, 2013). In particular, members of the different groups have to renegotiate power in order to enable this type of "creative challenging" (Levina & Vaast, 2008).

The boundary-spanning lens has been applied and developed in many settings, but, more often than not, it is used to study such naturally diverse settings as scientific collaboration (e.g. Star, 1989; Star & Griesemer, 1989; Swan et al., 2007; Nicolini et al., 2012), engineering product development (e.g. Carlile, 2002, 2004; Bechky, 2003), factory floors (Hsiao et al., 2012), and consulting (e.g. Hargadon & Sutton, 1996; 1997; Levina & Vaast, 2005; Ewenstein & Whyte, 2009). Consulting contexts is particularly relevant to our study of open innovation since consultants are typically seen as a source of new ideas for the organization and, in some cases, they are expected to transform existing practices and knowledge in organizations. Next, we review the literature on consultants and how they are seen in this role.

Management Consultants as Knowledge Brokers

Some of the management literature focusing on knowledge highlights the importance of bringing in outsiders to create new practices within organizations. Management consultants are often described as such (see Sahlin-Andersson & Engwall, 2002, and Clegg et al., 2004, for reviews). In that sense, management consultants are described in similar terms to boundary spanners in other literature. For instance, Hargardon & Sutton (1997) define consultants as "knowledge brokers" who can bring different and new perspectives to organizations. This external expertise can be technical or process focused (Werr & Stjernberg, 2003; Armbrüster, 2006). Consultants as knowledge brokers develop practices to translate new ideas and introduce them to their clients (e.g. Hargardon & Sutton, 1997; Suddaby & Greenwood, 2001; Kitay & Wright, 2004; Sahlin-Andersson & Engwall, 2002; Hargadon & Bechky, 2006). While many studies focus on the role of consultants as innovators, in some cases, their added value is not so much in the novelty or the difference of the perspective they bring to their clients, but more in the legitimation they provide to the organization as outsiders (Sturdy et al., 2009). Hence, as noted by Sturdy et al. (2009), consultants as knowledge brokers and boundary spanners often engage in both translation and legitimation activities based on their status as outsiders. While this outsider status seems central to the successful role of consultants as boundary spanners, studies have highlighted the challenges facing consultants as knowledge brokers: the lack of a common language (Semadeni, 2001; Kieser, 2002) or the degree of novelty of the knowledge (Armbrüster & Kipping, 2002). While time and development of long-term relations might help in creating a common identity and practice, as well as renegotiating old practices (Levina & Vaast, 2005), we are not familiar with studies looking at these kinds of issues in the context of short-term engagements, especially in cases where most participants are collaborating for the first time. Yet, in this day and age, many projects involving both consulting organizations and crowdsourcing platforms are short-term engagements, where participants may lack the time or desire to develop interpersonal relations and invest in building new practices. Moreover, in the case of crowdsourcing platforms, collaboration often takes place in online communities and not in traditional organizations. While such communities tend to have fluid membership and a great number of participants, which might make collaboration challenging, we do have growing evidence that collaboration is possible to achieve in such environments.

Collaborative Production in Online Communities

Online communities are increasingly regarded as important venues for promoting learning across the boundaries of time, space, and formal organization (Sproull & Faraj, 1995; Ahuja & Carley, 1999; Butler, 2001; Gray & Tatar, 2004; Herring, 2004; Fayard & DeSanctis, 2005, 2008; Faraj et al., 2011; Faraj et al., 2016). These communities provide a setting for participants from varied backgrounds to come together to share information and, in some cases, develop new ways of knowing. They offer examples of collaborative production between people who are separated by various boundaries—organizational, occupational, experiential, national—and who do not rely on traditional organizational structures for collaboration (Fayard & DeSanctis, 2005; Faraj et al., 2011; Faraj et al., 2016). In spite of some examples of success, both transactive and collaborative boundary spanning can be difficult to realize in the context of online communities (Faraj et al., 2011; Faraj et al., 2016).

Research on online communities has highlighted a number of factors that explain the success of some online communities in overcoming barriers to collaboration. There is an extensive literature examining what motivates contribution from diverse participants so as to enable the variety of viewpoints necessary to stimulate innovation (Wasko & Faraj, 2000; Lakhani & Von Hippel, 2003, Blanchard & Markus, 2004, 2005; Faraj & Johnson, 2011). We know that to sustain collaboration in such communities it is important to have facilitators and experts who can stimulate conversation (Gray & Tatar, 2004), develop communicative practices that would reflect their legitimacy and authority (Galegher et al., 1998), and facilitate identity expression to reinforce social rules (Finholt & Sproull, 1990). Importantly, online community research highlights the importance of developing and enacting multiple, adaptable, discursive, and interactive practices to create varied opportunities for information sharing (Fayard & DeSanctis, 2008, 2010). Arguing that most of the research on online communities has focused on structural mechanisms, Faraj et al. (2011) suggest focusing on the fluid nature of online communities arising due to the constant changing of boundaries, norms, participants, and foci over time. They make a call for future research on how collaboration ensues in situations where boundaries change dynamically and are not known a priori. In this chapter, we attempt to fulfill this call by examining practices in online communities focused on collaboration production that have fluid membership and boundaries.

Crowdsourcing for Innovation

Given that the phenomenon of crowdsourcing for innovation is quite new, little work has been done in the area to date. In particular, we do not yet understand how organizations develop practices that benefit from the diversity of ideas offered by the crowd, while also making them actionable locally. Several practitioner focused books and articles have mentioned the importance of such organizational practices (Chesbrough, 2003; Boudreau & Lakhani, 2009; Terwiesch & Ulrich, 2009). Yet, the majority of work in the area of crowdsourcing for innovation focuses on motivating the "crowd" to contribute their best ideas, rather than on how to make these ideas fit into the organizational context (Afuah & Tucci, 2012; West & Bogers, 2014). Some recent studies have explored the organizational perspective, but with a focus on the adoption of crowdsourcing as an approach to innovation. For example, a recent study (Fayard et al., 2016) has explored how organizational culture, in particular epistemic stance, frames its interpretation of crowdsourcing, while another study looked at organizational learning issues (Schlagwein & Bjorn-Andersen, 2014). Others have mapped the steps involved in crowdsourcing for innovation as well as designing software to support such steps for internal crowdsourcing (Leimeister et al., 2009).

Still, we know relatively little about the process of problem formulation, understanding and selecting a solution, and even less about adapting the solution back to the context in which the problem arose. Generally, these processes are meant to be handled by the client's organization (Wallin et al., 2018); however, some work indicates that the crowd can also be quite efficient in combining diverse solutions (Nickerson et al., 2009). Moreover, while innovation contests are relatively new, other forms of crowdsourcing production, such as open-source software development and user-generated product sites (e.g. Wikipedia, Open Source software), have been quite successful, not only in gathering contributions from diverse participants, but also in combining them in unique and useful ways (reviewed in Faraj et al., 2011; and Faraj et al., 2016). West & Sims (2018) discuss the differences between online communities, crowds, and what they define as hybrid crowds (where a network of contributors share some purpose, an identity, and/or some form of governance) and show how firms can leverage these different networks of contributors for innovation.

It is also unclear how collaboration practices in these settings compare with those used by consultants focused on brokering knowledge and designing collaborative solutions. In this chapter, we propose to probe these gaps in our understanding by exploring this phenomenon in situ through ethnographic field studies. We focus our exploration on boundary-spanning practices and the role of boundary spanners and boundary objects in these contexts. In particular, we are interested in whether and how collaborative boundary spanning takes place in short-term traditional or virtual engagements.

METHODS AND RESEARCH SETTINGS

This chapter presents two in-depth field studies of innovation consulting organizations addressing boundary-spanning challenges through online and offline means as they engage with their clients (problem owners or sponsors). One study focuses on an open innovation platform that we are calling "DeltaCommunity.com" (or "DC.com"),[1] a crowdsourcing platform with a focus on social innovation that was launched by Delta, an innovation consultancy. We have observed several client engagements happening on this platform. The other study focuses on Gamma, an innovation consultancy in the science and engineering space, using a globally distributed workforce as well as a network of "on-call" sub-contractors with specific subject matter expertise. The different ways in which each organization approaches boundary-spanning challenges offers a rich opportunity for understanding traditional organizational versus digital platform-mediated ways of enabling boundary spanning.

Research Sites

Case 1: DC.com. DC.com, a crowdsourcing platform, was launched a few years ago by Delta, a global innovation consultancy with a lot of experience in

---

[1] Names of all organizations are disguised to protect site confidentiality.

intense cross-disciplinary project work. Delta traditionally had delivered its services through small teams of designers, social scientists, and other professionals who had been socialized into its very strong culture of collaborative innovation, using its well-developed innovation process. By contrast, the platform was open to all people, designers or not, to brainstorm and collaborate on social innovation challenges. To date, there are about 100,000 members on DC.com, located all around the world. Some (but not the majority) are designers, and others have backgrounds in various fields such as management, architecture, marketing, non-profit, public policy, entrepreneurship, and technology. They are invited in a form of open public call to participate in challenges set by public and private organizations. Participation is completely voluntary, and there are no prizes or awards. These challenges are all related to social innovation, and address issues such as how technology can improve health or education in developing countries, how we can develop better urban communities, or how to support social entrepreneurship. The topic itself, social innovation, is prone to attracting a large number of people. Challenges are publicized on the DC website, on the sponsors organizations' websites, as well as by the members of the community via Twitter, Facebook, emails, and blogs. All the ideas and concepts that are contributed on the site are visible to the public, and anybody who is registered on the platform can comment on them. Moreover, participants can vote on each other's ideas. The site has a phased approach to solution generation, where several ideas are selected by the Delta DC team and clients to be developed further. While community vote matters in idea promotion, it is not the final say. A few ideas that are the most appealing to the DC team and the sponsor team are recognized as "winning ideas" with no monetary prizes. The whole process usually takes two to three months.

As the community involves a broad range of participants with different expertise, crafting the "challenge brief" is crucial so that it is broad enough to inspire and attract a large crowd, but clear and precise enough to allow the development of specific solutions. There is a small team of dedicated Delta specialists (both technical and business folks) involved in developing and supporting the crowdsourced platform. The DC team works with the client to understand the client's needs, design the brief, and evaluate ideas. They are also actively involved on the platform and engage with the community. DC.com has been hailed by the media as a great example of how to build upon a vast community of distributed participants (with a broad set of expertise) to develop creative, potentially implementable ideas for social impact.

Case 2: Gamma. Gamma is an innovation consulting firm offering its science and engineering consulting services to major multinational companies. The services are delivered by small teams of highly trained and extremely diverse scientists and engineers located in the USA (20 percent) and Europe (80 percent), as well as a network of over 7,000 "on-call" specialists engaged on an as-needed basis through Gamma's proprietary rolodex ("knowledge network"). In order to span boundaries across diverse technological and scientific domains, Gamma specialists rely heavily on the company's own proprietary methodology. The methodology was developed over decades and continues to evolve. It includes over a dozen highly codified techniques for understanding, abstracting out a client's problem, performing various market analyses, and then reformulating a problem in a way that can be related to diverse areas of science and technology, where ready-made solutions may already exist for this type of problem. The whole process is enabled by proprietary problem modeling language, which takes many years to master, along with various techniques involved in making the language useful. Eventually, multiple solutions are proposed to the customer on the basis of these various methods.

Gamma typically engages with clients in multiple phases (ideation, conception, and prototyping). Many engagements involve solving the client's "hardest technological problems" by applying the methods in small (four to five people) project teams on a fixed-price, fixed-time basis (e.g. 3 months). During the engagement, efforts of individual consultants (most of them PhDs in science or engineering domains) are supplemented by specific ways of searching proprietary and public databases of technical materials and contacting experts from the knowledge network when the team needs to learn something it does not know in a specific area.

Data collection and analysis. In both cases, we used a qualitative approach with a mix of ethnographic observations and open-ended interviews.

For the DC.com case, the data was collected by the second author over a three-year period of participant observation and from interviews with multiple stakeholders (i.e. DC team, community members, and challenge sponsors). It focuses on understanding the practices through which the team cultivates the DC.com community. Specifically, it focuses on how the team grew the community to foster a breadth of ideas and manages said community to improve the quality of the ideas through various forms of collaboration between online community participants, the DC.com team, and sponsor representatives.

For the Gamma case, the data was collected by the first author over the course of a four-year period (several interviews a year with key informants), with an intense period of data collection focusing on a specific client engagement. The intense data collection involved getting access to the client organization, which authorized the study at a time when the client was not yet sure whether it would hire engineering consultants or not, but was in the process of defining its strategy for open innovation. The client company was a green technology startup (GreenCo) located on the opposite coast of the USA from Gamma's headquarters. The period of intensive data collection, which included following all major meetings of GreenCo's open innovation team and its interaction with Gamma, as well as using an open innovation platform (RDInnovaiton.com), lasted nine months. Multiple semi-structured interviews with participants on both sides were recorded.

Each author developed a case study of their own setting and did the first exploratory analysis of the observations and interviews to define emerging themes. The authors then met regularly to discuss emerging themes and start comparing findings across sites and in the light of the literature on boundary spanning, consulting, online communities, and crowdsourcing.

FINDINGS

Our analysis highlighted two crucial types of boundaries that participants needed to span: (1) the boundaries between idea contributors and the client/sponsors and (2) the boundaries among idea contributors (consultants and/or crowd members). We will first present emergent themes, separately, for each case, highlighting each type of boundary involved.

Case: DC.com

The development of DC.com by Delta illustrates boundary-spanning practices, both transactive and collaborative. Delta as a consultancy plays the role of boundary spanner by creating DC.com (understood as the combination of the process, the community, and the web platform) to help sponsors to access the diverse and distributed knowledge of the DC community. In this case, we focus on how DC.com provides resources for boundary spanning in order to transform existing ways of knowing and develop creative concepts for social innovation.

The DC.com team has developed practices and built into the platform mechanisms to manage the multitude of diverse ideas generated by the community. These practices and mechanisms include the process underlying the platform, active community managers, and a collaborative culture, as well as some technical features. We will discuss the practices that have enabled boundary spanning to occur, focusing on two main elements (boundary objects and boundary spanners).

The DC.com process. The cornerstone of how the platform helps diverse participants to come together was the "innovation process" orchestrated by the DC.com team and enacted collectively by all participants. The platform mimicked the innovation process of Delta, which involved three stages: discover, ideate, and deliver. Each challenge on DC.com was structured around four (instead of three) phases:[2] *discovering*, during which members were invited to do some research on the challenge and share their ideas; *ideating*, during which members produced concepts by building upon the insights collected in the discovering phase; *specifying*, during which community members were invited to give feedback and collaborate in developing 15 to 20 concepts (selected by the DC.com team with the challenge sponsors) in order to make them more easily implementable; and *appraisal*, during which the community was invited to evaluate the concepts based on three or four specific criteria defined jointly by the DC.com team and the sponsors. At the end, the sponsors of the challenge and the DC.com team selected about ten winning ideas. During each of the four phases (which took place online), the crowd was invited to participate and generate diverse ideas within the structure of pre-defined themes for discovery or ideation.

All new participants in the platform, including the clients, were socialized into the practices of the platform by learning what the process meant. Indeed, the interaction and collaboration practices involved in participating on the DC.com platform sometimes needed to be explained to new members. For example, it was not always clear to newcomers why they needed to "discover" before they could start proposing ideas. In fact, what "discovering" meant and how different it was from "ideating" was difficult to grasp for many participants. Part of socializing into the process therefore involved understanding these subtle differences and learning what constituted a contribution in a particular stage. We also noticed that after a few days participating in a challenge, a new member's style evolved and they learned to provide feedback in a constructive way with lots of encouragement and positive effects. The process was enabled by both the DC.com team and the "core" community members, who participated in several challenges and developed a clear idea of what it meant to do things the "DC.com" way.

Boundary spanners-in-practice and boundary objects-in-use. The DC.com team ("the team") played the crucial boundary-spanner role with clients. The team consisted of Delta employees, who worked with the sponsors and participated in the challenge as community managers. The key boundary object used by the team was the DC.com website itself, which provided access to the members of the community, the team, and the clients. It provided a shared repository of information about the challenge (the brief, various updates on the blog, insights, and concepts posted by different members) as well as a tool to comment and collaborate on others' ideas. It also provided some features such as the "connecting" feature, which encourages members to connect different ideas and acknowledge their ideas via a drag-and-drop action. Not only did the website represent a common identity

---

[2] The labels are not the labels used on the platform.

of the participants as DC.com members, but it also supported almost all other crucial boundary objects. In this sense, it created an infrastructure (Star & Ruhleder, 1996).

One of the key boundary objects supported by the website was the symbolic representation of the four-phased DC.com process. The process was clearly depicted on the main webpage and was underlying the information architecture of the site (e.g. you could drill down on each phase). As new members entered the community, they started socializing into the practices of the community by understanding the meaning of each phase. While that meaning was different for each participant, it did have some common identity across participants who were socialized into the practice. Thus, the process itself can be seen as a symbolic boundary object key to the collaboration process.

The key boundary-spanning role both between the sponsors and the community and among community members was played by community managers, who were themselves active participants on the platform, engaged in community management tasks and officially managing the relationship with the client. At first, the team worked with the sponsor in defining and framing the main "challenge question" and the "challenge brief." The challenge question and the challenge brief were important boundary objects used by crowd participants to understand what the client needed.

As the idea generation and development process unfolded through various phases, with fewer and fewer ideas moving on to the next round, the DC.com team and the sponsor worked together to "funnel" the contributions of the community. Between each of the main online stages (discovering, ideating, specifying, and appraising), which could be described as phases of divergent thinking, the DC.com team and the sponsor worked together to converge and define the themes for ideating and selecting concepts. These sessions were offline sessions quite similar to Delta traditional brainstorming sessions, with all the ideas being mapped out and voted upon. During these workshops, the DC.com team focused on framing ideation topics and feedback to help the community members to translate their ideas in an impactful way and thus develop concepts that could be implemented. They also negotiated some of the directions of the challenge that shape the themes for the next phase in a way that recognized both the passion of the community members and the interests and constraints of the sponsor.

Criteria for selecting the concepts for the appraisal phase and the winning concepts were defined collaboratively by the DC.com team and the sponsors. They varied depending on the challenges, but they always focused on the potential impact of concepts, thus including the feasibility and the ease of implementation by the sponsor or even by community members. During the evaluation phase, community members were asked to evaluate the concepts based on a series of criteria defined by DC.com and the sponsors, and these evaluations were also taken into account. Thus, these criteria also became boundary objects used by community members. In making final judgments on which ideas to promote, the team also drew on its knowledge of who constituted the core group of contributors (from challenge to challenge) and whether and how the specific individuals who had posted the ideas considered were likely to contribute in the future. Team members used this knowledge in integrating and comparing concepts.

Community managers were not only engaged in spanning the boundary between the sponsor and the community, but they also facilitated the work among community members, much like moderators in online forums (Gray & Tatar, 2004; Fayard & DeSanctis, 2005). They were very active in framing and managing the conversation and creating a shared set of communicative and collaborative practices for all participants on the platform.

Thus, having the responsibility for spanning both the boundary with sponsors and among community members, community managers engaged in channeling contributors' energies in the direction that would be of interest to the client. They used a variety of practices to achieve this difficult task. These included commenting on the ideas of contributors, selecting featured ideas and concepts, and creating blog posts related to the challenge. In addition to the challenge brief created by the client-interfacing team, community managers also created "design-guiding principles," offering insights into the direction in which the client wanted the project to evolve.

The principles were useful, but not sufficient to enable effective communication, due to the wide diversity of people's backgrounds and their desire to take the project in their own direction. As a result, community managers kept inventing new means and approaches to explain to contributors the client's context. For example, in a challenge sponsored by an NGO to develop solutions to help political prisoners, many of the community members initially took a direction focusing on the potential detainees and came up with solutions involving microchip implants to be inserted under the skin of people at risk. The community managers highlighted in their comments the potential risks for people with the chip implants and pointed out that this direction of ideation was not consistent with the design-guiding principles for this project. They also created a blog post where they highlighted the broad range of technology that could be considered—RFID, social media, radio, letter writing, etc. This blog post aimed to suggest low-technology paths for developing ideas that contributors were not thinking of exploring.

This short example illustrates that there were numerous objects that emerged in any given challenge to support collaborative work. Some of the objects that DC.com participants experimented with became boundary objects and helped to enable collaboration, while others did not. Similarly, some research insights and concepts ended up becoming symbolic boundary objects for the specific challenge (and not for the community at large). Community members would rally around these specific concepts and would collaborate on developing them by providing each other with feedback on how they would work and tie into the challenge brief.

In some challenges, members of the sponsor team became participants on the platform, posting and commenting on ideas. In such cases, these individuals had to learn the practices of the DC.com community and gain legitimacy as members of the community. While their profile information revealed that they were part of the sponsor team, this was not as pertinent to the impact of their comments as their participation behaviors. They tended not to justify their comments on posts by claiming their identity as sponsors, instead focusing on content-based arguments. In this way, they emerged as additional boundary spanners between the sponsor and the community members who were engaged in that particular challenge. They drew on boundary objects (e.g. process steps) that were already established in the DC.com practices, and either introduced or reshaped objects that were specific to their challenge (e.g. leading concepts on their challenge).

Transactive and collaborative boundary spanning. The community managers and the DC.com team succeeded in creating a community with a collaborative culture, which was key in providing feedback and making connections across ideas. The DC.com team created more than a technology platform to collect hundreds of ideas from distributed participants; they also created an online community supporting the collaborative development of ideas. The exchange of ideas on this platform was enabled by the common experiences that members had in a variety of institutionalized settings/fields such as healthcare, western society, technology use, etc. All the exchanges took place in English and relied on commonly used vocabulary. A lot of the transactive practices focused on helping members new to a specific context (e.g. healthcare in the developing world) to learn about these contexts using rich descriptions, videos, pictures, and feedback provided on concepts that did not take context into account.

DC.com boundary-spanning practices were not only transactive, i.e. exchanging and translating information across fields (Levina & Vaast, 2013), but also, and mostly, collaborative, i.e. where participants challenged each other's prior views. The DC.com team, in particular the community managers, in their boundary-spanning roles, not only translated between the sponsors and the community, but they also negotiated meaning and understanding while defining the brief, themes for subsequent phases, and criteria for refinement. For example, when participants who had no exposure to political prisoners suggested ideas that had little relevance to the context, these ideas were not ignored, but rather were commented on by the community managers in ways that allowed idea contributors to refine their ideas to match the context of the situation and the interests of the sponsor. Because of the community voting mechanisms, the ideas that were very different from the sponsor's original ways of thinking or understanding of the context were not immediately dismissed, but instead, if they gained broad support from community members, were given the light of day in the discussion with the sponsor.

Thus, DC.com created a set of practices, through the features of the platform and the feedback and role modeling of the community managers, which supported a collaborative production of work, not only between the community and the sponsors, but among community members as well. Several members reported enjoying this collaboration, noting that they learned a lot and did not see the concept as an individual effort but rather as a truly shared production. This sense of collaborative work is very visible through the dialogue around ideas, which emerged for some concepts.

Collaborative boundary spanning between the contributors and the sponsors implies that the concepts would be impactful enough to transform the sponsor's practice, whether by implementing some of the concepts, or even by rethinking their ways of solving problems and developing new ideas. Impact was at the core of the DC.com mission, but it was not always easy to achieve or measure. In some cases, sponsors were able to implement some of the concepts and solutions right after the challenge took place. In other cases, the sponsor did not jump into implementing the ideas, but rather developed new practices such as organizing Hackathons to refine and prototype some of the concepts posted on the website.

There were also cases where some community members chose to take some of the concepts and prototype them in their communities. For example, three participants from Central America, after participating in a challenge on how to improve health in low-income communities, were inspired by two winning ideas. They combined the two ideas and created a social enterprise offering quality healthcare to low-income communities in their region. Their knowledge of the local context helped them to develop a workable solution.

Collaborative boundary spanning between the contributors and the sponsors required deep involvement by the sponsors (continuously encouraged and supported by the DC.com team). This was crucial in helping community members to understand the context of the challenge, in which the sponsor had expertise. When community members implemented some of the ideas in their own context (something encouraged by DC.com), it was because of their deep knowledge of the context, which allowed them to span boundaries between the community and the local constituents.

Case: Gamma

Gamma's business model focused on two premises: namely, that innovation can come from bringing solutions from one context into another context; and that this can be done in a "disciplined" way by using specific methodologies that would reframe client problems in ways that would allow consultants to see new solutions, potentially from other domains of science, engineering, and industry (henceforth, "technological domains"). The key boundaries involved in the Gamma work were not only those between clients and consultants and those between different technological domains, but also those between technology and business, because Gamma was typically hired to provide a solution to a technology problem embedded in a business domain (e.g. reducing costs, creating new products that would attract customers, scaling technologies from prototypes, etc.).

The Gamma process. The work of Gamma was highly technical and involved a large degree of understanding of the client's technological processes and, often, its business models. For example, an engagement with GreenCo required that within a month, Gamma would have developed sufficient understanding of a chemical engineering process so as to suggest how to address the technical problems faced in scaling this process. At the same time, the consultants needed to figure out what alternative processes existed and how they would relate to GreenCo's business model. In GreenCo's case, the client indicated that it wanted advice on the business model and not only, or necessarily, a solution to the technological problem.

The Gamma process involved working with clients in workshops and reviewing client documentation for a better understanding of current technological processes and problems. This was followed by a series of structured analyses of the information obtained in these interactions, such as identification of the client's business drivers, benchmarking of technologies against these business drivers, analysis of technological evolution within a particular industry, engineering system analysis tools, solution-generation techniques that involved comparing abstracted problem reformulation to similar problems in other technological domains, and ranking of potential solutions based on business drivers and feasibility of implementation.

While some aspects of these processes could be explained ("taught") to clients in a reasonable period of time (e.g. within a month of joint work or during an intensive week-long course), mastery of these processes took up to three years. Some of the tools were also much easier to understand, as they built upon commonly used concepts in engineering (e.g. cause and effect analysis or benchmarking), while others were much more esoteric and specific to Gamma, so that by the end of the engagement, clients hardly knew what the tools were meant to do.

Boundary spanners and boundary objects in use. The key boundary spanners between the clients and consultants were the client partner (the lead person involved in managing the client relationship) and the project managers (one collocated with the client partner in US headquarters and another located near the consultants developing the solution in Europe). As the project progressed, other "line" consultants assigned to the team also became boundary spanners with the clients, irrespective of whether they had or did not have direct interaction with the client representatives. They all had to understand the client's problem and participate in generating analyses and solutions. All of these boundary spanners were scientists (with PhDs) with varying degrees of process mastery. The client-facing team typically had long tenure at Gamma. While earlier in their careers, Gamma consultants were specialized, once they joined Gamma, they gave up their specializations and became generalists; they were exposed to multiple technological domains in their daily work and needed to learn quickly and integrate ideas from diverse domains.

In addition to consultants, some members of the client team were also asked to play the role of boundary spanners. Depending on the project, several technical and business specialists from the client's organization would get involved with Gamma as project sponsors and point-of-contact people for asking questions. They would help to articulate the business objectives, the current state of technology, and the history of technology development and approaches to the problem tried thus far. The point-of-contact people would interact with consultants on a regular basis in workshops, as well as in between, to respond to questions, vent ideas, etc. On the GreenCo project, for example, three scientists and two business leaders were continuously involved with Gamma in these roles. Additional people would join them (up to ten in total) during workshops.

Gamma and its clients used a variety of boundary objects to establish a common understanding as well as to integrate ideas from diverse technological domains. For example, they used PowerPoint slides extensively with various representations of their process to communicate to the client how the work would proceed and what different tools meant. Similarly, the client's team used PPT Slides to communicate to Gamma about the business and technology challenges, what had been done, etc. In fact, during the GreenCo process, the GreenCo team came up with a new boundary object that enabled communication between business and technical participants from GreenCo's side, as well as among scientists. It explicated some of the technological decisions that were taken by GreenCo in the past and illustrated which approaches were not explored. This "decision tree" was constantly referenced in problem formulation. Because this was a chemical engineering domain, chemical formulas and diagrams of the engineering process were constantly used to elaborate on the problem and current technological approaches. These served as critical boundary objects between clients and consultants and within each team. While consultants tried to elaborate on their process and demonstrate in numerous slides how the analysis was performed, in the GreenCo project, the client's team got a sense for the Gamma process but did not become deeply familiar with it, focusing mostly on the results of the analysis and ideas.

As various technological analyses started producing "results," certain diagrams depicting these results began to be referenced by the whole team and thus also became boundary objects. More importantly, specific technological solutions (the use of such and such technical process) acquired a label and a joint meaning. These specific solutions were subject to contestation as consultants argued for their value, while some client representatives argued against them as either scientifically invalid or not worth pursuing for business reasons. In the heated debates about which solution(s) to adopt, clients and consultants engaged in dialogue and joint meaning making around the specific technology involved. While multiple representations of the solution were used (e.g. various chemical formulas, energy balance calculations, risk analyses), the key boundary object was the solution idea itself.

Finally, in the work done on the Gamma side, it was often the same sets of objects that enabled joint working around GreenCo's problem. At the same time, consultants were more immersed in various analyses using the tools, some of which became boundary objects for the consulting team. Moreover, consultants involved external subcontractors (who were part of the 7,000 rolodex of "specialists-on-call") both to learn more about the client problem and to help to generate solutions. Specifically, these on-call specialists were not informed about the specific client or the problem, but instead were asked to explain how a particular technology identified as relevant to the problem worked. They might also be asked to perform specific scientific tests and/or calculations.

It was not always necessary to employ these specialists, as a lot of their expertise was codified in various scientific papers and patent databases. Thus, Gamma had an information department whose role it was to identify relevant sources of information pertinent to the project. Consultants working on the project would then read relevant papers and extract necessary details to build their understanding of the client problem. In this sense, such documents (scientific papers and patents) were boundary objects between the consulting team and the various technological domains that were involved in the project.

The key set of boundary objects enabling collaboration between consultants involved in problem analysis and solution generation were enabled by Gamma's tools and techniques. The names of these tools and techniques served as common symbolic objects, defining what was common among technological domains and allowing for differences between domains to be elaborated in the process of work. The specific representations used on the project (e.g. flow diagrams of GreenCo's process) tied Gamma tools to the client's context.

Transactive and collaborative boundary spanning. The Gamma process as well as the consultants themselves, with their broad expertise and their knowledge of the process, were able to span boundaries of diverse technological domains as well as the boundary with the clients. This was aided by the common institutionalized practices in science and engineering.

For example, at the beginning, the exchange of information (transactive mode of boundary spanning) was enabled by the common language and practices in science and engineering. In the GreenCo project, everybody relied on their common knowledge of chemical processes and formulas, engineering production processes, and the specific industry in which GreenCo operated. This same common language enabled consultants to engage with the on-call subcontractors to explicate what these specialists needed to do as well as to understand scientific papers and industry reports within particular technological domains. Similarly, institutionalized practices in management consulting and business analysis enabled communication between clients and consultants.

Collaborative boundary spanning was harder to accomplish. It occurred mostly in client–consultant interactions (workshops or personal meetings), where consultants offered alternative perspectives on the client's technology (they suggested, for example, that certain technological problems were inherent in technology design and could not be solved within the bounds of the same technology). In such settings they also offered their ideas for technological directions worth pursuing (e.g. using a different chemical from the one used in the current process). Finally, they proposed that the client should invest resources into an entirely different technological domain. These alternative ideas were not welcomed by many members of the client team and thus required joint dialogue to have an impact. It was very difficult for consultants to signal that they had achieved sufficient understanding of the client's technological and business context for these ideas to be seen as legitimate. They were more successful on the business front, where boundary objects used by consultants (e.g. benchmarking, trend analysis) were seen as more legitimate, eventually helping GreenCo business leaders to transform their ways of thinking and pursue new strategic directions.

Finally, within the consulting team, consultants worked jointly to figure out how to analyze client's technology and reformulate the problem using the tools. Not all the tools that were part of the methodology toolkit were used or found to be useful by consultants. However, some tools helped consultants take ideas from one context and apply them into another. Most of this translational and transformational work, however, was accomplished tacitly through consultants' exposure and study of diverse technological domains.

DISCUSSION

In this chapter, we analyzed boundary-spanning practices that were enacted by participants in our two case study sites: DC.com, an open innovation platform managed by an innovation consultancy that plays the role of intermediary between the sponsors of the challenge and a distributed community of about 100,000 members of various backgrounds and skills; and Gamma, a consultancy that addresses client problems using a hybrid model of teams of broadly trained scientists and engineers and a network of over 7,000 specialists engaged on an as-needed basis through Gamma's proprietary database.

Across the board, transactive boundary-spanning practices among idea contributors and between idea contributors and clients were first and foremost enabled by practices (and languages) that were already shared among these diverse actors. Thus, in the DC.com study, a large amount of transactive boundary spanning was enabled by the fact that people had a basic under-standing of the practices that they were trying to design (e.g. healthcare, imprisonment of political opposition, etc.). This enabled people to understand each other's ideas. Similarly, common practices in science, engineering, and business enabled transactive boundary spanning within Gamma projects.

Transformative boundary spanning among diverse contributors was enabled by shared practices built specifically by each organization. The DC.com team has facilitated development of shared practices that community members under-stood and enacted collectively along with community managers. These practices supported boundary spanning among community members across all pro-jects and could be said to constitute a new joint field of practice for DC.com. Similarly, Gamma enacted a set of unique practices that were shared by consultants and supported by a variety of boundary objects that made sense only to them. These practices were specifically targeted at relating diverse technological domains.

DC.com enacted joint practices that were easy to learn and were targeted at spanning any number of undefined boundaries in some way. They could help people from different countries and professions, but with similar backgrounds, such as in healthcare or human rights, to come together to establish a shared understanding and engage in collaboration. They focused much more on collaborative ways of interacting (e.g. allowing time for discovery, commenting on ideas, and evaluating ideas) than on creating a unique language for communicating and transforming ideas coming from diverse contexts. For example, the newcomers to the community had to learn that building on somebody else's idea was both allowed and, in fact, recommended.

This is in contrast to Gamma's practices, which worked for a more limited number of boundaries—broadly, those pertaining to engineering systems—and would not work for other boundaries, at least not without modification. However, Gamma practices, which took a very long time to learn, worked for establishing an understanding and transforming diverse ways of knowing in cases where shared professional fields (e.g. science and engineering) were not sufficient.

Boundary Spanning with Clients

Some of the most interesting and challenging boundary-spanning practices concerned boundary spanning with the client. The idea of engaging either of these open innovation providers is to learn something different from what clients already know and in this way to transform clients' knowledge-in-practice. Thus, it was of utmost importance that throughout the collective engagement of various participants, clients' understanding of their problems and potential approaches to them were transformed.

In both cases, open innovation providers tried to educate the client about the processes they enacted within their virtual and physical organizations. In both cases, the processes remained somewhat murky to most of the clients. In some cases, however, some clients engaged more deeply with the providers and learned the process in question. Moreover, some clients truly made an attempt to become legitimate peripheral participants (LPP) in the practices of their providers so as to engage in collaborative boundary spanning.

In order to harness the power of diversity, each project had to enable creation of new ideas that tied to the client's context, yet informed it in a new way. In both cases, transactive boundary spanning that allowed contributors to learn about the client's context (i.e. "the background") was enabled by a variety of documents, charts, pictures, etc. The elaboration of the background was facilitated by a variety of boundary spanners in translating roles. It then continued with contributors representing what they were learning in various ways and having clients react to that with feedback (e.g. Gamma participants presented what they were learning to the clients and heard their feedback).

The transformative boundary spanning with the clients started to emerge on the projects when new ideas were being offered by contributors (consultants and community). There was pushback to these ideas from the clients in both cases—as expected by boundary spanning theory. In the Gamma case, boundary spanners had to negotiate with the clients to get their ideas heard. The DC.com team also had to do the same. In some cases, the client problem was such that community members could also implement the idea independently, as we have illustrated in case of the Central American team starting a social enterprise. This was sometimes the case with Gamma projects, but most of the time the client owned complementary assets necessary to implement the new ideas or the IP required to use them.

Online Collaboration Practices for External Consumption

Enabling collaboration with an "open crowd" (Viscusi & Tucci, 2018) such as the DC.com challenges engenders several practices similar to those that have been found by previous research on online communities, such as the importance of (implicit and explicit) community norms, formalizing of certain roles, assignment of community managers, and facilitation of feedback mechanisms (e.g. Faraj et al., 2011; Faraj et al., 2016). However, there are important differences, especially because the aim of the collaboration is not simply knowledge sharing like in many online communities (Wasko & Faraj, 2005; Fayard &

DeSanctis, 2005, 2008). The goal here is to develop concepts that will help to solve a problem and will have an impact, i.e. will be implemented by the sponsors or other actors such as community members. In that sense, the aim is to produce an outcome for "external consumption"—the sponsor and ultimately the end users (i.e. people for whom the solutions are being developed.)

A few online communities have the goal of producing an outcome for external consumption. The open-source community is one of the most famous examples of such a community, which aims to create a product (Kogut & Metiu, 2001; Lakhani & Von Hippel, 2003; Metiu & Kogut, 2004). While it can be used by all, most of the programmers in the kernel are also users. On the contrary, DC.com members are usually not directly concerned by the issues at stake in the challenge, and even if they are, there is a sponsor who has a clear agenda. In fact, the sponsor could think of them as an extended workforce of Delta. They want to post a challenge on DC.com because of the Delta name, expertise, and process, but also because of the access to DC.com. For the DC.com team, the perspective is different; the community is not an extended workforce or even subcontractors—as is the case with the experts in the Gamma network—and thus, they do not have the power relation that allows them to state clearly the rules of the game. This is what makes the role of the community managers as boundary spanners even more important, as they are translators and negotiators of meaning for both the sponsors and the community, who they guide through comments and inspired features, as well as transforming the definition of ideation themes into directions, useful to the sponsor, that will increase the chance of implementation of the concepts.

As highlighted by Levina & Vaast (2005, 2013), boundary-spanning practices, collaborative ones in particular, imply the redefinition and renegotiation of power relations. From a power sharing perspective, online challenges are more egalitarian in enabling collaboration across contributors. Yet, they are not egalitarian in enabling collaboration with the client. While the client is invited and welcome to engage with the community, and community members are also eager to have feedback from the sponsors, there was rarely direct feedback and involvement from the sponsors. Thus, the DC.com team took on a crucial translator role in that relation, especially as the challenges were short and there was little time for sponsors to develop a relationship with the community members. While clients are free to ignore ideas in the case of Gamma or Delta traditional projects, there is a lot of interaction between the two groups, giving "voice" to the new ideas.

Our comparative case studies provide some responses to the issues raised by Faraj et al. (2011) for knowledge collaboration in online communities. Specifically, they have highlighted the importance of being able to change boundaries dynamically in fluid settings such as online communities. Our analysis suggests that this boundary work becomes even more complex when online communities participate in open innovation contexts, as several new boundaries have to be managed: the boundary between the sponsor/client and the community (and not only between the client and the consultant), and the boundary created for each new challenge, which, because of its specific focus, brings in a new group of experts interested in that topic but not necessarily aware of the DC.com community practices. More generally, our analysis of DC.com has highlighted the practices developed by the DC.com team to encourage or discourage certain actions from the community members at certain times.

CONCLUSIONS AND FUTURE RESEARCH

In this chapter, we examine one of the major questions associated with open innovation: how to integrate expertise and solutions across organizational boundaries when tapping into a very diverse base of experts and contexts. To a large degree these organizations rely on shared contexts or institutional fields (with the associated shared practices and languages) in which their contributors already practice. However, to enable collaborative boundary spanning, innovation consultancies develop emergent capabilities that span both virtual and traditional organizations. DC.com has implemented a specific process and has involved its team members, along with sponsor representatives, to serve as glue that helps to evaluate, filter, and integrate ideas. It has also focused on building a community (rather than a simple network for participants online) to enable collaboration. On the other hand, Gamma, which dealt with problems that required a great depth of professional expertise in multiple domains, has invested in a proprietary method that allows its broadly trained employees both to integrate ideas while working in close-knit teams with clients and also to tap into a wider network of experts for specialized expertise. The unique sets of practices that each organization have developed have enabled integration and transformation of diverse ideas without relying on a traditional organizational form. Moreover, these practices have enabled collaboration among people who did not know each other and were working together in short-term engagements.

We contend that in the future, we will see a variety of boundary-spanning practices that diverse innovation platforms and intermediary organizations would evolve and foster to address the boundary-spanning challenges involved in open innovation. Future research may be able to identify, categorize, and better understand those practices and what makes them most effective, in addition to understanding the circumstances under which different types of innovation platforms and intermediaries work best with the wide variety of boundary-spanning practices, and indeed organizations.

REFERENCES

Afuah, A. (2018). Crowdsourcing: A primer and research framework. In C. Tucci, A. Afuah, & G. Viscusi (eds.), *Creating and Capturing Value Through Crowdsourcing.* Oxford: Oxford University Press, pp. 11–38.

Afuah, A. & Tucci, C. (2012). Crowdsourcing as a solution to distant search. *Academy of Management Review, 37*(3), 355–75.

Ahuja, M. & Carley, K. (1999). Network structure in virtual organizations. *Organization Science, 10*(6), 741–7.

Armbrüster, T. (2006). *The Economics and Sociology of Management Consulting.* Cambridge: Cambridge University Press.

Armbrüster, T. & Kipping, M. (2002). Types of knowledge and the client- consultant interaction, in K. Sahlin-Andersson & L. Engwall (eds.). *The Expansion of Management Knowledge—Carriers, Flows and Sources.* Stanford, CA: Stanford University Press.

Anand, N., Gardner, A. J. K., & Morris T. (2007). Knowledge-based innovation: Emergence and embedding of new practice areas in management consulting firms. *Academy of Management Journal, 50*(2), 406–28.

Barrett, M. & Oborn, E. (2010). Boundary object use in cross-cultural software development teams. *Human Relations, 63,* 1199–221.

Bartel, C. & Garud, R. (2009). The role of narratives in sustaining organizational innovation. *Organization Science, 20*(1), 107–17.

Bechky, B. (2003). Sharing meaning across occupational communities: The transformation of understanding on a product floor. *Organization Science, 14*(3), 312–30.

Blanchard, A. L. & Markus, M. L. (2004). The experienced "sense" of a virtual community: characteristics and processes. *The Data Base for Advances in Information Systems, 35*(1), 64–71.

Boudreau, K. J., Lacetera, N., & Lakhani, K. R. (2011). Incentives and problem uncertainty in innovation contests: An empirical analysis. *Management Science, 57*(5), 843–63.

Boudreau, K. J. & Lakhani, K. R. (2009). How to manage outside innovation. *MIT Sloan Management Review, 50*(4), 69–76.

Butler, B. S. (2001). Membership size, communication activity, sustainability: a resource-based model of online. *Information Systems Research, 12*(4), 346–62.

Carlile, P. R. (2002). A pragmatic view of knowledge and boundaries: Boundary objects in new product development. *Organization Science, 13*(4), 442–55.

Carlile, P. R. (2004). Transferring, translating, and transforming: An integrative framework for managing knowledge across boundaries. *Organization Science, 15*(5), 555–68.

Clegg, S. R., Kornberger, M., & Rhodes, C. (2004). Noise, parasites and translation—theory and practice in management consulting. *Management Learning, 35*(1), 31–44.

Chesbrough, H. (2003). *Open Innovation: The New Imperative for Creating and Profiting from Technology.* Cambridge MA: Harvard Business Press.

Dougherty, D. (1992). Interpretive barriers to successful product innovation in large firms. *Organization Science, 3*(2), 179–202.

Espinosa, J. A., Cummings, J. N., Wilson, J. M., & Pearce, B. M. (2003). Team boundary issues across multiple global firms. *Journal of MIS, 19*(4), 157–90.

Ewenstein, B. & Whyte, J. (2009). Knowledge practices in design: the role of visual representations as epistemic objects. *Organization Studies, 30,* 7–30.

Faraj, S., Jarvenpaa, S. L., & Majchrzack, A. (2011). Knowledge collaboration in online communities. *Organization Science, 22*(5), 1224–39.

Faraj, S. & Johnson, S. L. (2011). Network exchange patterns in online communities. *Organization Science, 22*(6), 1464–80.

Faraj, S., von Krogh, G., Monteiro, E., & Lakhani, K. R. (2016). Special Section Introduction—Online community as space for knowledge flows. *Information Systems Research, 27*(4), 668–84.

Fayard, A-L. & DeSanctis, G. (2005). Evolution of an online forum for knowledge management professionals: A language game analysis. *Journal of Computer-Mediated Communication, 10*(4), article 2.

Fayard, A-L. & DeSanctis, G. (2008). Kiosks, clubs and neighborhoods: The language games of online forums. *Journal of the Association for Information Systems, 9*(10), article 2.

Fayard, A-L. & DeSanctis, G. (2010). Enacting language games: the development of a sense of 'we-ness' in online forums. *Information Systems Journal, 20*(4), 383–416.

Fayard, A-L., Gkeredakis, E., & Levina, N. (2016). Framing innovation opportunities while staying committed to an organizational epistemic stance. *Information Systems Research, 27*(2): 302–23.

Finholt, T. & Sproull, L. (1990). Electronic groups at work. *Organization Science, 1* (1), 41–64.

Galegher, J., Sproull, L., & Kiesler, S. (1998). Legitimacy, authority, and community in electronic support groups. *Written Communication, 15* (4), 493–530.

Gray, J. & Tatar, D. (2004). Sociocultural analysis of online professional development: a case study of personal, interpersonal, community, and technical aspects, in S. A. Barab, R. Kling, & J. Gray (eds.). *Designing for Virtual Communities in the Service of Learning.* New York: Cambridge University Press, pp. 404–36.

Jeppesen, L. B. & Lakhani, K. R. (2010). Marginality and problem-solving effectiveness in broadcast search. *Organization Science, 21*(5), 1016–33.

Hardy, C., Lawrence, T. B., & Grant, D. (2005). Discourse and collaboration: The role of conversations and collective identity. *Academy of Management Review, 30*(1), 58–77.

Hargadon, A. & Sutton, R. I. (1996). Brainstorming groups in context: Effectiveness in a product design firm. *Administrative Science Quarterly, 41*(4), 685–718.

Hargadon, A. & Sutton, R. I. (1997). Technology brokering and innovation in a product development firm. *Administrative Science Quarterly, 42*(4), 716–49.

Hargadon, A. B. & Bechky, B. A. (2006). When collections of creative become creative collectives: A field study of problem solving at work. *Organization Science, 17*(4), 484–500.

Herring, S. C. (2004). Computer-mediated discourse analysis: an approach to researching online behavior, in S. A. Barab, R. Kling, & J. A. M. Gray (eds.). *Designing for Virtual Communities in the Service of Learning.* New York: Cambridge University Press, pp. 338–76.

Howe, J. (2006). Crowdsourcing: A definition, http://crowdsourcing.typepad.com/cs/2006/06/crowdsourcing_a.html (accessed April 12, 2017).

Hossain, M. (2015). Crowdsourcing in business and management disciplines: an integrative literature review. *Journal of Global Entrepreneurship Research*, 5(1), 1–19.

Hsiao, R.-L., Tsai, D.-H., & Lee, C.-F. (2012). Collaborative knowing: The adaptive nature of cross-boundary spanning. *Journal of Management Studies*, 49(3), 464–91.

Isaacson, W. (2011). *Steve Jobs*. New York: Simon & Shuster.

Kane, A. A. & Levina, N. (2017). "Am I still one of them?" Bicultural immigrant managers navigating social identity threats when spanning global boundaries. *Journal of Management Studies*, 54, 540–77.

Kelley, T. (2005). *The Ten Faces of Innovation: IDEO's Strategies for Beating the Devil's Advocate & Driving Creativity Throughout your Organization*. New York: Currency/Doubleday.

Kieser, A. (2002). On communication barriers between management science, consultancies and business organizations, in T. Clark and R. Fincham (eds.). *Critical Consulting*. Oxford: Blackwell.

Kitay, J. & Wright, C. (2004). Take the money and run? Organisational boundaries and consultants' roles. *The Service Industries Journal*, 24(3), 1–18.

Kogut, B. & Zander, U. (1992). Knowledge of the firm, combinative capabilities, and the replication of technology. *Organization Science*, 3(3), 383–97.

Kogut, B. & Metiu, A. (2001). Open source software development and distributed innovation. *Oxford Review of Economic Policy*, 17(2), 248–64.

Kogut, B. & Zander, U. (1996). What firms do? Coordination, identity, and learning. *Organization Science*, 7(5), 502–18.

Lakhani, K. R., Lifshitz-Assaf, H., & Tushman, M. (2013). Open innovation and organizational boundaries: Task decomposition, knowledge distribution, and the locus of innovation, in A. Grandori (ed.). *Handbook of Economic Organization: Integrating Economic and Organization Theory*. Cheltenham, UK: Edward Elgar, pp. 355–82.

Lakhani, K. R. & Von Hippel, E. (2003). How open source software works: Free user-to-user assistance. *Research Policy*, 32(6), 923–43.

Leimeister, J. M., Huber, M., Bretschneider, U., & Krcmar, H. (2009). Leveraging crowdsourcing: Activation-supporting components for IT-based ideas competition. *Journal of Management Information Systems*, 26(1), 197–224.

Levina, N. (2005). Collaborating on multiparty information systems development projects: A collective reflection-in-action view. *Information Systems Research*, 16(2), 109–30.

Levina, N. & Vaast, E. (2005). The emergence of boundary spanning competence in practice: Implications for implementation and use of information systems. *MIS Quarterly*, 29(2), 335–63.

Levina, N. & Vaast, E. (2006). Turning a community into a market: A practice perspective on IT use in boundary-spanning. *Journal of Management Information Systems*, 22(4), 13–38.

Levina, N. & Vaast, E. (2008). Innovating or doing as told? Status differences and overlapping boundaries in offshore collaboration. *MIS Quarterly*, 32(2), 307–32.

Levina, N. & Vaast, E. (2013). A field-of-practice view on boundary spanning in and across organizations: Transactive and transformative boundary-spanning practices, in J. Langan-Fox and C. Cooper (eds.). *Boundary Spanning in Organizations*. New York: Routledge, Taylor & Francis Group, pp. 285–307.

Levina, N., Fayard, A. L., & Gkeredakis, E. (2014). Organizational impacts of crowdsourcing: What happens with not invented here' ideas? *Proceedings of Collective Intelligence Conference*, Massachusetts Institute of Technology, June 10th.

Malone, T. H., Laubacher, R., & Dellarocas, C. (2010). The collective intelligence genome. *MIT Sloan Management Review*, Spring, 21–31.

Malone, T. H., Laubacher, R., & Johns, T. (2011). Big idea: The age of hyperspecialization. *Harvard Business Review*, 89(7/8), 56–65.

Metiu, A. & Kogut, B. (2004). Distributed knowledge and creativity in the international software industry. *Management International Review*, 44(3), 27–56.

Nickerson, J., Zhner, D., Corter, J., Tversky, B., & Yu, L. (2009). Matching mechanisms to situations through the wisdom of the crowd. *Proceedings of the International Conference on Information Systems*, Phoenix, AZ.

Nicolini, D., Mengis, J., & Swan, J. (2012). Understanding the role of objects in cross-disciplinary collaboration. *Organization Science*, 23(3), 612–29.

Orlikowski, W. J. (2002). Knowing in practice: Enacting a collective capability in distributed organizing. *Organization Science*, 13(3), 249–73.

Pawlowski, S. D. & Robey, D. (2005). Bridging user organizations: Knowledge brokering and the work of information technology professionals. *MIS Quarterly*, 29(4): 645–72.

Sahlin-Andersson, K. & Engwall, L. (2002). Carriers, flows and sources of management knowledge, in K. Sahlin Andersson and L. Engwall (eds.). *The Expansion of Management Knowledge: Carriers, Ideas and Circulation*. Stanford, CA: Stanford University Press.

Schlagwein, D. & Bjørn-Andersen, N. (2014). Organizational learning with crowdsourcing: The revelatory case of LEGO. *Journal of the Association for Information Systems*, 15(11), 754–78.

Semadeni, M. (2001). Towards a theory of knowledge arbitrage: Examining management consultants as knowledge arbiters and arbitragers, in A. F. Buono (ed.). *Current Trends in Management Consulting: Research in Management Consulting*. Greenwich, CT: Information Age Publishing, pp. 43–67.

Sproull, L. & Faraj, S. (1995). Atheism, sex and databases: The net as social technology, in Keller, B. K. J. (ed.). *Public Access to the Internet*. Cambridge, MA: MIT Press, pp. 62–81.

Star, S. L. (1989). The structure of ill-structured solutions: Boundary objects and heterogeneous distributed problem solving, in M. Huhn and L. Gasser (eds.). *Readings in Distributed Artificial Intelligence*. Menlo Park, CA: Morgan Kaufman, pp. 37–54.

Star, S. L. & Griesemer, J. R. (1989). Institutional ecology, translations and boundary objects: Amateurs and professionals in Berkeley's Museum of Vertebrate Zoology 1907–39. *Social Studies of Science*, 19(3), 387–420.

Star, S. L. & Ruhleder, K. (1996). Steps toward an ecology infrastructure: Design and access for large information spaces. *Information Systems Research*, 7(1), 111–34.

Sturdy, A., Clark, T., Fincham, R., & Hadley, K. (2009). Between innovation and legitimation—boundaries and knowledge flow in management consultancy. *Organization*, 16(5), 627–53.

Suddaby, R. & Greenwood, R. (2001). Colonizing knowledge—Commodification as a dynamic of jurisdictional expansion in professional service firms. *Human Relations*, 54(7): 933–53.

Swan, J., Bresnen, M., Robertson, M., & Newell, S. (2007). The object of knowledge: The role of objects in interactive innovation. *Human Relations*, 60, 1809–37.

Terwiesch, C. & Ulrich, K. T. (2009). *Innovation Tournaments: Creating and Selecting Exceptional Opportunities*. Boston, MA: Harvard Business Press.

Van der Vegt, G., de Jong, S., Bunderson, S., & Molleman, E. (2010). Power asymmetry and learning in teams: The moderating role of performance feedback. *Organization Science*, 21(2), 347–61.

Viscusi, G. & Tucci, C. (2018). Three's a crowd? In C. Tucci, A. Afuah, & G. Viscusi (eds.), *Creating and Capturing Value Through Crowdsourcing*. Oxford: Oxford University Press, pp. 39–57.

Wallin, M., von Krogh, G., & Sieg, J. (2017). A problem in the making: How firms formulate sharable problems for open innovation contests. In C. Tucci, A. Afuah, & G. Viscusi (eds.), *Creating and Capturing Value Through Crowdsourcing*. Oxford: Oxford University Press, pp. 39–57.

Wasko, M. & Faraj, S. (2000). It is what one does: why people participate and help others in electronic communities of practice. *Journal of Strategic Information Systems*, 9, 155–73.

Wasko, M. & Faraj, S. (2005). Why should I share? Examining knowledge contribution in electronic networks of practice. *MIS Quarterly*, 29, 1–23.

Werr, A. & Stjernberg, T. (2003). Exploring management consulting firms as knowledge systems. *Organization Studies*, 24(6), 881–908.

West, J. & Bogers, M. (2014). Leveraging external sources of innovation: A review of research on open innovation. *Journal of Product Innovation Management*, 31(4), 814–31.

West, J. & Sims, J. (2018). How firms leverage crowds and communities for open innovation. In C. Tucci, A. Afuah, & G. Viscusi (eds.), *Creating and Capturing Value Through Crowdsourcing*. Oxford: Oxford University Press, pp. 58–96.

10

Co-Creation from a Telecommunication Provider's Perspective

A Comparative Study on Innovation with Customers and Employees

*Milica Šundić and Karl-Heinz Leitner**

Abstract

Recently, a number of co-creation approaches and techniques have been proposed for supporting innovation processes. These range from traditionally organized ideation workshops within an organization, to implementation of open innovation methods that allow the involvement of various external and globally distributed partners. Particularly in dynamic and emerging industries, innovation seems necessary, with both closed and open approaches being applied. This chapter provides an empirical study on idea contests with customers and employees of a large telecommunications provider in Austria, and provides insight into the commercial feasibility of ideas, their origin and likelihood, as well as how social media tools support community building during idea generation. Aiming at developing basic managerial implications on how to apply crowdsourcing effectively, we compare the outcomes of open, semi-open, and closed co-creation approaches, and discuss the importance of lead users and idea-sponsors. We find evidence for offline community building and other aspects supporting organizational crowdsourcing.

* This chapter represents the views of the authors and does not necessarily reflect the views of A1 Telekom Austria.

INTRODUCTION

Taking the lead in advanced technologies usually requires innovation, and this in turn requires tools and methods that can cope with the high dynamics and flexibility of the innovation process. Among recent developments in the field of organization and management of innovation, open and collaborative ideation methods—such as *Crowdsourcing* (Howe, 2008)—that include both experts and developers from within, as well as external suppliers and customers with little or no industry knowledge, are applied widely and studied in the literature. The role of such co-creation and communities in "creating, shaping, and disseminating innovation activities" (Hautz et al., 2010) is strongly affecting the management of innovations. As argued widely, the new forms of innovation communities have taken an important role in product development and corporate innovation activities, which is why co-creation and innovation with customers have attracted substantial interest from commercial management and academic research.

The topics related to innovation communities are challenging also in terms of user motivation and incentive systems. For example, it is important to note that crowdsourcing research is often related to exploring and analyzing behavior of online volunteers and their motivation and incentives within idea contests. In past years, a broad body of knowledge has evolved from studying the success and failure of online communities. Referring to these research areas as well as to common community success factors in literature, i.e. amount and quality of content, loyalty of customers, technological infrastructure, or marketing (Leimeister & Sidiras, 2004; Assmann et al., 2009), this paper focuses strongly on the quality of the content and on the dynamics and relations among participants of idea contests, i.e. user behavior.

Boudreau & Lakhani (2013) argue that *"despite a growing list of success stories, only a few companies use crowds effectively—or much at all."* We therefore explore crowdsourcing methods and their applicability within the organization process—in terms of process efficiency or commercial feasibility of the ideas. The purpose of this chapter is to contribute to the literature stream of idea contests, and at the same time to provide basic managerial implications on how to use crowds effectively. To answer this question, we conducted an in-depth case study (Yin, 1999).

While some case studies dealing with public crowdsourcing and idea contests have been conducted in the past, only few references to internal crowdsourcing within companies can be found. Recent studies tend to discuss and analyze how companies address their customers as well as employees to develop ideas (West & Sims, 2018). We contribute to this field by analyzing both public and internal crowdsourcing approaches from the same source and developing comparative results. We selected and categorized an open, a semi-open, and a closed co-creation process and performed a fine-grained analysis of user behavior, participation, and performance within the different processes to relate our insights to other industry examples and academic studies. The three approaches originate from A1 Telekom Austria, including: (i) the open, external co-creation approach with customers and users of A1 Support Community, (ii) the semi-open, internal tool-based co-creation approach with selected employees, and (iii) the internal offline co-creation approach with employees, which can be described as similar to a traditional, closed innovation (Chesbrough, 2003).

TOWARDS OPEN INNOVATION

The Rise of Openness and Co-Creation

Both the Internet, as known in its original form as a passive information medium before "Web 2.0," as well as the relationship between consumers and companies have changed rapidly over past years. Apparently, the Internet has transformed into an interactive platform with users that actively provide content and shape the World Wide Web. The new web has fostered the involvement of customers and other partners—the so-called *prosumers*—into various business processes, such as marketing, testing, product development, as well as innovation management. As often argued in the literature, companies increasingly initiate communication and review processes with their current and future customers and already involve them in the early stages of the innovation process. Nowadays, innovation processes are often carried out externally, for example in crowdsourcing communities or innovation platforms, e.g. based on the approach of *crowd wisdom* (Surowiecki, 2004), through interactive *innovation toolkits* (von Hippel, 2001), in various forms of *idea contests* (Bullinger & Möslein, 2010) or *idea tournaments* (Terwiesch & Ulrich, 2009).

The crowd is usually encouraged to participate through either financial incentives or non-monetary rewards. However, the approach is often criticized as it may lead to controversial or exploitative labor market practices. From a business perspective, it is crucial to provide the right incentives and intrinsic motivators, e.g. by addressing and motivating a large group of participants over a longer period to increase the number of good ideas. Eventually, setting up a customer community can provide a competitive advantage, which is important especially in challenging economic times. A strong customer community allows the company to expand the breadth of ideas, opportunities, and know-how while minimizing the technical and market risks associated with innovation.

As discussed by Bröring & Herzog (2008), companies often have limited resources to embed innovation activities into the organization, which often leads to undercutting of innovation processes. In order to optimize business processes, companies tend to focus on their (present) internal issues and may not manage to join future opportunities or technologies that are needed for a competitive position on the market. Yet, when applying open business models, *"it's important to be able to retain an open attitude that embraces how people and organizations can collectively solve a problem, rather than squabbling over how to split the potential reward"* (Carrero, 2009).

Open innovation can be extremely valuable and a source of significant competitive advantage, but it needs to be crafted, based on the organization's structure, size, culture, hiring practices, and other factors. According to Soni (2008): "necessary enablers of innovation could be grossly categorized into People, Process and Technology." But, albeit that a strong supporting culture and strategic intent within a company are necessary, external technology enablers, such as tools and platforms that enable creation and collaboration within groups or crowds, as well as innovation catalysts that connect companies with crowds of potential innovators or problem solvers (e.g. InnoCentive or NineSigma), play an important role in the implementation of open innovation.

Open Innovation in Firms

The implementation of open innovation within a company refers not only to a group or crowd of people outside of the organization supporting the innovation efforts, but also involves the work that must be done within a company to prepare, receive, and utilize ideas from outside. Engaging in open innovation must therefore be approached in a holistic and strategic manner (Kelley, 2011). For many years, open innovation has been described as the outsourcing of internal research and development activities. Recently, new concepts and methods, such as crowdsourcing, have been developed and are further starting to replace traditional contracting (Afuah, 2018) and marketing tools for identifying new customers, technology trends, or potential market channels. Such crowd oriented collaboration can be described as outsourcing of the innovation process through idea insourcing. Thereby the organization's relations with external actors, such as customers, researchers, suppliers, and other stakeholders are fostered; and vice versa, strong relations with partners are of high value towards further collaboration and crowdsourcing.

Innovation programs can be introduced to companies in many different ways. On the one side, senior management might see the need to become (more) innovative in order to accelerate innovation through the value chain. On the other, innovation is more likely to be approached by managers that are willing to take the risk of implementing a change or a novelty within the organization—the so-called *intrapreneurs* (Pinchot, 1985). Also, innovation is social—it usually happens in teams or groups and is not done by sole inventors. In fact, the activity of transforming ideas and useful intentions into valuable solutions is very social and requires a team that will work on proposals and suggestions and involve their own experience and ideas. Therefore, by involving an interdisciplinary team of innovators, on the one side, ideas and suggestions can reach the right experts (i.e. engineers or specialists) that will analyze and prove the feasibility of the ideas; and on the other side, reach the right people that will help to break down internal barriers within the organization. It is clear that within companies, innovation activities must be supported across hierarchies, by various stakeholders, departments, or divisions.

Particularly if there are no established metrics, best practice, or process to build on, the new program on developing and managing innovation is related to a cycle of trial and error. If the initial rollout is done company-wide, mistakes that result from trial and error cycles can be very costly and even lead to an eventual termination of the innovation program. Hence, when implementing a corporate innovation program, it is beneficial to initiate the activities within a selected department and include other units into the process at a later stage.

To ensure that networks and bridges between various functions and departments of the company are built and the open innovation approach is anticipated by the employees, it is crucial to identify potential employees who will support or foster the innovation process. Möslein (2013) classifies three types of innovators that are involved when a company opens up the innovation process beyond the traditional outsourcing of research and development activities:

(1) *Core inside innovators*, that are employees of a company and developing new products, services, strategies, or business models by their job specification; they are therefore *innovating professionally*. While these positions were mostly seen in the research and development department in traditional approaches, nowadays many other divisions contribute to innovation activities and participate in co-creation workshops.

(2) A group of *peripheral inside innovators*, that includes all other employees across all levels and units that generate new ideas in terms of intrinsic motivation and special engagement into business processes. These employees are not involved in the innovation process formally, but they act as innovators and provide possible solutions as well.

(3) Eventually, a group of *outside innovators* is composed of all external actors, including customers, suppliers, strategic partners, as well as academic institutions, research staff, or start-ups and competitors. This group builds a promising pool for generating design ideas, innovation concepts, or other solutions.

To complement internal innovation activities with an external perspective, various actors can be integrated into the innovation process. However, approaches that include a large pool of innovators combined with innovation tools into well-integrated, effective, as well as efficient business models, are currently a matter for experimentation and exploration. Hence, we contribute to this field by analyzing and sharing our insights on different operating models of co-creation that include tools, platforms, and large pools of users and innovators.

Business Model Innovation

There is an emerging literature about new business models that are particularly proposed in the context of open forms of innovation (e.g. Chesbrough, 2006; Osterwalder & Pigneur, 2010). The definition and implementation of a new business model, which not only includes a specific new offer to the customer or partners but also is associated with the adaptation of the entire value chain, is considered as business model innovation in literature (Gassmann et al. 2014).

Just as any other types of innovation activities, business model innovations usually encounter and have to overcome different types of barriers. Particularly they face organizational and cultural inertia, which requires the involvement of top management of the company. The definition and adoption of a new business model within a company and on the market is hence similar to open innovation, a holistic and strategic task which needs to be embedded in the strategy management processes.

One example of business model innovation is the "freemium" model, which is often discussed in the literature. It is described as the offer of a free basic product or service, which customers or beneficiaries can use without being charged or within a limited trial period, with the opportunity to upgrade to a full, premium package with extra services (Gassmann et al. 2014). Many services offered for free on the Internet follow this recipe. Another well-known business model is the "razor and blades" strategy, whereby a basic product or service is offered at a bargain price below production cost, or even for free, but additional products that are necessary to use it are priced higher. Gillette and Nespresso are given examples, though, even if the idea of complementary goods is well known from the theory of economics, the process of using singular, custom-built coffee capsules or selling coffee in boutiques was new to the coffee market.

INNOVATION WITH CROWDS

Innovation Communities

As the innovation settings shift from closed to open, the process of innovation must change as well. This includes emerging organizational and managerial challenges when shifting towards new, interactive operating and business models; new innovation strategies and adaptations to corporate policies; as well as the rise of individuals, communities, user-driven content, or platforms to support the transformation process.

The corporate challenges and needs for continual optimization, innovation, and competitiveness have also reinforced organizational learning and knowledge management approaches. In the organizational context, communities of practice or COPs (first coined by Wenger in 1999) are "informal groups of people seeking knowledge and information so as to solve problems in their specific fields of work" (Leal & Baeta, 2006) or aiming to create and share knowledge and problem solving (Wenger et al., 2002). Hence, communities of practice are described as tools for capturing valuable knowledge, generating new ideas, as well as for supporting innovation activities. Such communities and their members possibly emerged into potential innovation contest groups and networks within large companies.

From an organizational perspective, the use of information technology has fostered collaborative approaches and combining or production of knowledge and new ideas. In contrast with traditional work groups, communities of practice are not defined by targets, time schedules, objectives, or workday schemes (Leal & Baeta, 2006). Also, viewed from a global perspective, face to face relationships in large, multinational companies are almost impossible, so virtual groups or communities build a great alternative for (real-time) knowledge and information exchange. This fact again points out the need for tools that support internal communities and idea exchanges.

When setting up an innovation community, there are several parameters and stages that influence the initial realization and the success of the community at a later stage. For example, Füller et al. (2004) suggest a four-step process, which includes: (1) determining the relevant attributes that users need to participate in the innovation task or challenge; (2) identifying users as well as where they might most probably be found; (3) designing the interaction with users efficiently; as well as (4) enabling access for users and encouraging them to take part in the co-development process. This approach of "community-based Innovation" (Füller et al., 2004) includes three stages: *idea generation, design and engineering,* as well as *test and launching.* The benefit of this approach is argued by the authors as follows: "*By integrating selected community members more than once or iteratively in different stages these users may even get the status of development advisors what (sic) strengthens the idea of collective invention and trust building*" (Füller et al., 2004). In a similar approach, Hautz et al. (2010) consider innovation communities as networks with focus on special interaction possibilities. In their study, the authors identify differing community roles by combining user behavior, relationships, and user-generated content. Based on the underlying studies, the results by Hautz et al. (2010) include "motivators," "attention attractors," "passive users," or "idea generators" as crucial roles in communities. To some extent they refer to the five community roles recommended by Kim (2000): "visitors," "novices," "regulars," "leaders," and "elders"—arguing that each role is described by specific community tasks, roles, or rights.

In our study, we discuss the importance of different roles within communities and idea contests and define roles that are needed for each of the three analyzed operating models of co-creation. Also, we find evidence that community building as well as social networks positively support co-creation activities by enlarging the target group, or by keeping track of the achieved activities and forthcoming process steps. Therefore, as the abilities of communities and social networks have recently achieved crucial importance in many businesses, we add to this work the aspect of understanding social networks, i.e. social media as well as how it can be applied to support open innovation activities. A conclusion on what types of social media are applicable for corporate innovation contests and co-creation with employees and customers is also part of our study results.

Super Users

Researchers are continually paying attention to users' behavior and diversity within social networks, which we will refer to in the results section of this chapter. We find that some users of online communities have changed and advanced into so-called "gatekeepers" or "opinion leaders" (Fiege, 2012). These users can influence large groups of friends or communities of topic followers. Both friends and followers regard their recommendations as of particular importance. The term opinion leaders, or *super users* is used in our research to analyze whether ideas are rated or perceived differently, depending on who is their author. In addition, we match the characteristics of super users to lead users (von Hippel, 1986), as both groups seem to: (i) face needs for new products or services a long time (months or years) before these are introduced to marketplaces; (ii) expect to benefit significantly by finding a solution to their needs; and (iii) often develop new products or services themselves because they cannot or do not want to wait for them to become available commercially. Table 10.1 describes the similarities between the two user groups.

Referring to the current literature, we argue that searching for and identifying super users in a community is affiliated with searching for users with lead user characteristics. By identifying users at the front end with novel ideas and needs for cutting-edge offers, companies can collaborate with them to create products and services which fit highly with user needs. Based on previous findings, we observed communities, their users and super users, in order to see if some user groups or their ideas are privileged. Although we initially suppose that super users and strong content providers within a community are more visible than other community users—i.e. through highlights of their posts or finding

Table 10.1. Link between lead users (von Hippel, 1986) and super users.

Lead users (as described in the literature)	Super users (evolved from the study)
Lead users are at the front end of market trends, and so experience early needs that will later be experienced by mainstream users and markets.	Super users often participate in testing products or services earlier than other customers. Hence, they are using and experiencing cutting-edge products and face the need to use, improve, or develop ideas on these products.
Lead users expect benefits from finding or building a solution to their needs, and therefore they innovate— e.g. to find appreciation or because they seem impatient to wait for market maturity.	Super users are provided with beneficial user roles within the community, so they encounter topics or discussions earlier than other community users. Hence, they are treated as valuable idea creators and important players in the product development process.

their names in top user lists—this work shows that the ideas of super users are preferred to ideas of other users. We limit the findings in this chapter to creating and capturing value through crowdsourcing and we propose further research to determine, whether the ideas of super users: (a) are higher rated because of their presence, or (b) truly score better, because these users are at the front end of product development and idea creation. This inequality is one of the risks of crowd involvement, which are discussed in the next section.

Intra-Corporate Crowdsourcing

In the literature, the process of involving employees in idea creation and product development in large enterprises based on software tools is also described as "enterprise crowdsourcing" (Vuković, 2009) or "intra-corporate crowdsourcing" (Villarroel & Reis, 2010). Based on the example of IBM (Vuković, 2009; Stewart et al. 2009) or Siemens (Wiener et al., 2012), the discipline of software development and the need to resolve urgent requests by finding the right experts within globally distributed teams and departments can be argued as one of the main origins of internal crowdsourcing. Nowadays, large companies are motivated to set up so-called "stock markets for innovation" (Villarroel & Reis, 2010), continuous improvement processes, or employee crowdsourcing and idea contests for many other purposes, such as to find and gather knowledge and acknowledge ideas from individuals across all areas of the company.

Internal activities and employees are considered as the most important source of innovation for companies in the traditional innovation literature. There is a vast literature investigating the implementation of idea generation or employee suggestion schemes within companies and how to set incentives for the participation of employees in product development processes (Lewin & Mitchell, 1992).

Gradually the use of information technologies, the Internet and social media, has also allowed involvement by different, or all, groups of employees across organizational and hierarchical levels, which is particularly relevant for large and globalized firms. Companies often develop and use tools which combine information technology, communication, networking, and social media features to share information and communicate with employees. Besides professional idea management software or innovation toolkits, so-called "enterprise webs" (Vuković, 2009), which combine social platforms and working tools, can also be used for various activities like development of ideas, problem solving, and co-creation.

Current communication practices in companies can be categorized within two distinct methods. First, the channels—given the example of email and instant messaging—can be used by everyone to share and distribute digital information, but the shared data is only accessible by a restricted circle of people. The second group of platforms is vice versa, as the information is generated by a smaller group of users but can be accessed by large groups of people. The use of such *Enterprise 2.0* tools and platforms (McAfee, 2006) can be seen as a first step towards an internal opening which can lead to extended external opening in terms of open innovation. It leverages the way to collaborate, share, and organize information between employees.

In order to achieve a wide acceptance of internal crowdsourcing technologies, they have to be easy to use with no or low training efforts. Employees should not feel dictated to in how to work or structure the information they share. Instead, the structure of information as well as the art of how it is shared and linked to other topics should emerge as the content grows. Hence, autonomous and individual peers should build a distributed platform with changing structures (McAfee, 2006).

A recent study in 95 Austrian industrial firms reveals empirical evidence about the use of different sources and methods for idea creation (Leitner et al. 2015). The study shows that: analysis of completed projects and processes, internal suggestion programs, and regular meetings for creative search of new ideas, are the most used internal sources to gather information and ideas (see Figure 10.1). More than 50 percent of firms have declared that these sources are used to a large or very large extent for their knowledge gathering.

Risks of Openness and Crowd Involvement

Howe (2008) states that *"Given the right set of conditions, the crowd will almost always outperform any number of employees–a fact that companies are becoming aware of and are increasingly attempting to exploit."* From the

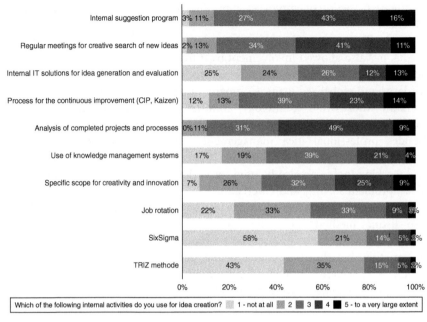

Figure 10.1. Use of internal sources and methods for idea creation (N = 95).

crowd's perspective, the right rewards and incentives are crucial in voluntary participation. Inappropriate compensation may force many participants into abandoning crowdsourcing activity, leaving a small group of actors which emerge, that submit similar ideas and approaches repeatedly (Šundić & Leitner, 2013). Formal registration to the innovation platform might have a negative impact on the number of solvers, but it is a nice way to select supposedly motivated solvers. As already argued, having a large crowd is critical, since a small group of registered customers might manipulate the image of the market and customer demands, or even distort ideas and solutions.

From the corporate perspective: "Pushing problems out to a vast group of strangers seems risky and even unnatural, particularly to organizations built on internal innovation. [...] But excluding crowdsourcing from the corporate innovation tool kit means losing an opportunity" (Boudreau & Lakhani, 2013). Also, arguments exist that wrong mode of user innovation or crowd-sourcing may force companies into "falling behind in the relentless race" (Pisano & Verganti, 2008). Still, one of the reasons why companies resist user innovation or crowdsourcing is that managers don't clearly understand the benefits of crowds and how to manage the process and external crowd of volunteers to achieve set results. Hence, this work aims to highlight the risks and potentials of crowdsourcing within corporate settings and decrease the managerial reluctance that is connected with new forms of innovation. Considering the structure and organizing principles of the relationship between a company and the crowd, Pisano & Verganti (2008) call for a "collaborative architecture," which distinguishes between open and closed collaboration modes and strongly relates to the company's strategy.

As organizations become more porous—with more outsourcing, freelancers, and crowdsourcing—risks rise along with potential rewards. We therefore discuss a critical situation where the crowd gets off track through the example of TED's open licensing model. TED (which stands for technology, education, and design or "ideas worth spreading") was initially launched in 1984 as a single annual conference in California to share inspiring ideas, and has since grown into a global phenomenon. Since 2006, all talks are available for free on the Internet and most are translated by a crowd of volunteers into more than 90 different languages—which again points to a benefit of crowd collaboration. Soon after the beginning, TED organizers ventured to "democratize the idea-spreading process by letting licensees use its technology and brand platform" (Merchant, 2013), allowing people around the world to further spread ideas by organizing local, independent TEDx events. Since 2009, more than 5,000 TEDx events have taken place around the world, with around 2,700 of them in 2012 (Merchant, 2013). By setting up an independent, decentralized (sub-)community, TED saved millions of dollars they would have had to have spent through their initial business model. However, because it allowed nearly anyone to contribute, the total control of the content was no longer possible. TEDx licensees began hosting inappropriate events under its brand, which caused negative comments and articles (Quora, 2010). As a result, TED revoked their license, keeping some important parts of the organization closed. This approach is described in three levels by Merchant (2013): *open, semi-open, and closed*. Besides using the example of TED to point to the risk of losing control in crowd-oriented projects, we further use the three levels of openness to classify the different co-creation approaches by A1 Telekom Austria in our case study.

As argued in this chapter, numbers of interactions between companies and crowds on innovation projects in different industries, such as industrial engineering, software engineering, media processing, gaming and apps, as well as new forms of marketing, are rising and they play an important role when business models are generated or designed. Since crowdsourcing is moving into the mainstream, being aware of the best form of user involvement and co-creation, as well as knowing the basic rules of crowdsourcing is helpful in addressing concerns and finding the best possible ideas and solutions. Particularly, by knowing the risks and combining the benefits of both closed and open innovation methods, innovating companies can generate potential profits and achieve growth and a sustainable market position, as well as relocating the intensive trial and error process towards finding their customers' needs directly to the customer. Eventually, both innovation seekers and solution providers must find a balance between their competing and shared interests.

CASE STUDY

Research Framework and Questions

Qualitative research is particularly affected by the digital and technological revolutions that have shaped the beginning of the twenty-first century. Computer software, digital recorders, IP-telephony, and other digital tools are used for conducting and recording interviews and focus groups as well as analyzing qualitative data. Given the widespread use and access to this medium, it is no surprise that the Internet has been discovered as an object of research and also as a tool to use for research (Flick, 2009). To answer the proposed research questions of co-creation and user behavior in communities, we collected data from three co-creation approaches, including: timelines and important timestamps, detailed user information, content, ideas, reviews and votes to ideas, comments, as well as other meta-information. Based on our first data observation and empirical analysis, we derived three research questions which considered the content, user participation or behavior, and eventually the influence of social networks on idea contests and co-creation.

Given that crowdsourcing projects are always promoted to the entire community of Internet users, a large number of the submissions will not meet the required demands or quality. The principle to "remember the Sturgeon's Law" (Howe, 2008) recalls that "90 percent of everything is crap" (leaving only around ten percent of usable ideas). Hence, the path towards finding a suitable solution to the idea contest at an expected quality is analyzed as follows: (1) *What is the impact of the level of specificity of the submission criteria on the commercial feasibility of the submitted ideas?*

Once the submission criteria for the ideation contest is defined sufficiently, it's crucial to find the right users to participate. Active users of online communities increasingly gain professional experience as they become accustomed community members, and some of them even become opinion leaders or leading members. We agree with Assmann et al. (2009) that "*[visitors and new users] interact less with other members of the community and have fewer and weaker ties within the community than members who have been in the community for some time.*" Therefore, the impact of advanced users or opinion leaders on other participants in the community is explored in this work. As argued before, we particularly consider such advanced community members or opinion leaders as users with lead user characteristics. Gaining a deeper insight on how ideas are rated and selected, we explore the impact of lead users in our communities as follows: (2) *Do individual characteristics of idea creators (lead users or opinion leaders) influence the likelihood of idea selection?* Analogous to lead users, the influence of idea seekers (sponsors) or third parties on the ideation process is studied in parallel.

With reference to Kaplan & Haenlein (2010), social media is ever present today, allowing companies to "engage in timely and direct end-consumer contact at relatively low cost and higher levels of efficiency." Social Media and Web 2.0 provide important and new communication pathways and opportunities for companies. However, to make social media a useful support for crowdsourcing initiatives, several challenges arise. Hence, we included side-research on social media tools and social networks: (3) *How do social media tools and social networks support co-creation activities within the three studied approaches?*

Three Co-Creation Approaches from an Austrian Telecommunication Provider

As discussed in the literature, crowdsourcing generally takes one of the distinct high-level forms: idea contests, innovation markets, or collaborative communities. After exploring crowdsourcing projects in and around Austria, idea contests within existent communities were perceived as the common form in corporate settings. With reference to Bullinger & Möslein (2010), who find a majority of contests from a rather random sample of innovation contests conducted by firms (43 out of 57), a large-enterprise platform was selected among firms that provide online crowdsourcing activities. The community selection criteria are adapted from Franke & Shah (2003): "to observe community-related innovation behavior, the community as a whole or some community members should be engaged in innovative activities." Hence, A1 Support Community operated by A1 Telekom Austria was identified, and among various community threads, the idea contest "Mein A1 einfach machen" (transl.: simplifying my A1) was selected for deeper analysis to answer the research questions. Similar to this approach, innovation activities or idea contests that are organized internally within a company and involve employee participants were identified and selected as counterparts to the study. We compare three co-creation approaches: (i) the *open* external co-creation with "anyone," i.e. members of the A1 Support Community; (ii) the *semi-open* internal tool-based approach with employees; and eventually (iii) the internal offline co-creation with selected employees, which we describe as *closed* co-creation. Hence, the public crowdsourcing with A1 Support Community members, including both A1 customers and non-customers, is compared to the two internal crowdsourcing approaches. Hereby, we use the same underlying company as a common source to search for ideas and solutions in the field of digital, customer-oriented information and telecommunication.

Based on the identified data source, the following A1 Support Community data sets were selected for the study: the project forum, idea forums including metadata, leader board pages, as well as the A1 Facebook fanpage. The data were observed and collected in September 2013. As the idea contest finished during the first quarter of 2013 and the archived content had not been changed or modified, a specific date stamp for collection of the forum content does not seem crucial. However, to collect meta-information on community members from the so-called "leader board page," we find a collection date stamp (09-2013) to be strongly important. In order to include all relevant postings on Facebook that refer to the idea contest "Mein A1 einfach machen," the collected data set includes postings that go back to November 2011, to the project start. The internal data sources were collected in October 2013 and include data (i.e. ideas and submissions) that were created and documented during 2013. The corporate data from the internal crowdsourcing contests were collected by exporting data from the idea management tool on one side, and manually collecting the innovation workshops documentation from other online resources otherwise.[1]

Eventually, we studied and interpreted the data and research proposals to evaluate the content of submitted ideas and solutions, as well as possibilities of incorporating external groups into the collaborative innovation process. The presumptions call for addressing the right target group on the one side, but also addressing a large and diverse group of customers on the other, in order to maintain the level of novelty and a vivid and dynamic community atmosphere. Eventually, the influence of social media was added to the study. We discuss the results in the next chapter, after introducing the three approaches.

Open co-creation with customers. A1's social support program including the crowdsourcing community was launched in 2011 and envisioned as a vital community for customers and a constantly growing platform for co-creation and cooperation with users in various game workshops and interactions. A1 Telekom Austria's social media channels are further illustrated in Table 10.2.

Table 10.2. A1 Telekom Austria's social media outreach in September 2013.[2]

Type of channel	Link	Facts
A1 blog	http://www.a1blog.net/	22 categories, 60 stories
Youtube	http://www.youtube.com/user/EinfachA1	2,500+ followers
Facebook	https://www.facebook.com/A1Fanpage	270,000+ page fans
Twitter—@A1Telekom	http://www.twitter.com/A1Telekom	2,600+ followers
A1 Support Community	http://www.a1community.net/	160,000+ members

---

[1] The sources were approved and provided by counterparts at A1 Telekom Austria. In terms of corporate privacy, detailed sources that provide insight into organizational, strategic, or systematic methods are not included in the publication.

[2] Source: content channels and profile pages, unless otherwise specified.

When comparing the incumbent to other competitors in the Austrian telecommunications market, A1 holds the leading position with a Facebook fan-share of 59 percent (Lithys, 2013b). Three full-time customer care agents support through Facebook and other channels by providing fast and exclusive customer support, two additional agents are responsible for product-related postings, special offers, and news. A1's social media channels are linked and provide target-group oriented content, such as offers, lotteries, and product information particularly for the youth target group. A1's most popular age group on Facebook is formed by 18- to 24-year-olds (source: A1 Facebook page, 2013). The contests and social commitment on the Facebook page intensify the relationship between A1 and its fans and enforce a strong attachment to the brand. Eventually there is a strong community commitment of the A1 fans as they help other customers and share their experience with A1, resulting in exchange of experience or even problem solving among A1 customers.

Besides the cooperation and co-creation with customers in a rather gaming atmosphere, A1 Support Community acts as a further front door channel for customers of A1, its purpose is to generate a high substitution rate. In 2012, a real substitution value of 25 percent was reached. This sums up to around 168,000 saved interactions—such as community postings and search requests—during the period of one year. The community provides a notable case reduction with the use of efficient engaging processes, with around 26 percent of the community users finding their solution within the first minutes of their visit and a crowd ratio of 80 percent whereof 20 percent of the content is created by the most active users, i.e. super users (Lithys, 2013a).

Finally, it is notable that all these community activities push and enable outsourcing of key activities to the crowd and lead to a digital service shift, as well as to reducing development and beta testing expenses. Seeking to increase customer satisfaction, A1 involves "super users" in service and product development processes to guarantee the best results for both customers and the company. We compare super users with lead users (von Hippel, 1986), as they are at the front end of market trends, experiencing early needs that will later be experienced by mainstream users and markets and finally expecting benefits from innovating, i.e. finding or building a solution to their needs.

Even the launch of the A1 Support Community has itself been shaped by the community. Sixteen neatly selected users were involved in beta testing activities and feedback on functions and appearance of the platform, resulting in attention to small bugs that would not have been found without the support of the so-called "superfans" in this short time. Superfans (super users) of the A1 Support Community build an essential part of the entire community concept. They are particularly dedicated and competent customers, helping other community members and heavily volunteering their private time and commitment. As often described in the literature, community members differ in age, gender, educational background, or interests. Members of the

A1 Support Community are distinct, ranging from a student from Salzburg to a professional application developer from Styria. In particular, A1 was awarded the "Lithys best superfan story" in 2012 for co-creation with Simon, a 15-year-old boy and very committed community member. After attending a design co-creation workshop, Simon wrote 150 posts and received 56 kudos within the community, and was eventually hired by A1 to support the team (Lithys, 2012). This fact also corresponds with the common finding in the literature that intrinsic motivation to participate in ideation contests and eventually being hired by the idea seeking company exists widely in both crowdsourcing and open source contests.

In February 2012, A1 had launched the ideation project "Mein A1 einfach machen" within their support community. The aim of this project was to redesign online services and develop a new self-care area and thereby co-create with community members and potential customers. Besides enforcing a positive atmosphere and a strong brand awareness through social media channels, customer experience is at high importance within A1 Telekom Austria. Therefore, A1 had involved community members in the development process of the new "Mein A1" self-care portal in order to achieve the best-in-class user experience. Users were invited to provide new ideas and participate in the development and beta testing of products and solutions. In the first step, the community was invited to an idea generation process (MeinA1, 2012). The ideas and solutions provided were then transformed into scribbles and prototypes, which were eventually reviewed and rated by the community in an interactive feedback approach before being incorporated into customer applications (Lithys, 2013b). From A1's perspective (Lithys, 2013b), customer benefits include: (1) the opportunity to take part in an innovation process; (2) prospective realization of individual ideas; (3) exchange of thoughts and ideas with other users; as well as (4) incentives and awards for participating in the idea contest. Benefits on the company's side include: (1) direct communication with users; (2) interaction with the support community; (3) identification of consumer needs; and essentially, (4) the opportunity to integrate consumers into the realization process.

The project itself as well as the workshop outcomes were communicated within the community and promoted on the company's social media channels, such as Facebook. Technically, the project was enabled by Lithium's Ideas component, which supports crowdsourcing through idea exchange and by soliciting and identifying the best ideas. The invitational letter was posted in the A1 Support Community, saying: "Dear Community, the team of A1 Support Community is convinced that pioneering online service can only come hand in hand with our customers. We therefore want to find new ways to collect your valuable inputs. Therefore, on February 17th [2012] we will start the project 'Mein A1 einfach machen.' In this project, you, dear members of the A1 Support Community, are experts and decision-makers of how future online services should look like. [...]" (MeinA1, 2012). The preparation activities and the project setup had started months before the external project kickoff and communication. The total project duration was estimated to be eight months, the external project was set up in four phases: (1) *idea generation and project sharpening*, including the introduction and a detailed project scope; (2) *co-creation workshops*, which involved ten super users to support the A1's core team and co-develop the prototype; (3) *feedback on the prototypes* by all members of the community, including commenting and rating the results; as well as the final phase (4) *prototype release & polishing/feedback on the project*, including a revision of the prototypes according to the community feedback and a review feedback session back to the community.

Semi-open co-creation with employees. Internally within A1 Telekom Austria, various prototypes and web-based crowdsourcing tools have been tested in different departments over past years, including the teams and groups from network or information technology divisions, sales and solutions, customer service, and even human resources teams and experts. Hence, a centralized tool that is available to all employees company-wide was targeted and conceived by the end of 2012. The established crowdsourcing tools, as well as best-practice approaches from other telecommunication providers were considered during the project realization. Besides Hyve, one of the leading innovation and idea-management providers in the German-speaking countries, other end-to-end innovation management software and innovation solutions, known and unknown out-of-the-box and customized solutions have been shortlisted and selected as potential partners. Capabilities of such crowdsourcing platforms should potentially include idea evaluation workflows and decision-making support tools, in order to support the transformation of plain ideas into actionable results and sustainably drive innovation across organizations.

To point out the potential of crowdsourcing in the telecommunication industry, two examples of telecommunication incumbents from Germany and Switzerland are mentioned in particular through looking at their crowdsourcing best-practice:

- *Deutsche Telekom*: In 2011, employees submitted close to 11,000 suggestions for improvement using the genial@telekom ideas platform, which had been introduced several years before. The savings generated by these improvements came to 116 million Euro and 244 registered patents in the reporting period (Deutsche Telekom, 2011).
- *Swisscom*: In 2011, the company integrated an ideation platform on the Swisscom Labs website and opened the innovation process in order to better meet their customers' needs (Swisscom Community, 2011). Hereby, website visitors as well as Swisscom customers could take part in the innovation process and share their ideas and concepts directly with Swisscom's innovation team. Eventually, the collected ideas were rated, commented on, and co-developed by other users.

The global telecommunication industry has shown great potential by applying crowdsourcing and hosting idea contests and product development and co-creation platforms with their customers. Some successful examples of worldwide crowdsourcing initiatives in this industry are: Cisco's iPrize, Nokia Concept Lounge and Beta Labs, LG's Design the Future, Community Support at Bouygues Telecom in France (analogous to A1's Support Community), Vodafone's Betavine, and many other platforms (Crowdsourcing Examples, 2011). However, most of these initiatives are customer oriented and focus on novel ideas—leaving only a small percentage of practicable and feasible ideas that are commercially realized.

When dealing with internal organizational crowdsourcing, it is important to mention, that submitted ideas and postings in fact focus on improvements and issues that increase the company's efficiency and provide a better approach to an existing situation in the company, therefore only little space is left for creating breakthrough ideas, as the study will prove. In particular, only a small percentage of employees are dealing with innovation or idea generation activities on a daily basis. Eventually, at A1 Telekom Austria, idea management was set up as a lean process and initially involved selected employees from different departments—a group of *peripheral inside innovators* (Möslein, 2013) that generated new ideas based on self-motivation, engagement, intrinsic interest, confidence, even though they were not involved on a daily basis. Beyond that, a virtual network of expert employees across departments existed, focusing on trend and market research, innovative technologies or benchmarks, and best-practice from the telecommunication industry. Essentially, one of the main driving factors for implementing the corporate idea management tool was the need for a centralized, transparent idea base, available and accessible to all employees.

Closed offline co-creation. Besides the ICT-tool supported innovation and idea-management approach within A1 as described in the last section, several offline workshops are organized and hosted in the company. Some of these workshops include residential or business customers; however within this study, the term *offline co-creation* refers to innovation workshops with exclusively employee participants (from technology departments), neither supported by an online community, nor innovation toolkits, social media, or any other forms of digital support. These workshops are organized and carried out with paper material such as flipcharts, post-it stickers, books, journals, and other physical equipment.

During spring 2012, three offline co-creation workshops aimed at addressing future technology topics were hosted within one of the technology departments, including 86 participants from various groups and teams: *"[. . .] a moderated future workshop will take place, where we look ahead into the future and identify trends and their potential impact on our work. We hope to develop ideas for optimal positioning and maximizing the contribution of our department to our company. Take your chance and share your creativity with us . . . let's draw a picture of 2017 together!*" (Source: A1). Compared to the two other co-creation approaches that are supported by online tools, it is important to notice that the offline workshops are characterized by a concentrated inspiration and brainstorming momentum right on the spot. The kick-off always begins with a rather mind-opening impulse and trend key-note, which is followed by a brainstorming session on the following question: *Which trends are relevant for us five years ahead?* Then, the identified topics are mapped to the social, cultural, economic, or technological trends and rated by the sticking points method (each participant receives a fixed amount of points (voting stickers) to be placed on their preferred ideas). Selected ideas are then elaborated in group work and eventually presented to the other participants and the management team. The main goals of the ideation workshops are to look into the future and identify trends (social, cultural, economic, or technological), identify new, relevant technologies, and derive innovative ideas, as well as identifying the top three innovation topics.

RESULTS

This section includes explanatory results and discussions of our case study and of the three analyzed co-creation approaches. The results for the research questions are interpreted comparatively in this section. The remainder of the results section is organized as following: (1) analysis of the commercial feasibility of the submitted ideas; (2) user participation and impact of super users or idea sponsors to the community: and finally, (3) exploration of the social media influences on different co-creation activities and prospective community building.

Prior to answering the research questions, we point out that within the open co-creation with customers, a certain number of users were identified as lead users (i.e. super users), as defined in literature (von Hippel, 1986). These users were selected based on their expertise or their community roles by: (1) comparing the list of participants of the idea contest to the list of "category experts" and the "Kudo high score list"; and (2) analyzing their community roles (i.e. highlighting users with super user icons). As a counterpart, participants of the semi-open and closed approaches, i.e. employees of A1 with von Hippel's lead user characteristics were coined as opinion leaders, as their need to strive for and develop innovative ideas is an essential part of their profession.

Commercial Feasibility of Ideas

The main result with regard to the first research question is that the level of specificity of the submission criteria is found to be related to the commercial

Table 10.3. Main results: Commercial feasibility of ideas.

Research question	Open co-creation with customers	Semi-open co-creation with employees	Closed co-creation with employees
Definition of submission criteria	Detailed definition	Loose verbal definition, internal company context is a premise	Medium definition level, internal company context is a strong premise
Set of defined criteria	• Usability (usable by a large target group) • Applicability (it is a solution) • Feasibility	• Customer value • Profitability • Feasibility	• Related to the (future) core business • Related to corporate strategy • Profitability
Submitted ideas	7	113	27 ideas + 15 innovation topics
Fit of ideas	Strong	Medium	Medium
Implemented ideas[3]	6	5	3 implementations + 4 line activities
Commercial feasibility	High	Medium	Medium

feasibility of the submitted ideas. Particularly in the case of open co-creation with customers, the detailed submission criteria have led to a close fit with the ideas as well as high commercial feasibility with further implementation of the solutions. Further, all submissions indicate that the author had provided his or her personal ideas. Each submission comprises specific and individual suggestions for improvement that differ from the previous. Compared to this, within the two intra-corporate co-creation approaches, the defined submission criteria were characteristically loose, and although profitability was among the defined criteria, only a very small number of ideas were implemented at a later stage. Also, the fit of ideas is lower than in the customer-oriented approach. The results of the first research question are summarized in Table 10.3.

User Participation and Behavior

To answer the second research question about user participation and preferences, it is important to point out the main differences between the size and composition of the target groups:

---

[3] Implemented submissions or ideas are considered as commercially feasible submissions.

- *Open co-creation with customers*: involves a large target group of existing and potential users (> 150,000 community members). The presence of lead users or experts is prominently visible.

- *Semi-open co-creation with employees*: includes a mid-sized target group of employees within a corporate setting (>2,500 active users in 2013). The presence of lead users as defined by von Hippel (1986) was not obvious during the study; however, some participants were identified as "innovation experts" or "competent jury members" and therefore have a special role in the innovation process.

- *Closed offline co-creation*: involves a small, closed group of employees (< 40 participants at a workshop). The presence of so-called opinion leaders (i.e. managers or experts) is notably low, but lead users as defined in literature are not remarkable in this approach. We can add that opinion leaders are present and influence the co-creation process.

The results for the second research question are summarized in Table 10.4.

Regarding the origin of an idea and its likelihood of being selected as the best idea and subsequently being implemented, interesting evidence was found. Within co-creation with customers, the role of super users was found to be crucial and they are prominent and heavily involved in co-creation. Also, the ideas of lead users are generally preferred in the community, as well as in the particular idea contest. If observed as a timeline, the difference between numbers of votes and comments between the first and last submitted idea by the crowd is clearly notable. It is further important to note that the first two submitted ideas in the open co-creation approach take more than 50 percent (17 out of 32) of the given votes. The second posted idea was rated best with a total of ten kudos, whereas none of the ideas has remained uncommented or without a vote.

Besides the inequality regarding super users and preference for their ideas over others, we explored the role of idea sponsors. The role of idea sponsors (users with the "A1_" name prefix) was found to be a crucial factor in the success of idea contests, particularly in the open co-creation approach with the A1 community. These users act as moderators who control and actively promote activities in the community and motivate members to contribute.

Also, when comparing the two community-based approaches (open and semi-open co-creation), the fact that employees are also allowed to post anonymously can be put on the same level as aliases and nicknames in the public community, keeping the author unknown to other participants. Notably, the possibility of posting a submission anonymously in the internal co-creation approach was seen as beneficial by participants. Some users chose not to be identified by direct colleagues or supervisors who perhaps paraphrase idea creation as pleasure and not work. As described in the literature, the process of innovation within a large enterprise should be strongly linked to strategy, and demands a strong commitment to innovation from top

Table 10.4. Main results: User participation and behavior.

Research question	Open co-creation with customers	Semi-open co-creation with employees	Closed co-creation with employees
Target group	Large target group of existing and potential users (> 150,000 community members). Experts or lead users are prominent.	Large target group of employees (> 2,500 active users) within a corporate setting. Experts are identified, the presence of lead users is unknown.	Closed small group of employees (< 40 participants at a workshop). The presence of lead users or experts is unknown.
Defined roles	• Lead users • Active participants (incl. submissions) • Reviewers • passive visitors (readers)	• Idea sponsor(s) • Moderators • Experts (participate in rating the best ideas) • active participants • passive visitors	• Moderator • Manager(s) • All other participants *User roles are pre-defined and clearly set before the workshop.*
Total active participants	22	Estimated at 500	86 (25–35 per workshop)
Lead user ratio	50%[4]	Unknown	Low
Influence of idea-sponsors	*Strong* influence and visibility in the community	*Low or no* influence, no presence on the platform	*Medium*, observing presence at the workshops
Role of lead users ("opinion leaders" within closed innovation)	Lead users are prominent, their ideas are *preferred* to ideas of other users.	Lead users are not (yet) existent or perceivable[5]	Opinion leaders (similar to lead users) are rather *passive observers* and the content provided by them is minor.
User behavior in the community	Community members are treated according to their status (e.g. super users own admin rights). Super Users and sponsors (A1 agents) support other members and reply or solve most issues.	Idea sponsors and experts rarely visit the platform and have no interaction with the idea providers. Although there is no registration level and the access to the platform is granted to all employees, the number of active users is low (~20 percent).	During the workshop the defined topics or shared ideas are redirected or adapted. During the selection phase, small groups (i.e. communities) are formed to review ideas of other participants.

[4] The large ratio of lead users can be explained as follows: participants of this particular idea contest were selected among previously identified lead users, i.e. super users of the community, customers, and Facebook fans.

[5] Lead users are probably not perceivable because of the early stage (pilot) of this approach.

management, as well as making the internal crowdsourcing process a part of the holistic strategy and corporate innovation process. Based on our insights, we conclude that internal crowdsourcing and co-creation processes require acceptance across departments and hierarchies, and eventually defined user roles, as described in Table 10.4.

As argued by Villarroel & Reis (2010), ideas submitted to intra-corporate crowdsourcing contests are often provided by employees ranked lower in the corporate hierarchy. This state of lower ranking in the corporate hierarchy being an innovative advantage, so-called rank marginality, can be explained through one of the following implications: (1) lower ranked employees face customers or operational problems on a daily basis and therefore have applicable ideas and solutions to common problems; (2) lower ranked employees hold specific or unique information and can prove to be valuable knowledge-holders when answering intra-corporate questions; and finally, (3) the possibility that lower ranked employees see the co-creation process as an alternative path for receiving acknowledgment for their knowledge, ideas, and contributions—which we proved in our study as well. We also found evidence that most of the internal ideas were submitted by employees from Customer Care, Marketing, or other customer-oriented departments and teams.

Eventually, open co-creation with customers clearly highlights the role of customers and involves these in the value chain of innovation. Whereas exploration of the semi-open co-creation approach indicates that idea sponsors and experts do not necessarily visit the platform or join the ideation process, a closer look at the closed offline approach shows that all participants are required to actively participate, engage in the co-creation process, and act in their different roles.

Social Media Tools for Communities

To answer the supplementary question about social media, we have analyzed A1's public Facebook page and the internal corporate communication channels. Social media support is interpreted as following:

- *Open co-creation with customers* is strongly supported by social media tools, such as Facebook, Youtube, A1 blog, etc., and provides a large outreach to fans, potential customers, and others.
- *Semi-open co-creation with employees* is supported by the internal communication channels, including blogs, news channels, or a newspaper/magazine for employees.
- *Closed offline co-creation* is obviously not supported by Web 2.0; the content, including comments, voting, or sharing is done offline but documented with common office tools. However, community building is thereby strongly supported through acquaintances between employees.

Eventually, it is important to note that common crowdsourcing and idea management tools all offer social media features, such as profile pages, inter-active messaging and commenting, liking and sharing content, as well as tagging and participation statistics, or high score listings. In general, the three approaches include an environment that is more related to gamification than hard working and reaches out to a large group of participants by motivating them to be part of the game, and at the same time incentivizing them intrinsic-ally as well as extrinsically, i.e. by providing professional acknowledgments, coupons, or monetary awards.

DISCUSSION

To explore the impact and benefits of crowdsourcing and co-creation in large enterprises, as well as to contribute to both commercial management and academic research with implications on how to use crowds effectively, we summarize our main insights and study results for each of the three analyzed approaches—open, semi-open and closed co-creation.

Open Co-Creation with Customers

Studies and explorations of crowdsourcing and idea contests usually focus on the motivation of participants and on how to identify them and offer the right incentives to retain a vibrant and committed crowd which might grow into a community of innovators. In our case, the platform itself, the call for crowdsour-cing, and the specific idea contest was initiated by the idea-seeking company, without third parties or intermediaries. It was therefore obvious that customers of A1 were strongly involved in the crowdsourcing initiative and provided most of the ideas and comments. Besides the highly motivated crowd outside of the organization, crowdsourcing and co-creating products and services with cus-tomers requires effort that must be done within the company—before, during, and after the idea contest. In particular, open co-creation with customers indicated the importance of lead users (super users), which caertainly acted as an essential part of the product development process at A1.

When setting up and launching a crowdsourcing campaign or contest, we find that highly specified submission criteria are profitable for the ideation process itself, as well as for conceiving ideas with a high commercial feasibility. In this study, ideas with a high fit or commercial value were created in response to detailed submission criteria, whereas fewer responses to lower specified or open idea calls had subsequently been implemented commercially.

Our study shows that lead users participate intensively and submit ideas, and in general, their ideas are rated better over other ideas and thus implemented as a result. On the other hand, the presence of idea seekers, i.e. dedicated employees who moderate crowdsourcing activities, was crucial during the ideation process to guide and coordinate the interactions. Next to idea sponsors and active idea providers (including super users), we see potential for a third group of participants—the observers or passive users. The third group is usually reading the content, rating ideas, or sharing the information with others, without submitting their own content. Hence, we find evidence that social media positively supports crowdsourcing activities by enlarging the target group with additional observers, or by keeping a track of the achieved activities and forthcoming process steps.

Semi-Open Co-Creation with Employees

When setting up a crowdsourcing community—either with a public crowd or only among internal employees—we suggest defining the process of innovation and idea management in a holistic manner and integrating it into the corporate strategy and business processes. To some extent, crowdsourcing and other open innovation methods create the impression of brainstorming for creative ideas, pleasure, and gamification, rather than hard work. However, submitted ideas and solutions as well as the authors behind these submissions are crucial and of a great value for the company and its innovation and product development value chain. Besides identifying the right crowd of experts, lead users, supporters, or idea sponsors and offering them the right incentives, it is important to secure support from across all hierarchies and departments within a company, particularly from the top management level.

In the case of semi-open co-creation with employees, i.e. intra-corporate crowdsourcing, the submitted ideas must match corporate strategy, goals, or values. The developed ideas are proposals for improvement and concepts that contribute to internal company processes, or to a large extent processes that involve customers. In addition, the profitability or emerging costs are very important criteria. Hence, it remains to be further studied whether an internal idea management process or ideation workshop is the appropriate mechanism for breakthrough ideas and cutting-edge innovations—or if these are rather less radical and non-disruptive. Some of the key effects of internal crowdsourcing at A1 are: (1) reaching a higher degree of openness and transparency towards employees; (2) adopting a lean method that fosters thinking outside of one's department, hierarchy, or responsibilities; (3) introducing a platform for sharing valuable ideas and solutions that one employee could not implement without others; and (4) finding and connecting the right idea recipients and partners, as well as sharing ideas and solutions in order to get noticed, acknowledged, and possibly rewarded by others. To some extent, internal crowdsourcing fosters creative and collaborative work and may even break silos or internal barriers.

Closed Offline Co-Creation

In contrast with the two online (tool-based) approaches, personal interactions and talks during offline workshops are beneficial and are used to adjust and redirect the process of idea generation towards finding and developing ideas with a better fit and a higher applicability or practicability. The possibility of interacting and adjusting or changing direction during the offline ideation workshops is further perceived as a factor that keeps the community vibrant and committed.

The fact that participants are well known to each other at the beginning of the workshop is positive, because the time needed to set up a comfortable co-creation environment or build up an innovation community is much shorter or zero. Participants can start developing ideas immediately after receiving the key facts. The examples of closed innovation or co-creation in our study prove that at some point, participants start building small groups and sub-communities during idea creation, similar to how online innovation communities are organized.

CONCLUSIONS AND FUTURE RESEARCH

Many factors lead to a new socio-economic viewpoint on crowdsourcing and active involvement of consumers in the value creation and innovation processes. Even though open innovation is often described as the outsourcing of internal research and development activities, modern and interactive methods such as crowdsourcing have emerged and can identify new customer needs and technology trends or potential market channels. The corporate change towards openness and co-creation with customers, partners, researchers, suppliers, and other stakeholders, can be argued as a tool to change and enrich corporate business processes and employees' mindsets, and bring companies and consumers closer together. Consumers are often highly interested in chasing trends, being part of communities, and proactively developing ideas and solutions, for a variety of reasons. Firms should therefore focus on retaining them as loyal customers by attracting their attention and offering for them to actively participate in value creation and innovation. Essentially, "identification with an organization strongly affects the willingness of individuals to engage in activities favorable for this entity" (Franke et al., 2013).

A willingness to provide effort and to support corporate product development and innovation has been demonstrated in our study, particularly by the loyal customers, i.e. super users of the A1 Support Community. We have observed the submissions of super users while we have identified them as lead users and see them taking an essential role in the value creation and innovation process of A1. We also agree with the findings of Kratzer et al. (2016), arguing that lead users can be found in social networks, as they are positioned as bridges between different social groups, i.e. at a high level of "betweenness centrality." This approach may also help companies to identify lead user candidates quickly and at low cost (Kratzer et al., 2016), the effectiveness of which could be explored further in future research.

As described by Afuah & Tucci (2012), including both experts and non-experts—which we refer to as internal employees and external customers—can be a valuable resource of knowledge for ideation and contributing to idea development. Either way, crowds perform best when the problem or the call for ideas can be broken down into simple, understandable modules. While we find that customers' ideas outperform the ideas of employees in levels of novelty and target fit, Horn et al. (2018) discuss that the internal experts perform much better in innovation management tasks than the external, non-expert participants. This might be explained through the maturity of the innovation process and the participants' readiness to share their ideas to the community or the public crowd.

As argued by Poetz & Schreier (2012), numerous literature studies reveal that commercially significant products have initially been developed by users rather than by manufacturers. In fact, user innovations are often found in sports, clothing, computer innovations, or scientific instruments, and some of these products highly exceed the conventionally developed products in terms of sales (Ogawa & Piller, 2006). Hence, the results of this work can be rudimentarily compared to other literature findings. Our work indicates that ideas that have been developed and co-created by external users have a stronger fit to market and fit to customer, as well as a higher commercial feasibility (based on the number of particularly realized ideas) than ideas that were developed in-house, whereas Poetz & Schreier (2012) argue their results for ideas that were created by users as "higher in novelty and customer benefit, but lower in feasibility." It is important to note further that our study includes a comparison of co-creation approaches with a similar questioning. A comparison of ideas by users and employees to exactly the same contest is something that could also be explored in future research. Similar to the experiment by Franke & Shah (2003), which is related to innovation activities of sports enthusiasts in communities, the fact that helpful information or assistance is provided free of charge is confirmed in our study. Eventually, Franke et al. (2013) also show that: *"potential contributors not only want a good deal, they also want a fair deal"* when participating in co-creation or idea contests—which is strongly committed in the A1 Support Community.

An essential part of our study deals with intra-corporate crowdsourcing. We argue that crowdsourcing contests within a company are limited by office hours and employees' motivation to make additional efforts. In contrast to a public crowd, employees might need explicit permission to participate in an idea generation process if it is not part of their job description. Our work proves that the largest group of innovators in a public contest are outside innovators, and peripheral inside innovators within the intra-corporate contest. Hence, tolerating and actively encouraging employees to submit ideas and solutions is crucial if we affiliate to the statement that outsiders have an unbiased approach to problems and beneficially contribute to crowdsourcing activities (Lakhani et al., 2006).

Clearly, technology that has fostered crowdsourcing is still relatively new, but it opens up space for novel strategies and integration of the crowd to meet today's innovation challenges. This paper contributes to innovation management research by providing insight into the idea generation stage, i.e. an early-stage of innovation processes within an incumbent. Specific conditions which should be considered during the ideation process are identified in this study, such as involving a large target group of potential participants, as well as a group of (high-performing) lead users. Essentially, no matter whether crowdsourcing and innovation communities in organizational settings are analyzed in an academic, commercial, entrepreneurial or social context, the topics merit further research.

REFERENCES

A1 Facebook page (2013). https://www.facebook.com/A1Fanpage

A1 Support Community (2013). http://www.a1community.net

Afuah, A. (2018). Crowdsourcing: A primer and research framework. In C. Tucci, A. Afuah, & G. Viscusi (eds.), *Creating and Capturing Value Through Crowdsourcing.* Oxford: Oxford University Press, pp. 11–38.

Afuah, A. & Tucci, C. (2012). Crowdsourcing as a solution to distant search. *Academy of Management Review, 37*(3), 355–75.

Assmann, J., Sandner, P., & Ahrens, S. (2009). Users' influence on the success of online communities. *Proceedings of the 42nd Hawaii International Conference on System Sciences* (HICSS), Big Island, Hawaii, IEEE, January 5–8. doi: 10.1109/HICSS.2009.490.

Boudreau, K. J. & Lakhani, K. R. (2013). Using the crowd as an innovation partner. *Harvard Business Review, 91*(4), 61–9.

Bröring, S. & Herzog, P. (2008). Organizing new business development: Open innovation at Degussa. *European Journal of Innovation Management, 11*(3), 330–48.

Bullinger, A. C. & Möslein, K. M. (2010). Innovation contests—Where are we? *AMCIS 2010 Proceedings*, Paper 28, http://aisel.aisnet.org/amcis2010/28/ (accessed October 29, 2017).

Carrero, M. (2009). Innovation for the Web 2.0 Era. *IEEE Computer Society*, 42(11), 96–8.

Chesbrough, H. (2006). *Open Business Models: How to Thrive in the New Innovation Landscape*. Boston: Harvard University Press.

Chesbrough, H. W. (2003). *Open Innovation: The New Imperative for Creating and Profiting from Technology*. Boston, MA: Harvard Business School Press.

Crowdsourcing Examples (2011). *Brand-Sponsored Crowdsourcing Initiatives*, http://crowdsourcingexamples.pbworks.com/w/page/16668397/Brand-sponsored% 20crowdsourcing%20initiatives

Deutsche Telekom (2011). *Ideas Management, 2011 Corporate Responsibility Report*, http://www.cr-report.telekom.com/site12/indicators/social-indicators/ideas-management#atn-1431-1962

Fiege, R. (2012). *Social Media Balanced Scorecard*. Wiesbaden: Springer Verlag.

Flick, U. (2009). *An Introduction to Qualitative Research*, 4th edn. London/Thousand Oaks, CA/Dehli: Sage.

Franke, N., Keinz, P., & Klausberger, K. (2013). "Does this sound like a fair deal?" Antecedents and consequences of fairness expectations in the individual's decision to participate in firm innovation. *Organization Science*, 24(5), 1495–516.

Franke, N. & Shah, S. (2003). How communities support innovative activities: An exploration of assistance and sharing among end-users. *Research Policy*, 32, 157–78.

Füller, J., Bartl, M, Ernst, H., & Mühlbacher, H. (2004). Community based innovation— A method to utilize the innovative potential of online communities. In *Proceedings of the 37th Hawaii International Conference on System Sciences*. IEEE, January 5–8, Big Island, HI. doi: 10.1109/HICSS.2004.1265464.

Gassmann, O., Frankenberger, K., & Csik, M. (2014). *The Business Model Navigator: 55 Models That Will Revolutionise Your Business*. Harlow, UK: FT Publishing.

Hautz, J., Hutter, K. Füller, J., Matzler, K., & Rieger, M. (2010). How to establish an online innovation community? The role of users and their innovative content. *43rd Hawaii International Conference on System Sciences*. IEEE, January 5–8, Honolulu, HI. doi: 10.1109/HICSS.2010.221.

Horn, C., Bogers, M., & Brem, A. (2018). Prediction markets for crowdsourcing. In C. Tucci, A. Afuah, & G. Viscusi (eds.), *Creating and Capturing Value Through Crowdsourcing*. Oxford: Oxford University Press, pp. 292–309.

Howe, J. (2008). *Crowdsourcing—Why the Power of the Crowd is Driving the Future of Business*. New York: Crown Business, Random House.

Kaplan, A. M. & Haenlein, M. (2010). Users of the world, unite! The challenges and opportunities of social media. *Business Horizons*, 53(1), 59–68.

Kelley, B. (2011). The importance of a strategic approach to open innovation, in P. Sloane (ed.). *A Guide to Open Innovation and Crowdsourcing: Advice from Leading Experts*. London: Kogan Page.

Kim, A. J. (2000). *Community Building on the Web*. Berkley: Peachpit Press.

Kratzer, J., Lettl, C., Franke, N., & Gloor, P. A. (2016). The social network position of lead users. *Journal of Product Innovation Management*, 33(2), 201–16.

Lakhani, K. R., Jeppesen, L. B., Lohse, P. A., & Panetta, J. A. (2006). The value of openness in scientific problem solving. HBS working paper 07–050. Harvard, MA, Harvard Business School.

Leal, W. L. M. & Baêta, A. M. C. (2006). The contribution of communities of practice in an innovative enterprise. *Journal of Technology Management & Innovation*, *1*(4), 22–9.

Leimeister, J. M. & Sidiras, P. (2004). Success factors of virtual communities from the perspective of members and operators: An empirical study. In *Proceedings of the 37th International Conference on System Sciences*. IEEE, January 5–8, Big Island, HI. doi: 10.1109/HICSS.2004.1265459.

Leitner, K-H., Felder, C., Kasztler, A., & Rhomberg, W. (2015). *Neue Innovationsmodelle: Potentiale und Herausforderungen für die österreichische Wirtschaft und Innovationspolitik*. Vienna: AIT-IS-Report.

Lewin, D. & Mitchell, D. J. B. (1992). Systems of employee voice: Theoretical and empirical perspectives, *California Management Review*, *34*(3), 95–111.

Lithys (2012). *A1 Telekom Austria—Best SuperFan Story*, http://lithosphere.lithium. com/t5/lithys-social-customer/Lithys-2012-A1-Telekom-Austria-Best-SuperFan-Story/ idi-p/41830

Lithys (2013a). *A1 Telekom—Best Business ROI*, http://lithosphere.lithium.com/ t5/lithys-social-customer/Lithys-2013-A1-Telekom-Best-Business-ROI/idi-p/78124

Lithys (2013b). *A1 Telekom—Best Social Support Program*, http://lithosphere.lithium. com/t5/lithys-social-customer/Lithys-2013-A1-Telekom-Best-Social-Support-Program/ idi-p/78132#M274

McAfee, A. E. (2006). Enterprise 2.0: The dawn of emergent collaboration. *MIT Sloan Management Review*, *47*(3), 21.

MeinA1 (2012). *A1 Support Community: Unser Projekt: Mein A1 einfach machen*, http://www.a1community.net/t5/Unser-Projekt-Mein-A1-einfach/ct-p/ideas-pj1

Merchant, N. (2013). When TED lost control of its crowd. *Harvard Business Review*, *91*(4), 78–83.

Möslein, K. M. (2013). Open innovation: Actors, tools, and tensions, in A. S. Huff, K. M. Möslein, & R. Reichwald (eds.). *Leading Open Innovation*. Cambridge, MA: MIT Press, pp. 69–86.

Ogawa, S. & Piller, F. (2006). Reducing the risks of new product development. *MIT Sloan Management Review*, *47*(2), 65.

Osterwalder, A. & Pigneur, Y. (2010). *Business Model Generation*, Hoboken: Wiley.

Pinchot, G. (1985). *Intrapreneuring: Why You Don't Have to Leave the Corporation to Become an Entrepreneur*, 2nd ed. Wiesbaden, Germany: Berrett-Koehler Publishers.

Pisano, G. P. & Verganti, R. (2008). Which kind of collaboration is right for you? *Harvard Business Review*, *86*(12), 78–86.

Poetz, M. K. & Schreier, M. (2012). The value of crowdsourcing: Can users really compete with professionals in generating new product ideas? *Journal of Product Innovation Management*, *29*(2), 245–56.

Quora (2010). *Is Randy Powell saying anything in his 2010 TEDx Charlotte talk?* http://www.quora.com/TEDx/Is-Randy-Powell-saying-anything-in-his-2010-TED xCharlotte-talk-or-is-it-just-total-nonsense

Soni, P. (2008). Open innovation: A strategic imperative for non-linear growth. In: *Proceedings of the 2008 IEEE ICMIT*. IEEE, 21–4 Sept, 2008, Bangkok, Thailand. doi: 10.1109/ICMIT.2008.4654357.

Stewart, O., Huerta, J. M., & Sader, M. (2009). Designing crowdsourcing community for the enterprise. In *Proceedings of the ACM SIGKDD Workshop on Human Computation*, Proceeding, HCOMP '09, pp. 50–3, Paris, France, June 28 - 28, 2009, ACM, New York, NY. doi: 10.1145/1600150.1600168.

Šundić, M. & Leitner, K-H. (2013). Crowdsourcing as an innovation strategy: A study on innovation platforms in Austria and Switzerland. *Digiworld Economic Journal*, 89(1), 55–72.

Surowiecki, J. (2004). *The Wisdom of the Crowds*. New York: Doubleday.

Swisscom Community 2011. *Gemeinsam Ideen entwickeln*, http://www.swisscom.ch/de/ghq/media/mediareleases/2011/03/20110329_MM_Ideenbereich.html

Terwiesch, C. & Ulrich, K. T. (2009). *Innovation Tournaments: Creating and Selecting Exceptional Opportunities*. Boston, MA: Harvard Business School Press.

Villarroel, J. A. & Reis, F. (2010). Intra-corporate crowdsourcing (ICC): Leveraging upon rank and site marginality for innovation. Presented at CrowdConf 2010, 04 October 2010, San Francisco, CA, https://www.researchgate.net/publication/228458949_Intra-Corporate_Crowdsourcing_ICC_Leveraging_Upon_Rank_and_Site_Marginality_for_Innovation (accessed October 29, 2017).

von Hippel, E. (1986). Lead users: A source of novel product concepts. *Management Science, 32*, 791–805.

von Hippel, E. (2001). User toolkits for innovation. *Journal of Product Innovation Management, 18*(4), 247–57.

Vuković, M. (2009). Crowdsourcing for enterprises. In *World Conference on Services*, pp. 686–92. IEEE, July 6–10, Los Angeles, CA. doi: 10.1109/SERVICES-I.2009.56.

Wenger, E., McDernott, R., & Snyder, W. M. (2002). *Cultivating Communities of Practice: A Guide to Managing Knowledge*. Boston, MA: Harvard Business School Publishing.

West, J. & Sims, J. (2018). How firms leverage crowds and communities for open innovation. In C. Tucci, A. Afuah, & G. Viscusi (eds.), *Creating and Capturing Value Through Crowdsourcing*. Oxford: Oxford University Press, pp. 58–96.

Wiener, C., Acquah, I. N., Heiss, M., Mayerdorfer, T., Langen, M., & Kammergruber, W. C. (2012). Targeting the right crowd for corporate problem solving: A Siemens case study with TechnoWeb 2.0. In *Technology Management Conference (ITMC)*, 2012 IEEE International. IEEE, June 25–27, Dallas, TX. doi: 10.1109/ITMC.2012.6306350.

Yin, R. (1999). *Case Study Research: Design and Methods*, Thousand Oaks, CA: SAGE Publications. "Single case study," pp. 38ff, "Multiple case study," pp. 44ff.

Part IV

Hybrids: Tournament-Based and Collaboration-Based Crowdsourcing

11

Co-opetition in Crowdsourcing: When Simultaneous Cooperation and Competition Deliver Superior Solutions

Allan Afuah

Abstract

In tournament-based crowdsourcing, members of a crowd compete to solve a problem and the agent with the best solution wins. In collaboration-based crowdsourcing, members of a crowd cooperate to solve a problem, bringing their collective expertise to bear on the problem. Each can yield extraordinarily high-value solutions. This raises a question: Can crowdsourcing co-opetition—simultaneous cooperation *and* competition to solve a problem via crowdsourcing—deliver even higher-value solutions than either tournament-based or collaboration-based crowdsourcing alone? I argue that simultaneous competition to solve modules of a decomposable problem and collaboration to aggregate the module solutions produces a higher-value solution to the problem than collaboration alone. And simultaneous cooperation to reduce crowdsourcing frictions and competition to solve a non-decomposable problem yields a higher-value solution than competition alone.

INTRODUCTION

Value creation and capture are fundamental to strategy, and a critical part of the creation is problem solving (Nickerson et al., 2012). Over the years, an important strategy question has been whether to solve such problems through hierarchies, markets, or hybrids (Leiblein & Miller, 2003; Nickerson & Zenger, 2004; Williamson, 1985). In exploring this question, work on the use of markets for problem solving has focused on finding designated solvers to serve as contract suppliers. Much less attention has been paid to another form of markets—crowdsourcing—a phenomenon that Howe defined as "the act of taking a job traditionally performed by a designated agent (usually an employee) and outsourcing it to an undefined, generally large group of people in the form of an open call" (2006: 1).

Subsequent research exploring the phenomenon has identified two types of crowdsourcing: Tournament-based and collaboration-based crowdsourcing (Afuah & Tucci, 2012; Bauer & Gegenhuber, 2015). In tournament-based crowdsourcing, an actor with a problem that it wants solved broadcasts the problem to a crowd whose members self-select to *compete* to solve the problem with no ex ante contracts, and the highest value solution wins (e.g. Bayus, 2012; Girotra et al., 2010; Jeppesen & Lakhani, 2010; Lampel et al., 2012; Terwiesch & Xu, 2008; Terwiesch & Ulrich, 2009). Anecdotal examples and preliminary research findings suggest that tournament-based crowdsourcing can deliver phenomenally high-value solutions to some problems (Brabham, 2008; Jeppesen & Lakhani, 2010; Morgan & Wang, 2010). For example, the solutions that GoldCorp obtained through tournament-based crowdsourcing enabled the firm to find so much gold on its property at low cost that its market value shot up from $300 million to $9 billion in just a few years (Marjanovic et al., 2012; Tapscott & Williams, 2006; Tischler, 2002).

In collaboration-based crowdsourcing, members of a crowd self-select to *cooperate* to solve a problem with no ex ante contracts, bringing their collective expertise to bear on the problem (Afuah & Tucci, 2012; Bauer & Gegenhuber, 2015). Collaboration-based crowdsourcing can also deliver phenomenal performance (Afuah, 2018). For example, Wikipedia has used collaboration-based crowdsourcing to produce the world's most used encyclopedia which is also free.

This remarkable success of tournament-based crowdsourcing in which solvers compete to solve a problem with no seeker–solver ex ante contracts, and collaboration-based crowdsourcing in which solvers cooperate to solve a problem, raises an interesting question: can co-opetition—simultaneous cooperation and competition—during crowdsourcing deliver even higher-value solutions than either tournament-based or collaboration-based crowdsourcing alone? If so, when? This is an important question, especially to those strategy scholars who see performance differences and value creation/capture as central to strategy research. Below, I present a framework for exploring when and how *co-opetition*-based crowdsourcing—crowdsourcing in which solvers simultaneously compete *and* cooperate in solving a problem—is likely to deliver higher-value solutions than either tournament-based or collaboration-based crowdsourcing alone.

In particular, I argue that simultaneous competition to solve modules of a decomposable problem and collaboration to aggregate the module solutions produces a higher-value solution to the original problem than collaboration alone. Also, simultaneous cooperation to reduce crowdsourcing frictions or build relevant capabilities, and competition to solve a non-decomposable problem yield a higher-value solution than competition alone.

My primary contribution is in developing a framework for exploring when and how co-opetition during crowdsourcing delivers higher-value solutions than either cooperation or competition alone. To the extent that understanding performance differences—especially from value creation and capture—is a pillar of strategy research, and crowdsourcing is a demonstrated superior mechanism for getting some problems solved, such a framework can contribute to advancing knowledge in strategic management. A secondary contribution is in introducing a new arena for co-opetition. Co-opetition has traditionally been about a focal firm simultaneously cooperating and competing with its rivals or members of its ecosystem to create and capture value, with the focal firm at the center of the value creation (Brandenburger & Stuart, 1996; Gnyawali & Park, 2011). In crowdsourcing co-opetition, the center of value creation is away from the focal firm that wants a problem solved. That is, although value is being created for the focal firm, the focal firm itself is not directly involved with many of the value-creating activities. I show how value creation for a focal firm—by solving problems through crowdsourcing away from the firm—can be higher when created through co-opetition by solvers than through either cooperation or competition alone.

Note that throughout, I will refer to an individual, firm, or any other entity that has a problem that it wants to get solved as the *seeker*, and any actor that could solve the problem as a *solver*. The problem that a seeker wants to see solved can be to isolate a new chemical compound, produce a free encyclopedia, translate a website, tell a company where to dig for gold on its property, design a new car, design a museum building, and so on (Afuah, 2018; Afuah & Tucci, 2012). Solving any of these problems is tantamount to value creation. A seeker or solver can be an individual, team, firm/organization, country or any other entity.

BACKGROUND LITERATURE: CO-OPETITION AND WHY CROWDSOURCING

Before exploring when and how co-opetition during crowdsourcing is likely to deliver higher-value solutions than either tournament-based or collaboration-based crowdsourcing alone, it is useful to do two things. First, it is important to distinguish between: (1) traditional co-opetition, in which a firm with a problem (seeker) cooperates and competes with suppliers, complementors, competitors, and customers to solve the problem; and (2) crowdsourcing co-opetition, in which solvers cooperate and compete to solve a problem from a seeker with no ex ante solver–seeker contracts (Figure 11.1). Second,

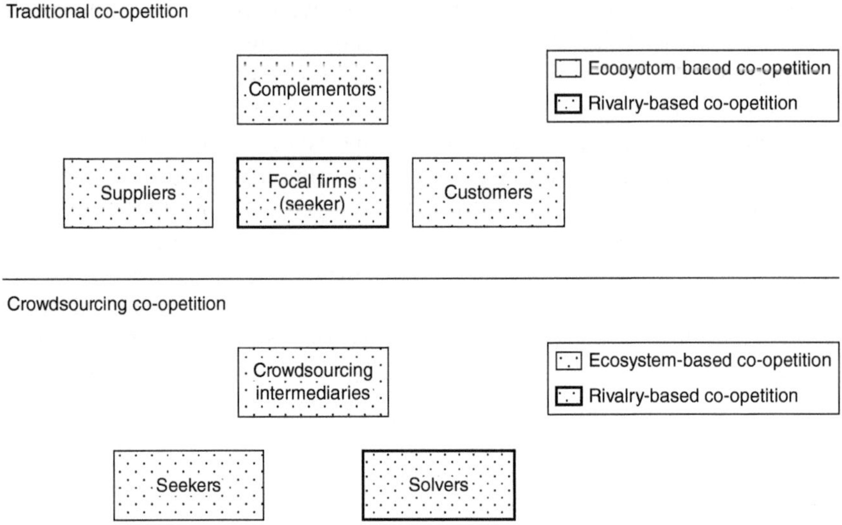

Traditional co-opetition

Crowdsourcing co-opetition

Figure 11.1. Types of co-opetition: traditional versus crowdsourcing.

it is critical to quickly explain why a seeker would want to crowdsource a problem rather than solve it or contract the job to a designated solver. Both pieces of information are critical to understanding the causal logic of the framework for exploring the central.

Traditional Co-opetition

In traditional co-opetition, a firm (seeker) has a problem which it wants to get solved, and simultaneously cooperates and competes with rivals, suppliers, complementors, competitors or customers to solve the problem (Brandenburger & Stuart, 1996; Bengtsson & Kock, 2000; Gnyawali et al., 2006: Figure 1). This simultaneous cooperation and competition—in which the focal firm (seeker) is the center of attention—can be rivalry based or ecosystem based (Figure 11.1).

Rivalry-based co-opetition. In rivalry-based co-opetition, the focal firm (seeker) and its rivals pursue cooperation at one stage of a problem-solving value chain, while competing at another stage (Bengtsson & Kock, 2000; Gnyawali & Park, 2011; Lado, Boyd & Hanlon, 1997). For example, firms in an industry can cooperate to develop a new technology, and then each firm can use the technology in its own branded products to compete against others in product markets—that is, rivals can cooperate at one stage of the value chain while simultaneously competing at the other (Gnyawali & Madhavan, 2001). For example, the joint venture between Toyota and General Motors from 1984 to

2010—called the New United Motor Manufacturing, Inc. (NUMMI)—allowed the two automobile firms to cooperate in manufacturing while simultaneously competing in automobile product markets. In some co-opetition cases, co-operation is downstream rather than upstream (Gnyawali et al., 2006). For example, firms can compete in developing competing technologies and other assets but combine them in a joint venture to offer joint products. Firms can also cooperate in one product market but compete in another.

Ecosystem-based co-opetition. In the ecosystem-based view, co-opetition is in the broader ecosystem of suppliers, rivals, complementors, customers, and any other institutions that participate in value creation and capture in the ecosystem (Adner & Kapoor, 2010; Afuah, 2000; Brandenburger & Nalebuff, 2011; Brandenburger & Stuart, 1996; Lavie, 2007: Figure 1). That is, simultaneous cooperation and competition are not limited to rivals. The rationale behind ecosystem-based co-opetition is simple. Because the value (benefits) that customers perceive in a product from a firm depends critically on the activities of suppliers, customers, complementors, and rivals—on the activities of all the members of its value system—the firm may be better off cooperating and competing with other members of its ecosystem, rather than with only its rivals as is the case with rivalry-based co-opetition (Afuah, 2000; Brandenburger & Stuart, 1996; Porter, 1985; Stabell & Fjeldstad, 1998). One example of ecosystem-based co-opetition involves owners of games consoles (platforms) such as Microsoft, Nintendo, and Sony. Each of these platform owners cooperates with game developers by giving them the critical proprietary information about the platforms that they need to develop the games to run on the platforms. At the same time, platform owners also develop their own games to compete with those from the developers that they cooperate with.

Crowdsourcing Co-opetition

In co-opetition during crowdsourcing, solvers cooperate and compete to solve a problem with no ex ante contract with the seeker (Figure 11.1). As is the case with traditional co-opetition, simultaneous competition and cooperation during crowdsourcing can also be rivalry based or ecosystem based. However, whereas in traditional co-opetition, rivalry is among competing focal firms, in crowdsourcing co-opetition, rivalry is among solvers (Figure 11.1). And whereas in traditional co-opetition, an ecosystem consists of suppliers, customers, complementors, and rivals, in crowdsourcing co-opetition, an ecosystem consists of solvers, seekers, and crowdsourcing intermediaries, with solvers at the core (Figure 11.1). Below, I will have a lot more to say about crowdsourcing co-opetition when I explore the central question of when and how is co-opetition during crowdsourcing likely to deliver higher-value solutions than either tournament-based or collaboration-based crowdsourcing alone? But before exploring the question, I first explain why a firm would want to crowdsource a problem (see also Afuah, 2018).

Why Crowdsource a Problem?

The answer to why a seeker would crowdsource a problem rather than solve it or outsource it to a designated contractor is deeply rooted in the theories of the firm, especially the resource-based view (RBV), transaction costs economics (TCE), and behavioral theories of the firm (e.g. Barney, 1991; Conner & Prahalad, 1996; Cyert & March, 1963; Williamson, 1985). How? According to RBV, *for example*, resources and knowledge are heterogeneously distributed and, importantly, can be valuable, rare, immobile, inimitable, and non-substitutable (VRIIN) (Barney, 1991; Dierickx & Cool, 1989; Mahoney & Pandian, 1992; Peteraf, 1993).

Therefore, there are going to be times when a seeker has a problem that requires VRIIN resources that the seeker neither owns nor has access to (Chesbrough, 2003; 2006). Importantly, the seeker may not know who out there has the resources/knowledge to solve the problem, and locating that potential solver is synonymous with finding a needle in a haystack. That is, locating who has the resources and knowledge required to solve the problem is tantamount to distant search—search that can be problematical to cognitively limited seekers (Afuah & Tucci, 2012; Cyert & March, 1963; Leiblein & Macher, 2009). Because finding a solver with the right resources/knowledge can be so difficult, such a seeker may be better off crowdsourcing the problem rather than pursuing the alternatives of solving it in-house or having a designated contractor do it (Afuah & Tucci, 2012; Surowiecki, 2005). In crowdsourcing, the seeker broadcasts the problem so that the needle in the haystack will "find" itself (Afuah, 2018).

Having distinguished between co-opetition in the traditional sense and crowdsourcing co-opetition, and explained why a seeker would prefer crowdsourcing over alternative mechanisms for solving problems, we can now return to the primary question: when and how does co-opetition during crowdsourcing deliver higher-value solutions than tournament-based or collaboration-based crowdsourcing alone?

FRAMEWORK FOR EXPLORING THE IMPACT OF CO-OPETITION ON CROWDSOURCING PERFORMANCE

A framework for exploring the impact of co-opetition—the impact of simultaneous cooperation and competition by solvers—on crowdsourcing performance is shown in Figure 11.2. In the framework, a seeker has already decided to crowdsource a problem, rather than solve it internally or contract it to a designated solver, but must take a series of decisions including whether to pursue either tournament-based or collaboration-based crowdsourcing. Details of the components of the framework and the relationships among them are provided below. Briefly, however, the choice of how to pursue crowdsourcing—the choice of whether to employ tournament-based or collaboration-based crowdsourcing—is driven by the decomposability of the problem (Figure 11.2). The relationship between pursuing tournament-based crowdsourcing (competition by solvers) and the likelihood of obtaining a superior-value solution for the problem is moderated by cooperation by solvers to reduce crowdsourcing frictions (Figure 11.2). That is, co-opetition here is the simultaneous competition by solvers to solve a problem and cooperation to reduce the frictions that would otherwise compromise the crowdsourcing process.

The relationship between pursuing collaboration-based crowdsourcing—a cooperative undertaking—and the likelihood of obtaining a superior-value solution, is moderated by competition to reduce problem module solution inefficiencies (Figure 11.2). We now turn to the details of the framework.

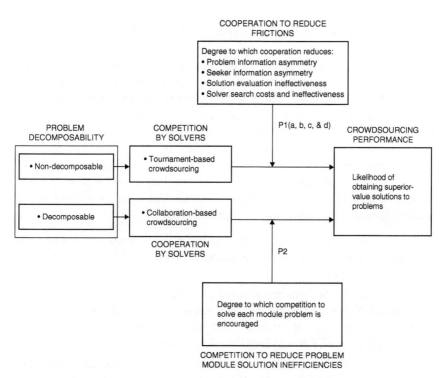

Figure 11.2. Framework for exploring the impact of co-opetition on the superiority of solutions to problems.

Problem Decomposability

The choice of whether to pursue tournament-based or collaboration-based crowdsourcing depends critically on whether or not the problem being solved is decomposable (Brusoni et al., 2007; Hoetker, 2006; Schilling, 2000). If a problem is decomposable, collaboration-based crowdsourcing can be used, since the problem can be parceled out into modules, and each solver can self-select to solve a module. The module solutions can then be (re)assembled to obtain a solution to the original problem (Figure 11.2). That is, solvers cooperate when each solver solves a module of a problem and all the module solutions are (re)assembled to obtain the solution to the original problem (Bauer & Gegenhuber, 2015). For example, the problem of raising a certain amount of money for a venture—by crowdsourcing it to the public in the form of an open call—can be parceled out into raising smaller amounts. The amounts raised are combined to achieve the original target amount.

If the problem is non-decomposable—that is, it cannot be parceled out into modules—each potential solver in a crowd *competes* to solve the whole problem, and the highest-value solution wins the competition (Figure 11.2).

Competition by Solvers: Tournament-Based Crowdsourcing

Choosing to pursue tournament-based or collaboration-based crowdsourcing is an important first step. But there are other significant steps in a crowdsourcing process (Afuah, 2018; Afuah & Tucci, 2012). The seeker must delineate and broadcast the problem to the chosen crowd, potential solvers in the crowd must self-select to solve the problem, the solution must be accurately evaluated, and the winning solution(s) assimilated by the seeker into its value creation and capture activities (Afuah, 2018; Afuah & Tucci, 2012; Franke et al., 2013; Poetz & Schreier, 2012). Now consider a seeker firm that has decided to get a problem solved through tournament-based crowdsourcing in a world in which the following assumptions hold.

Assumption 1: Complete and perfect information about seekers and the problems that they broadcast is available to all potential solvers. (No search costs for solvers.)

Assumption 2: Seekers are rational enough to accurately delineate and broadcast the problem to the right crowd. All solvers are cognitively endowed with what it takes to understand the problems broadcast to them, and to make rational decisions about self-selecting to solve problems.

Assumption 3: Problem-solving resources (expertise, time, and tools) and incentives are heterogeneously distributed.

Assumption 4: Evaluation of solutions and their transfer from solvers to seekers is accurate and costless.

In such a perfect crowdsourcing world, a broadcast problem gets to all potential solvers who now have complete and perfect information, not only about the problem and its seeker, but also about other solvers' incentives and capabilities—enough information to decide whether to self-select and solve problems with no ex ante contracts with seekers. For example, a solver can use the perfect and complete information to determine whether its expected cost of pursuing the solution is below its reservation cost for each problem. (Recall that a solver's reservation cost during tournament-based crowdsourcing is the maximum hit (cost) that it can afford in pursuing the problem, since losers are paid nothing and have to "eat" their own costs.)

Effectively, each solver can use the perfect and complete information to self-select to compete to deliver the best solution to the whole non-decomposable problem. Because problem-solving resources and incentives are heterogeneously distributed among solvers (Assumption 3), the quality of solutions that they produce is likely to vary from solver to solver, with some solvers producing superior solutions. And because evaluation of solutions and their transfer from solvers to seekers is accurate and costless (Assumption 4), all the solutions generated by solvers can be accurately evaluated, increasing the likelihood of finding the highest-value solution in the crowd. Thus, *tournament-based crowdsourcing* can deliver optimal solutions to non-decomposable problems in the frictionless world of Assumptions 1 to 4.

Unfortunately, we do not always live in the perfect crowdsourcing world of Assumptions 1 to 4. Crowdsourcing activities can be anything but frictionless, and therefore that optimal solution is often but a dream, a goal. Frictions during crowdsourcing often lead to violations of Assumptions 1, 2, and 4, and stand in the way of that dream. Thus, if the effects of these frictions are not mitigated, the superiority of the solutions that can be obtained through tournament-based crowdsourcing can be compromised. This is where *cooperation to reduce frictions* comes in (Figure 11.2). Cooperation can mitigate the effects of frictions, increasing the likelihood that the superiority of solutions from tournament-based crowdsourcing will not be compromised.

Moderating Role of Cooperation to Reduce Frictions

In Figure 11.2, I have modeled *cooperation to reduce frictions* as a construct that moderates the relationship between tournament-based crowdsourcing and the likelihood of obtaining superior-value solutions to problems. In particular, the relationship is moderated by the degree to which cooperation reduces problem information asymmetry, seeker information asymmetry, solution evaluation inefficiencies, and solver research costs and ineffectiveness (Figure 11.2).

Problem information asymmetry. For several reasons, the information about the problem that solvers receive from a seeker is likely to be incomplete and imperfect, thereby creating crowdsourcing frictions. First, the medium that a seeker uses to broadcast a problem may be ineffective or inefficient. For example, a seeker that decides to broadcast a problem by posting it only on its website risks not reaching those potential solvers that do not visit the site frequently. Another seeker who chooses to use a network with structural holes as a broadcast medium, risks being confronted with the inefficiencies/ineffectiveness associated with opportunistic actors who bridge the structural holes (Burt, 2001).

Second, even if all the problem information from a seeker were to reach all solvers, the knowledge distance between the seeker and solvers may prevent solvers from understanding the problem. For example, if the problem is in communications codes or technical language that solvers cannot understand, the likelihood of these solvers understanding the problem well enough to self-select and solve it is decreased (Monteverde, 1995).

These information asymmetries about a problem—between a seeker and solvers—can be mitigated by cooperation among rivals, or cooperation in a crowdsourcing ecosystem of seekers, intermediaries, and solvers. The resulting co-opetition—simultaneous cooperation and competition among solvers—increases the likelihood of producing higher-value solutions to problems. How? Take rivalry co-opetition. Solvers can cooperate by trading information about the problem, knowing full well that they are simultaneously competing against each other in the tournament to deliver the best solution to the problem (Schrader, 1991). A special issue of an academic journal offers a good example. Recall that rather than write their own articles or outsource the writing to designated writers, academic journals often crowdsource the task to anyone, anywhere, who can write the type of articles publishable in the journals. In a special issue of such a journal, potential authors can cooperate and compete simultaneously. They can cooperate to understand what the editors are looking for in the special issue, but at the same time, each author writes his or her own paper and submits it for the tournament to get published in the special issue. Such cooperation can take advantage of any social ties or other relationships that solvers have (Hansen, 1999).

Ecosystem-based co-opetition can also mitigate information asymmetry frictions. For example, rather than cooperate with rivals, solvers can also join the two-sided network of an intermediary such as InnoCentive—a network with solvers on one side and seekers on the other. Thus, not only can the intermediary help solvers to understand a problem, solvers can also enjoy the network effects of the two-sided network (Afuah, 2013; Parker & van Alstyne, 2005).

Proposition 1a: The more that solvers *cooperate* with rivals or members of their ecosystem to reduce *problem information asymmetry frictions,* the more that *tournament-based crowdsourcing* is likely to produce *superior-value solutions to problems.*

Stated differently, the more that solvers simultaneously cooperate with rivals or members of their ecosystem to reduce *problem information asymmetry frictions,* and compete to produce a solution (through tournament-based crowdsourcing), the higher would be the likelihood of producing a higher-value solution than pursuing competition (tournament-based crowdsourcing) alone. That is, co-opetition-based crowdsourcing is better than tournament-based crowdsourcing alone.

Seeker information asymmetry. During tournament-based crowdsourcing, a critical piece of information for solvers—when they decide whether to self-select and tackle a problem with no ex ante contracts—is whether the seeker will evaluate the solutions fairly and pay the prize promised for the winning solution. In the perfect world of Assumptions 1 to 4, solvers have perfect and complete information about seekers and can tell, ex ante, which solver will evaluate solutions fairly and deliver the reward promised to the winner. In a less than perfect world, solvers may not know if seekers can be trusted. Thus, because solutions are often primarily information, the solver may run into the Arrow (1962) paradox, in which the seeker needs the solution for evaluation. But once it has the solution and now knows it, an opportunistic seeker may decide not to pay the advertised contest prize. Therefore, information about the seeker—about whether it is opportunistic or trustworthy—can be a critical component of the information that a solver needs to make its decision on whether to self-select and solve a problem.

A solver can mitigate the effects of this seeker information asymmetry through either rivalry-based or ecosystem-based co-opetition. In rivalry-based co-opetition, competing solvers can cooperate to obtain information about the seeker. For example, if a solver is connected through social ties to rival solvers, it can use the ties to obtain or divulge information about the seeker—information about whether the seeker is trustworthy or not and what winning would mean to the solvers (Burt, 2001). (Authors can exchange information about the guest editors of a special issue of a journal and what being published in the special issue could mean to their careers.) In ecosystem-based co-opetition, competing solvers can cooperate through a crowdsourcing intermediary (Figure 11.1). Because an intermediary mediates between solvers and seekers, it can give solvers the assurances that they need to self-select and solve problems. For example, InnoCentive all but guarantees that solvers whose solutions win will be awarded the prizes promised.

> **Proposition 1b:** The more that solvers *cooperate* with rivals or members of their ecosystem to reduce *seeker information asymmetry frictions,* the more that *tournament-based crowdsourcing* is likely to produce *superior-value solutions to problems.*

Stated differently, this says the more that solvers simultaneously cooperate with rivals or members of their ecosystem to reduce *seeker information asymmetry frictions*, and compete to produce a winning solution (through tournament-based crowdsourcing), the higher would be the likelihood of producing a higher-value solution than pursuing competition (tournament-based crowdsourcing) alone.

Solution evaluation ineffectiveness. It is not always the case that a seeker can accurately and costlessly evaluate all the solutions that are submitted to it for evaluation, as suggested by Assumption 4. Why? The seeker may not have the untainted expertise or time required to evaluate the solution, the criteria for determining a winner may be very subjective, and there may be too many solutions for the seeker to evaluate cost effectively (e.g., Piezunka & Dahlander, 2015). These hurdles can decrease the likelihood of obtaining superior solutions to problems. Rivalry-based co-opetition among solvers can mitigate the hurdles. How? Consider the case in which the seeker has neither the expertise nor time to evaluate all the solutions submitted during tournament-based crowdsourcing. Competing solvers can also collaborate to evaluate the solutions. This is rivalry co-opetition. Take the academic journal example again. Authors who submit manuscripts to a special issue of a journal usually also review other authors' manuscripts. Authors who submit for the special issue may know more about the special topic than the average referee for the journal, and therefore would be better at evaluating the papers than other references.

When evaluation of solutions involves subjective judgments, a seeker may also be better off having competing solvers cooperate to evaluate the solutions. For example, a seeker's taste for T-shirt designs may be very different from that of the customers to whom the shirts will be sold (Brabham, 2008). Thus, having the seeker evaluate which T-shirts customers are likely to prefer may not be a good idea. The seeker may be better off having customers cooperate in the "solution evaluation" by voting to choose a winner.

> **Proposition 1c:** The more that solvers *cooperate* with rivals or members of their ecosystem to *reduce solution evaluation ineffectiveness*, the more that *tournament-based crowdsourcing* is likely to produce *superior-value solutions to problems*.

That is, the more that solvers simultaneously cooperate with rivals or members of their ecosystem to *reduce solution evaluation ineffectiveness*, and compete to identify a winning solution (through tournament-based crowdsourcing), the higher would be the likelihood of producing a higher-value solution than pursuing competition (tournament-based crowdsourcing) alone. That is, co-opetition-based crowdsourcing is better than tournament-based crowdsourcing alone.

Solver search costs and ineffectiveness. In the crowdsourcing perfect world of Assumptions 1 to 4, solvers have no search costs since information about problems and seekers gets to all potential solvers. In the real world, however, search costs can be very high, especially if solvers have to search beyond their immediate neighbors—that is, search costs can be very high when solvers have to conduct distant search so as to find problems to solve (Katila & Ahuja, 2002; Piezunka & Dahlander, 2015). For example, a scientist in India may have to search through the websites of numerous potential seekers or call them up to find out if these seekers have problems that they want to get solved through crowdsourcing. Such searches can be very costly.

Cooperation by solvers can reduce their search costs. How? By joining an intermediary's community of solvers and seekers. For example, in InnoCentive's two-sided network of seekers and solvers, problems from solvers are broadcast to the solvers in the community, limiting solvers' search costs to the time it takes to turn to the pages in the community's website where problems are listed. Reducing search costs can mean increasing the number of solvers who can participate in the tournament to solve the problem, thereby increasing the likelihood of producing that superior solution.

There is another potential increase in the number of solvers who self-select to solve a problem that has nothing to do with lower search costs—the increase due to network effects (Afuah, 2013; Katz & Shapiro, 1986). When solvers cooperate by joining the solver side of a two-sided seeker–solver network, they are also increasing the value of the network, since the more seekers that join the network, the more valuable the network becomes to solvers because they are now more likely to find the problem that they want to solve. And the more solvers there are in the network, the more valuable the network becomes to seekers since they are now more likely to obtain a high-value solution from solvers.

Effectively, cooperation by joining an intermediary reduces search costs and may kick in network effects, both of which are likely to increase the number of solvers who participate in the tournament to deliver the best solution. This simultaneous cooperation to reduce search costs or leverage network effects, and competition to solve a problem, is more likely to deliver a higher-value solution than competition (tournament-based crowdsourcing) alone.

Solver search costs are not the only frictions that solvers face in an imperfect crowdsourcing world. The solvers in a crowd targeted by a cognitively limited seeker may not possess the right combination of resources and incentives needed to deliver superior solutions to a problem. Thus, in a crowdsourcing tournament with solvers from such a crowd, winning solutions may be less than optimal. For example, because designing T-shirts is part art and part science, some winners in a T-shirt contest may be a little short on the art side, while others may be a little short on the science part. By asking these winners to cooperate, they may be able to combine their complementary expertise to deliver a superior design. That is, co-opetition—competition followed by cooperation—is more likely to deliver higher-value solutions than competition alone. The top contestants in the Netflix Challenge were encouraged to collaborate to produce an even better solution.

> **Proposition 1d:**   The more that solvers *cooperate* with rivals or members of their ecosystem to *reduce solver search costs and ineffectiveness*, the more that *tournament-based crowdsourcing* is likely to produce *superior-value solutions to problems*.

Put differently, the more that solvers simultaneously cooperate with rivals or members of their ecosystem to *reduce solver search costs and ineffectiveness*, and compete to produce a winning solution (through tournament-based crowdsourcing), the higher would be the likelihood of producing a higher-value solution than pursuing competition (tournament-based crowdsourcing) alone.

Taken together, these four propositions amount to the following overarching proposition.

> *Simultaneous competition by solvers to solve a problem and cooperation to reduce crowdsourcing frictions delivers higher-value solutions than either competition alone or cooperation alone.*

Cooperation by Solvers: Collaboration-Based Crowdsourcing

Now, suppose the problem that a seeker wants to crowdsource is decomposable (Figure 11.2). For example, Wikipedia's problem of providing the world with a free encyclopedia is decomposable into module problems of providing entries for different topics. In a perfect crowdsourcing world of Assumptions 1 to 4, each potential solver has perfect and complete information about the modules from the decomposable problem, what resources are needed to solve each module, information about other solvers who want to solve the modules, as well as information about the seeker. With this perfect and complete information, each rational solver can compute which module problem it can solve better than all other solvers. Thus, each solver self-selects to solve only the module that it is best equipped to solve and also has the most incentive to solve. Less qualified and less motivated solvers do not bother tackling modules that they know someone else can solve better. That is, in the perfect crowdsourcing world of Assumptions 1 to 4, each module of the decomposed problem will be solved by the best qualified and most motivated solver, and the module solutions will be costlessly aggregated to deliver an optimal solution to the original problem. This is collaboration-based crowdsourcing at its best.

Moderating Role of Competition to Reduce Problem Module Solution Inefficiency

Unfortunately, we do not live in a perfect crowdsourcing world—that is, Assumptions 1 to 4 do not always hold. Solvers are boundedly rational and do not have perfect and complete information about much. Take the Wikipedia example. A writer of an entry does not typically know everyone else who could write the entry. Nor do they have the cognitive ability, resources, and time to evaluate and compare their own ability to produce the entry against the abilities of all other potential writers of the same entry so as to determine who will produce the best entry. Rather, because they are boundedly rational, solvers search in their immediate neighborhoods for information about what encyclopedia entries need to be written, what expertise is needed, which authors might choose to write the entries, and their abilities to write the entries. That is, each author makes his/her decision to write an entry by conducting local search—search that may leave out a lot about other potential solvers and entries (Katila & Ahuja, 2002; Piezunka & Dahlander, 2015).

Each solver who self-selects to produce a solution to a problem module brings a different combination of resources (expertise, time, and tools) and incentives to bear on the problem. One of these solvers has the combination that will deliver the highest-value module solution, but neither that solver nor any other solver is likely to know, since they are cognitively limited and depend on local search. No one knows ex ante who is likely to deliver the best solution for the module problem.

Degree to which competition to solve each module problem is encouraged. One way to increase the likelihood of selecting the module solution from the solver with the best combination of resources and incentives for the task is competition—contests in which each solver competes to solve a problem module, and the best solution for the module problem is selected. This process is repeated for all the modules from the decomposed problem to pick the best module solutions. These best module solutions are then aggregated through cooperation to produce a high-value solution for the original problem. That is, simultaneous competition to produce solutions to the modules of a decomposable problem, and cooperation to aggregate the module solutions, produces higher-value solutions than either competition or cooperation alone. This is rivalry-based crowdsourcing co-opetition. Again, Wikipedia offers a good example. Writers compete to produce each entry, and the winning entries become part of the encyclopedia (Malone et al., 2010).

However, there is a small issue with using competition to select the best module solution. Because seekers and solvers are in an imperfect crowdsourcing world, evaluation of the many module solutions to pick winners may be very costly or the module solutions selected as winners may be the wrong ones.

To make matters worse, the number of evaluations can grow incredibly large when we multiply the number of modules by the number of contestants per module. One quick fix is ecosystem-based co-opetition, in which solution modules are evaluated through cooperation between seekers and solvers. Take the translation of a document from one language to another by a crowd. The document is usually parceled out into passages for translation. Each translator of the passage produces his/her own translation of the passage. A crowd that includes some translators votes on which translation they believe is the most accurate and elegant. The winner is selected as the translation for the passage. The winning translations of all the passages in the document can then be combined to produce the translation of the document. Effectively, ecosystem co-opetition between a seeker and solvers is used to evaluate competing module solutions from rivalry co-opetition.

> **Proposition 2:**   The more that solvers *compete* with rivals or members of their ecosystem to *produce the best module solutions*, the more that *collaboration-based crowdsourcing* is likely to produce *superior-value solutions to problems*.

Put differently, the more that solvers simultaneously compete with rivals or members of their ecosystem to produce the best solutions to module problems, *and* cooperate to aggregate the module solutions (through collaboration-based crowdsourcing) to produce the solution, the higher would be the likelihood of producing a higher-value solution to the problem than pursuing collaboration-based competition alone.

CONCLUSIONS AND FUTURE RESEARCH

Although crowdsourcing academic research is still in its infancy, anecdotal evidence—some of which goes as far back as 1714—suggests that the value created during tournament-based crowdsourcing (when solvers compete) or collaboration-based crowdsourcing (when solvers cooperate) can be remarkably high. The expectations associated with such high-value solutions make crowdsourcing alluring to those scholars who maintain that understanding performance differences is fundamental to strategy research. The fact that co-opetition in the non-crowdsourcing world has been shown to improve value creation, raises an interesting question: Can co-opetition—simultaneous co-operation and competition by solvers—deliver even higher-value solutions than either competition (tournament-based crowdsourcing) or cooperation (collaboration-based crowdsourcing) alone? In this essay, I have presented a framework for exploring this question.

In the framework, I have argued that for a non-decomposable problem, simultaneous cooperation by solvers to reduce crowdsourcing frictions or build problem-solving capabilities, and competition (through tournament-based crowdsourcing) to select a winning solution, are more likely to produce high-value solutions than cooperation or competition alone. For a decomposable problem, simultaneous competition to solve problem modules and cooperation to aggregate the solution modules delivers higher-value solutions than either cooperation or competition alone. These are provocative propositions, especially to those strategy scholars who believe that strategy is rooted in understanding performance differences and their sources and consequences (Rumelt et al., 1991).

Effectively, previous research has demonstrated that co-opetition—simultaneous cooperation and competition—delivers high-value solutions to some of the problems that are central to value creation and capture. Here we have taken the research one step further by exploring when and how co-opetition during crowdsourcing—simultaneous cooperation and competition by solvers—can also improve value creation and capture. However, there are a few cautionary notes, especially for future research.

First, to keep the causal logic of the framework tractable, I have focused on the value-creating aspects of co-opetition in crowdsourcing, neglecting the costs. But the interplay of cooperation and competition can be costly. Take cooperation during tournament-based crowdsourcing in which rival solvers cooperate to reduce information asymmetry about the problem that they are competing to solve. In obtaining the information, each solver usually gives away information, some of which may help a rival become a more formidable competitor. Then there is also the opportunity cost component—time spent giving away information is time that could have been spent solving the problem. Thus, exploring the cost of co-opetition would make for a good research topic, given that most of the research in cooperation—especially strategic alliances—has traditionally focused on the benefits of cooperation and neglected its costs.

Second, as shown in Figure 11.2, both decomposable and non-decomposable problems are solved through markets (crowdsourcing). But the problem-solving view (PSV)—consistent with transaction cost economics—asserts that non-decomposable problems are more efficiently solved through hierarchies rather than markets (Nickerson & Zenger, 2004; Felin & Zenger, 2014; Sanchez & Mahoney, 1996; Schilling, 2000; Zenger et al., 2011). These rather contrasting predictions about where to get non-decomposable problems solved are the basis for an interesting debate and future research. Third, early work in co-opetition was rooted in neoclassical economics' cooperative game theory (Brandenburger & Nalebuff, 2011; Brandenburger & Stuart, 1996, 2007). This essay has taken a multidisciplinary approach, drawing on both the resource-based view (RBV) and behavioral theories of the firm. Future research could explore the implications of such a multidisciplinary approach relative to those more specialized.

The low cost and pervasiveness of information and communications technologies have facilitated the rediscovery of crowdsourcing as a means to obtain high-value solutions to some problems. I suggest that simultaneous cooperation and competition during crowdsourcing may be able to deliver even higher-value solutions to such problems than competition or cooperation alone. To the scholars who see value creation as fundamental to strategy, co-opetition during crowdsourcing may be worth pursuing.

REFERENCES

Adner, R. & Kapoor, R. (2010). Value creation in innovation ecosystems: How the structure of technological interdependence affects firm performance in new technology generations. *Strategic Management Journal, 31*(3), 306–33.

Afuah, A. (2000). How much do your "co-opetitors" capabilities matter in the face of technological change? *Strategic Management Journal, 21*(3), 387–404.

Afuah, A. (2013). Are network effects really all about size? The role of structure and conduct. *Strategic Management Journal, 34*(3), 257–73.

Afuah, A. (2018). Crowdsourcing: A primer and research framework. In C. Tucci, A. Afuah, & G. Viscusi (eds.), *Creating and Capturing Value Through Crowdsourcing*. Oxford: Oxford University Press, pp. 11–38.

Afuah, A. & Tucci, C. L. (2012). Crowdsourcing as a solution to distant search. *Academy of Management Review, 37*(3), 355–75.

Arrow, K. J. (1962). The economic implications of learning by doing. *Review of Economic Studies, 29*(3), 155.

Barney, J. B. (1991). Firm resources and sustained competitive advantage. *Journal of Management, 17*(1), 99–120.

Bauer, R. M. & Gegenhuber, T. (2015). Crowd-based sourcing: Global search and the twisted roles of consumers and producers. *Organization, 22*(5), 661–81.

Bayus, B. L. (2012). Crowdsourcing new product ideas over time: An analysis of the Dell IdeaStorm community. *Management Science, 59*(1), 226–44.

Bengtsson, M. & Kock, S. (2000). "Coopetition" in business networks—to cooperate and compete simultaneously. *Industrial Marketing Management, 29*(5), 411–26.

Brabham, D. C. (2008). Crowdsourcing as a model for problem solving an introduction and cases. Convergence. *The International Journal of Research into New Media Technologies, 14*(1), 75–90.

Brandenburger, A. M. & Nalebuff, B. J. (2011). *Co-opetition*. New York: Doubleday.

Brandenburger, A. M. & Stuart, H. W. (1996). Value-based business strategy. *Journal of Economics and Management Strategy, 5*(1), 5–24.

Brandenburger, A. M. & Stuart, H. W. (2007). Biform games. *Management Science, 53*(4), 537–49.

Brusoni, S., Marengo, L., Prencipe, A., & Valente, M. (2007). The value and costs of modularity: a problem solving perspective. *European Management Review, 4*(2), 121–32.

Burt, R. S. (2001). Structural holes versus network closure as social capital. Ronald S. Burt, in N. Lin, K. Cook, and R. S. Burt, in *Social Capital: Theory and Research*.

Sociology and Economics. Controversy and Integration series. New York: Aldine de Gruyter, pp. 31–56.

Chesbrough, H. (2003). *Open Innovation: The New Imperative for Creating and Profiting from Technology.* Boston, MA: Harvard Business School Press.

Chesbrough, H. (2006). *Open Business Models: How to Thrive in the New Innovation Landscape.* Boston, MA: Harvard Business Press.

Conner, K. R. & Prahalad, C. K. (1996). A resource-based theory of the firm: Knowledge versus opportunism. *Organization Science,* 7(5), 477–501.

Cyert, R. M. & March, J. G. (1963). *A Behavioral Theory of the Firm.* Englewood Cliffs, NJ: Prentice-Hall.

Dierickx, I. & Cool, K. (1989). Asset stock accumulation and sustainability of competitive advantage. *Management Science,* 35(12), 1504–11.

Felin, T. & Zenger, T. R. (2014). Closed or open innovation? Problem solving and the governance choice, *Research Policy,* 43(5), 914–25.

Franke, N., Poetz, M. K., & Schreier, M. (2013). Integrating problem solvers from analogous markets in new product ideation. *Management Science,* 60(4), 1063–81.

Girotra, K., Terwiesch, C., & Ulrich, K. T. (2010). Idea generation and the quality of the best idea. *Management Science,* 56(4), 591–605.

Gnyawali, D. R., He, J. Y., & Madhavan, R. (2006). Impact of co-opetition on firm competitive behavior: An empirical examination. *Journal of Management,* 32(4), 507–30.

Gnyawali, D. R. & Madhavan, R. (2001). Cooperative networks and competitive dynamics: A structural embeddedness perspective. *Academy of Management Review,* 26(3), 431–45.

Gnyawali, D. R. & Park, B. R. (2011). Co-opetition between giants: Collaboration with competitors for technological innovation. *Research Policy,* 40(5), 650–63.

Hansen, M. T. (1999). The search-transfer problem: The role of week ties in sharing knowledge across organizational subunits. *Administrative Science Quarterly,* 44(1), 82–111.

Hoetker, G. (2006). Do modular products lead to modular organizations? *Strategic Management Journal,* 27(6), 501–18.

Howe, J. (2006). Crowdsourcing: A Definition. Wired Blog Network:Crowdsourcing, 2006, http://crowdsourcing.typepad.com/cs/2006/06/crowdsourcing_a.html (accessed March 21, 2017).

Jeppesen, L. B. & Lakhani, K. R. (2010). Marginality and problem-solving effectiveness in broadcast search. *Organization Science,* 21(5), 1016–33.

Katila, R. & Ahuja, G. (2002). Something old, something new: A longitudinal study of search behavior and new product introduction. *Academy of Management Journal,* 45(6), 1183–94.

Katz, M. L. & Shapiro, C. (1986). Technology adoption in the presence of network externalities. *Journal of Political Economy,* 94(4), 822–41.

Lado, A. A., Boyd, N. G., & Hanlon, S. C. (1997). Competition, cooperation, and the search for economic rents: a syncretic model. *Academy of Management Review,* 22(1), 110–41.

Lampel, J., Jha, P. P., & Bhalla, A. (2012). Test-driving the future: How design competitions are changing innovation. *Academy of Management Perspectives,* 26(2), 71–85.

Lavie, D. (2007). Alliance portfolios and firm performance: A study of value creation and appropriation in the US software industry. *Strategic Management Journal*, *28*(12), 1187–212.

Leiblein, M. J. & Macher, J. T. (2009). The problem solving perspective: A strategic approach to understanding environment and organization. *Advances in Strategic Management*, *26*, 97–120.

Leiblein, M. J. & Miller, D. J. (2003). An empirical examination of transaction- and firm-level influences on the vertical boundaries of the firm. *Strategic Management Journal*, *24*(9), 839–59.

Mahoney, J. T. & Pandian, Jr (1992). The resource-based view within the conversation of strategic management. *Strategic Management Journal*, *13*(5), 363–80.

Malone, T. W., Laubacher, R., & Dellarocas, C. (2010). The collective intelligence genome. *MIT Sloan Management Review*, *51*(3), 21.

Marjanovic, S., Fry, C., & Chataway, J. (2012). Crowdsourcing based business models: In search of evidence for innovation 2.0. *Science and Public Policy*, *39*(9), 318–32.

Monteverde, K. (1995). Technical dialog as an incentive for vertical integration in the semiconductor industry. *Management Science*, *41*(10), 1624–38.

Morgan, J. & Wang, R. (2010). Tournaments for ideas. *California Management Review*, *52*(2), 77–97.

Nickerson, J. A., Yen, C. J., & Mahoney, J. T. (2012). Exploring the problem-finding and problem-solving approach for designing organizations. *Academy of Management Perspectives*, *26*(1), 52–72.

Nickerson, J. A. & Zenger, T. R. (2004). A knowledge-based theory of the firm—The problem-solving perspective. *Organization Science*, *15*(6), 617–32.

Parker, G. & Van Alstyne, M. (2005). Two-sided network effects: a theory of information product design. *Management Science*, *51*(10), 1494–504.

Peteraf, M. A. (1993). The cornerstones of competitive advantage: a resource-based view. *Strategic Management Journal*, *14*(3), 179–91.

Piezunka, H. & Dahlander, L. (2015). Distant search, narrow attention: How crowding alters organizations' filtering of suggestions in crowdsourcing. *Academy of Management Journal*, *58*(3), 856–80.

Poetz, M. K. & Schreier, M. (2012). The value of crowdsourcing: can users really compete with professionals in generating new product ideas? *Journal of Product Innovation Management*, *29*(2), 245–56.

Porter, M. E. (1985). *Competitive Advantage: Creating and Sustaining Superior Performance*. New York: Free Press.

Rumelt, R. P., Schendel, D., & Teece, D. J. (1991). Strategic management and economics. *Strategic Management Journal*, *12*(S2), 5–29.

Sanchez, R. & Mahoney, J. T. (1996). Modularity, flexibility, and knowledge management in product and organization design. *Strategic Management Journal*, *17*(S2), 63–76.

Schilling, M. A. (2000). Toward a general modular systems theory and its application to interfirm product modularity. *Academy of Management Review*, *25*(2), 312–34.

Schrader, S. (1991). Informal technology transfer between firms: Cooperation through information trading. *Research Policy*, *20*(2), 153–70.

Stabell, C. B. & Fjeldstad, Ø. D. (1998). Configuring value for competitive advantage: On chains, shops, and networks. *Strategic Management Journal, 19*, 413–37.

Surowiecki, J. (2005). *The Wisdom of Crowds*. New York: Anchor Books.

Tapscott, D. & Williams, A. D. (2006). *Wikinomics: How Mass Collaboration Changes Everything*. New York: Penguin Books.

Terwiesch, C. & Ulrich, K. T. (2009). *Innovation Tournaments: Creating and Selecting Exceptional Opportunities*. Boston, MA: Harvard Business Press.

Terwiesch, C. & Xu, Y. (2008). Innovation contests, open innovation, and multiagent problem solving. *Management Science, 54*(9), 1529–43.

Tischler, L. (2002). He struck gold on the net (really). *Fast Company*, https://www.fastcompany.com/44917/he-struck-gold-net-really (accessed October 29, 2017).

Williamson, O. E. (1985). *The Economic Intstitutions of Capitalism*. New York: Simon and Schuster.

Zenger, T. R., Felin, T., & Bigelow, L. (2011). Theories of the firm–market boundary. *Academy of Management Annals, 5*(1), 89–133.

12

Prediction Markets for Crowdsourcing

Christian Horn, Marcel Bogers, and Alexander Brem

Abstract
Crowdsourcing is an increasingly important phenomenon that is fundamentally changing how companies create and capture value. There are still important questions with respect to how crowdsourcing works and can be applied in practice, especially in business practice. In this chapter, we focus on prediction markets as a mechanism and tool to tap into a crowd in the early stages of an innovation process. In line with the growing interest in open innovation, we also investigate the difference between using internal or external sources in the context of prediction markets. We apply one example of a prediction market, a virtual stock market, to open innovation through an online platform, and show that using mechanisms of internal crowdsourcing with prediction markets can outperform the use of external crowds under certain conditions.

INTRODUCTION

Crowdsourcing is becoming an increasingly important mechanism for creating and capturing value by tapping into external sources of knowledge (Afuah & Tucci, 2012, 2013; Afuah, 2018b). Originally coined by Howe (2006), the term "crowdsourcing" describes the act of outsourcing a function once performed by employees to an undefined and generally large network of people in the form of an open call—mostly published on the Internet. The act of opening up to external knowledge sources is also in line with the growing interest in open innovation (Bogers et al., 2017; Chesbrough et al., 2006; Dahlander & Gann, 2010). Open innovation can be defined as "a distributed innovation process based on purposively managed knowledge flows across organizational boundaries, using pecuniary and non-pecuniary mechanisms in line with the organization's business model" (Chesbrough & Bogers, 2014, p. 17). Indeed, the growing base of evidence on how to leverage external sources of innovation has identified a variety of mechanisms, that allow organizations to obtain knowledge from the outside (West & Bogers, 2014). As one such mechanism, crowdsourcing specifically describes how to leverage the knowledge of large groups of external people ("crowds") to thereby accelerate the internal value creation and capture processes. Recent evidence has accordingly shown that crowdsourcing can indeed be beneficial under certain circumstances (Jeppesen & Lakhani, 2010; Poetz & Schreier, 2012).

Along with the growing interest in crowdsourcing, the complexity of the phenomenon is also becoming more apparent. For example, Afuah & Tucci (2012), who defined crowdsourcing as "the act of outsourcing a task to a 'crowd' rather than to a designated 'agent' [...] in the form of an open call" (p. 355), distinguish two types of crowdsourcing. First, "tournament-based crowdsourcing" describes how the crowd self-selects how to work on a problem, with the best solution winning some type of reward. Second, "collaboration-based crowdsourcing" describes how certain members of the crowd work together to offer a solution to a certain problem. Besides, Poetz & Schreier (2012) show that outsourcing idea generation to a crowd of users generates ideas that score significantly higher (compared to professionals generating similar ideas) in terms of novelty and customer benefit, but that they score lower in terms of feasibility. Jeppesen & Lakhani (2010), moreover, showed that the marginality of the problem solver (being further away from the problem domain) increased problem-solving effectiveness in broadcast search.

In this chapter, we address a particular mechanism to implement crowdsourcing in an organization, namely the use of prediction markets. Prediction markets can be seen as an information technology (IT) resource that can act as a platform to conduct crowdsourcing with the particular aim of forecasting the outcome of certain organization processes. We build on evidence that prediction markets are useful in predicting the outcome of, for example, political events (Berg et al., 2008, Forsythe et al., 1992) or sports results (Servan-Schreiber et al., 2004). At the same time, prediction markets are also gaining some interest in the context of strategic management and new product development (Matzler et al., 2013; Stieger et al., 2012).

In the remainder of this chapter, we will specifically describe how prediction markets can be used to tap into the crowd in the early stages of the innovation process, especially in the idea evaluation phase and for market forecasting. We will develop a framework that considers different attributes of prediction markets to show under what conditions prediction markets with the crowd will outperform those with internal professionals. Given that prediction markets, like any crowdsourcing tool, require the organization to invest resources and attention to facilitate the process, these findings have important implications not only for how to create value from crowdsourcing but also how to efficiently capture that value through prediction markets.

CROWDSOURCING FOR KNOWLEDGE IN
INNOVATION MANAGEMENT

In his book *The Wisdom of Crowds*, Surowiecki (2005) gave popular examples of how users can be employed in tasks that are useful for an organization with popular applications such as "the mechanical Turk," where tasks are fulfilled solely by agents recruited online. In their study on innovation management, Poetz & Schreier (2012) show that crowdsourcing can be a useful concept in the first few stages of new product development, specifically in the generation of good new product ideas. Especially idea contests seem to be a domain of crowdsourcing with external stakeholders (Leimeister et al., 2009). Leimeister et al. (2009) also test their concept with the help of lead users and see them as most valuable informants in the idea generation process (see Bogers et al., 2010 and von Hippel, 2005 for an overview of these arguments). Others have shown that in the early stages of the innovation process, especially in the idea creation and evaluation phase, crowdsourcing with the help of prediction markets can be a powerful tool (Chen & Plott, 2002; Soukhoroukova et al., 2012; Stieger et al., 2012; Cowgill & Zitzewitz, 2014). For marketing planning and innovation management, we go one step ahead of using merely internal resources of crowdsourcing for innovation management support.

The main idea of this chapter is to describe how to use "the crowd" to solve the problem of forecasting future market conditions and product success values efficiently in the very early stages of the innovation process. Many authors postulate that new product development is a domain for experts, such as professionals from marketing, marketing research, or product management (Ulrich, 2007; Ulrich & Eppinger, 2008). Schulze & Hoegl conclude that by "relying on the method of asking buyers to describe potential future products, big leaps to novel product ideas are generally not likely" (Schulze & Hoegl, 2008: 1744). In other contexts, it has been shown that high levels of self-explicated or ascribed profession in a certain field of research do not necessarily result in better solutions of certain problems. Jeppesen & Lakhani (2010) show, for instance, that keeping more distance from the field where experts are seen as experts positively influences the capabilities of individuals to solve complex problems in many different areas of scientific research. For example, a biologist is more likely to solve a complex problem in chemistry than a researcher with his main domain in chemistry research (Jeppesen & Lakhani, 2010). Although employees in companies are seen as experts in their fields, the crowd may help to manage forecasting in innovation management more efficiently than the persons that have been in an expert role before.

While other prediction market systems in companies only use internal "crowd" sources, it will be described how crowdsourcing allows a company to integrate "the crowd" besides experts or lead users from outside and uses their knowledge, as Poetz & Schreier (2012) postulate in their publications about crowdsourcing with users and consumers. Forecasts generated by these groups can be more efficient than forecasts with experts from within the company. Afuah & Tucci postulate that crowdsourcing is likely to be used by organizations when five requirements are fulfilled: (*1*) *the problem is easy to delineate and broadcast to the crowd*; (*2*) *the final solution is easy to evaluate and integrate into the focal agent's value chain*; *and* (*3*) *information technologies are low cost and pervasive in the environment that includes the focal agent and the crowd*, (*4*) *the knowledge required to solve the problem falls outside the focal agent's knowledge neighborhood* (*requires distant search*); *and* (*5*) *the crowd is large, with some members of the crowd motivated and knowledgeable enough to solve the problem* (Afuah & Tucci, 2012).

In applying these requirements to prediction markets, most of them fit with our prediction market framework: Requirement (1) can be met by prediction markets, as innovation process questions can usually be translated into virtual stock questions. They can be easy to understand (Christiansen, 2007) and the results of crowdsourcing with prediction markets can be easily integrated into the innovation process (requirement 2). Companies like Ford are using prediction markets exactly for this reason, to integrate the employees into their internal idea evaluation processes. Already in 2011 the company integrated 1,300 employees to real-time shift in production planning successfully. Later the usage was shifted to forecast future consumer and market trends. Several applications of prediction markets and a framework for the technical application of prediction markets (e.g. Soukhoroukova et al. (2012) show that requirement (3) can be satisfied. With the help of the crowd, complex tasks and forecasting problems can be solved. In the innovation process, experts such as managers and industry members are traditionally seen as persons from a knowledge neighborhood of innovation-related forecasting tasks. Those persons are usually seen as having all the necessary capabilities to be better in problem solving for innovation-related forecasting. Following Afuah & Tucci, using the knowledge neighborhood of the crowd, which can be anonymously required via the Internet for a prediction market, would produce more efficient results (requirement 4).

Thus, we try to use prediction markets, not only with experts, but we integrate "the crowd" into prediction markets instead of employees and compare the results with internal experts markets. With our configuration of prediction markets, we want to combine the principles of crowdsourcing with prediction market principles that are described in the following.

PREDICTION MARKETS AND CROWDSOURCING

Foundations for the use of prediction markets were laid by Hayek (1945) and Fama (1970). With the help of the market price, knowledge that lies dispersed among informants and evaluations of an uncertain future outcome can be organized and reflected by one number—the market price of a (virtual) asset. The market price can, for example, represent the price for an actual good, or prices can reflect expectations about an uncertain event, such as product success or the market entry of a competitor.

One basic concept that underpins the information aggregation mechanisms of markets in general and also prediction markets is the theory of marginal traders. Marginal traders on all kinds of markets have a high(er) knowledge about the problem and influence the market price through their transactions ino the "right" direction (McManus & Blackwell, 2011; Berg et al., 2008). In contrast, a usually larger number of "noise traders" with little knowledge are active on the same markets, too, e.g. towards the right forecasting of the later sales success of a certain product. It is necessary to have an asymmetric distribution of "good" knowledge in order to keep the markets liquid; noise traders will sell goods or virtual stocks on markets that are rational for them, but this gives them a disadvantage compared to better-informed marginal traders. For example, noise traders are willing to sell contracts on the prediction market although, with higher expertise or better information, it wouldn't be rational to sell. As an example, trading contracts about the success of new products, those traders with less information about the target groups' taste and needs will be willing to sell e.g. virtual stocks on products that would be successful later. Thus, marginal trades can buy these contracts for a lower price and through this be more successful in the long run. With their success, they accumulate virtual capital and can, in many market environments, have more influence on the virtual market outcome because they can leverage their opinion better with virtual capital.

Prediction markets have been extensively and successfully used for the forecasting of political events, such as presidential or gubernatorial elections (Forsythe et al., 1992; Berg et al., 2008; Hanson, 2006), macroeconomic contexts (Gürkaynak & Wolfers, 2005), or forecasting sports results (Rosenbloom & Notz, 2006; Servan-Schreiber et al., 2004).

There is a rising number of prediction markets publications in academic research, also for use in companies. Snowberg et al. (2012) gave an overview of numerous possible uses in economic forecasting, such as macroeconomic measures. Rieg and Schoder (2011) mention Google, Deutsche Lufthansa, or Eli Lily as examples of companies that make creative use of internal prediction markets for forecasting, e.g. in logistics or in financial markets.

Table 12.1 shows an overview of scientific publications about prediction markets in business use. A comprehensive synopsis and classification of publications about prediction markets can be found in the *Journal of Prediction Markets* (Horn et al., 2014).

Yet we still see a lack of empirical evidence of usage in the innovation process, especially with the involvement of customers as "the crowd."

Table 12.1. Prediction markets for business use.

Company	Duration	Traders involved	Further information	Questions in the field of...
Adidas	1 hour (this analysis)/ 1 month	24 employees 14–20 customers	This chapter	Demand forecasting, assesment of product concepts, external events
Carl Zeiss	36 days	Employees	Soukhoroukova et al. (2012)	Idea sourcing and filtering
Ford	Several days	902 selected employees	Cowgill & Zitzewitz (2014)	Auto demand forecasting
General Electric	22 days	Employees	LaComb et al. (2007)	Technology assessment
Google	Up to >2.5 years	1,465 employees	Cowgill & Zitzewitz (2014)	Project success, demand forecasting
Hewlett Packard	7 days	Employees	Chen & Plott (2002)	Sales figures
Siemens Basic materials company	3 months >5 years (analysis for 15 days)	Employees 57 employees	Ortner (1998) Cowgill & Zitzewitz (2014)	Project management Commodity prices, political outcomes
Technology company	1 hour/36 days	Employees/ customers	Soukhoroukova et al., (2007)	Technology assessment
Communications company	n/a	Employees	Spann & Skiera . (2003)	Sales figures
Finance company	22 days	Employees	Van Bruggen et al. (2010)	Sales figures
movie industry	1 month	public	Spann et al. (2009)	Lead user identification

Note: Based on Horn and Ivens (2014).

Although the number of publications has increased in the last few years, Graefe's statement (2011) about prediction markets used in companies, that there are very few publications that were written with actual company data, is still true. Data that are used for empirical studies are often generated by experimental setups instead of real-world conditions. Horn et al. (2014) show a comprehensive synopsis about prediction markets research streams which underlines this statement.

So far, there have mainly been four steps where prediction markets have been seen as possibilities for helping companies to innovate (Dahan & Hauser, 2002): idea generation and screening, building product concepts and testing them, product testing, and product launch. The steps can be specified as pre-launch phases and post-launch phases. The first two phases face problems associated with the development and evaluation of ideas, the product testing phase deals with product alternatives. Ortner (1998) shows prediction markets inside the Siemens company to forecast project deadlines. LaComb et al. (2007) use prediction markets at General Electric, Soukhoroukova et al. (2012) establish prediction markets in the early stages of the innovation process. The last phase where prediction markets can support the innovation process is the forecasting of sales figures before (Skiera & Spann, 2011) and continuous sales forecasting after the launch as part of the marketing planning information system. In our case, we focus on product and concept evaluation and forecasting tasks in the early stages of the innovation process. Matzler et al. (2013) showed that forecasting can be successfully done with prediction markets in that stage. Chen and Plott (2002) had shown previously how HP used prediction markets to forecast printer sales successfully.

EMPIRICAL ANALYSIS: CASE AND METHODOLOGY

Prediction markets have mainly been used by companies to integrate informants from inside the company. But how prediction markets can be used successfully for real "crowd"-sourcing to support the innovation process is a field to be discussed too. For empirical investigation we concentrated on Adidas, the international sporting goods and fashion company.

With their main brand, "Adidas Sports Performance" and other popular brands such as "Reebok" or "Taylormade," their worldwide turnover in more than 60 countries was 19.3 billion Euro in 2016. In our study, we found that 100 percent of the crowd members were aware of the brand "Adidas" by a questionnaire after participation in the prediction market. Adidas has more than 60,000 employees, 10 percent of the employees worked in marketing or research and development functions. The studies took place at their Germany-based company headquarters.

Adidas has implemented forecasting systems and as in most consumer markets, the reduction of flop rates of new products is still a major goal. The task was to establish an innovation supporting system that helps to improve the existing and well-established innovation management, strategic marketing planning, and product management tools. Information about other operand resources is not the subject of this article; we focus on the use of prediction markets.

First, the test environments will be outlined. After that, the results will be presented and discussed.

Empirical Studies

In the following, the four studies that were conducted to test the performance of prediction markets are described. Data collection procedure 1 (Market

Table 12.2. Prediction market designs.

Market type	Internal experts (market setup 1)	The crowd (market setup 2)
Trading time	1 hour	
Recruitment	Invitation via email with login data, encouraged by management.	Invitation via email with login data to students from graduate/ undergraduate courses.
Number of stocks	12 virtual stocks	
Demand outcome scenarios	Value of stock for certain product feature, market share totals, sales volumes, sales prices.	
Design market parameters	Double auction mechanisms and simple betting mechanisms (for €/$ rate). The initial capital for each player was 500 virtual $ and the initial shares of each product were put into participants' depots.	
Market outcomes	Stock prices at market closing.	
Participants' earnings	Lottery with higher winning probabilities for participants with the highest virtual portfolio values.	
Encouragement of active trading	Encouraged by management. Employees got free time hours to take part. A ranking showed the traders with the highest portfolio value.	A ranking showed the traders with the highest portfolio value. A lottery system with small incentives was established.

setup 1) produced the initial data and was performed with internal experts from the company. Market setup 2 integrated groups of customers instead of internal experts; two of the approaches that are described in Šundić & Leitners' (2018) chapter in this book (see Table 12.2).

Market setup 1: Internal corporate prediction markets. In the first study, stock markets were set up to be run with Adidas employees as traders. As described above, internal markets in companies have been tested and used for different purposes. In our design, we followed the design criteria for the application of virtual markets by Soukhoroukova et al. (2012).

The virtual stocks in the prediction markets represented questions that were important for the innovation process of the partnering company. Numerical values of the stock prices represented values such as *sales prices*, *sales volumes*, or other numerical values that could clearly be assigned to the values in question. For example, a stock value of "5" represented an estimated sales number of 5,000 units in a specific sales period. In other cases the optimum sales price for a polo shirt was represented by a virtual stock market price of 75,89 €. This design also follows Matzler et al. (2013). Stock prices at the end of the trading time were taken as final forecasting values.

Prediction market topics. Each trading group was confronted with the following forecasting questions: (1) *How much additional earnings can be made with additional product feature Z?* (Z = one other sports shirt); (2) *What would be the ideal sales price for product X?* (X = four different sports shirts); (3) *What will be the sales volumes for products Y?* (Y = five other different sports shirts); (4) *What will be the sales volumes for product X?* We also asked (5) *What will be the euro-dollar exchange rate on day T?* (T = date in future, after closing the trading phase). Additionally, we asked other questions which are not relevant for this analysis, such as the prediction of popular sports results in order to motivate the participants in all groups. For reasons of confidentiality, product names and absolute figures had to be changed, but numbers do reflect the correct relations. In total, the participants could trade on 12 different topics.

Starting the markets and trading phase. The markets were initiated by the provision of a certain amount of resources to each market player. Both groups traded the virtual stocks with virtual play money. The play money was issued by placing 500 virtual dollars and an initial amount of virtual stocks in each player's depot. Thus, each player could begin buying or selling stocks to maximize their own personal portfolio value. Also, using play money avoids regulatory risks that can arise from a gambling character in the markets in the case where real money with a chance to win or lose for the participants has been used. Also, the perceived risk of the market participants stays lower.

The transactions were matched by continuous double auctions or betting market mechanisms. Participants can place buy and sell orders that are executed immediately, with corresponding orders on the other side of the order book (Madhavan, 1992). Orders with no matching bids are cued in an order book and executed as soon as a matching order is sent. The 12 markets were set up simultaneously for two groups of ten and seven active traders. Each group had their own market environment and was not able to interact with persons from the other group on the markets. Research has shown that this number of persons can result in efficient markets (Borison & Hamm, 2010). Forty-nine persons were invited for each market (average age 31.3 years), 27 signed in and placed orders, but only those persons with at least three transactions were considered as active traders. Orders which were not executed on the virtual markets because they didn't match other orders were not taken into consideration. During the firm-internal markets, 254 transactions were performed in total, 15 per person on average. With this market, we generated benchmark data from 24 prediction markets to compare this data to the forecasting accuracy set up by the crowd.

Each participant was invited via a personal email address and the login data was provided before the trading phase. The motivation of the trading persons is an important topic in prediction markets. As the equilibrium price changes with each transaction, a minimum number of transactions are needed and more transactions can improve the quality of outcome (Berg et al., 2008). Intrinsic motives can result in higher trading volumes for company internal agents, as well as for the crowd. Fun on the "game" as well as the need to help in completing the task and in solving the question can be motives for intrinsic motivation (Kapp, 2012; Borison & Hamm, 2010). To motivate the participants in all of the markets and stimulate them to actively participate in the markets, incentives in the form of *Amazon.com gift cards*, ranging from 10 to 100 Euro, were distributed among trades with the best results and in a lottery. This form of motivation represents a competitive component and the setup is a form of competitive crowdsourcing or tournament-based crowdsourcing. In tournament-based crowdsourcing, a task is set up and only the best solution(s) can win the prize(s) for completing the task (Afuah 2018a, b). In our setup, each trader had the chance to win one of the 40 gift cards in each trading environment, but the better the portfolio values were, the higher was the probability of winning one of the incentives. In each scenario, the participants could win the same amount of prizes. The trading activity resulted in 254 transactions on the markets during the one-hour trading time and produced results for 23 of the 24 forecasting scenarios among the 12 topics. For one market, the number of transactions was too small, thus it was not analyzed. The trading platform included a profile section, a portfolio overview section, and a high score ranking list to inform traders about their success in the markets. The traders were asked not to interact with each other aside from the market platform.

Market setup 2: The crowd. In this data collection period, the setup of study three was taken over with small, but relevant modification. Five groups from 14 to 20 persons (mainly students from graduate and undergraduate courses) were tested in our markets in contrast with the internal experts. The group of students was not seen as experts in sporting goods and apparel, as they were drawn randomly from several classes and distributed amongst the trading groups. Following West & Sims' (2018) chapter, the participants formed a crowd, not a community, as they were self-selected and randomly drawn to one of the groups and there were no traces that they shared a common goal or collaborated to perform the tasks. The distribution of age and gender of the participants also form the Adidas professionals (average age 24.5 years, $\sigma = 2.47$). In this study, all tests took place at the computer science lab at the university campus. The groups did not trade on all markets in order not to have too many open questions within the one hour trading time. Other conditions were kept *ceteris paribus*. The results that are shown are parts of a larger series of prediction market research activities in real business environments as well as under controlled conditions. Other aspects such as more detailed market designs and empirical results can be found in Horn (2015) and Horn and Ivens (2014).

Evaluating the prediction markets. All of the stock questions addressed innovation-related topics that could not be known at the time of running of the markets, and would only be assessed empirically after market closing to create benchmarks for later evaluations of the accuracy of the answers and to calculate prediction errors. The mean absolute prediction error (MAPE) is calculated for every scenario to calculate errors, because MAPE is commonly used to assess prediction markets (Skiera & Spann, 2011), or as a general performance measure in business and economics forecasts (Russel & Adam Jr, 1987; Armstrong & Collopy, 1992). It is unit-free and measures the deviation between the benchmark values and the values of the markets' closing prices. Specifically, it is calculated using the following equation:

$$\text{MAPE} = \frac{1}{|S|} \sum_{s=1}^{S} \left| \left(\frac{P_{s,t} - B_s}{B_S} \right) \right|, \tag{12.1}$$

where
S = the number of different observations in trading group n;
B = the value of the benchmark of the sth stock;
P = the price of the sth stock in the market at time point t;
t = the closing time of the market.

To interpret the value of the MAPE, it can be considered that the smaller it is, the smaller the deviation of the market outcomes compared to the benchmark value, and thus the better the accuracy of the market. We compare the performance of the different types of market designs to the real-life market outcomes as benchmarks. The company provided the realized, actual market data after the experiments and the forecast events. Those were, for example, after several months, the sales figures or the market share of the products that were traded in the virtual markets. According to interviews with managers by the partner company, 10 percent errors are excellent forecasts, and 20 percent are still very good results in this industry, as seasonal changes and fast fashion trends challenge all forecasting methods. Matzler et al. (2013) find an average Mean Absolute Error of 2.74 percent to 9.09 percent in their study on forecasting and use a similar method to present their results. The differences in the absolute values and means are commonly used to present forecasting errors, as do Matzler et al. (2013) in their study.

Table 12.3 reports the MAPEs of the different market design setups (columns) and for each of the innovation-related questions (rows) that were investigated. The first virtual stock type in the table is "Specific product features." This question represents the valuation of the market for certain product features to be helpful for later market success. The second virtual stock shows the MAPE for the market outcomes of the evaluation of the later market share for a certain range of products. The other virtual stocks follow the same scheme.

Table 12.3. Mean absolute prediction error (MAPE) results from the markets.

Virtual stock	Market design 1	Market design 2
Specific product features	0.490	0.418
Market share product 1	0.499	0.872
*Market share product 2**	5.15	9.06
*Market share product 3**	3.10	1.37
Market share product 4	0.120	0.250
Market share product 5	0.093	0.762
Price product 6	0.014	0.042
Price product 7	0.064	0.073
Price product 8	0.076	0.108
Price product 9	0.092	0.241
Price product 10	0.093	0.191
Future Euro/Dollar exchange rate	0.109	0.030
Total MAPE	**0.165**	**0.299**
Total *MAPE with all stocks**	**0.82**	**1.12**

* "Market share product 2" and "Market share product 3" represented the only two products/markets from non-domestic markets for the participants. They are shown in the table to give an overview over the complete data set but are not taken into consideration for the analysis of the data and conclusions.

CONCLUSIONS AND FUTURE RESEARCH

The results suggest that a crowd can produce valuable results in forecasting innovation-related questions effectively. The groups, the non-experts crowd as well as the internal markets with Adidas experts, demonstrate that forecasting market success in innovation management can be done by internal experts as well as with the help of external sources of knowledge. This demonstrates that the crowd is capable of producing valuable results in the tested innovation tasks with this market setup. As postulated by Afuah (2018b) and discussed by Šundić & Leitner (2018), the knowledge from non-expert persons can also be a valuable resource of knowledge in the innovation process and in crowdsourcing especially. Thus, it not only makes sense to involve non-experts, but in specific circumstances their evaluations even outperform expert opinions.

Taking a closer look at the results, they show that the internal experts perform much better in the innovation management tasks than the external, non-expert participants. It turns out that non-experts can be useful sources, but are outperformed by internal experts under *ceteris paribus* conditions with the use of prediction markets. As such, our findings contribute to the larger domain of open innovation in which it has become clear that companies increasingly need to rely on external sources of innovation to accelerate their innovation processes (Chesbrough, 2006; Chesbrough & Bogers, 2014;

West & Bogers, 2014). We thus show that crowdsourcing in general and the use of prediction markets in particular can be a powerful resource in implementing open innovation.

In the area of crowdsourcing, there are still important aspects to be investigated in future research. The empirical analysis was performed on consumer products, as seen in Matzler et al. (2013) or Spann and Skiera (2003). Replication studies in other industries could suggest limitations in the ability of firms to employ virtual markets for solving difficult business decisions with the help of the crowd. Although we did not externally test the participants on their knowledge about the topics that were addressed in the prediction markets, it should be noted that only the information that exists within the marginal traders' minds can be gathered by the markets. Thus, for lesser known products, such as industrial goods or other business-to-business markets, results may look different. It is true that all of the participant traders in our studies were knowledgeable about the products traded. As a consequence, similar study designs may produce different results for samples of crowds who are asked to trade stock for products they are less familiar with. However, the fact that participants do not need to be high-level experts in the field produces opportunities for the use of prediction markets in many contexts. Prediction markets in panel-like setups for business forecasting, especially with employees, are still under-researched and could potentially offer a large field of contributions for scholars and a high practical use. However, it is necessary to spend some time finding the right target group for the internal market, as recent research on differences has shown, e.g. in the individual degree of risk aversion of the persons trading (Boulu-Reshef et al., 2016).

Over decades, scholars as well as practitioners have made tremendous efforts to develop instruments that allow the prediction of future developments in markets to improve the innovation process. This is also true for the field of new product development at the intersection between marketing and innovation management (Brem et al., 2011). Crossing different domains may also help in developing new tools and frameworks to enable cross-fertilization of knowledge within and between organizations (Bogers & Horst, 2014), which may also become applicable outside of the traditional corporate setting (e.g. Eftekhari & Bogers, 2015).

The results show that design variables for prediction markets that have been discussed in other contributions are relevant for our use, too (Christiansen, 2007; Borison & Hamm, 2010). The level of expertise and knowledge is one of the relevant design variables. For managers, it may be concluded that prediction markets—if designed carefully with regard to the latest scholarly knowledge—can be effective tools for providing important insights with respect to key questions in the innovation process. The selection of the right kinds of "experts" is still a key design element for successfully applying crowdsourcing with prediction markets.

When designing prediction markets, firms need to decide whether to use customers as informants, or their own employees, or other stakeholder groups. As discussed, the alternatives differ with respect to costs of setup and incentives that are required to motivate participation. Additionally, in many cases, confidentiality may be required in order to prevent competitors from learning about development projects too early. Confidentiality and ease of implementation would be two main arguments in favor of employees participating. On the other hand, the participation of employees does not necessarily yield better insights into future market developments when compared with the use of other stakeholder groups, as the outcomes depend on the level of expertise. This means that prediction markets can help to gather information and support the innovation process without employees spending time on related tasks. They can be implemented as an alternative tool for conducting market research with current and potential customers. On the other hand, prediction markets do not yield less valuable insights into market phenomena as compared with answers gleaned from customers. Given the traditional argument in marketing that firms should conduct market research among customers in order to understand customer value expectations and needs, this is an interesting result and worthy of further work in the area. It allows questioning whether customers are truly required as reference points for new product development in all situations. Rather, it seems that firm employees' "myopia" may not be as strong as sometimes suggested. It is likely that firms should mix different sources of information when attempting to understand market developments via crowdsourcing.

ACKNOWLEDGMENTS

The authors would like to thank Björn Sven Ivens from the Department of Marketing at Otto-Friedrich-University of Bamberg for his valuable support and comments. We are also grateful for the support we received from the editors of this volume and for the comments that we received from the participants of the "Crowd" volume workshop in Lausanne, Switzerland on November 27, 2015.

REFERENCES

Afuah, A. (2018a). Co-opetition in crowdsourcing: When simultaneous cooperation and competition deliver superior solutions. In C. Tucci, A. Afuah, & G. Viscusi (eds.), *Creating and Capturing Value Through Crowdsourcing*. Oxford: Oxford University Press, pp. 271–91.

Afuah, A. (2018b). Crowdsourcing: A primer and research framework. In C. Tucci, A. Afuah, & G. Viscusi (eds.), *Creating and Capturing Value Through Crowdsourcing.* Oxford: Oxford University Press, pp. 11–38.

Afuah, A. & Tucci, C. (2012). Crowdsourcing as a solution to distant search. *Academy of Management Review*, 37(3), 355–75.

Afuah, A. & Tucci, C. L. (2013). Value capture & crowdsourcing. *Academy of Management Review*, 38(3), 457–60.

Armstrong, S. J. & Collopy, F. (1992). Error measures for generalizing about forecasting methods: Empirical comparisons. *International Journal of Forecasting*, 8, 69–80.

Berg, J. E., Forsythe, R., Nelson, F., & Rietz, T. A. (2008). Results from a dozen years of election futures market research, in Plott C. R. & Smith V. (eds.). *Handbook of Experimental Economic Results.* Amsterdam: Elsevier Science.

Bogers, M., Afuah, A., & Bastian, B. (2010). Users as innovators: A review, critique, and future research directions. *Journal of Management*, 36(4), 857–75.

Bogers, M. & Horst, W. (2014). Collaborative prototyping: Cross-fertilization of knowledge in prototype-driven problem solving. *Journal of Product Innovation Management*, 31(4), 744–64.

Bogers, M., Zobel, A.-K., Afuah, A., Almirall, E., Brunswicker, S., Dahlander, L., Frederiksen, L., Gawer, A., Gruber, M., Haefliger, S., Hagedoorn, J., Hilgers, D., Laursen, K., Magnusson, M. G., Majchrzak, A., McCarthy, I. P., Moeslein, K. M., Nambisan, S., Piller, F. T., Radziwon, A., Rossi-Lamastra, C., Sims, J., & Ter Wal, A. L. J. (2017). The open innovation research landscape: Established perspectives and emerging themes across different levels of analysis. *Industry and Innovation*, 24(1), 8–40.

Borison, A. & Hamm, G. (2010). Prediction markets: A new tool for strategic decision making. *California Management Review*, 52(4), 125–41.

Boulu-Reshef, B., Comeig, I., Donze, R., & Weiss, G. (2016). Risk aversion in prediction markets: A framed-field experiment. *Journal of Business Research*, 69(11), 5071–5.

Brem, A., Sherif, H., Katzenstein, L., Voigt, K.-I., & Lammer, D. (2011). R&D, innovation and marketing—Strategies for internal and external communication of technological innovations, in M. Hülsmann & N. Pfeffermann (eds.). *Strategies and Communications for Innovations.* Heidelberg: Springer, pp. 193–208.

Chen, K. -Y. & Plott, C. R. (2002). Information aggregation mechanisms: Concept, design and implementation for a sales forecasting problem. *Working Paper No. 1131*, California Institute of Technology, Pasadena.

Chesbrough, H. (2006). Open innovation: A new paradigm for understanding industrial innovation, in H. Chesbrough, W. Vanhaverbeke, & J. West (eds.). *Open Innovation: Researching a New Paradigm.* Oxford: Oxford University Press, pp. 1–12.

Chesbrough, H. & Bogers, M. (2014). Explicating open innovation: Clarifying an emerging paradigm for understanding innovation, in H. Chesbrough, W. Vanhaverbeke, & J. West (eds.). *New Frontiers in Open Innovation.* Oxford: Oxford University Press, pp. 3–28.

Chesbrough, H., Vanhaverbeke, W., & West, J. (eds.) (2006). *Open Innovation: Researching a New Paradigm.* Oxford: Oxford University Press.

Christiansen, J. D. (2007). Prediction markets: Practical experiments in small markets and behaviours observed. *The Journal of Prediction Markets*, 1(1), 17–41.

Cowgill, B. & Zitzewitz, E. (2014). Corporate prediction markets: Evidence from Google, Ford, and Firm X. *The Reviews of Economic Studies*, *82*(4), 1309–41.

Dahan, E. & Hauser, J. R. (2002). The virtual customer. *Journal of Product Innovation Management*, *19*(5), 332–53.

Dahlander, L. & Gann, D. M. (2010). How open is innovation? *Research Policy*, *39*(6), 699–709.

Eftekhari, N. & Bogers, M. (2015). Open for entrepreneurship: How open innovation can foster new venture creation. *Creativity and Innovation Management*, *24*(4), 574–84.

Fama, E. F. (1970). Efficient capital markets: A review of theory and empirical work. *Journal of Finance*, *25*(2), 383–417.

Forsythe, R., Nelson, F., Neumann G. R., & Wright J. (1992). Anatomy of an experimental political stock market. *The American Economic Review*, *82*(5), 1142–61.

Graefe, A. (2011). Prediction market accuracy for business forecasting, in Vaughan Williams (ed.). *Prediction Markets*. New York: Routledge, pp. 87–95.

Gürkaynak, R. & Wolfers, J. (2005). Macroeconomic derivatives: An initial analysis of market-based macro forecasts, uncertainty, and risk. *IZA Discussion Papers 1899*, Institute for the Study of Labor (IZA), Bonn, Germany.

Hanson, R. (2006). Designing real terrorism futures. *Public Choice*, *128*(1–2), 257–74.

Hayek, F. A. (1945). The use of knowledge in society. *American Economic Review*, *35*(4), 520–30.

Horn, C. F. (2015). *Prediction Markets in der betriebswirtschaftlichen Anwendung. Eine empirische Analyse*. Lehrstuhl für Marketing. Dissertation. Universität Bamberg.

Horn, C. F. & Ivens, B. S. (2014). Corporate prediction markets for innovation management – Theoretical foundations and practical examples for business use, in A. Brem & E. Viardot (eds.). *Adoption of Innovation—Balancing Internal and External Stakeholders in the Marketing of Innovation*. Cham, Switzerland: Springer International Publishing.

Horn, C. F., Ohneberg, M., Ivens, B. S., & Brem, A. (2014). Prediction markets—a literature review 2014. *Journal of Prediction Markets*, *8*(2), 89–126.

Howe, J. (2006). The rise of Crowdsourcing. *Wired*, (14/6), http://archive.wired.com/wired/archive/14.06/crowds.html (accessed September 2014).

Jeppesen, L. B. & Lakhani, K. R. (2010). Marginality and problem solving effectiveness in broadcast search. *Organization Science*, *21*(5), 1016–33.

Kapp, K. M. (2012). *The Gamification of Training: Game-Based Methods and Strategies for Learning and Instruction*. San Francisco: Pfeiffer & Co., John Wiley & Sons.

LaComb, C. A., Barnett, J. A., & Pan, Q. (2007). The imagination market. *Information Systems Frontiers*, *9*(2–3), 245–56.

Leimeister, J. M., Huber, M., Bretschneider, U., & Krcmar, H. (2009). Leveraging crowdsourcing: Activation-supporting components for IT-based ideas competition. *Journal of Management Information Systems*, *26*(1), 197–224.

Madhavan, A. (1992). Trading mechanisms in securities markets. *Journal of Finance*, *47*, 607–41.

Matzler, K., Grabher, C., Huber, J., & Fuller, J. (2013). Predicting new product success with prediction markets in online communities. *R&D Management*, *43*(5), 420–32.

McManus, T. C. & Blackwell, C. (2011). An exploration of market efficiency and the marginal trader hypothesis. *Undergraduate Economic Review*, *7*(1), 9.

Ortner, G. (1998). Forecasting markets—An industrial application. *Mimeo*. Technical University of Vienna.

Poetz, M. & Schreier, M. (2012). The value of crowdsourcing: can users really compete with professionals in generating new product ideas? *Journal of Product Innovation Management*, 29(2), 245–56.

Rieg, R. & Schoder, R. (2011). Corporate prediction markets: Pitfalls and barriers. *Foresight: The International Journal of Applied Forecasting*, 21, 35–40.

Rosenbloom, E. & Notz, W. (2006). Statistical tests of real-money vs. play-money prediction markets. *Electronic Markets*, 16(2), 63–9.

Russel, T. D. & Adam, E. E. (1987). An empirical evaluation of alternative forecasting combinations. *Management Science*, 33(10), 1267–76.

Schulze, A. & Hoegl, M. (2008). Organizational knowledge creation and the generation of new product ideas: A behavioral approach. *Research Policy*, 37(10), 1742–50.

Servan-Schreiber, E. Wolfers, J., Pennock, D., & Galebach, B. (2004). Prediction markets: Does money matter? *Electronic Markets*, 14(3), 243–51.

Skiera, B. & Spann, M. (2011). Using prediction markets in new product development, in L. Vaughan Williams (ed.). *Prediction Markets: Theory and Applications*. London: Routledge, pp. 75–86.

Snowberg, E., Wolfers, J., & Zitzewitz, E. (2012). *Prediction Markets for Economic Forecasting*. National Bureau of Economic Research, Working Paper w18222, http://www.nber.org/papers/w18222 (accessed October 29, 2017).

Soukhoroukova, A., Spann, M., & Skiera, B. (2007). Creating and evaluating new product ideas with idea markets. In *Produktinnovation mit Informationsmärkten*, Dissertation, University of Passau, May, pp. 73–93.

Soukhoroukova, A., Spann, M., & Skiera, B. (2012). Sourcing, filtering, and evaluating new product ideas: An empirical exploration of the performance of idea markets. *Journal of Product Innovation Management*, 29(1), 100–12.

Spann, M., Ernst, H., Skiera, B., & Soll, J. H. (2009). Identification of lead users for consumer products via virtual stock markets. *Journal of Product Innovation Management*, 26(3), 322–35.

Spann, M. & Skiera, B. (2003). Internet-based virtual stock markets for business forecasting. *Management Science*, 49(10), 1310–26.

Stieger, D., Matzler, K., Chatterjee, S., & Ladstaetter-Fussenegger, F. (2012). Democratizing strategy: How crowdsourcing can be used for strategy dialogues. *California Management Review*, 54(4), 44–68.

Šundić, M. & Leitner, K-H. (2018). Co-creation from a telecommunication provider's perspective: A comparative study on innovation with customers and employees. In C. Tucci, A. Afuah, & G. Viscusi (eds.), *Creating and Capturing Value Through Crowdsourcing*. Oxford: Oxford University Press, pp. 236–70.

Surowiecki, J. (2005). *The Wisdom of Crowds*. New York: Random House.

Ulrich, K. T. (2007). *Design: Creation of Artefacts in Society*. Philadelphia: Pontifica Press.

Ulrich, K. T. & Eppinger, S. D. (2008). *Product Design and Development*, 4th edn. New York: McGraw-Hill.

Van Bruggen, G. H., Spann, M., Lilien, G. L., & Skiera, B. (2010). Prediction markets as institutional forecasting support systems. *Decision Support Systems*, 49(4), 404–16.

von Hippel, E. (2005). *Democratizing Innovation*. Cambridge, MA: MIT Press.

West, J. & Bogers, M. (2014). Leveraging external sources of innovation: A review of research on open innovation. *Journal of Product Innovation Management*, *31*(4), 814–31.

West, J. & Sims, J. (2018). How firms leverage crowds and communities for open innovation. In C. Tucci, A. Afuah, & G. Viscusi (eds.), *Creating and Capturing Value Through Crowdsourcing*. Oxford: Oxford University Press, pp. 58–96.

13

Ethics in Crowdsourcing: Revisiting and Revising the Role of Stakeholder Theory

Daniel Curto-Millet and Arsalan Nisar

Abstract

Stakeholder theory is one of the predominant theories on ethics for guiding the inclusion of stakeholders for organizations to balance their interests ethically. However, emerging phenomena, such as the increasing importance of organizations adopting novel forms of engagement like crowdsourcing, challenge stakeholder theory in substantial ways, primarily induced by the vagueness of the term "crowd" and how it could or should relate to the organization. In this chapter, we revise the extent to which stakeholder theory is applicable to crowdsourcing by identifying its limitations, so as to allow for a better understanding of the ethical challenges surrounding crowdsourcing. By so doing, we substantiate some of the ethical consequences of crowdsourcing and propose recommendations on how stakeholder theory can provide a response to such ethical dilemmas. We provide one of the first attempts to debate the role of stakeholder theory for future research directions in the context of crowdsourcing.

INTRODUCTION

Stakeholder theory is outlined as a combination of heterogeneous narratives (Miles, 2017) with multi-contextual interpretations and applications. While it is well over 30 years since the seminal work of Freeman (1984), some authors (e.g. Laplume et al., 2008) are suggesting that stakeholder theory is entering a maturity phase; it thus becomes important to consider the role of stakeholder theory in the context of growing discussions on ethics in emerging phenomena such as crowdsourcing. Ethics is a primary concern in crowdsourcing and features prominently in crowdfunding (Beaulieu et al., 2015; Hossain & Oparaocha, 2015); in open source culture (Benkler, 2011; Mingers & Walsham, 2010); in crowdsourcing projects (Brabham, 2013; Coleman, 2014); in citizen science (Resnik et al., 2015); in open innovation (Henkel et al., 2014); and in collaborative spaces involving shared commons (Hess & Ostrom, 2011). To study the applicability of stakeholder theory to crowdsourcing, we first offer a definition and illustrate how it encompasses a wide range of phenomena (Doan et al., 2011), centering on three aspects of novel means of production. These three aspects challenge the pre-dominant understanding of the firm as a well-determined entity, with clearly assigned roles and ownership rights (Benkler, 2011). This challenging stance is similar (although with different intensities) to that offered by some readings of stakeholder theory (e.g. Crane & Ruebottom (2011) and Savage et al. (2010)), which prompts us to examine how applicable the theory is to explaining crowdsourcing. Points are offered later, where the theory is limited in its analytical force.

What is Crowdsourcing?

In this study, we consider a rather broad notion of crowdsourcing, and in so doing we risk generalizing—and perhaps even over-simplifying—a number of phenomena that enact their own idiosyncrasies and should be treated in their own terms. However, since the purpose of this study is to argue for the applicability of stakeholder theory to new methods of production that involve the "crowd" as a novel form of stakeholder, we take this risk to contend that stakeholder theory is malleable enough to accommodate these new phenomena.

Crowdsourcing is an increasingly important phenomenon that revolves around the fluid concept of "the crowd" (Orlikowski & Scott, 2015). As Orlikowski & Scott point out, the crowd is neither nameless nor necessarily a general and passive mass (as customers would be in a mass market). Instead, the "crowd" in crowdsourcing follows four characteristics: it is a generative, distributed, predominantly online, problem-solving collaborative effort (Doan et al., 2011; Lukyanenko et al., 2014; Straub et al., 2015; Butticè et al., 2018). There are many movements that incorporate this particular idea of the crowd, including open source (Howe, 2006), open innovation (Davis et al., 2015), crowdfunding (Mollick, 2014), and even in- and out-sourcing (Ågerfalk & Fitzgerald, 2008).

There is debate over what movements constitute the crowdsourcing phenomenon and whether or not it should be viewed as an entirely new concept (Zhao & Zhu, 2012). For example, some authors exclude open source software projects from crowdsourcing by arguing that open source communities have more control than firms (Brabham, 2013; Schlagwein & Bjørn-Andersen, 2014).[1]

---

[1] Although communities are a crucial element of open source (Stewart 2005; Shaikh & Cornford 2009), there is an increasing participation of commercial companies within open source movements that mitigates this assertion (Bonaccorsi et al., 2007).

Some authors say there is little or no difference (Doan et al., 2011; Mergel & Desouza, 2013). Others point out that the differences between these models (beyond several common features) are degrees of intensity (Albors et al., 2008). Additionally, crowdsourcing itself is attributed many different definitions emphasizing one aspect over another. Consolidating some 200 definitions, Estellés-Arolas & González Ladrón de Guevara (2012: 197) define crowdsourcing as (our emphasis):

> A type of participative *online activity* in which an individual, an institution, a non-profit organization, or company proposes to *a group of individuals* of varying knowledge, heterogeneity, and number, via a flexible open call, *the voluntary undertaking of a task*. The undertaking of the task, of variable complexity and modularity, and *in which the crowd should participate* bringing their work, money, knowledge and/or experience, always entails mutual benefit. The user will receive the satisfaction of a given type of need, be it economic, social recognition, self-esteem, or the development of individual skills, while the crowd-sourcer will obtain and utilize to their advantage what the user has brought to the venture, whose form will depend on the type of activity undertaken.

Just like crowdsourcing is debated, the meaning of those other movements bearing resemblance to those crowdsourcing characteristics such as open innovation, are also discussed along the related lines of the four characteristics emphasized in the quote (the generative, distributed, pre-dominantly online, problem-solving collaborative effort). For example, when comparing open innovation, open standards, and open source, West (2007) emphasizes the central role of firms and their interest in profit, where they will have a more direct say in which problem should be resolved. Similarly, de Laat (2007, p. 172) indicates that for the Linux project, membership is "reserved for external partners like firms and universities," casting shadows over definitive statements regarding the marginalization of commercial firms by communities.[2] It is difficult to offer a definitive definition of crowdsourcing, partly because there is an inherent fluidity in the emerging concepts based on digital innovation (Yoo et al., 2010). Especially in new media, there is a continuous and ongoing process of distinctiveness taking place where identities are not stable and are often relative to others (Vaast et al., 2013).

Should crowdsourcing, open source, open innovation, and other phenomena be regarded as the same? Far be it from us to accept the reductionist urge and say that all these different movements are equal; they are not.[3] However,

---

[2] The Linux Foundation produces every year a report on the origin of contributions. Last year, the majority of contributors came from sponsoring firms.

[3] Kelty (2008), for example, firmly argues for the differentiation of open source (especially from "free software" which requires derivative works to be licensed as the original work), emphasizing its capacity to be what he calls a "recursive public" which allows the public to build its own self-sustaining infrastructure and propagate its cultural identity from its own use.

for the purposes of this study, we consider they can be treated as such by generalizing their characteristics. In this way, we can argue for the applicability of stakeholder theory and its ability to deal with such complexities. These four characteristics (i.e. generative, distributed, pre-dominantly online, problem-solving collaborative effort) make the phenomenon of crowdsourcing novel and counter to traditional ways of doing business and understanding ethics. Essentially, these characteristics create three challenges: a challenge to traditional views of the firm; debate over the evidence of property rights and ownership; and, discussion over the role of involved actors, their heterogeneous needs, and their expectations (Chua et al., 2015; Feller et al., 2012).

Locus of Control

Brabham (2013) argues for an interplay and balance in the locus of control between organizations and the crowd. For example, in some cases like Threadless, the organization has a clear policy on intellectual property (IP) that is fair to both the organization and crowd. Once any member from the crowd has made a submission to Threadless, the submitter offers the commercial rights to Threadless for 90 days and any design that is printed results in prize money. However, if the submission is not selected, the submitter retains the IP rights. In crowdsourcing "the locus of control for the creation of goods and ideas must reside between the organization and the community, in a shared space that maximizes the benefits of top-down traditional management with the benefits of bottom-up, open creative production" (Brabham, 2013: 4).

Likewise, one of the central aspects in open innovation is its explicit challenge to established methods of production that would traditionally have stayed inside the firm to avoid high transaction costs (Donaldson & Preston, 1995; Benkler, 2006; Feller et al., 2012). This effectively blurs the lines between the organization and its stakeholders (Levina & Ross, 2005; Fleming & Waguespack, 2007). Why this de-centralization works is due, in part, to the paradoxical agreement between individuals, going so far, for some, as to become neither producer nor consumers, but peers (Benkler, 2006). The locus of control between a community and the firms involved is somewhere in between, instead of being in the firms' hands.

This displaced locus of control is favorable for arguing with actors who, in traditional, hierarchical organizations, would hold a dominant position. In some cases, the crowd can have the upper hand and "crowdslap" the firm that infringes some deeply held values, such as free speech (Brabham, 2013). Also, in open source, a similar control mechanism exists in the form of an "invisible hand" which pushes community members to create a "fork"—a competitive development project which uses as a basis the code of the original project, but under a new governance. There have been a number of successful forks which have managed to wrestle companies away from their grip over a project. LibreOffice is such an example and came into being after the owners of the original project were distrusted (Gamalielsson & Lundell, 2014).

Internet mediation makes it difficult to understand who are the involved actors and what they want, and thus the accompanying social constructions of meaning. In their study of TripAdvisor—a website that crowdsources opinions about venues—Orlikowski & Scott (2014) show how managers struggle to grasp how they should take into account online feedback in comparison with the traditional expert reviews seen as more standard. This uncertainty around the identity of the actors that participate in crowdsourcing projects poses a problem for the ethical management of firms and communities, since the identity of the "crowd" is uncertain, leading to an ethical dilemma.

The three issues—challenge to the traditional view of the firm; challenge to the evident nature of property rights; and uncertainty over the identity and role of new actors that are, in some cases, crucial to the firm—are related. They point towards new thinking for management to understand their firm as more open than before, able to create strong relations with actors who do not necessarily have a contract, and are normally seen as outsiders. In summary, these challenges need to be visited in the light of a theory that can explain some of these ethical dilemmas in the context of crowdsourcing.

CORE CONCEPTS OF STAKEHOLDER THEORY

Stakeholder theory has remained the predominant theory in ethics since Freeman's (1984, 2010) seminal contribution. The literature has discussed and debated its core aspects in detail (e.g. Hörisch et al., 2014), but rarely in the context of crowdsourcing. In this section, we examine three elements of the theory that can be associated with the study of ethics in crowdsourcing: a de-centralized view of the firm and its stakeholders; its capacity for holistic explanations and guidance over ethical issues; and an emerging and multiple notion of stakeholder identity.

A De-Centralized View of the Firm

Freeman (2010: 52) defines stakeholders as "groups and individuals who can affect, or are affected by, the achievement of an organization's mission." The theory is originally concerned with a view of a central firm made of relations with stakeholders. Although prominent stakeholder theorists have posited a view where the firm is central (e.g. Freeman, 2010), others have argued for a de-centralization (Pajunen, 2006). The centralist theories have explicitly contested the assumed alignment between the firm, the managers in their role of caretakers for the firm's interests (Fassin, 2008), and the various stakeholders. Stakeholders, thus, hold different interests in the firm, which are not necessarily aligned with management. The necessity to account for stakeholders ultimately questions the purpose of the firm and its traditional emphasis on shareholder value maximization (Sundaram & Inkpen, 2004).

The theory suggests that, instead of pursuing narrow economic objectives (Strand & Freeman, 2015), organizations should accommodate for the variety of stakeholder interests without resorting to tradeoffs (Bowie, 2012). Whether tradeoffs can be overcome at all (Jensen, 2002) depends largely on philosophical assumptions behind the application of stakeholder theory and the independence and degree of sharing of concepts (Siltaoja & Lähdesmäki, 2015).

Depending on the philosophical position, some stakeholders will be more valued than others, and also more determined in their definition. For some authors, to be considered as such, stakeholders must be "persons or groups that have, or claim, ownership, rights, or interests in a corporation and its activities" (Clarkson, 1995: 106). Stakeholders, thus, must be able to make a claim and, depending on the strength of that claim, be considered relatively close to or distant from the firm and its ethical obligation to them. More critical research, in contrast, would argue for the need to look to those whose voice cannot be heard (Jensen & Sandström, 2011; Derry, 2012).

The stakeholder theory literature is complete with classification systems; some are static, others dynamic. The static ones are usually ordered as hierarchical systems and based on economic terms (Crane et al., 2011): Clarkson (1995) categorizes stakeholders depending on their criticality to a firm's functioning; similarly, Freeman (2010) depicts internal and external actors relative to the firm (Fassin, 2009; Jensen & Sandström, 2011); Post et al. (2002) order stakeholders along three rings that move further away from the central corporation (resources; industry structure; and social political arena). Within the hierarchies, stakeholders are ordered flatly as equals, with little guidance over the evaluation of stakeholder closeness to the firm, and little attention has been given to the relations between stakeholders (Paul, 2015).

These classifications tend to be static. Other studies, instead, take a dynamic approach to understanding the relative distance between the firm and the stakeholders. These approaches depend on Mitchell et al.'s (1997) concept of "salience" in which the relative closeness of the stakeholder is evaluated in time around three concepts: legitimacy, urgency, and power. Certain stakeholders will take the opportunity to become more involved and closer to the firm, thus moving between stakeholder categories (Fassin, 2010). The fluctuations of stakeholders along these three categories as identified by management underpins an idea of uncertainty and emergence which necessitates further research into managerial perceptions of stakeholders and their subsequent response to change (Neville et al., 2011).

Holistic Analysis and Guidance

The methods in which these perceptions and their focal points are adopted and applied (e.g. managerial) are influenced by the practitioners' or researchers' ontological understanding of the environment (Santana, 2012). These philosophical assumptions carry further consequences when judging the extent of the explanation the theory can provide. To clearly separate facts from values, or business from ethics limits the network of actors that participate in a firm's value creation (Purnell & Freeman, 2012). As such, the theory's open-endedness and simplicity—although criticized as vague (Fassin, 2008)—offers opportunities to understand contemporary events and dilemmas. There is a larger societal trend that requires analysis to move beyond the nucleus of the firm (Jensen & Sandström, 2011). Stakeholder theory, in its insistence on finding out "who or what really counts" (Freeman, 1994: 412), is especially instructive in questioning the status quo (Jones & Felps, 2013), and even the central place afforded to the firm (Derry, 2012).

Consideration of the importance of the stakeholder involves the holistic analysis of three issues, those of: value creation; ethics; and the managerial mindset, all combined together (Parmar et al., 2010). Stakeholder theory's concern for these three problems shows its holistic capacity to move beyond narrow economic analyses (Dienhart, 2008; Strand & Freeman 2015). Instead of separating domains of enquiry—for example, considering managers purely as agents of the firm—stakeholder theory is able to analyze the complex dilemma of modern organizations and their challenges in changing contexts (Crane, 2010).

Nevertheless, there is a discrepancy in the literature on the extent to which these three issues are independent from one another. For some, the theory is decidedly ethical in its premise, prioritizing its normative capacity (Donaldson & Preston, 1995). Others, yet, discuss the reality of stakeholder theory and its descriptive and instrumental validity (e.g. the debate between Treviño & Weaver, 1999; and Jones & Wicks, 1999). Perhaps it is the theory's open-endedness that is the cause of this discrepancy: it is widely applicable, yet not necessarily applied; it thus competes with other views of the firm that are closer to shareholder theory (e.g. Mansell, 2013).

In Pursuit of Identity

The focus of the theory on stakeholders and their interests implies that a firm either knows them, or ought to know them. In this sense, the principle of finding "who or what really counts" Freeman (1994: 412) is not necessarily a deontological imperative, but a call to understand the existence and the relationship between social entities that make up an organization. The theory guides—practitioners and researchers alike—in the search for realities, but does not impose an objective value system based on rules (Siltaoja & Lähdesmäki, 2015). This reasoning is in line with a large part of the work on social constructivism in the social sciences (Bijker et al., 2012), in which actors are not considered as settled, but socially enacted. This ontological flexibility has important ramifications that stakeholder theory has been arguing for.

Similarly, stakeholder theory proves to be useful in understanding the development of social identities and their relation to the organization (Crane et al., 2011). The shift towards considering the firm as a de-centralized organization allows the study of emerging elements that would otherwise be left in the background, or accounted for as a miscellaneous element in the "community" category (Pajunen, 2010; Crane et al., 2011). The firm's dominating perspective can also be detrimental to searching for and understanding stakeholder identities (Crane et al., 2011), especially given the specific nature of co-production in organizations other than commercial firms (Cordella et al., 2018). By considering that the firm is not a unified kernel, it thus has to negotiate its central position with a number of stakeholders (Fassin, 2008), where the identity is not evident (Crane et al., 2011).

Such a strand of research is inherently opposed to calls that aim to separate the conduct of business from considerations of ethics (e.g. Sandberg, 2008), and ultimately questions the possibility of objectively defining moral behavior (e.g. Loviscky et al., 2007). Separating business prerogatives and ethical considerations would ignore potential stakeholders who would have a say concerning what those prerogatives should be, and at what cost (Derry, 2012). Instead, things take shape in emergent processes in which meaning is continuously applied to business objectives and ethical considerations (Tsoukas & Chia, 2002; Bolton et al., 2011). Similarly, the identities of emerging stakeholders can be dynamic and unexpected (Fassin, 2010).

This emergence in the meaning of things is a core aspect of stakeholder theory. When firms engage with stakeholders (be they shareholders, employees, or "community" members), this perspective believes that their collective identities will come out changed, even challenged (Savage et al., 2010). Stakeholder theory allows questioning of the overbearing position that the firm can have by allowing actors outside of it to have a say in its conduct (Scherer et al., 2016). The consequence is that it is not only the stakeholder's identity that is likely to change, but also the identity of the organization, emphasizing the need to reconsider the central position of the firm (Barraquier, 2013).

THE APPLICABILITY OF STAKEHOLDER THEORY FOR CROWDSOURCING

From the core features of stakeholder theory, a number of aspects are applicable to crowdsourcing activities, be it their similarity or their shared perspectives.

In particular, three seminal points for the understanding of crowdsourcing stand out: a shared challenge to the traditional view of the firm; a complex understanding behind ownership and property rights and the rules with which they are attributed; and evolving stakeholder identities.

Challenging Traditional Notions of the Firm

The latent ethical consciousness in crowdsourcing—the push for a more open, collaborative method of production—relates well with the theory's emphasis on pluralist notions of normative *cores* (Machold et al., 2008). Crowdsourcing has a number of competing values within project organizations and between stakeholders (Carillo & Okoli, 2008; Kelty, 2009). The value of "freedom" is positioned differently by free software advocates (staunch supporters of restrictive licenses, where derivations of the code must be licensed as the original), and open source advocates (fewer restrictions on use) (Perens, 2005). In this sense, the purpose of an organization in crowdsourcing movements can be deeply debated and, just as stakeholder theory argues (Lopez-De-Pedro & Rimbau-Gilabert, 2012), the consequences and boundaries of the effects of a crowdsourcing movement—both within and outside a firm— may be less straightforward than one might imagine. Stakeholder theory can be useful for understanding the reach of different normative cores and how they give voice to or silence certain actors in the organization.

Closely related to challenging traditional notions of the firm as a monolithic institution is the increasing necessity to look for sources of innovation outside their traditional boundaries (Gould, 2012). The importance of external actors for innovation confronts the idea that dealing with outside sources is—as transaction costs would indicate—inefficient, requiring employment within the firm (Benkler, 2002). It is under this open light that legitimate claims can be made by stakeholders, which may otherwise have been seen as less legitimate, external actors. Stakeholder theory can evaluate those claims by understanding better the stakeholders' relations and contributions to an organization and whether the organization's behavior corresponds with the values shared by the stakeholders, and considered to be ethical. For example— beyond practical concerns of stakeholder participation and the degree to which the community shares interests with the project's goals (Wenger & Snyder, 2000; Dunham et al., 2006)—what is considered as an organization's adequate conduct could change by, say, involving new stakeholders (Fassin, 2010). When a crowdsourcing project becomes increasingly commercial, there may be a backlash from the existing community, which may challenge values and their claims of legitimacy to the organization (O'Mahony & Bechky, 2008; Ferraro & O'Mahony, 2012). To engage in crowdsourcing activities ethically, firms, communities, and organizations need to account (and be able to do so) for those stakeholders that are beyond the means of direct contractual obligations or employment relations, and take into account distributed modes of production (Benkler, 2006).

Similar to stakeholder theory, at the core of crowdsourcing movements lies an explicit challenge to traditional views of the firm (Benkler, 2002), centralized organizations (Chesbrough, 2007), and society in general (Stallman, 1985), with traditional organizational boundaries becoming blurred (Viscusi & Tucci, 2018). Stakeholder theory can help to explain crowdsourcing's challenge to existing practices and push actors such as the government to support alternative organizational structures with different stakeholders that may be in line with policy. For example, the current wave of open access and citizen science aims to democratize publicly-funded research and emancipate a wide range of stakeholders (Matten & Crane, 2005), that can legitimately participate in novel forms of emerging organizations (Dahlander, 2007). These forms challenge the monolithic and hierarchical views of firms as "owned" in a tight-fisted way (Dahlander & Magnusson, 2005).

Complex Ownership Rules

The explanatory capacity of stakeholder theory is based on its understanding of complex rules of ownership and appropriation of property (Donaldson & Preston, 1995). The degree to which stakeholders are considered as such depends on their ability to claim to own an interest in the firm (Clarkson, 1995). This right for stakeholders to own a firm's interest (as opposed to shareholders) is historically attributed to the de-centralized view that the theory proposes. In this line, Donaldson & Preston (1995: 84) argue for a pluralistic notion of rights, making the connection between property and stakeholder theory explicit: "the 'stake' of long-term employees who have worked to build and maintain a successful business operation is essentially based on effort. The stake of people living in the surrounding community may be based on their need, say, for clean air or the maintenance of their civic infrastructure." In this sense, stakeholder theory provides liberty to understand ownership of property rights as something that is economical, social, or personal (Gibson, 2012; Hörisch et al., 2014). The way stakes are "owned" does not necessarily depend on predominant, Western, economic views (Orozco & Poonamallee, 2014). For example, Ortega & Rodríguez (2011) relate the indigenous concept of *potlatch*—the exchange of physical gifts for social and political capital—with current trends of gift giving in open access movements, where contributors exchange articles for (potential) reputation by disseminating their work openly. The form that the ownership of a stake may take is thus not universal.

What form these stakes can take and how ownership is enacted depends on their institutional context. When Elinor Ostrom studied the social construction of rules in her studies on commons-based pool resources—the building block of open source software and many crowdsourcing-like communities (Benkler, 2011; Schweik & English, 2012)—she found that the resources were unlike those usually studied. These did not fall under traditional institutional regimes: either markets or central government (Ostrom, 1990); they were even contrary to mainstream perceptions (e.g. Hardin, 1968). Stakeholders, it was believed, were not capable of understanding their context to create or adapt rules to suit their conditions. To confirm the existence of a third way, she implicitly used a stakeholder perspective: in the cases she studied, institutions of great complexity were invented and sustained by communities built around accepted definitions of roles of stakeholders. The way that stakeholders are defined—their rights, their obligations, their closeness to the resources—is the principal way in which stakeholder theory can help us to understand the creation and sustainability behind crowdsourcing projects and the new ethical conundrums they pose.

Much of the way the rules of ownership in commons-based systems are applied is contingent on their sustainability. This is a problem deeply rooted in commons, where rules about who can appropriate resources and in what quantity are dependent on the specificities of the context (Ostrom, 1990). The Valencian *huertas*—irrigated, cultured lands—have used and evolved a system to regulate the legitimate use of various water sources by recognizing specific groups of farmers contingent on abundance of water. Similarly, as noted by Clarkson (1995: 110), a firm's survival "depend[s] upon its ability to fulfil its economic and social purpose" in a way that "each primary stakeholder group continues as part of the corporation's stakeholder system." In this sense, stakeholder theory changes the way firms are thought of and organized, so that they can embody ethical rules and assume the plurality of legitimate stakeholder groups to sustain their existence (Agle et al., 2008).

As stakeholder theory surmises, the rules need not be based on narrow economic values (Jones & Felps, 2013), and some are based on multiple philosophical views, such as utilitarian or libertarian positions (Coleman, 2012). In many commons-based systems—such as the Valencian *huertas*—they involve elements of trusts that make up the management of complex systems. Its monitoring would otherwise be too expensive if contracted out. Instead, they have evolved autonomous management practices to take into account the many factors that affect and ultimately define the stakeholders involved and legitimate distribution of wealth (Ostrom, 1990). Among others, they include: the origin of land ownership from the days of the *reconquista* (the *hereters*); the type of land (irrigated, dry, or dependent on rainfall); an elected *syndic* acting as chief executive; an executive committee to consult with the *syndic*; ditch-riders which monitor the use of water; a system of irrigation the turning of which defines the order of irrigation and the autonomy of farmers to water their lands as long as no wastage is produced; or a water tribunal to expedite fines for unlawful use of water.

Even though stakeholder theory stems from a critique of shareholder dominance, it is flexible enough to contemplate and apply a variety of philosophical perspectives to the determination of what is a legitimate "right" (Santana, 2012). In a sense, this is due to the historical position we are in, and a changing economy that increasingly challenges traditional, dominating positions, whether scientific (Latour, 2004), economical (Savage, 2014), or societal (Corsín Jiménez, 2014).[4] Equally, crowdsourcing involves a variety of ways of determining ownership rights, from critical thought (Levy, 2010), to Kantian principles (Klang, 2005). This flexibility of thought allows both stakeholder and crowdsourcing theories to be used in contexts which involve rapid change, such as digital (Yoo et al., 2010).

Evolving Stakeholder Identities

Like stakeholder theory, crowdsourcing is inherently preoccupied with ethical participation (Donaldson & Preston, 1995). Some of the views applied— utilitarian, libertarian, etc.—help to define the extent to which different stakeholders are linked to and how they participate with the organization they form. Debian—an open source distribution of the Linux kernel—has always been wary of financial contributions, claiming that they disrupt meritocratic, technical contribution (Coleman, 2012). The technical proficiency of actors is important if they want their stake to be recognized as legitimate (Iivari, 2009). Without a view concerned with the identification of stakeholders, these volunteer contributions could be ignored because, in many cases, no formal ties exist between the project and contributors (Amrit & van Hillegersberg, 2010). In this sense, in some projects the closeness to the organization—the strength of the claim—will depend on perceived meritocracy of the stakeholder, and stakeholder theory can help in analyzing the relative relevance of those claims.

With this emphasis on merit, much of open innovation goes counter to the mainstream, established players in the way organizational ties are created, both to the market and to public bodies. Lead-user innovation, for example, often takes place without the consent of the producer (Gould, 2012). Yet these users develop products that can create important market niches or open up new markets (Urban & von Hippel, 1988; von Hippel, 2007). Yet for a long period of time, these users/creators would remain invisible and treated as

---

[4] No doubt by creating other dominant positions (Morozov, 2012).

outside of the primary concerns of the firm. It is in the identification of vague actors that stakeholder theory, by teasing out the situational meaning of "the community," can give them a place within novel views of the firm of active contributors that partake in its success (Dunham et al., 2006; Crane et al., 2011; Paul, 2015). Social media is another example of crowdsourced marketing done by the users of the firm's products. If they engage in a way favorable to the firm, how should they be viewed?

The importance in crowdsourcing applications of stakeholders' evaluation of a firm and its ethical conduct reflects on the project's goals and its alignment with stakeholders' personal interests (Hu et al., 2015). This forces the organizations to dynamically search and discover who the *potential* stakeholders are (Fassin, 2010), and not only those who press their claim at a precise moment in time. This level of uncertainty around their identity (since it is an ongoing matter) affects the organization's own products. For example, the incorporation of "stretch goals," even when a project is already funded online due to demand by backers, is a relevant way to provision stake-holder needs better (Scholz, 2015). Although a similar process of re-invention and re-positioning often occurs for traditional companies in the market (Doganova & Eyquem-Renault, 2009), change is continuous in digital innovation (Yoo et al., 2010), inviting the use of flexible approaches for understanding an organization's stakeholders. Stakeholder theory can thus become instrumental to crowdsourcing managers so that they may skillfully evaluate stake-holder needs appropriately and consequently tailor their relationship with solvers; an area which has been identified as requiring further attention (Ghezzi et al., 2017).

CHALLENGES: STAKEHOLDER THEORY AND CROWDSOURCING

In spite of the aspects that make stakeholder theory a useful heuristic in understanding the growing phenomenon of crowdsourcing, two main issues can limit its applicability. First, some roles in crowdsourcing are either attributed an inordinate amount of power, or the stakeholders are relative and distributed minorities with little strength to press claims unless organized into collectives. Second, stakeholder theory treats the firm as the traditional organizational kernel, rarely contemplating other types of organizations, such as communities, foundations, not-for-profit, etc. (Moriarty, 2014), allowing for a dominant view of the ownership of property to be based on the individual, which can limit the application of stakeholder theory to novel forms of collaborative work.

Uncertainty of Roles

There is a problem with the uncertainty behind many of the roles participating in crowdsourcing, making the avoidance of tradeoffs (or even their limitation) difficult. Although some have proposed that stakeholder theory treat all stakeholders as intrinsically equal (Donaldson & Preston, 1995; Freeman, 2010), others have sought to tease the meaning of legitimate relationship with the firm more precisely. Some authors have, for example, argued that some stakeholders are more central than others (Post et al., 2002). In crowdsourcing, though, the way roles hold different degrees of stake within a project can reach extremes, coming to resemble the figure of the shareholder and challenging the more democratic undertones of stakeholder theory. In open source, for example, there is the figure of benevolent dictator for life (BDFL) which could, if one is not cautious, be understood as the ultimate owner of the project (Ljungberg, 2000), but rarely exercises unilateral decision making, concentrating instead on coordination (Coffin, 2006), as would a board (Kaufman & Englander, 2011). Nevertheless, many projects have shown that this role, in spite of its title, holds more of a last-ditch decision-making aspect. Cornford et al. (2010) have shown how Linus Torvalds, the original creator of Linux and also its BDFL, was pushed and forced to switch to an open source code management program for the kernel's development. The dictatorship status is thus usually limited to technical decisions concerning the project's development. Nevertheless, it is striking how the BDFL can come to resemble a traditional shareholder or owner view of the organization.

Other stakeholders in crowdsourcing are more vulnerable, having little voice unless organized. Such can be the case for investors in large crowdfunding projects such as in Kickstarter. These crowdsourcing projects pose a challenge to stakeholder theory's capacity to articulate stakeholders who are large in number and with particular idiosyncrasies. Unless these groups form collectives, there is little chance that they would have a voice to press their claim as stakeholders.

Internet-mediated collaboration can also hinder the management of stakeholders due to the dis-intermediation between actors in such projects. With no clear organization to which to attribute the responsibility of an ethical conduct, how much can stakeholder theory illustrate beyond the descriptive depictions of such distributed organizations? To be useful in such contexts, stakeholder theory would have to understand that the manner in which claims are made (or not) depends on values, which may be difficult to communicate or understand equally for all stakeholders involved. Additionally, it is noted that the non-physical presence of stakeholders can limit possible social interactions, reduce trust (Hinds & Mortensen, 2005), and render more difficult the use of stakeholder theory. The consequence is that the distinction between different categories of stakeholders (which, like in any classification system, are far from static (Bowker & Star, 2000)), and the evaluation of an organization will be problematic to *both* managers and the stakeholders themselves.

In addition to the uncertainty of the roles held by actors, some of the dominant philosophical assumptions in some crowdsourcing movements can limit the applicability of stakeholder theory. There is, for example, ambiguity in the importance of democracy versus the prevalent concept of meritocracy, clearly biasing the legitimate claims towards some actors over others. This puts in question the degree of influence that stakeholder theory can have over crowdsourcing projects that do not support democratic governance (Moriarty, 2014), potentially foregoing one of the theory's early principals to accommodate all stakeholders (Freeman, 1994).

The philosophical assumptions are important because they influence who is considered a legitimate stakeholder. It is particularly consequential in crowdsourcing movements because a large aspect of these movements concerns defining the extent accorded to the notion of "openness" and who can collaborate. This is perhaps paradoxical but in most projects, it is considered that there are different limits to participation. The meritocratic approach of open source, Ostrom's description of commons-based pool resources, tiered-crowdsourcing efforts, explicitly all come to exclude or limit some forms of usage and interaction by certain actors, be they governments, volunteers, or commercial actors. The lack of contracts in some crowdsourcing projects and the general volunteering nature of open innovation makes the assignation of stable roles difficult (Benkler, 2006), and thus the rules surrounding the claiming of legitimate stakes are, by derivation, themselves unstable. In other crowdsourcing movements where such contracts do exist, careful management of legal issues (e.g. infringement of third-party intellectual property) is necessary and is not evident (Brabham, 2013).

Novel Notions of Rights Ownership

In spite of its flexibility in the definition of organizational actors, stakeholder theory has mainly involved itself with the analysis of traditional, for-profit firms (Moriarty, 2014). This is, perhaps, because the links between stakeholders and organization are more easily defined, as they emphasize the importance of property rights to stakeholder theory. It gives a sense that property rights are evident, but for many activities in crowdsourcing, it is not. This is not the case for crowdsourcing in general, where the meaning of these rights and their organization is debated vigorously (Stallman, 1985; Barrett et al., 2013). Some resources, over which claims of proprietorship can be made, even when contractual, are difficult to implement and their meaning can vary.

In considering the firm as the traditional kernel of organization, stakeholder theory has developed a conception of property rights which is also traditional and which does not contemplate changes in the notion of what constitutes a "property." Property rights have tended towards an interpretation, which sees them as private property that is clearly owned. Conflating private rights and property rights, Donaldson & Preston (1995: 83–4) argue that there is "considerable agreement" on the concept of private property and that it "clearly does not ascribe unlimited rights to owners and hence does not support the popular claim that the responsibility of managers is to act solely as agents for the share-owners." Some who critique the unproblematic reading of proprietorship do so in order to emphasize the clearer relation with property that shareholders have above other actors, and to which the firm owes a deontological duty. For example, Mansell (2013: 584) argues that *"the normative theories of the firm[…], including variations of 'social contract' theory, distributive justice and fairness, are either inconsistent with rights to property and contract that underpin any market economy, or can logically support only a shareholder theory of the firm."*

In contrast, in many applications of crowdsourcing, the development of ownership is not settled and is, indeed, one of the main points of contention (Alspaugh et al., 2010). It is worth debating whether a stakeholder perspective that is, say, based on Kantian thought that gives preferential weight to share-owners, managers, and other actors who have a clear relation of duty to the firm (Mansell, 2013), would work at all to explain crowdsourcing organizations. There are two reasons for this, and both rely on the debated notion of ownership rights and private property. First, there is a deep rejection of the technical superiority of private proprietorship in large parts of the crowdsourcing movement, even by libertarians, who embrace the philosophical underpinnings of Friedman's perspectives (e.g. Raymond, 2001). In this sense, to be useful to crowdsourcing, stakeholder theory would have to be capable of analyzing unclear, non-obvious, novel forms of production, many (if not all) of which are cultural products that escape and even challenge traditional conceptions.

Second, many of the actors involved, even those who have financially invested in a project through crowdfunding (and thus have a quantifiable stake), have little legal status. In the case of Kickstarter—one of the most important crowdfunding platforms—the organization is only expected to fulfill its promise.[5] In the case of open source projects, contributors of code often assign copyright to a foundation, blurring the stake that the author has, since there is no longer an ownership of rights (O'Mahony & Bechky, 2008). The GNU Public Licenses (GPL), for example, one of the most used licenses to define the conditions of use of software, says the following [emphasis added]:

---

[5] https://www.kickstarter.com/help/faq/kickstarter+basics (accessed October 29, 2017).

Our lawyers have told us that to be in the best position to enforce the GPL in court against violators, we should keep the copyright status of the program as simple as possible. We do this by asking each contributor to *either assign the copyright on his contribution to the FSF [Free Software Foundation], or disclaim copyright on it and thus put it in the public domain.*[6]

How can stakeholder theory define the "stake" of the original author if his copyright belongs to the foundation?

CONCLUSIONS AND FUTURE RESEARCH

The study explained how stakeholder theory is one of the most widely accepted theories in business ethics, primarily for its holistic exploratory capacity, able to offer descriptive, instrumental, and normative explanations to ethical dilemmas. We expanded on the limited application of stakeholder theory to the phenomenon of crowdsourcing. By assessing the theory's capacity to explain ethical dilemmas arising from crowdsourcing, the objective was to connect two important bodies of work from which to gain a better understanding of the role of organizations and their distributed capacity to avoid and resolve ethics issues.

The study demonstrated and examined three elements of stakeholder theory—a decentralized view of the firm and its stakeholder; its capacity for holistic explanations and guidance over ethical issues; and a multiple notion of stakeholder identity—that can be associated with research on ethical dilemmas in crowdsourcing. Further, this study extended on the applicability of stakeholder theory to crowdsourcing to filter some of the tradeoffs that organizations encounter in crowdsourcing. This resulted in a detailed discourse on the mismatch between traditional organizational forms and novel forms of engagement such as crowdfunding, citizen science, and open innovation initiatives. In so doing, this study described a considerable number of ethical challenges—complex ownership rules; evolving stakeholder identities; and traditional notions of the firm—when positioning crowdsourcing in the background of stakeholder theory.

To conclude, in this study we have synthesized the challenges that crowdsourcing brings to stakeholder theory and how stakeholder theory can be revised in the light of these challenges. These challenges shed light on the major ethical dilemmas that organizations and the crowd face: ownership rules; quality control; hierarchy; uncertainty of roles; task assignment; and

---

[6] https://www.gnu.org/licenses/gpl-faq.html

crowd selection. Future research in this area is then a two-way street. Stake-holder theory can play a more prominent role in crowdsourcing research, and may be applied differently to the different organizational forms and engage-ment outlined above. Furthermore, research in stakeholder theory itself is likely to be influenced when incorporating nuances of the phenomena discussed in this study.

REFERENCES

Ågerfalk, P. J. & Fitzgerald, B. (2008). Outsourcing to an unknown workforce: Explor-ing opensourcing as a global sourcing strategy. *MIS Quarterly, 32*(2), 385–409.

Agle, B. R., Donaldson, T., Freeman, R. E., Jensen, M. C., Mitchell, R. K., & Wood, D. J. (2008). Dialogue: Toward superior stakeholder theory. *Business Ethics Quarterly, 18*(2), 153–90.

Albors, J., Ramos, J., & Hervas, J. (2008). New learning network paradigms: Commu-nities of objectives, crowdsourcing, wikis and open source. *International Journal of Information Management, 28*(3), 194–202. doi:10.1016/j.ijinfomgt.2007.09.006.

Alspaugh, T. A., Scacchi, W., & Asuncion, H. U. (2010). Software licenses in context: The challenge of heterogeneously-licensed systems. *Journal of the Association for Information Systems, 11*(11), 730.

Amrit, C. & van Hillegersberg, J. (2010). Exploring the impact of socio-technical core-periphery structures in open source software development. *Journal of Information Technology, 25*(2), 216–29. doi:10.1057/jit.2010.7.

Barraquier, A. (2013). A group identity analysis of organizations and their stake-holders: Porosity of identity and mobility of attributes. *Journal of Business Ethics, 115*(1), 45–62. doi:10.1007/s10551-012-1363-x.

Barrett, M., Heracleous, L., & Walsham, G. (2013). A rhetorical approach to IT diffusion: Reconceptualizing the ideology-framing relationship in computerization movements. *MIS Quarterly, 37*(1), 201–20.

Beaulieu, T., Sarker, S., & Sarker, S. (2015). A conceptual framework for understanding crowdfunding. *Communications of the Association for Information Systems*, Vol. 37, Article 1, http://aisel.aisnet.org/cais/vol37/iss1/1/ (accessed October 29, 2017).

Benkler, Y. (2002). Coase's Penguin, or, Linux and the nature of the firm. *Yale Law Journal, 112*(3), 369.

Benkler, Y. (2006). *The Wealth of Networks: How Social Production Transforms Markets and Freedom.* Newhaven, CT: Yale University Press.

Benkler, Y. (2011). *The Penguin and the Leviathan: How Cooperation Triumphs over Self-Interest.* New York: Crown Business.

Bijker, W. E., Hughes, T. P., Pinch, T., & Douglas, D. G. (2012). *The Social Construction of Technological Systems: New Directions in the Sociology and History of Technology.* Cambridge, MA: MIT Press.

Bolton, S., Kim, R., & O'Gorman, K. (2011). Corporate social responsibility as a dynamic internal organizational process: A case study. *Journal of Business Ethics, 101*(1), 61–74. doi:10.1007/s10551-010-0709-5.

Bonaccorsi, A., Lorenzi, D., Merito, M., & Rossi, C. (2007). Business firms' engagement in community projects: Empirical evidence and further developments of the research. In *First International Workshop on Emerging Trends in FLOSS Research and Development (FLOSS'07: ICSE Workshops 2007)*, 13. IEEE. doi:10.1109/FLOSS.2007.3.

Bowie, N. E. (2012). Stakeholder theory: The state of the art. *Business Ethics Quarterly*, *22*(1), 179–85.

Bowker, G. & Star, S. L. (2000). *Sorting Things Out*. Cambridge, MA: MIT Press.

Brabham, D C. (2013). *Crowdsourcing*. The MIT Press.

Butticè, V., Franzoni, C., Rossi-Lamastra, C., & Rovelli, P. (2018). The road to crowdfunding success: A review of extant literature. In C. Tucci, A. Afuah, & G. Viscusi (eds.), *Creating and Capturing Value Through Crowdsourcing*. Oxford: Oxford University Press, pp. 97–126.

Carillo, K. & Okoli, C. (2008). The open source movement: A revolution in software. *The Journal of Computer Information Systems*, *49*(2), 1–9.

Chesbrough, H. (2007). Open innovation and strategy. *California Management Review*, *50*(1), 57–76.

Chua, R. Y. J., Roth, Y., & Lemoine, J.-F. (2015). The impact of culture on creativity: How cultural tightness and cultural distance affect global innovation crowdsourcing work. *Administrative Science Quarterly*, *60*(2), 189–227. doi:10.1177/0001839214563595.

Clarkson, M. E. (1995). A stakeholder framework for analyzing and evaluating corporate social performance. *Academy of Management Review*, *20*(1), 92–117. doi:10.5465/AMR.1995.9503271994.

Coffin, J. (2006). An analysis of open source principles in diverse collaborative communities. *First Monday*, *11*(6) (June), http://journals.uic.edu/ojs/index.php/fm/article/view/1342/1262

Coleman, G. (2012). *Coding Freedom: The Ethics and Aesthetics of Hacking*. Princeton, NJ: Princeton University Press.

Coleman, G. (2014). *Hacker, Hoaxer, Whistleblower, Spy: The Many Faces of Anonymous*. London: Verso Books.

Cordella, A., Palletti, A., & Shaikh, M. (2018). Renegotiating public value with co-production. In C. Tucci, A. Afuah, & G. Viscusi (eds.), *Creating and Capturing Value Through Crowdsourcing*. Oxford: Oxford University Press, pp. 181–203.

Cornford, T., Shaikh, M., & Ciborra, C. (2010). Hierarchy, laboratory and collective: Unveiling Linux as innovation, machination and constitution. *Journal of the Association for Information Systems*, *11*(12), 809–37.

Corsín Jiménez, A. (2014). The right to infrastructure: Prototype for open source urbanism. *Environment and Planning D: Society and Space*, *32*(2), 342–62. doi:10.1068/d13077p.

Crane, A. (2010). From governance to governance: On blurring boundaries. *Journal of Business Ethics*, *94*, 17–19. doi:10.1007/s10551-011-0788-y.

Crane, A. & Ruebottom, T. (2011). Stakeholder theory and social identity: Rethinking stakeholder identification. *Journal of Business Ethics*, *102*(1), 77–87.

Crane, A., Gilbert, D. U., Goodpaster, K. E., Miceli, M. P., Moore, G., Reynolds, S. J., Schminke, M., Waddock, S., Weaver, G. R., & Wicks, A. C. (2011). Comments on

BEQ's Twentieth Anniversary Forum on new directions for business ethics research. *Business Ethics Quarterly, 21*(1), 157–87.

Dahlander, L. (2007). Penguin in a new suit: A tale of how de novo entrants emerged to harness free and open source software communities. *Industrial and Corporate Change, 16*(5), 913–43.

Dahlander, L. & Magnusson, M. (2005). Relationships between open source software companies and communities: Observations from Nordic firms. *Research Policy, 34*, 481–93.

Davis, J. R., Richard, E. E., & Keeton, K. E. (2015). Open innovation at NASA. *Research Technology Management, 58*(3), 52–8. doi:10.5437/08956308X5803325.

De Laat, P. B. (2007). Governance of open source software: State of the art. *Journal of Management and Governance, 11*(2), 165–77. doi:10.1007/s10997-007-9022-9.

Derry, R. (2012). Reclaiming marginalized stakeholders. *Journal of Business Ethics, 111*(2), 253–64. doi:10.1007/s10551-012-1205-x.

Dienhart, J. W. (2008). The separation thesis: Perhaps nine lives are enough. *Business Ethics Quarterly, 18*(4), 555–9.

Doan, A., Ramakrishnan, R., & Halevy, A. Y. (2011). Crowdsourcing systems on the World-Wide Web. *Communications of the ACM, 54*(4), 86–96. doi:10.1145/1924421.1924442.

Doganova, L. & Eyquem-Renault, M. (2009). What do business models do? Innovation devices in technology entrepreneurship. *Research Policy, 38*(10), 1559–70.

Donaldson, T. & Preston, L. E. (1995). The stakeholder theory of the corporation: Concepts, evidence, and implications. *Academy of Management Review, 20*(1), 65–91. doi:10.5465/AMR.1995.9503271992.

Dunham, L., Freeman, R. E., & Liedtka, J. M. (2006). Enhancing stakeholder practice: A particularized exploration of community. *Business Ethics Quarterly, 16*(1), 23–42.

Estellés-Arolas, E. & González-Ladrón-de-Guevara, F. (2012). Towards an integrated crowdsourcing definition. *Journal of Information Science, 38*(2), 189–200. doi:10.1177/0165551512437638.

Fassin, Y. (2008). Imperfections and shortcomings of the stakeholder model's graphical representation. *Journal of Business Ethics, 80*(4), 879–88. doi:10.1007/s10551-007-9474-5.

Fassin, Y. (2009). The stakeholder model refined. *Journal of Business Ethics, 84*(1), 113–35. doi:10.1007/s10551-008-9677-4.

Fassin, Y. (2010). A dynamic perspective in Freeman's stakeholder model. *Journal of Business Ethics, 96*, 39–49. doi:10.1007/s10551-011-0942-6.

Feller, J., Finnegan, P., Hayes, J., & O'Reilly, P. (2012). "Orchestrating" sustainable crowdsourcing: A characterisation of solver brokerages. *Journal of Strategic Information Systems, 21*(3), 216–32. doi:10.1016/j.jsis.2012.03.002.

Ferraro, F. & O'Mahony, S. (2012). Managing the boundaries of an "open" project, in J. F. Padgett and W. W. Powell (eds.). *The Emergence of Organizations and Markets.* Princeton, NJ: Princeton University Press, pp. 545–65.

Fleming, L. & Waguespack, D. M. (2007). Brokerage, boundary spanning, and leadership in open innovation communities. *Organization Science, 18*(2), 165–80. doi:10.2307/25146092.

Freeman, R. E. (1984). *Strategic Management: A Stakeholder Approach.* Cambridge: Cambridge University Press.

Freeman, R. E. (1994). The politics of stakeholder theory: Some future directions. *Business Ethics Quarterly*, 4(4), 409–21.

Freeman, R. E. (2010). *Strategic Management: A Stakeholder Approach*. 25th Anniversary Edition. Cambridge, UK: Cambridge University Press.

Gamalielsson, J. & Lundell, B. (2014). Sustainability of open source software communities beyond a fork: How and why has the libreoffice project evolved? *Journal of Systems and Software*, 89, 128–45. doi:10.1016/j.jss.2013.11.1077.

Ghezzi, A., Gabelloni, D., Martini, A., & Natalicchio, A. (2017). Crowdsourcing: A review and suggestions for future research. *International Journal of Management Reviews*, January, n/a-n/a. doi:10.1111/ijmr.12135, http://onlinelibrary.wiley.com/doi/10.1111/ijmr.12135/full (accessed October 29, 2017).

Gibson, K. (2012). Stakeholders and sustainability: An evolving theory. *Journal of Business Ethics*, 109(1), 15–25. doi:10.1007/s10551-012-1376-5.

Gould, R. W. (2012). Open innovation and stakeholder engagement. *Journal of Technology Management & Innovation*, 7(3), 1–11.

Hardin, G. (1968). The tragedy of the commons. *Science*, 162(3859), 1243–8. doi:10.1126/science.162.3859.1243.

Henkel, J., Schöberl, S., & Alexy, O. (2014). The emergence of openness: How and why firms adopt selective revealing in open innovation. *Research Policy*, 43(5), 879–90. doi:10.1016/j.respol.2013.08.014.

Hess, C. & Ostrom, E. (eds.) (2011). *Understanding Knowledge as a Commons: From Theory to Practice*. Cambridge, MA: MIT Press.

Hinds, P. J. & Mortensen, M. (2005). Understanding conflict in geographically distributed teams: The moderating effects of shared identity, shared context, and spontaneous communication. *Organization Science*, 16(3), 290–307. doi:10.1287/orsc.1050.0122.

Hörisch, J., Freeman, R. E., & Schaltegger, S. (2014). Applying stakeholder theory in sustainability management links, similarities, dissimilarities, and a conceptual framework. *Organization & Environment*, 27(4), 328–46. doi:10.1177/1086026614535786.

Hossain, M. & Oparaocha, G. O. (2017). Crowdfunding: Motives, definitions, typology and ethical challenges. *Entrepreneurship Research Journal*, 7(2). doi: https://doi.org/10.1515/erj-2015-0045.

Howe, J. (2006). The rise of crowdsourcing. *Wired*, 14(6), 1–4.

Hu, M., Li, X., & Shi, M. (2015). Product and pricing decisions in crowdfunding. *Marketing Science*, 34(3), 331–45. doi:10.1287/mksc.2014.0900.

Iivari, N. (2009). "Constructing the users" in open source software development: An interpretive case study of user participation. *Information Technology and People*, 22(2), 132–56. doi:10.1108/09593840910962203.

Jensen, M. C. (2002). Value maximization, stakeholder theory, and the corporate objective function. *Business Ethics Quarterly*, 12(2), 235–56.

Jensen, T. & Sandström, J. (2011). Stakeholder theory and globalization: The challenges of power and responsibility. *Organization Studies*, 32(4), 473–88. doi:10.1177/0170840611400290.

Jones, T. M. & Felps, W. (2013). Stakeholder happiness enhancement: A neoutilitarian objective for the modern corporation. *Business Ethics Quarterly*, 23(3), 349–79. doi:10.5840/beq201323325.

Jones, T. M. & Wicks, A. C. (1999). Regarding "convergent stakeholder theory." *Academy of Management Review, 24*(4), 621–3. doi:10.5465/AMR.1999.12600876.

Kaufman, A. & Englander, E. (2011). Behavioral economics, federalism, and the triumph of stakeholder theory. *Journal of Business Ethics, 102*(3), 421–38. doi:10.1007/s10551-011-0822-0.

Kelty, C. M. (2008). *Two Bits: The Cultural Significance of Free Software*. Durham, NC: Duke University Press.

Kelty, C. M. (2009). Conceiving open systems. *Washington University Journal of Law and Policy, 30* (Open Source and Proprietary Models of Innovation: Beyond Ideology), 139.

Klang, M. (2005). Free software and open source: The freedom debate and its consequences. *First Monday, 10*(3) (March).

Laplume, A. O., Sonpar, K., & Litz, R. A. (2008). Stakeholder theory: Reviewing a theory that moves us. *Journal of Management, 34*(6), 1152–89.

Latour, B. (2004). *Politics of Nature: How to Bring the Sciences into Democracy*. Cambridge, MA: Harvard University Press.

Levina, N. & Ross, J. W. (2005). From the vendor's perspective: Exploring the value proposition in information technology outsourcing. *MIS Quarterly, 27*(3), 331–64.

Levy, S. (2010). *Hackers: Heroes of the Computer Revolution*. Garden City, NY: O'Reilly Media.

Ljungberg, J. (2000). Open source movements as a model for organising. *European Journal of Information Systems, 9*(4), 208–16.

Lopez-De-Pedro, J. & Rimbau-Gilabert, E. (2012). Stakeholder approach: What effects should we take into account in contemporary societies? *Journal of Business Ethics, 107*(2), 147–58. doi:10.1007/s10551-011-1029-0.

Loviscky, G., Treviño, L., & Jacobs, R. (2007). Assessing managers' ethical decision-making: An objective measure of managerial moral judgment. *Journal of Business Ethics, 73*(3), 263–85. doi:10.1007/s10551-006-9206-2.

Lukyanenko, R., Parsons, J., & Wiersma, Y. F. (2014). The IQ of the crowd: Understanding and improving information quality in structured user-generated content. *Information Systems Research, 25*(4) 669–89. doi:10.1287/isre.2014.0537.

Machold, S., Ahmed, P., & Farquhar, S. (2008). Corporate governance and ethics: A feminist perspective. *Journal of Business Ethics, 81*(3), 665–78. doi:10.1007/s10551-007-9539-5.

Mansell, S. (2013). Shareholder theory and Kant's "duty of beneficence." *Journal of Business Ethics, 117*(3), 583–99. doi:10.1007/s10551-012-1542-9.

Matten, D. & Crane, A. (2005). What is stakeholder democracy? Perspectives and issues. *Business Ethics: A European Review, 14*(1), 6–13. doi:10.1111/j.1467-8608.2005.00382.x.

Mergel, I. & Desouza, K. C. (2013). Implementing open innovation in the public sector: The case of challenge.gov. *Public Administration Review, 73*(6), 882–90. doi:10.1111/puar.12141.

Miles, S. (2017). Stakeholder theory classification: a theoretical and empirical evaluation of definitions. *Journal of Business Ethics, 142*(3), 437–59.

Mingers, J. & Walsham, G. (2010). Toward ethical information systems: The contribution of discourse ethics. *MIS Quarterly, 34*(4), 833–54.

Mitchell, R. K., Agle, B. R., & Wood, D. J. (1997). Toward a theory of stakeholder identification and salience: Defining the principle of who and what really counts. *Academy of Management Review*, *22*(4), 853–86. doi:10.5465/AMR.1997.9711022105.

Mollick, E. (2014). The dynamics of crowdfunding: An exploratory study. *Journal of Business Venturing*, *29*(1), 1–16. doi:10.1016/j.jbusvent.2013.06.005.

Moriarty, J. (2014). The connection between stakeholder theory and stakeholder democracy: An excavation and defense. *Business & Society*, *53*(6), 820–52. doi:10.1177/0007650312439296.

Morozov, E. (2012). *The Net Delusion: How Not to Liberate the World*. London: Penguin.

Neville, B., Bell, S., & Whitwell, G. (2011). Stakeholder salience revisited: Refining, redefining, and refueling an underdeveloped conceptual tool. *Journal of Business Ethics*, *102*(3), 357–78. doi:10.1007/s10551-011-0818-9.

O'Mahony, S. & Bechky, B. A. (2008). Boundary organizations: Enabling collaboration among unexpected allies. *Administrative Science Quarterly*, *53*(3), 422–59. doi:10.2189/asqu.53.3.422.

Orlikowski, W. J. & Scott, S. V. (2014). What happens when evaluation goes online? Exploring apparatuses of valuation in the travel sector. *Organization Science*, *25*(3), 868–91. doi:10.1287/orsc.2013.0877.

Orlikowski, W. J. & Scott, S. V. (2015). The algorithm and the crowd: Considering the materiality of service innovation. *MIS Quarterly*, *39*(1) 201–16.

Orozco, D. & Poonamallee, L. (2014). The role of ethics in the commercialization of indigenous knowledge. *Journal of Business Ethics*, *119*(2), 275–86. doi:10.1007/s10551-013-1640-3.

Ortega, F. & Rodríguez, J. (2011). *El Potlatch Digital: Wikipedia Y El Triunfo Del Procomun Y El Conocimiento Compartido*. Madrid: Catedra.

Ostrom, E. (1990). *Governing the Commons: The Evolution of Institutions for Collective Action Political Economy of Institutions and Decisions*. Cambridge: Cambridge University Press.

Pajunen, K. (2006). Stakeholder influences in organizational survival. *Journal of Management Studies*, *43*(6), 1261–88. doi:10.1111/j.1467-6486.2006.00624.x.

Pajunen, K. (2010). A "black box" of stakeholder thinking. *Journal of Business Ethics*, *96*, 27–32. doi:10.1007/s10551-011-0940-8.

Parmar, B. L., Freeman, R. E., Harrison, J. S., Wicks, A. C., Purnell, L., & de Colle, S. (2010). Stakeholder theory: The state of the art. *The Academy of Management Annals*, *4*(1), 403–45. doi:10.1080/19416520.2010.495581.

Paul, K. (2015). Stakeholder theory, meet communications theory: Media systems dependency and community infrastructure theory, with an application to California's cannabis/marijuana industry. *Journal of Business Ethics*, *129*(3), 705–20. doi:10.1007/s10551-014-2168-x.

Perens, B. (2005). The emerging economic paradigm of open source. *First Monday*, http://www.firstmonday.dk/ojs/index.php/fm/article/view/1470/1385 (accessed October 29, 2017).

Post, J. E., Preston, L. E., & Sachs, S. (2002). Managing the extended enterprise: The new stakeholder view. *California Management Review*, *45*(1), 6–28.

Purnell, L. & Freeman, R. E. (2012). Stakeholder theory, fact/value dichotomy, and the normative core: How Wall Street stops the ethics conversation. *Journal of Business Ethics*, 109(1), 109–16. doi:10.1007/s10551-012-1383-6.

Raymond, E. S. (2001). *The Cathedral and the Bazaar: Musings on Linux and Open Source by an Accidental Revolutionary*. North Sebastopol, CA: O'Reilly Media.

Resnik, D. B., Elliott, K. C., & Miller, A. K. (2015). A framework for addressing ethical issues in citizen science. *Environmental Science & Policy*, 54, 475–81.

Sandberg, J. (2008). Understanding the separation thesis. *Business Ethics Quarterly*, 18(2), 213–32.

Santana, A. (2012). Three elements of stakeholder legitimacy. *Journal of Business Ethics*, 105(2), 257–65. doi:10.1007/s10551-011-0966-y.

Savage, M. (2014). Piketty's challenge for sociology. *The British Journal of Sociology*, 65(4), 591–606. doi:10.1111/1468-4446.12106.

Savage, G., Bunn, M., Gray, B., Xiao, Q., Wang, S., Wilson, E., & Williams, E. (2010). Stakeholder collaboration: Implications for stakeholder theory and practice. *Journal of Business Ethics*, 96, 21–6. doi:10.1007/s10551-011-0939-1.

Scherer, A. G., Rasche, A., Palazzo, G., & Spicer, A. (2016). Managing for political corporate social responsibility: New challenges and directions for pcsr 2.0. *Journal of Management Studies*, 53(3), 273–98. doi:10.1111/joms.12203.

Schlagwein, D. & Bjørn-Andersen, N. (2014). Organizational learning with crowd-sourcing: The revelatory case of LEGO. *Journal of the Association for Information Systems*, 15 (Special Issue).

Scholz, N. (2015). *The Relevance of Crowdfunding: The Impact on the Innovation Process of Small Entrepreneurial Firms*. Wiesbaden, Germany: Springer Gabler.

Schweik, C. M. & English, R. C. (2012). *Internet Success: A Study of Open-Source Software Commons*. Cambridge, MA: MIT Press.

Shaikh, M. & Cornford, T. (2009). Innovating with open sourcing: Governance concerns for managers. Presented at the 15th Americas Conference on Information Systems (AMCIS), January, https://ulir.ul.ie/handle/10344/1843 accessed October 29, 2017).

Siltaoja, M. & Lähdesmäki, M. (2015). From rationality to emotionally embedded relations: Envy as a signal of power in stakeholder relations. *Journal of Business Ethics*, 128(4), 837–50. doi:10.1007/s10551-013-1987-5.

Stallman, R. (1985). The GNU manifesto. *GNU Project—Free Software Foundation*, https://www.gnu.org/gnu/manifesto.en.html (accessed October 29, 2017).

Stewart, D. (2005). Social status in an open-source community. *American Sociological Review*, 70(5), 823–42.

Strand, R. & Freeman, R. E. (2015). Scandinavian cooperative advantage: The theory and practice of stakeholder engagement in Scandinavia. *Journal of Business Ethics*, 127(1), 65–85. doi:10.1007/s10551-013-1792-1.

Straub, T., Gimpel, H., Teschner, F., & Weinhardt, C. (2015). How (not) to incent crowd workers. *Business & Information Systems Engineering*, 57(3), 167–79. doi:10.1007/s12599-015-0384-2.

Sundaram, A. K. & Inkpen, A. C. (2004). The corporate objective revisited. *Organization Science*, 15(3), 350–63.

Treviño, L. K. & Weaver, G. H. (1999). The stakeholder research tradition: Converging theorists+not convergent theory. *Academy of Management Review, 24*(2), 222–7. doi:10.5465/AMR.1999.1893930.

Tsoukas, H. & Chia, R. (2002). On organizational becoming: Rethinking organizational change. *Organization Science, 13*(5), 567–82. doi:10.1287/orsc.13.5.567.7810.

Urban, G. L. & von Hippel, E. (1988). Lead user analyses for the development of new industrial products. *Management Science, 34*(5), 569–82.

Vaast, E., Davidson, E. J., & Mattson, T. (2013). Talking about technology: The emergence of a new actor category through new media. *MIS Quarterly, 37*(4) (January).

Viscusi, G. & Tucci, C. (2018). Three's a crowd? In C. Tucci, A. Afuah, & G. Viscusi (eds.), *Creating and Capturing Value through Crowdsourcing*. Oxford: Oxford University Press, pp. 39–57.

von Hippel, E. (2007). Horizontal innovation networks—by and for users. *Industrial and Corporate Change, 16*(2), 293–315.

Wenger, E. C. & Snyder, W. (2000). Communities of practice: The organizational frontier. *Harvard Business Review, 78*(1) (January).

West, J. (2007). Seeking open infrastructure: Contrasting open standards, open source and open innovation. *First Monday, 12*(6), http://firstmonday.org/ojs/index.php/fm/article/view/1913/1795

Yoo, Y., Henfridsson, O., & Lyytinen, K. (2010). The new organizing logic of digital innovation: An agenda for information systems research. *Information Systems Research, 21*(4), 724–35. doi:10.1287/isre.1100.0322.

Zhao, Y. & Zhu, Q. (2012). Evaluation on crowdsourcing research: Current status and future direction. *Information Systems Frontiers, 16*(3), 417–34. doi:10.1007/s10796-012-9350-4.

Index

Note: 'f' indicates the reference is to material in a figure. 't' indicates the reference is to material in a table.